**Mass Media and the Shaping of American Feminism
1963–1975**

Mass Media
and the Shaping of
American Feminism
1963–1975

Patricia Bradley

University Press of Mississippi / Jackson

www.upress.state.ms.us

The University Press of Mississippi is a member of the Association of
American University Presses.

11 10 09 08 07 06 05 04 03   4 3 2 1

∞

Library of Congress Cataloging-in-Publication Data
Bradley, Patricia, 1941–
    Mass media and the shaping of American feminism, 1963–1975 / by Patricia Bradley.
        p. cm.
Includes bibliographical references and index.
    ISBN 1-57806-612-3 (alk. paper) — ISBN 1-57806-613-1 (pbk. : alk. paper)
    1. Feminism and mass media. I. Title.
    P96.F46B73 2003
    070.4'4930542—dc21   2003010747

British Library Cataloging-in-Publication Data available

To Laurie, for making this work possible

Contents

List of Abbreviations   ix
Introduction   xi

1. The Legacy of *The Feminine Mystique*   3
2. Marching for the Media: NOW and Media Activism   29
3. The Left at Center   48
4. The Practice of the Craft   77
5. August 1970   104
6. Media and Mitigation: Soothing Sexual Angst   123
7. Gloria Steinem   143
8. *Ms.* and the Success of Liberal Feminism   167
9. Efforts to Reform the Media: Print   194
10. Reform Redux: Broadcast   222
11. Rise of the Opposition   247

Conclusion: A Moment of Triumph   273
Works Cited   287
Index   309

List of Abbreviations

AA	Advertising Age	*JC*	Journal of Communication
ABC	American Broadcasting Company	*JQ*	Journalism and Mass Communications Quarterly
Ain't	Ain't I a Woman	*LHJ*	Ladies' Home Journal
BC	Broadcasting	**MTR**	Museum of Television and Radio, New York
BF-SLRI	Betty Friedan Papers, Arthur and Elizabeth Schlesinger Library on the History of Women in America at the Radcliffe Institute for Advanced Study, Cambridge, Massachusetts	**NARB**	National Advertising Review Board
		NBC	National Broadcasting Company
		NOW	National Organization for Women
BG	Boston Globe	*Nswk*	Newsweek
BMR	Big Mama Rag	*Nwsday*	Newsday
CBS	Columbia Broadcasting Company	*NYT*	New York Times
		NYTM	New York Times Magazine
ChicTrib	Chicago Tribune	*oob*	off our backs
CJR	Columbia Journalism Review	*PrinInk*	Printer's Ink
CPB	Corporation for Public Broadcasting	*PSR*	Phyllis Schlafly Report
		PW	Publisher's Weekly
CSM	Christian Science Monitor	*Spokes*	The Spokeswoman
CSMC	Critical Studies in Mass Communication	**USNWR**	U.S. News and World Report
		Voice	Village Voice
DN	New York Daily News	**VTA**	Television News Archives, Vanderbilt University
E&P	Editor and Publisher		
Esq.	Esquire	**WMM**	Women, Men, and Media
EvenBull	Philadelphia Evening Bulletin	*WP*	Washington Post
FCC	Federal Communications Commission	*WSJ*	Wall Street Journal
HB	Harper's Bazaar		
JB	Journal of Broadcasting; Journal of Broadcasting and Electronic Information		

Introduction

This is a study of the intersection between mass media and the second wave of the women's movement, a period I have defined as ranging from 1963, the year of publication of *The Feminine Mystique*, to 1975, when the initial energy of the movement was over, at least as far as mass media was concerned. I have represented the high point of media attention as the Billie Jean King–Bobby Riggs tennis match in 1973, a popular culture event of national proportions that provided the media definition that the women's movement was most about permitting women entry into the male bastions of the workplace.

Entry into the workplace was indeed high among feminists' goals, but for many of the early feminists it was just one of the panoply of issues that aimed at examining gender roles and gender relationships. Second-wave activists not only sought entry for women into new areas of the workplace and an end to gender barriers generally but also sought to put on the public agenda issues of how women's secondary nature in U.S. society adversely reflected attention to women's health, child support concerns, rape and legal protections, and domestic abuse—issues that were discrete problems to be corrected as well as related to the overall pattern of culture. As long as the pattern remained, these activists argued, solutions would be impermanent or subverted.

This larger discussion slipped away as job equity came to dominate other ways of examining American life. Once it seemed assured that women would be allowed to enter what had been forbidden parts of the workplace, mass media's interest in the women's movement markedly dropped. The *New York Times*, the setter of the nation's news agenda, drastically curtailed its coverage of the National Organization for Women after 1975, despite the organization's ongoing efforts on behalf of passage of the Equal Rights Amendment, the use of challenges against broadcast licenses, efforts to implement Title VII of the Civil Rights Act and Title IX of the Education Act and other feminist issues (Barker-Plummer 2002: 192). By its own account, the Associated Press covered the Equal Rights Amendment "as if it were the culmination of a trend, but the movement for women's rights is one of the continuing 'trend' stories of the time. In this case, it may be too late to correct the shortcoming in coverage" (APME 1982: 168). When the "trend" story of women's rights

x

was covered, it shifted to "first-women stories"—women who became the first of their gender to enter previously male occupations. Such attention served to emphasize the definition that the women's movement had been most about seeking entry into the workplace, or, as it was framed, equal pay for equal work, although, as we know, entry into the workplace and equal pay are not the same thing.

As the media turned their attention to stories of women in new jobs, the activism related to the movement's philosophical discussions of male and female power relationships (and the overall uses of those power relationships to the culture) found limited expression, most often in separatism or social welfare activism. Now on the margins, the issues of the second wave were activated in the founding of shelters for battered women, law projects, abortion clinics, academic refuges, and child-care centers. Set apart as local and independent projects, joined loosely if at all, the new groups set out to find ways to ensure the survival of concerns that were not considered to be of national importance. With the exception of abortion services, such efforts, with their reverberations of women's-sphere reform activism, were generally perceived as nonthreatening and returned the women's movement to the "soft news" category from whence it had emerged. The issues of the second wave, if they survived at all, joined the begging bowl that came to define U.S. "human services" in the 1980s and thereafter. Political activism continued but increasingly faced the formidable opposition of the political right: to seek public attention for feminist goals was to prompt ever-enlarging counteractions from the antifeminist community. Attempts to retain, much less enlarge, the second wave beyond the accepted definition of the workplace not only did not strengthen feminism but rather served to promote antifeminism and the new conservative agenda that it ushered in.

In short, what had been put forward as a beginning position—job equity—came to be the major definer of the second wave's entire meaning. And once discriminatory hiring was presented as wrongful behavior, mass media's interest in the second wave disappeared. Women's entry into the workplace became the media product of the second wave, while other discussion slipped into niches or disappeared altogether from the cultural landscape. When feminists attempted to go beyond the beginning position, as in the campaign to pass the Equal Rights Amendment, the feminist "story," from the mass media perspective, already had been told. And since the "story" was about job equality, other feminist successes—notably abortion rights—were open to attack. The concern here is not simply to make the point that mass media limited the agenda of the women's movement but also to provide an account of why mass media, anchored in business values and the journalistic traditions that most often serve to uphold them, could not do otherwise. Mass media function as a double-edged sword, providing rapid dispersal of messages but ones that are necessarily constrained by mass media's systemic levers. For historians of the second wave, this account provides one explanation for its rapid rise, peak, and disappearance from the public agenda.

In seeking an explanation for both the shape and short period of the second wave, this work looks at the interplay of influences in one particular triumvirate: the media activism of the second wave, the journalistic craft that filtered it, and the uses of both by the U.S. mass market industry. I begin with the not-so-surprising proposition that mass media operate in a market-driven model and suggest that at every stage in coverage of the second wave, market forces played a pivotal role—whether attracting a new suburban audience for *The Feminine Mystique*, providing media products with many layers of meanings so no audience member would be turned away, or building on the large female audience that ABC had already garnered by the time of the King–Riggs tennis match.

Despite the overweening presence of mass media as a business, the second wave emerged at a time when attention from the mass media was commonly held to be imperative for the setting of a political agenda and for influencing national values. In assessing the media strategies of the second wave, these strategies were influenced by the notion that mass media vehicles were powerful enough, as sociologist Gaye Tuchman proposed at the time, to "symbolically annihilate" women (Tuchman 1978: 3).

Such beliefs were grounded in the successes of the civil rights movement as it unfolded on the nation's television screens and in the lush, large pages of the picture magazines. Young woman growing up during this era, too young to be connected to the first stage of feminism of the first part of the century, not surprisingly sought to promote change along feminist lines by way of the mass media. This tendency was encouraged by women activists professionally involved in media, who assumed they knew enough about media practices to achieve several ends—to disperse their messages through mass media vehicles, to utilize mass media pressure for the passage and implementation of legislation, and to replace negative images of women with those that would change the culture. By mass media's perceived abilities both to pressure and persuade, mass media were to be agents of change. This was a remarkable ambition for a collection of U.S. businesses, none of which had social change as its purpose.

Less understood at the time was that the powerful images of the civil rights movement had not spontaneously appeared on the mass media agenda. Rosa Parks, as we know, did not spark the Montgomery bus boycott by her sudden refusal to give up her seat for a white passenger but rather was selected by civil rights activists for her ability to present a media-sympathetic figure (Robnett 1998). In the same way, the clear narratives of right and wrong, as in the marches and confrontations mounted by civil rights media activists, similarly fit into journalistic standards that insured a sympathetic profile of the activists and, not incidentally, provided compelling content to maintain large audiences. Feminists could not be blamed for seeking the same kind of media attention.

But the feminist "story" was not the same as civil rights, and reporters, presented with less clear story narratives, made sense of the confusion by screening what seemed to them a jumble of new ideas through a familiar journalistic template. While a body of communication research exists that address "framing," "gatekeeping" and similar issues, sociologist Herbert Gans may be most useful for this discussion. Studying news decision making in the period, Gans found that news practitioners help maintain notions about the nation and society by shaping news content to fit into categories of what he called "enduring values," including small-town pastoralism, individualism, responsible capitalism, and moderation (Gans 1980: 42–52). Such categories had relevance for the second wave. The emphasis on the virtues of "small town pastoralism," for example, established those virtues as superior and even antithetical to those of urban life and, in the second-wave context, helped establish feminism as representing the less worthy city value. "Individualism," when reflected in news values, results in the shaping of news according to individual lives and defines success in terms of the individual success, thereby avoiding the discussion of systemic solutions. "Responsible capitalism" reinforces notions that a business ideology is the national ideology and puts what does not fit into that category outside the pale. And for news producers committed to the value of moderation, the demands of second-wave radicals meant there was no room for those demands to be framed other than as the breaking of boundaries. The breaking of boundaries thus became the story, while the story beyond the boundary was not so much discredited as disallowed.

Most unlike the civil tights model, however, was that the women's movement could never offer up a transcendent leader equal to Martin Luther King Jr. Although a multitude of women leaders certainly existed in the second wave, an insufficient number of them achieved national recognition of the scope that could usurp the media celebrity of Betty Friedan and Gloria Steinem, neither of whom represented a power bloc—the most traditional characteristic of leadership. The second wave struggled with leadership issues, as in the ongoing disputes between factions, which were reflected in news media as division and thus reason for dismissal of feminist issues.

For those who pay the bill—that is, the owners of mass media—the influences on media content are not as interesting at their impact on media audiences, who must be retained if media content is to exist at all. Despite media's emphasis on newness, new ideas, outside of the tweaking of ongoing stories, do not necessarily attract or maintain audiences. This is recognized by supervisors of mass media content, who seek to balance one view against another in news vehicles and find other ways to balance views in entertainment vehicles. Whatever programmers said at the time, the television programs *All in the Family* and *Maude* were not so much about the introduction of new ideas in the mass media marketplace as a way for traditional ideas to be reinforced as audiences picked up cues that were clearly available. Such responses to subtext provided (and continue to provide) a safe holding tank for views that, for the moment, were off the main agenda. Programmers, in the meantime, took advantage of timely topics as new content but did so in the comfortable frame of familiar values. Whether in entertainment programs or in journalistic products, U.S. postwar mass media sought to maintain their large and diverse audiences by emphasizing enduring values by means that could be overt but also otherwise.

Certainly, one proved audience pleaser in mass media terms has been the role of work as the expression of individual success. From the days of the Horatio Alger stories, the media have defined success as success in the marketplace when accomplished by individual effort (whether or not this is a realistic expectation—even Horatio Alger had significant help along the way). Such a media-designated "enduring value" played a significant role in the second wave as it shifted attention away from broad calls for change made by radical women and toward a familiar mode of American individualism. In her recent overview of the second wave, Barbara Epstein notes that what she sees as the reign of individualism in the United States today may have its roots in second-wave workplace demands that encouraged feminists to take on middle-class career aspirations to the detriment of other values. "The media image of feminist as careerists was not entirely invented by a hostile press," she writes, "but feminists are no more careerists than other members of the same class. If this is true, then we are admitting that we have lost a grip on the social vision that feminism originally embraced" (Epstein, B., 2002: 125).

An emphasis on individualism clearly shifts focus from the cooperative behavior needed for systemic change; it can encourage leadership on the basis of celebrity; it can claim victory on the basis of individual achievement, whether individual achievement is the norm or the exception and, as Epstein writes, it contributes to "a cold and selfish society" (Epstein, B., 2002: 124). All these modes of individualism were reflected in the media's representation of the second wave, often with the cooperation of activists but certainly insisted upon by mass media, which do not have a place for "cooperative behavior" on their encoding templates.

But women who viewed entry to the workplace as a beginning rather than an ending became characterized as "strident," so off-putting that even the word *feminism* is still rejected today by young women who continue to associate it with rejection of men personally rather than the rejection of oppressive power arrangements. Indeed, success in the workplace as a result of individual effort is so integrated into the U.S. outlook that choices that do not conjoin work and individual effort at the center of a national philosophy are hard to imagine. Even present readers, some of whom may have benefited from opportunities that resulted from the period, may ask why equal work for equal pay should not be considered the ultimate success.

One answer might be to consider that feminist success in gaining entry to the workplace came without addressing a power structure that found female employment useful for a society seeking the inexpensive labor of a service economy (on its way to the "information society" that would further dislocate the U.S. worker base), the ongoing usefulness of second incomes in a consumer society, or the new necessity (thanks to the service economy) of second incomes for the survival of working-class families. In making individualism and work the media "story," mass media defined feminism in its most limited meaning.

Nonetheless, the value of work was clearly part of the ideology of the women's movement, and much of the anger that accompanied the movement in the early days was clearly related to the frustration of women who were denied participation in a national value. The belief in the importance of female employment opportunities was so widely held among feminist leaders that when new options for work became available, only the most charismatic and contemplative leader could have expressed the idea that they came at the expense of other kinds of discussion. Meantime, the belief in work as the penultimate proof of an equal society also served to alienate women (and men) whose values did not center on employment or success in the marketplace. Given the overall American faith in work and the usefulness of a work ethic to American business as a simultaneous provider of workers and consumers, discussions of political, theoretical, and even practical aspects of feminism (Who is to provide childcare so women can work?) slipped away.

This account of media and the second wave begins with decision to publish *The Feminine Mystique* at a time when book publishers were seeking to take advantage of postwar female uneasiness (and the audience they represented) and Betty Friedan was able to shape her work by way of a familiar, mass media writing style. I then focus on how the early activities of the National Organization for Women were covered because NOW organizers chose its activities with an eye to the craft decisions of the industry. The "radicals," with as much belief in the power of media as anyone, took the same tack, choosing to mount their ideas in ways that were amenable to media demands. At the midpoint of the second wave, I look at how the mass media asserted power by defining a major event of the second wave, the August 1970 march to celebrate women's suffrage, as a city success that was antithetical to "small town pastoralism" and was not such a success outside of New York. In the final chapters, I suggest that mass media moved inexorably to the restoration of the values of the status quo—by including women as craft practitioners, by setting out the lesbianism of Kate Millett against the thoroughgoing heterosexuality of Germaine Greer, and by agreeing on a compromise: Gloria Steinem, whose own "packaging" signaled a reformer of seeming little danger to the power arrangements. Her rise was encapsulated in the media product *Ms.* magazine, which radicals dismissed as liberal feminism, even as it took its messages to the small towns that previous efforts had ignored. Finally, the acceptance of female workers, which I explore in terms of print and broadcast reform, leads to the question of how much the addition of female workers to a male workforce can change the final product. By the time of this occurrence, however, the question was moot: the conservatives had taken advantage of media craft traditions to facilitate a rise to power. In the final chapter, I put forward the King–Riggs tennis match as the national parable that asserts the supremacy of market-designated values.

When Billie Jean King beat Bobby Riggs in 1973, the American media demonstrated their success in defining the second wave in ways that did not challenge what Americans saw as their national ideology. In a remarkable diminishment of a social movement, second-wave feminism was put into an entertainment setting, which, as all agreed at the time, was of circus proportions, but nonetheless was one in which many feminists joined. What was not so clear at the time was that the match marked the decline of the second wave as a social protest movement.

Historians of social activism continue to struggle with how to assess the Damoclean sword of media attention. Bernadette Barker-Plummer, a scholar of second-wave media activism, writes that activists are not necessarily at the mercy of media but can come to a strategic understanding of journalistic practices in ways that will promote their own agenda (Barker-Plummer 1995). In assessing 1960s activism, Chad Raphael argues that even in light of the negative media coverage of that period, messages useful to the protest movement were communicated by mass media channels. Dominant hegemony is not a closed system, he argues; some gains can be made. Mass media remain useful, even in this time of the Internet, and media use should not be dismissed on an all-or-nothing basis: "a pyrrhic victory is different from a total loss" (Raphael 2000: 135). But Edward P. Morgan, also revisiting media coverage of the 1960s, notes how media "continually sought out the most deviant, flamboyant and outrageous behaviors in their coverage of antiwar protests" (2000: 97). Such coverage not only resulted in the loss of a public forum at the time, he writes, but remains in U.S. social memory in terms of nostalgia, failure, and/ or youthful excess, images that serve as a deterrent to present-day social activists because of the ease by which today's media (and the available news footage) can call up these formulaic images. Readers may consider how the images of the second wave continue to haunt feminism today.

Whatever the errors of the past, activists continue to utilize media but now do so in increasingly sophisticated ways that seek to match the changed media environment (Bonk 1999). Despite the changes in mass media during the past thirty years, mass media activism continues to draw interest from those who believe mass media attention is necessary for change. The National Organization for Women tracks images of women in mass media, one of its longtime interests, as evidenced by its 2002 "Feminist Prime Time Report" (NOW Foundation 2002). A much different organization, Concerned Women of America, tracks the role of media in what it views as media's promotion of pornography and homosexuality. A variety of family-interest groups maintain pressure on legislators, advertisers, and owners to reduce the sexual and violent content in mass media. Even in a mass media world that is characterized by convergence of ownership, new technology, and fragmented audiences, the belief in the importance of mass media remains.

As scholars of the second wave move beyond celebration to analysis, this work seeks to recast second-wave history by way of understanding the intersection between media and a social movement. While this account remains sympathetic to the women's movement that so fundamentally reshaped American society from the mid-1960s on, I also suggest that we need to examine the movement and its key players in new ways. No matter how seductive the attention, the public sphere operates on harsh and unforgiving ground, one that offers few protections but many opportunities for wrong turns. Redemption may not be impossible, but its difficulties are profound.

Mass Media and the Shaping of American Feminism
1963–1975

1. The Legacy of *The Feminine Mystique*

In 1962, the editor-in-chief of the New York publishing house W. W. Norton and Company was skimming *Harper's Magazine* in a routine trolling for possible Norton writers. What caught George Brockway's eye was an article predicting the consequences of a meltdown of the arctic ice cap—not such an odd subject for a nation already poised for the nuclear equivalent. "The piece was well organized and well written," he later wrote. "I thought Betty might have a book in her, although perhaps not on this particular subject. So I wrote her" (Brockway 1998).

What later arrived on Brockway's desk was the prospectus for Betty Friedan's *The Feminine Mystique*, titled the "The Togetherness Woman." "I fell in love with it at once," Brockway recalled nearly forty years later. "The title, of course, traded on *The Organization Man*, which then was, or had recently been, a best-seller; and one of the women's magazines had been running an ad campaign about the Togetherness Woman. I don't remember anything extraordinary or important that I did," Brockway wrote. "Betty knew what she wanted to say, and she said it well" (Brockway 1998).

It speaks to the book as a successful writing project that Brockway found no trace of the five years of struggle that Friedan had put into the preparation of the manuscript, seeking both to identify what she wanted to say in addition to saying it well. In fact, the book emerged from a confluence of competing influences—her background as a writer for the American Left, her experiences combining a career and domestic life, and her ambition to succeed on a commercial level. And once these influences had been negotiated sufficiently enough to find a mass media publisher, the book faced further difficulties. Published in the middle of a New York newspaper strike, turned down by the Book-of-the-Month Club, and without much publicity from Norton, the book nonetheless became the founding document of the second wave of feminism. Indeed, it became the founding event, responsible for engaging millions of women in feminist thought and turning Friedan into a celebrity, with accompanying ramifications for the leadership of the second wave.

The publication of *The Feminine Mystique* can be the only place to start in a study that examines the intersections of mass media and the second wave. Friedan's book signaled the importance of the role of media in the second wave, as its activists, even those who rejected Friedan as a leader, sought media attention to spread the feminist message. With Friedan's book as the opening salvo, the second wave of feminism was inextricably mounted to a midcentury belief in the mass media's ability to promote change. This intersection of feminism and media was furthered by women activists, many of whom were media professionals and operated out of the nation's news and information center, New York. And the media were ready to convey discussion of what was increasingly being intimated in the postwar years.

Beginning with *The Feminine Mystique*, mass media brought feminism to millions of women who otherwise might never have been connected to the movement at all. As a result of coverage of the movement by mass magazines, newspapers, and television, women across the nation turned to various forms of activism. Local and national opportunities for women enlarged in dramatic ways, the U.S. Supreme Court approved abortion, and prohibitions based on gender were challenged in the workplace, in education, in sports, and in other institutions. Then and now, most activists of the era would agree with Ellen Willis, who regarded—and still regards—mass media as being "absolutely crucial in building the feminist movement" (Willis 1998).

But there were consequences to mass media's role in the second wave. While the media abilities of many second-wave feminists meant that the movement was able to get on the nation's media agenda, organizational difficulties also shared the national spotlight. The movement's public identity soon became one of fragmentation, as if it were disintegrating before it was off the ground. And, as the movement broadened into a proliferating number of feminist goals, each with its own media agenda, the movement appeared less an overarching ideology represented by multiple forms of activism and more like bursts of confetti in a roiling wind. Partly to order information, news media adopted easy stereotypes—the most enduring of which was the strident woman—and gave to the movement the common denominator that feminism was about equal pay for equal work. Finally, the operation of the media's craft tradition—that is, the accepted form of practices as in the search for new leads—promoted the dispersal of points of view diametrically opposed to feminist ideas, which led to the rise of the powerful antifeminist movement and helped the conservative ascension to power in the 1970s and 1980s. By that time, the media—and perhaps much of the country—had become tired of the second wave. The women's movement had used up its media moment and, with it, opportunities for ongoing influence and development of the radical critique.

One way to understand the short shelf life of the second wave is to examine the role of mass media in the dispersal of second-wave feminism. Friedan's book fit the mass media business context of its time in its ability to reach a new audience, and her ability as a commercial writer allowed her to write a book that translated the cultural impulses of the period in ways that were acceptable to mass media. Moreover, her years of mass media involvement also gave her foresight into the role of marketing of media products, which, in the case of *The Feminine Mystique*, served to dispense feminist ideas by way of mass media vehicles. And, as a former left-wing radical, Friedan was a believer in the "powerful-effects" theory of mass media and helped establish that belief as a principle and lever of the second wave. For all of these reasons, *The Feminine Mystique* was an important factor in influencing media's packaging of feminism as a whole. Once feminism was found useful as a media product, its representation was set out on a trajectory that awaits all media products: rise, peak, and compromise. Feminism would find itself absorbed into a broader media culture, but only in ways that served other aspects of mass media.

Media Markets and a Changing Culture

The welcome Norton gave to the prospectus for Friedan's book illustrated the company's effort to reach the women who had settled in the suburbs following the postwar building boom. This market remained largely untapped by major book publishers, except in the area of cookbooks. This outreach for new markets was part of a larger reorganization of the book business in the 1950s and 1960s. After years of control by elite men, the book business at midcentury was increasingly responding to a commercial philosophy. Book content, whether in hardback or not, was, to some publishers, simply another product aimed at particular market niches. Thus, compilations of crossword puzzles, how-to books, books of cartoons—indeed, just about any subject matter that might have an audience—were sought out, sometimes invented, and thence mounted and marketed like any other consumer product. In 1962, Gloria Steinem's first book, *The Beach Book*, typified the trend. Here was a book that simply strung together illustrations of beaches to amuse for the moment—a satire of the usual portentous coffee-table book that was intended to have permanent appeal.

This willingness to look at book content in new ways was accompanied by the industry's acceptance of more aggressive marketing techniques. Norton's initial resistance to Friedan's marketing plans was out of step with the growing understanding that books needed to be marketed in innovative ways. "You can get almost anything published these days," well-known agent Lynn Nesbitt told a

New York Times reporter in 1967. "But it's what gets promoted that counts. Books get lost if they're not promoted" (*NYT* 3/20/67: 20).

Television in particular offered new opportunities for marketing books, usually at no cost, given the medium's need for material. Bennett Cerf, the president of Random House and a man who had made his firm a household name by his weekly appearances on the television quiz program *What's My Line?* was a great proselytizer for the role of television in the selling of books. "There's not a better aid to selling books than TV," he told an industry group in 1960. He noted that jackets of Random House books were designed with an eye to the television camera. The title of Moss Hart's autobiography, *Act One*, had been deliberately enlarged to be better transmitted by television. After Ed Sullivan held up a copy of the book on his program, bookstores sold out of the book within three or four days (*PW* 6/27/60: 50).

Under Cerf's leadership, Random House agreed to distribute books published by a new company, Bernard Geis and Associates, established for the single purpose of taking advantage of the free plugging opportunities offered by television. Geis sought only books that lent themselves to easy promotion. His authors' list was composed of celebrities—Joey Bishop, Debbie Reynolds, Art Linkletter, even Harry S. Truman—and included books that stretched contemporary standards for sexual explicitness by authors who were willing to take on endless promotion (*NYT* 3/22/59: 81; *NYT* 12/14/59: 35). Helen Gurley Brown, an ambitious advertising copywriter from Hollywood and author of one of Geis's early best-sellers, *Sex and the Single Girl*, met both requirements: a sexually frank book whose contents she was willing to discuss in any medium, particularly on the proliferating television talk shows. Brown, however, was a weak second to the promotional efforts put forth by another Geis author, Jacqueline Susann, whose *Valley of the Dolls* remained on best-seller lists for more than a year (and remarkably remains in print at this writing) in part because of a promotional campaign by Susann and her husband that may never be equaled (Korda 1999: 48). In a footnote that has some relevance for the women's movement, the campaign was organized by Geis's publicity director, Letty Pogrebin, later a founding editor of *Ms.* magazine (*E&P* 4/4/70: 45).

Such aggressive marketing challenged the policies of old-line firms, forcing them to develop markets that had previously been of little interest but now could be reached by savvy promotion. Doubleday tried reaching irregular book readers by advertising Harold Robbins's *The Carpetbaggers* in the news sections of newspapers rather than their book sections (*PW* 3/12/62: 94). However, the market that promised to be both sizable and reachable was composed of suburban women, who for years had subscribed by the millions to women's service magazines such as *Ladies' Home Journal*, *Good Housekeeping*, and *McCall's* but that had generally been ignored in the years since the great department stores had stopped selling books. As the suburban female audience again came to notice book retailer WaldenBooks set up shops in postwar malls. Doubleday Company did the same, while its publishing arm brought on board longtime magazine editor Margaret Cousins to help develop the audience who might be shopping in the new stores. In an effort to establish a beachhead on the promised new market, Cousins produced a collection of fiction, *Love and Marriage*, drawn from women's magazines. But this particular entry into the suburban sweepstakes failed, coming at a time when women were turning away from formulaic escapist fiction that Cousins's book encapsulated (and, in any case, surely were not going to pay dearly for what they could get for next to nothing in magazines) (Bradley 1995).

Emerging Themes

As tantalizing as the suburban female audience was to booksellers, it was not so easy to know exactly what content attracted female readers, especially for publishers who took their cues from the women's magazines. Even at a time when women were generally expected to work in the home and consume for the national good, mass media content was by no means monolithic. Domesticity was no longer the only realm of women's interest, according to the editor of *Redbook*: "We also want stories that reflect the wider range of a woman's concerns—social problems, business and community affairs, politics and so forth" (Blakemore 1964: 25, 26). *McCall's* expensive "Togetherness" campaign was found "downgrading of masculine prestige" and petered out (*PrinInk* 7/20/62: 25). Brown, who had ridden her success as a best-selling author to the editorship of *Cosmopolitan*, voiced the culmination of the new focus, noting her magazine was by then "aimed less toward the family and more toward the modern young woman. She can have a husband and children, but she doesn't live through them. We treat her as her own person, very involved in life" (Brown 1975: 20).

As a magazine writer, Friedan had taken advantage of these trends as they emerged, as in her 1955 article in *Charm* magazine, "Why I Went Back to Work." And although Friedan frequently claimed she had written a book because she could not say what she wanted to say in the women's magazines, her 1960 article in *Good Housekeeping*, "I Say Women Are People Too!" clearly raised the essential idea of the book, even to not being able to find a name for the discontent.

Friedan's *Good Housekeeping* article exemplified the mass media's attention to women's angst in the decade of the 1950s. *Life's* double edition in December 1956, "The American Woman: Her Achievements and Troubles," suggested the frustration of postwar women pulled between two poles. In the issue, prominent women approvingly marked the place career women had made for themselves while a male writer addressed the "Changing Roles in Modern Marriage: Psychiatrists Find in Them a Clue to Alarming Divorce Rise." By 1962, the tensions were sufficiently high to warrant the devotion of an entire issue of *Esquire* magazine to "The American Woman: A New Point of View," which included *Esquire's* version of a typical *Ladies' Home Journal* cover (*Esq.* 7/19/62: 71). What is interesting about *Esquire's* labored satire is that a woman's magazine was considered important enough to warrant such extensive attention in a men's magazine that sought to be on the cutting edge.

Less directly, the subject was also explored in a variety of subtexts in women's magazines of the 1950s and 1960s. On the one hand, women's magazines "presented a wide variety of options open to women and praised the women who had chosen to assert themselves as public figures" (Meyerowitz 1994: 237). But problems were represented in another theme—the frustration that accompanied such role modeling, as in articles, "How Do You Beat the Blues?" "What Do You Do When Worries Get You Down?" "I Can't Stand It Anymore," "Why Do Women Cry?" "How to Get Over Feeling Low," "Blues and How to Chase Them," and "Occupation Housewife" (Moscowitz 1996). Although Friedan claimed that women's magazines unilaterally promoted women's oppression, the postwar magazines are now seen to have represented some degree of unhappiness with home and hearth while also showcasing career women and work (Walker 2000).

The television industry's need to attract female viewers resulted in a kind of doublespeak that was even more pronounced than what existed in the women's magazines. Unlike the women's magazines and their all-female audience, television in general sought to attract female and male viewers at the same time. Television programming in this universal frame offered less privacy than the women's magazine field. Men were not likely to pick up a *Ladies' Home Journal* to read the regular column "Can This Marriage Be Saved?" with the implication that it could not. Television was more likely to have a drop-in audience from a larger profile than those for whom the programming was designed. Criticism of particular television programs, then and now, often comes at the behest of audiences who are not regular viewers. Even in the mass media setting of the fifties and sixties, not all content reached all audiences. Thus, as the nation's most conservative medium—a product of federal licensing, the advertising basis of the medium, and the broad audience made possible by the relative cheapness of the television set—television in the 1950s expressed the nation's most traditional views of women but did so with sufficient subtext to reflect the existing undertow of postwar American feminism.

These example were, for sure, fairly tentative. In an early television game show, ABC's 1951 *Ladies before Gentlemen*, a female guest was confronted by the regular six-member, all-male panel "wherein the female must successfully defend the woman's point of view to maintain her position on the pedestal." In NBC's *Ladies' Choice*, a 1953 summer replacement program, a woman talent scout provided her choice of undiscovered talent. Here was a recognition that women's points of view might not agree with those of male talent scouts but were nonetheless worthy of hearing. As early television programmers (and the furniture industry) made a place for the television set in the American living room, women were utilized as hosts of interview and entertainment shows and occasionally as lead characters. Lilli Palmer, Patti Page, Patrice Munsel, and Patricia Bowman hosted shows that bore their names (Terrace 1976: 2:28, 186–87). In a peculiar metaphor that attempted to disguise a real woman with a corporate image, the actress Adelaide Hawley Cumming was hired to give a face to the General Mills' character Betty Crocker and under that name hosted the half-hour *Betty Crocker Show* from 1950 to 1952 (*NYT* 12/25/98: B11).

The same year as the *Betty Crocker Show* closed, the adventures of the lead character in *My Little Margie*—a grown woman, it should be noted—played out against the supervision of her father. The year following, *I Love Lucy* emerged and introduced Lucy's constant subterfuge to combat her husband's supervision. (Ricky was Cuban born, some indication that American men no longer saw themselves as able to lay down the law quite as unequivocally as a foreign-born character.) The early situation comedies—*I Married Joan, My Little Margie, I Love Lucy* (in which all the titles indicate male possession)—most often put women in situations of domestic conflict. And while the plotline of the half hours always reasserted the authority of the male figure at the conclusion, the successful situation comedies of the period came to be remembered, like the noir films of the forties, for the fight of the female leads rather than the surrenders forced by the plots. Audiences tended to forget that Joan Crawford's Mildred Pierce in the film of the same name contritely returned to her husband; it was Joan Crawford *as* Mildred Pierce—assertive, square-shouldered, and successfully entrepreneurial—that became part of national memory. In the same way, Lucy, no matter how contrite at the end of the half hour, always seemed to be the winner.

The popular media in the United States are particularly interesting because of the varied interpretations that can be given to most of their products, even ones that seem at odds with the products' overt messages. Cultural studies scholars credit the empowerment of a subordinate audience for making oppositional readings, thereby resisting the identities contrived for them by those in charge. From a business perspective, however, the importance of the antics of Lucy or Margie might not be that they affirmed patriarchy as much as that they represented multiple views, or at least as many of those as it took to draw audiences. In other words, it was not necessary for audiences to read the comedies as opposite to the overt intent if the oppositional points of view were already embedded, there for the taking. Mass media may be defined as the timely distribution of similar content over a large audience, but mass media does not necessarily mean that content is similarly interpreted. Thus, even the conservative medium of television represented some degree of the discontent of the times. Women's roles in the game shows and in the situation comedies in venues of conflict alongside their demonstrated competence in entertainment shows gave voice to the same stirrings that were found in the women's magazines.

One upshot of the new female celebrities was a sudden increase in high-profile women. At a time when female film celebrities were largely untouchable and unconcerned with day-to-day life, female television provided—overnight it seemed—dozens of new voices of public and female authority. Not surprisingly, these new female celebrities were initially characterized in ways that diminished their own striving for power and acclaim. In *TV Guide*, well on its way to becoming as much a fixture in the living room as the television set it served, the new female stars proclaimed that their first devotion was to hearth and home. They had found themselves "propelled" or "elevated" to stardom, not by their own efforts but by happenstance or male mentorship; ritualistically, they stated that their worst nightmare was fear of "loss of femininity" (Altschuler and Grossvogel 1992: 135–36). The new television celebrities, who represented working women in the public sphere for many American women, explained their success in terms of finding balance between competing tensions. As the women's magazines had long counseled, these were questions—demons, even—with which women had to wrestle individually. No mass media venues of the time, any more than at present, suggested that these were also questions of equal opportunity, child care facilities, burden sharing, or, in short, anything out of the women's own individual ability to handle. The emphasis was on individual decision making rather than institutional levers or cultural practices. By the end of the fifties, however, the formula of having to explain away success as surprise happenstance did not fit with the reality of female celebrities who—whatever they said—gave every evidence of seeking the spotlight and wanting to remain there.

One of the women of the time, Helen Gurley Brown, understood these tensions, and she put that understanding in the context of a business acumen that realized that a growing service economy and its pink-collar women workers would provide an audience for *Sex and the Single Girl* and later for the reconstituted *Cosmopolitan* (Ouelette 1999). It was not just that women were a large part of the mass media audience—that was not new—but that women were coming into the workforce in ways that gave them independent buying power. When Brown published her book, women between ages twenty-five and fifty-four were on the cusp of exploding into the workforce, a group that increased 45 percent from 1962 to 1975 according to the U.S. Department of Labor (Taeuber 1991: B1–11). Prompted by the availability of consumer goods in the postwar period (and the accompanying advertising), the stirrings of feminism among these new working women may have had much to do with their desire to participate more fully in the U.S. consumer culture. Better jobs and commensurate pay was one way to insure that, but feminism was not the automatic corollary.

This summary seeks to place Friedan's book in a media culture that was clearly representing aspects of feminism, if only because of commercial entities' need to attract female consumers. But in whatever mass media incarnation, postwar feminism was hardly a clear voice, subjugated by the mass media characteristic of seeking to be acceptable to all by encompassing, in some way, all points of view, even if they had to be represented in symbolic ways.

Content in media can be driven by a variety of forces besides the commercial drive, of course—propaganda, artistic vision, special interest groups, public relations, cultural affirmation, and so on. All of these impulses found mass media expression in some form at midcentury. However, I argue that the desire to meet the demands of the postwar generation prompted commercial underwriters of mass media to seek an inclusive audience, which led to some expression of emerging ideas. The commercial base of media was not an iron curtain erected against the postwar feminist impulse; rather, the commercial base allowed for—even demanded—the inclusion of postwar feminism as part of a mix that aimed to please and to please as many as possible.

The Feminine Mystique as a Media Product

In her book, Friedan expanded on the themes already present in women's magazines and in other areas of popular culture, but she did so in ways that were familiar to readers. Like the shelves of postwar American supermarkets, the contents of *The Feminine Mystique* ran to abundance, culling evidence from recognizable brand sources—mass media, institutional icons, government reports, extracts from newspapers, and her famous Smith College survey. Friedan's work was far from sociological or scientific, but it presented the kinds of proofs that readers of service magazines had come to expect and trust. Friedan's Smith College survey, for example, would have had a familiar ring to readers of women's magazines, who were long familiar with reader surveys. Indeed, the book represented a compilation of magazine strategies—the professional voice of the advice columnist, the anecdotal and other "proofs" of the nonfiction articles, the small but achievable steps presented by the self-help articles, and the epiphanies that routinely climaxed romantic fiction. Overarching was Friedan's didactic tone, as authoritarian as any taken by editor Edward Bok in addressing *Journal* readers a half century before.

The Feminine Mystique was most like magazines, popular fiction, and television storytelling because it pointed to solutions on the basis of individual resolution rather than systemic correction. Friedan could be both expert and front-line crime fighter, but in the end, like the authors of *The Organization Man, The Man in the Gray Flannel Suit,* and *Marjorie Morningstar,* books that had also focused on difficulties in middle-class society, she could only point to individual roads. As in so much of magazine nonfiction, the book ended with a series of "steps" for the reader to take. In this approach, Friedan reflected the merging of the traditional self-help articles of the magazines with the postwar popularization of psychology. The book did not address in substantive ways political or legal resolutions.

The silences in *The Feminine Mystique* are considerable. Legal perpetrations of female inequality go unquestioned. Political activity is mentioned briefly in the historical terms of the first wave—the "passionate journey" in Friedan's language—rather than the ongoing activities of the Women's Party to pass the Equal Rights Amendment, the activities of the Business and Professional Women's Club, or the activity surrounding the establishment of the President's Commission on the Status of Women. Despite Friedan's history of involvement in the issues, race and class are ignored. Similarly passed over are the benefits of inexpensive female labor to American business, a major denial of her earlier work as a labor journalist. Finally, *The Feminine Mystique* did not reflect the optimism that emerged with presidency of President John F. Kennedy. In retrospect, the book seems hinged to the previous decade rather than to the one in which it was published.

These silences must be considered as strategic as any other part of her commercial skills and helped account for the book's attraction for women whose ideas had been shaped by the previous decade. As in her article on the arctic ice cap, for example, Friedan's brilliance as a commercial writer was demonstrated not only by her ability to introduce feminism by way of a familiar journalistic framework, including strategic silences, but also in the way she gathered up the themes of the period and incorporated them into her focus. Most telling is the organizing principle of *The Feminine Mystique*: feminism as a reaction against the difficult-to-define and only slowly understood "mystique." The book's framing was familiar not only in the way it gathered up the feminist strains that already existed in the magazines and its accessible anecdotal style but also in the way Friedan put in service to her theme a variety of Cold War fears that were marginally related to twentieth-century feminism, although meaningful to the readers of the time.

Women were, indeed, people, too, to recall Friedan's early article, and that meant that women as much as men were affected by the tensions of the time, including those outside of a feminist framing.

As we know from Brockway's account, the book was first to be called *The Togetherness Woman*, a title that would have reflected *McCall's* magazine slogan of the moment, the "magazine of togetherness." Apart from avoiding *McCall's* objections, Friedan's final title was also the better choice. In fact, its very vague exoticism may be thought to represent the Cold War undertow simmering below the surface of the decade's prosperous security. As we know, fear of the Bomb translated into a number of popular culture venues in the white America of the period, from alien invasion movies to the "invasion" of open sexuality in the crossover music emerging from rhythm and blues. The astonishing success of Mickey Spillane's novels has been connected to Mike Hammer, Spillane's hero, as the "ultimate Cold War warrior." After the 1960 U-2 spying incident, the anticommunism theme was carried forth by a new paperback hero, James Bond, now "a high-tech Mike Hammer" (Davis, K. 1984: 182, 286). In both cases, the anticommunist fighters were also sexist, racist, homophobic, misogynistic, and anti-Semitic. Not surprisingly, the anticommunist culture in the fifties carried overtones that had little to do with Soviet domination and played a role in the anxiety of the age. "For all their comforts," sociologist Todd Gitlin has written, "the middle-class parents were afflicted by 'insecurity,' to use another of the decade's code words." The apprehension could be found in several spheres: growth of the life insurance business, increased use of psychiatrists, and a series of best-sellers in which success had to be justified "as an instrument of self-fulfillment." Cutting across all its expressions, however, was the common terror: the Bomb: "Everything might be possible? So might annihilation" (Gitlin 1980: 17, 18, 22).

Although Friedan was to identify the amorphous dread that characterized so much of the 1950s as the "feminine mystique," the unsettledness of female suburban readers may have had to do with a multitude of factors that included but was not limited to the role of women in U.S. society. What may have accounted for the life-changing experience that the book prompted for so many readers was how Friedan challenged the "mystique," offering a virtual one-woman dismantling of the ultimate weapon. In hyperbolic prose (notably when she drew an analogy between American housewives and Nazi concentration camps, certainly one example where her style did not mesh with that of the service magazines), Friedan deconstructed and defused the "mystique" with as much confidence and with the same meat-cleaver approach as Mike Hammer. The mystique had taken hold because of a confluence of circumstances: Sigmund Freud and his followers, missteps in sociology, the anthropology of Margaret Mead, women's magazines, advertising, the glorification of housework. The damage was already considerable and could be seen in women's passivity and their suicidal tendencies, altogether a kind of viral sickening of American women in yet another translation of another fifties great fear, polio. Friedan was authority and diagnostician: "As a magazine writer I often interviewed women about problems with their children, or their marriages, or their houses, or their communities. But after a while I began to recognize the telltale signs of this other problem" (Friedan 1997: 20). Like the domestic communist threat, the mystique was insidious and unexpected.

Friedan had already tapped into the anxiety of the period in the "Coming of the Ice Age" article that had first attracted Brockway's eye. Here was a story filled with the ominous warnings of the end of the world. Its publication history gives evidence to Friedan's ability to popularize serious subjects by connecting them to themes of the age and suggests Friedan's driving commercial ambition, which enabled her to rescue a story dropped by *Collier's* (when it went out of business), overcome the objections of the two scientists who were so appalled by her popularization they refused to cooperate further, and, under her byline alone, carry the story triumphantly to the cover of the prestigious *Harper's Magazine* and subsequently to the profitable reprint offered by *Reader's Digest*. On a practical level, the article led to several offers from interested editors and agents and made the publication of *The Feminine Mystique* possible. On another level, it surely increased her confidence that complicated ideas—even those on a grand and historical scale—could be popularized.

By 1959, after the success of the ice age story, she was successful enough to be a panelist at an event sponsored by New York University and the Society of Magazine Writers. Her theory of successful writing, she told the group, was to find ideas that were personally meaningful: "The real secret of your article's success, really, is that it interests you enough to interest someone else in it." But interest alone was not enough, and her subsequent comments shed light on the commercial shadings her ideas took in *The Feminine Mystique*. "I mean, you cannot say, 'I'll do a piece about psychoanalysis.' You do, and nobody buys it. But, if you were to say, 'I have a story of two people who . . .' and you hardly mention the word psychoanalysis, that somehow focuses it a little differently" (BF-SLRI 1).

The Influence of the Left

Friedan's ability to accommodate her writing to the complications of 1950s mass culture mirrored how she had adopted herself to a suburban lifestyle after a ten-year period as a radical writer. Her own tensions in the 1950s were not so much the dread of Soviet domination but likely the fear of discovery, in her own country, of her former political affiliations. For a former leftist, a Jew, and a woman who was not classically attractive, the Cold War as an oppressive, shuddering presence provided a personal metaphor of entrapment. Adoption of the Cold War motif and her dismantling of it as a gender-based mystique, as well as the subsequent marketing of the book by presenting herself as a typical suburban housewife, were surely affected by her outsider background.

Nevertheless, she was most different from the suburban readers to whom the book was marketed because of the dozen years—1941–52—she had spent as a radical political activist and labor journalist. As documented in her papers at the Arthur and Elizabeth Schlesinger Library on the History of Women in America at the Radcliffe Institute for Advanced Study, an FBI informant identified her as a member of the Young Communist League who had evinced interest in joining the Communist Party (BF-SLRI 2). Friedan likely came to the attention of the FBI as a result of her romantic relationship with David Bohm, not only a communist but also a graduate student in physics and a protégé of Robert Oppenheimer at a time when he was involved in the development of the atomic bomb (Horowitz, Daniel 1998: 92; Hennessee 1999: 35). Friedan did not acknowledge this period in her life until her 2000 memoir, after biographers had brought it to light. Her ideas were also shaped by the eight weeks in 1941 she spent in Monteagle, Tennessee, at the Highlander Folk School, famous for its role in the training of a generation of civil rights and labor activists, not only in the nonviolence techniques that culminated in the Montgomery bus boycott of the civil rights movement but also in writing across various genres (Horowitz, Daniel 1998: 71).

Thanks to Daniel Horowitz's investigation, we now know Friedan put such training to work as a writer in the Left press in the 1940s and early 1950s, first for the Federated Press, a leftist news service representing labor, and then for the United Electrical, Radio, and Machine Workers, considered the most procommunist of all American unions in the postwar period.

The Communist Party had encouraged women's councils in the early 1930s, and women's membership in the party increased to almost 50 percent by the end of the decade, partly because of the party's attention to female concerns. As the party embraced the reforms of Franklin Delano Roosevelt and moved away from an emphasis on revolution and overthrow, women came to compose half of the membership by 1943. In 1945, during the period when Friedan was likely to be influenced, the party began to examine its position on women in ways that "laid important practical and theoretical groundwork for the women's liberation movements of the 1960s and 1970s" (Weigand 1994: 13). Friedan was likely familiar with Mary Inman's 1940 book, *In Woman's Defense*, which called for housework to be regarded as productive labor, a theme repeated in Friedan's call for a national strike of women's labor, including the work of housewives, in 1970. Similarly, Friedan knew the work of Left writer Elizabeth Hawes, whose criticism of media in defining women's consumption would be echoed by Friedan in *The Feminine Mystique* (Horowitz, Daniel 1998: 144).

In 1946, writing for the Left-oriented Federated Press, Friedan covered aspects of the founding of Congress of American Women, the American branch of a pro-Soviet organization, the Women's International Democratic Federation. Its national offices were close to her New York apartment; Friedan knew or knew of several of its leaders; and Friedan, in her role as reporter, would likely have been at its founding convention in New York, when the organization affirmed its opposi-tions to racism and anti-Semitism, its support for equal pay for equal work and further child care facilities, and its decision to include working-class women in women's rights activities. The congress' agenda was impressive, as it sought sys-temic solutions to the problems of American women rather than the individual solutions that were routinely offered by mass media. Within a year, the organiza-tion claimed a membership of a quarter of a million women. However, in 1948 the House Un-American Activities Committee investigated the group, and in 1950 it was ordered to register as a foreign agent; in the same year it disappeared (Horowitz, Daniel 1998: 145–49).

In 1952, by then working for the United Electrical Workers Unions, Friedan wrote the unsigned pamphlet, *UE Fights for Women Workers*, calling for an end to wage discrimination. The real reason for discrimination, she wrote, was to insure profit for big business. "It is no accident that big business all over the world opposed the movement for votes and equal rights for women.... The public acceptance of women's equality would mean the loss of a huge source of labor they could segregate and exploit for extra profit and as a means to hold down the wages of all workers" (United Electrical Workers 1952: 19).

As in her work for the Federated Press, Friedan's development of feminist ideas at the United Electrical Workers Union was framed by issues of world politics, his-torical change, and industrial and military production. *The Feminine Mystique,* however, ignored the connections between women's status and these contexts in favor of the individual step-by-step approach to salvation that the women's magazines favored. In an interview for a 1998 Cornell University publication, Horowitz's work already published, Friedan continued to deny that her feminism was influenced by her associations with the Left. Instead, she again insisted, her experience as a mass magazine writer led her to a sense of "a prevailing dissatisfac-tion among her female contemporaries that wasn't reflected in the magazines" (Myers 2002: 176). Despite Friedan's never-ending characterization that the book came to be written out of her suburban experience, her Left experience in her young adulthood makes it difficult to view her as the emerging, tentative feminist of "the problem that has no name" as described in *The Feminine Mystique.*

"Powerful Effects" of Media

For the purposes here, Friedan's Left influence is of particular interest because of the role she assigns mass media in the construction of the "mystique." Friedan never tired, both in the book and in later works, of bringing attention to the artificial way by which magazines constructed women. "I helped create this image," she wrote. "I have watched American women for fifteen years try to conform to it. But I can no longer deny my own knowledge of its terrible implications. It is not a harmless image. There may be no psychological terms for the harm it is doing. But what happens when women try to live according to an image that makes them deny their minds? What happens when women grow up in an image that makes them deny the reality of the changing world?" (Friedan 1963: 59). Underlying Friedan's view of the role of media image was what she construed as media power. What women read or see about themselves (she would later expand this to television), played a pivotal role in women's sense of identity or lack thereof and contributed to the mystique. If we consider her years of coming of age at the center of left thought in New York, Friedan's belief in the power of media was not just echoing popular wisdom but was clearly connected to Marxist understandings of mass media.

Friedan's belief in the power of media was not unusual for members of the postwar generation beginning to understand and elevate the role of propaganda in World War II. Propaganda scholars such as Harold Lasswell emphasized a "powerful effects" theory, but even subsequent researchers of the "limited effects" school, such as Paul Lazarsfeld and Robert K. Merton, warned of the power of manipulation by interest groups that were using, in the new phrase, "public relations" (Lazarsfeld and Merton 1957: 457). Left thinkers had long emphasized the detrimental influence of mass media and were more likely to see media as all-powerful. For the members of Columbia University's Frankfurt School, media were so influential that consumers were seen to adopt positions contrary to their own best interests.

The Frankfurt School's view of media became popular in American academic circles in the 1960s and 1970s, but it first came to the United States in the 1930s when its founders, Max Horkeimer and Theodor W. Adorno, fled Germany and reestablished their Institute for Social Research at Columbia University. Seeking answers to the Holocaust, Jewish intellectuals centered in the institute found partial answers in the role of German propaganda. Such studies led to the corollary that media could be instrumental in positive as well as negative ways. Influenced by the group, the Anti-Defamation League (ADL) of B'nai B'rith in the 1940s and 1950s mounted a public relations campaign that sought to encourage tolerance along racial and religious lines (Wyman 1984).

In 1945, Bess Myerson, the first Jewish Miss America, spent much of her reign on a speaking tour for the ADL, prompted in part by the anti-Semitism she had experienced both as a Miss America candidate and as the title holder (Dworkin 1998). The ADL campaign ranged from subway posters so subtle they featured a blond child's plea for acceptance to influences on major cultural productions such as the film *Gentleman's Agreement* and the musical *South Pacific.* By the end of the 1950s, however, the ADL concluded that the task was too enormous and expensive for a single public relations campaign, and the group turned to other activities that depended less on persuasive techniques (Svonkin 1997). As another writer argues, the emphasis on mass media in Jewish intellectual circles did not disappear, shifting from the promotion of assimilation, as in the ADL campaign, to the seeking mass media attention on the Holocaust as a way to promote the survival of the state of Israel (Novick 1999).

Friedan came of age both in the powerful-effects period of media and in circles that were influenced by the Marxist interpretations of the Frankfurt School as well as the ADL campaign, and her writings indicate that she saw in mass media both danger and its antidote. In her criticism of women's magazines, Friedan adopted the powerful-effects theory and attached it to the hegemonic notion that media were so powerful that consumers, given no other choices, fashion themselves in the images the media promote. Yet she would also believe, like the B'nai B'rith organizers, that mass media could provide an equally powerful counter, even if her message had to be shaped to the craft traditions of each medium.

The Suburbanite

By the time she wrote her UE pamphlets, Friedan was already moving into a new phase of her life. In 1952 Friedan closed out her life as a labor journalist and turned to mass-market writing. But even in the early 1950s, experimenting with new forms of writing, Friedan's life was not that of the average suburbanite. The family lived in a 650-unit housing complex in Queens, New York, that had been established with a four-hundred-thousand-dollar guarantee from the United Nations to insure that its African, Chinese, Indian, and other nonwhite families could find nondiscriminatory housing. In February 1952, the community's newsletter, the *Parkway Villager,* announced that Friedan was to be the short-term replacement as its editor. That announcement coincided with another notice that rents were about to be raised. In what would be typical of her organizational relationships, Friedan not only took over the permanent job of editor but turned the community newspaper into a bully pulpit against the rent increase when she became head of the publicity committee protesting the increases. Given the UN connection and the threat of protest, the dispute was considered sufficiently important that the *New York Times* gave it generous coverage from June through December 1952 (*NYT*-PV).

We should not assume that the *Times* came to the story without initial prompting, and, although she is not mentioned by name in the dozen stories, the ongoing source was likely Friedan. Her success in gaining coverage indicates not only her media connections but her largesse of vision, which did not hesitate to seek the media eye of the nation's premiere newspaper. Her involvement in the Parkway Village development also gave evidence to her continued interest in racial equality, a commitment, ironically, not widely recognized when she became a feminist leader. In February 1954, her last article as editor was an interview with Roy Wilkins, a member of the community who was just beginning to rise to prominence in civil rights circles (Friedan 1954).

At the same time she was writing and editing the *Parkway Villager*, Friedan also was attempting to break into mass-magazine writing. Her first major article suggests that she was experimenting with ways to take her ideas of social reform into mass media. In March 1955 *Redbook* published her "We Built a Community for Our Children," which showcased a community in South Norwalk, Connecticut, much like Parkway Village. In Friedan's mass media incarnation, the cooperative nature of the development was generally framed in terms of its cost-efficiency. But even in that framing, Friedan was unable to slip by a paragraph that indicated the interracial nature of the residents. In her final draft she noted the varied nature of the residents, including, in the terminology of the period, "Negro" families (BF-SLRI 2). In *Redbook*, this was abridged to "people with the widest range of cultural differences" (Friedan 1955: 62), leaving out what was clearly the most controversial part of the "range," the interracial nature of the development. Notes for an article on a female fashion designer (which was eventually framed in a way that played on U.S. jingoism vis-à-vis the French as "The Gal Who Defied Dior") suggest her original idea was to explore Mafia influence on the dress trade. By the time it appeared in *Town Journal*, "The Family Magazine of Home-Town America," such antecedents had disappeared. The final version of the article, "New Hampshire Love Story," which appeared in *Family Circle*, dropped the details about the reform positions taken by the female protagonist (BF-SLRI 3).

Her next chapter in suburban living was equally atypical of the kind experienced by most American families. In 1957, the family, now with three children, moved to a large Victorian house in the Rockland County village Grand-View-on-Hudson, not far from New York City. This was far from the suburbs of the postwar tract housing, which were often isolated from their adjacent cities and dependent on the automobile. Even in this elite setting, her reform impulse flourished. As in Parkway Village, Friedan took on an organizational role in paid leadership to bring progressive speakers to the community and came to know the upper-middle-class suburban women of her neighborhood as she had once known the international and radical women of her former circles (Hennessee 1999: 67).

By this period, however, her biographers point out that as a result of her involvement with psychotherapy—one of her major intellectual interests—she had come to understand herself outside of a purely radical frame (Horowitz, Daniel 1998: 228). As is clear in her 2000 memoir, her progressive nature did not minimize her enjoyment of middle-class married life with children, and after her divorce and her book's success, she sought the company of other celebrities who were generally not drawn from the feminist community. Nonetheless, on the basis of her residences in Parkway Village and Rockland County, Friedan subsequently characterized herself as a typical suburban housewife. As late as 1992, she returned to the rote recitation that *The Feminine Mystique* was written as a response to suburban living: "I gave up my ambitions and then my job in order to become a suburban housewife. Soon my life was PTA meetings and dinners and housecleaning and having coffee with my neighbors. Housewives were supposedly living this dream life, but, of course, there was something wrong" (Sheff 2002: 112). The reporters never questioned this approach, even in the *Playboy* interview, which was perhaps the most thorough of all her interviews. Nor did reporters ever delve into what exactly was entailed in writing for the "labor press," apparently not understanding the range of political ideologies represented there. Indeed, her connection to the "labor press" was not questioned nor clarified once in twenty-two articles (Sherman 2002).

Even ensconced in Rockland County, it was clear that Friedan had no intention of simply dabbling in the occasional article but regarded herself as a professional journalist. She had household help and set herself a regular writing schedule outside of the home. During this period, she learned to shape articles to serve the master of the moment, from venues as famous as *Harper's Magazine* to the modest *Rotarian,* but not without a struggle. Publication of her articles did not come easily, as many of her ideas could not escape their radical genesis and were not the stuff 1950s' editors sought. Her papers indicate the multiple drafts of articles she prepared and copies of prepared articles that she could not place. Nonetheless, she gradually began to place her articles and, with her evolving success, Friedan was an appropriate choice to write "How to Find and Develop Article Ideas" for the March 1962 issue of *The Writer.* Supporting her growing reputation as a professional writer were the several excerpts from *The Feminine Mystique* appearing in the mass press (Friedan, "Fraud of Femininity"; Friedan, "GI Bill for Women"). Yet at this juncture, her book seemed most related to her writing career rather than a polemic from her radical past in the clothing of popular writing. Indeed, she told would-be magazine writers that she thought the book would supply her with enough articles for four or five years to come. Nothing, she said, was ever wasted in terms of research. Even after the publication of the book, she wrote to Peter Wyden at *McCall's* proposing her new project, an attack on the "cool" look, certainly a subject far a field from developing feminism (BF-SLRI 4).

By the time she came to write *The Feminine Mystique*, Friedan had experienced a long apprenticeship in mass media writing. She had certainly learned the difficulty of trying to frame radical ideas in a popular format. Daniel Horowitz believes that her outlook had essentially changed in the ten years of mass media writing and believes that her account in *The Feminine Mystique* of her own struggle to combine domesticity with career not only served to conceal her radical antecedents but also represented a real struggle as she moved away from the ideology of her early adulthood (Horowitz, Daniel 1998: 217). If that change occurred, it suggests that what also changed was her initial impulse to pursue mass media writing as a way to get radical ideas into the mainstream. At this point, her drive to place her articles seems most related to career ambitions. The list of her mass media writing from the early 1950s to the early 1960s indicates that her articles moved away from the progressive thinking of her first attempts. Her most famous article in *Harper's*, the ice age piece that brought her to Norton's attention, had no particular connection to radical thought and certainly required nothing like the reframing of ideas she had had to do in her Parkway Village writing days. In fact, the arc of her writing career suggests that a need for public recognition and success may have been the essential ingredient in her desire to succeed in mass media writing. Surely evident in every sphere of Friedan's life was a desire and enjoyment of the limelight. Although her radical ideas simmered below the surface, her personal struggle may not have been so much about career versus domesticity as much as it was about ideology versus ambition.

This drive to be central in organizations with which she was associated had ramifications for the women's movement. At the same time, her drive and egotism also provided the engine to write the book, which, despite its mass media influences, still advanced feminist discussion in the mass media. However, the book clearly represents the lessons she had learned as a mass-magazine writer. Personal regeneration replaced the charges against big business found in her UE pamphlet; popular psychology took the place of own sophisticated and long-standing interest in the field; and the radical language of her youth—*oppression, capitalist class, workers*—found no home at all. In a book filled with personal anecdotes, none concerned her experiences in directly challenging class and race. There are the obligatory "steps to salvation," a writing technique for women's magazines that remains alive and well and can still be seen on the covers of many women's magazines.

What was new in Friedan's book was her energetic and angry personal voice, a kind that had not been applied to social change issues since the days of Upton Sinclair. And, as odd as the pairing appears, Friedan's style may have most in common with Brown's approach in the 1962 *Sex and the Single Girl.* While style and substance are enormously different, both women shared a willingness to integrate their personal voices into their subject. This style had some indebtedness to women's magazine writing but surely had not taken place to the risk-taking extent that Friedan and Brown used it. Nor was it put to use in other books on social mores written by male authors of the time. Friedan's voice was passionate, and her overstatements made her a personality that could not be ignored. Even as she held back important parts of her understanding of women, there was a urgent presence in the book to which readers could only respond. While the book called for personal regeneration rather than systemic change, Friedan nonetheless attacked recognized authorities such as Margaret Mead and media institutions. In its context of half a century ago, cultural icons such as Mead were not attacked in mass media, and Friedan's chapter on mass media came at a time when their ownership structure and profitability were unrecognized outside of business and radical circles. Those criticisms of mass media did not reach a general audience until the 1970s and did so then in part because of the radical critique in the women's movement.

What is compelling about her criticisms is a kind of recklessness, a willingness to bite the hand that fed her, to go out on the limb for the passion of her cause. These were characteristics of the old, hectoring Left that had been part of her coming of age, not of suburban housewives or of writers for American mass media. In the end, even in the comfortable dress of the mass media writing that she knew so well and with the inclusion of whatever changes she had made in her radical positions, Friedan's past was in the woof and warp of *The Feminine Mystique.*

The Paperback Revolution

The Feminine Mystique sold well in hardback—sixty thousand copies—but achieved best seller status of 1.5 million sales when it moved to paperback. The quick publication of the book in paperback also represented the intersection of the book with changes in the paperback market, whose sellers had discovered there was an audience for paperbacks beyond readers of seamy detective stories and westerns. Doubleday Anchor, for example, had had a great success with the 1963 publication of David Riesman's *The Lonely Crowd*, which was based on a sociological work first published by Yale University Press.

No publishing house was more involved in the paperback revolution than Friedan's paperback publisher, Dell, which was finding new profits in subjects that once had been the purview of hardback houses. This was no rush into academic publishing: Dell titles were "carefully edited to make exciting and understandable presentations that would interest the average readers" (Lyles 1983: 20). Friedan's book easily met this standard.

Nonetheless, the book was selected, according to editor Don Fine, primarily because of pressure "from every woman in my office." And at Dell and other paperback houses, there were, indeed, women in the office, and not only as secretaries. One of the differences between the paperback publishers and the hardback publishers was some openness to the employment of women in executive positions, largely because paperback publishing was not considered as prestigious or as important as publishing hardbacks. At Dell, opportunities for women meant that "every women in the office" carried some weight: the women included Arlene Donovan, former receptionist who had risen to be editor of Dell's First Editions; Marcia Nassatir, assistant editor at Dell Books; and, most formidably, the company's chief executive officer, Helen Meyer, once a file clerk but by this time the powerful, imperious, and demanding chief executive officer who was exerting new control over Dell's paperback roster. Under Meyer, Dell paperbacks had already broken new ground in publishing books by women who were not shy about writing about women's sexuality, as in Françoise Sagan's *A Certain Smile* and particularly the best-seller *Peyton Place*, by Grace Metalious, which sold nine million copies.

Despite Fine's claims to having been "bulldozed" into the decision to publish Friedan's work, the book's purchase price indicated that the house recognized the commercial possibilities. "We didn't pay much, but it was considered a lot for a book of its kind," Fine recalled. Fine's judgment quickly proved sound. "Within months after it was published, there was an interesting sign. I think it was Vassar that bought copies of the Dell edition for its freshman kits for the incoming class. That's a hell of a tip-off. It had already become something for young, intelligent women. And then it just spread. Garden clubs started calling to talk to Betty. She was all over the country. Again it was the exposure of the book. It sold millions of copies" (Davis, K. 1984: 104).

Publication in paperback offered new opportunities for marketing. From its initial publication, Friedan's understanding of media did not stop at that of a content producer. "I knew the book was big," Friedan recalled, "But it had to be promoted" (Wilkes 1970: 31). Friedan and her husband, Carl, who had an advertising and theatrical background, insisted that Norton hire a publicist, to which Brockway reluctantly agreed (Wilkes 1970). Even before the publicist was on board, however, the publication of the book was prominently noted in the introduction to her 1961 *Good Housekeeping* article "Women Are People Too!" Her agent arranged to have various parts of the book published as excerpts in *Mademoiselle, McCall's,* the *Saturday Review,* and *Ladies' Home Journal.*

She also promoted her book to the television audience, as in her two-part 1964 article for *TV Guide,* "Television and the Feminine Mystique." Although her celebrity was newly minted, the invitation to publish in *TV Guide* marked her rapid ascent from best-selling author to media-designated spokeswoman and dovetailed with *TV Guide*'s strategy of positioning itself as a watchdog of television rather than as a promotional magazine for the industry (Altschuler and Grossvogel 1992).

As she had found women's service magazines confining, Friedan's article found in television another example of how popular media inculcated women to accept and imitate a narrow world: "The whole world beyond her home—its politics, art, science, issues, and problems—is evidently beyond her comprehension. For not only is there no television image of a woman acting in the world, but the programming of daytime television and, increasingly, even in prime time, assumes she has no interest in it or ability to understand it. She lives only for love." Again she saw the media in terms of their power to influence its consumers: "Is it a coincidence that millions of real girls, who have grown up watching television—and seeing only that empty 'glamorous' housewife image of women—do not, in high school, have any goal in their own except being such a passive housewife?" (Friedan 1976: 50, 55).

In the meantime, publicist Tania Grossinger booked Friedan for interviews on a national promotional tour, smoothed over difficulties when Friedan insulted interviewers, and arranged for books to be purchased at Friedan's speaking engagements, a new method of marketing. All of these efforts brought the book to a generation of women who seemed to be waiting for it. Bella Stumbo, later a reporter for the *Los Angeles Times,* recalled the impact of Friedan's promotional stop there: "Betty Friedan came to town. She was promoting *The Feminine Mystique* and I got to do the interview. It was true love. I was an enlisted person in the army. The women's army. Crazy people feel that way when they hit a shrink's couch; there's finally someone who's willing to listen" (Ricchiardi and Young 1991: 86).

One episode in the marketing campaign deserves attention because it has been noted in subsequent writings by Friedan. Friedan was booked on a forerunner of national daytime talk shows, Virginia Graham's syndicated *Girl Talk*. The format was designed to be gossipy and informal, its spark generated by bringing unlike guests together. As Graham described it, her guests were "people who would never meet in life, never sit next to each other at a dinner party, never glare at each other in contempt or purr silken insults at each other" (Graham, V. 1966: 196). This concept led to a varied mix of guests—most were celebrities, but writers and professional women were also included—the primary necessity being able to talk easily and wittily. Graham's job was to bring out the opposite points of view in a lively, entertaining way while she took on a moderate or conservative road, presumably representing the point of view of her viewers or at least of the station managers who purchased the program. Subjects for the show often imitated what was appearing in the mass magazines of the day and like them sometimes had an undercurrent that questioned accepted practices. This was demonstrated in the subject of the first show: Should husbands and wives go on separate vacations? The topics reeled from the frivolous—the Gabor sisters were frequent guests—to the timely (for example, a program on LSD), each subject with a pro and con but in a chatty, conversational style from a comfortable living room set. Friedan appeared on the show in 1964, three years into the show's run, when the concept of spark by way of opposites was well established. Friedan was paired with the English comic actress Hermione Gingold (Graham, V. 1978: 106–8).

It was an odd combination—the supercilious and theatrical Gingold and the intense and humorless Friedan, alike only in that there was a slight resemblance between the two women. Graham instigated the spark, as she did with all her guests, and was delighted when "Hermione and Betty went after each other tooth and claw." In her second memoir, Graham remembered the program in terms of its entertainment values, "one of our funniest shows" (Graham, V. 1978: 172). Friedan, however, recalls Graham promoting confrontation by asking her audience, "Girls, how many of us really need bylines? What better thing can we do with our lives than do the dishes for the one we love?" In response, Friedan said she turned to the camera and said, "Don't listen to her. She needs you out there doing the dishes, or she wouldn't have the captive audience for the television program, whose byline she evidently doesn't want you to compete for" (Friedan 1976: 40).

Earlier, Friedan's recollection was sharper. Never hesitant to criticize women who did not share her point of view, Friedan called Graham an "Aunt Tom." "Once I was interviewed on television and said something about getting more satisfaction out of having a byline than out of washing dishes. And the hostess, a big, tough battle-axe who has worked ruthlessly for her success, smiled tenderly at the studio audience and said, 'Oh, girls. What does a byline mean? Don't we all know that being at home washing the dishes and caring for her loved ones is the most satisfying work a woman can do?' That's a real Aunt Tom" (Lear 1968: 50). As late as her 2000 memoir, Friedan still referred slightingly to the interview, having the last word (Graham then dead) by remembering Graham's name as "Vivian or something" (Friedan 2000: 141).

In terms of the program, Friedan's response was not any more confrontational than many on a show that sought lively and oppositional discussion. In collective memory, however, this early representation of feminism became an example of what would be viewed as Friedan's personality. The *Girl Talk* episode set out feminism as angry, with Friedan as its early standard-bearer, a frame from which the movement could never disassociate itself.

By 1964, Friedan was not simply promoting her book but was in demand as a paid speaker. Her booking firm, W. Colston Leigh, organized intense, tightly scheduled tours that included private schools, such as Smith, Colby, and Mt. Holyoke Colleges as well as Westbrook Junior College in Portland, Maine, and Modesto Junior College in Modesto, California. As in the placement of her articles, Friedan was a democrat, never fussy about the venue in which she spoke if it meant a paying audience. Friedan was a popular choice for nation's burgeoning junior colleges, which in the 1960s were experiencing a bulge of older women students, some of whom had undoubtedly begun or returned to college as a response to Friedan's book. Serving this nontraditional student population at what were sometimes out-of-the-mainstream institutions was a source of livelihood for Friedan and, soon thereafter, many other leading feminists. These tours also helped make feminism a national phenomenon. When Friedan became president of NOW in 1966, she used her speaking tours to recruit for NOW chapters, a form of rank-and-file organizing reminiscent of old-time socialists. Friedan's ongoing lecture tours—usually accompanied by a local media interview at each stop—provide one explanation for Friedan's continuing recognition as a leader of the women's movement long after her ties to movement organizations ceased. As late at 1999, a tribute to her organized by the Veteran Feminists of America was dominated by a stream of former NOW chapter presidents from the late 1960s.

The Issue of Stridency

In contrast to the favorable response to her on speaking tours, evidenced by her subsequent returns to the same venues, *Girl Talk* was fairly typical of her public face. The headline to a November 1963 *Life* magazine story characterized Friedan as an "Angry Battler for her Sex," accompanied by an unflattering photograph. (Interestingly, the photographs in which Friedan was in a housewifely setting—for example, dusting a bust of Lincoln—are flattering.) Nonetheless, it was a coup to have a spread in *Life*, made possible in part because of Friedan's willingness to use personal connections. In this case, angered by Norton's lack of attention to her book, she invited a *Life* editor and his wife to dinner on the tenuous connection that his wife, like Friedan, was a Smith College graduate (Friedan 2000: 140).

Although Friedan might find her way to media attention, she was not able to control the coverage, as when she appeared on a 1963 ABC-TV program, *Philco Presents the World's Girls*, purporting to examine women's power around the world. Accompanied by jolly music, a male commentator, and many shots of women in bikinis, the "special" found women's power not wanting. As in the *Life* article, Friedan was characterized in negative ways. Utilizing film clips from her speech to the National Women's Press Club, where, slim and well-groomed, appropriate for the suburbanite woman whom she sought to represent, Friedan spoke clearly and calmly about how the skein of gender expectations closed opportunities for young women. Friedan cast her comments in the familiar, framing the therapeutic sensibility so popular in women's magazines: "The terrible thing we are doing in the name of femininity. We are preventing them from their growth as human beings" (ABC 1963).

These comments, hardly revolutionary, nonetheless abutted an interview with Simone Signoret, who seemed to be directly answering Friedan, saying, "It's too complicated for me," as she affirmed her satisfaction with womanhood. "I'd rather be a woman," Signoret said, setting out what would be a frequent media representation of feminism as disaffection with female gender rather than the status of female gender.

There is no disagreement that Friedan was as difficult in professional circles as in her private life. As early as 1964, when invited to take part in the remaking of *Ladies' Home Journal*, even Friedan admitted that *Journal* editors found her difficult (Friedan 1976: 30). In a 1970 interview, when Friedan's reputation for stridency was well established, Friedan's early publicist, Grossinger, was quoted in a *New York Times Magazine* interview, "There were few stations that asked her back because she was a tough interview. I can remember her confronting Virginia Graham on 'Girl Talk' and screaming, 'If you don't let me talk I'll say orgasm ten times'" (Wilkes 1970: 30). Muriel Fox, who directed the initial public relations efforts for the National Organization for Women, found that one of her jobs was to make amends to those whom Friedan had alienated: "Betty was so hostile [that] I was sort of her ambassador to the rest of the world. That was an important part of what I did in the early days, not just to the press but to other NOW members who

Betty was so rude to that they'd say, 'It's not worth it,' and some of them quit and I talked them into staying or cooperating or whatever it was" (Fox, Muriel 1998). At a 1999 tribute Anne O'Shea, a former administrative assistant to Friedan, described her job as "trying to soothe the feathers Betty had ruffled."

Friedan's hostility finally resulted in her replacement in media circles by Gloria Steinem. However, Friedan's willingness to remain a public figure, coupled with her quick and angry tongue, made her ongoing copy for journalists and helped cement the theme of feminist stridency that was to be the ongoing stereotype of feminists of the second wave. There was indeed a reference to this aspect of her personality in all of her major interviews until the 1990s (Sherman 2000). Nonetheless, both in the 1963 publication of her book and in the founding of the National Organization for Women in 1966, Friedan's legacy to the women's movement was profound. Its most telling characteristic was the role she made for mass media in distributing the messages of the second wave, beginning with *The Feminine Mystique.*

2. Marching for the Media
NOW and Media Activism

In taking to the public stage to market *The Feminine Mystique*, Betty Friedan not only contributed to the success of the book but became famous herself, and the line between marketing the book and taking on the mantle of leadership of a burgeoning women's movement began to blur. In moving from a writer on social issues to a popular leader, Friedan is equaled only by Ralph Nader, whose *Unsafe at Any Speed* (1965) projected him to the leadership of the consumer movement. But elevation from best-selling author to reform leader is not the usual path for writers on social issues. Vance Packard, author of *The Hidden Persuaders* (1957), did not become a spokesman for reform of the advertising industry, nor did William Whyte, author of *The Organization Man* (1956), seek to change the way Americans do business. Friedan, however, gave up her stated ambition to attend law school once the manuscript was finished in favor of active involvement in a social change cause. Her willingness to take on the mantle of leadership, her unwillingness to fade into a media afterthought, and her passion for the cause, all on top of her celebrity, led to the formation of the most well known of second wave organizations, the National Organization for Women. From the beginning, NOW emphasized the role of the media as a lever for social change, a result of Friedan's experience and belief in media, the media women she gathered around her, and the willingness of women who came into the organization to utilize media avenues.

In Friedan's account of the genesis of NOW, the idea for the organization came in 1966, when she was in Washington researching a second book and came into contact with the leadership of the state organizations of the President's Commission on the Status of Women, established by President John F. Kennedy in December 1961. Despite the commission's announced purpose, combating prejudices and outmoded customs, there were several political motivations for its founding: to repay women who had supported Kennedy, to build a bloc of women for continued support, and to deflect attention from the Equal Rights Amendment, which was strongly opposed by organized labor, whose support was necessary for Kennedy's reelection (Harrison 1980). However, the Business and Professional

Women and the General Federation of Women's Clubs had long argued against the continuance of protective laws for women—the position of organized labor—and, at a time of increasing numbers of women in the postwar workforce, continued to lobby for the ERA. Concerned that the ERA might become a political issue, U.S. Rep. Emanuel Celler (D-N.Y.), a powerful opponent of the ERA, initially proposed the commission. Estelle Peterson, assistant secretary of labor in the Kennedy administration, who had a background in organized labor, brought it to fruition (Stewart 1980). The commission's final report in 1963 had no role for an equal rights amendment, but its attention to discriminatory labor practices fostered the passage of the 1963 Equal Pay Act and a presidential order requiring equality of hiring for career civil service positions (Harrison 1980). The commission was reappointed during Lyndon B. Johnson's administration, and, in a climate of social change, the president announced a campaign to put fifty women into high federal offices. Commission members, however, were frustrated by their lack of power. When the women at the 1966 national convention, the commission's third national gathering, were told they could not pass resolutions or take action, there was strong agreement that a new organization was needed, "an NAACP for women." According to Friedan, Sonia Pressman, an assistant to the general counsel of the Equal Economic Opportunity Commission, took Friedan aside to tell her that only she had the independence to do what had to be done: "You have to start a national organization to fight for women, like the civil rights movement for blacks" (Friedan 1976: 80).

This was an important juncture in the second wave—moving from activism on the inside to a protest model based on outsider status. The choice to move to the outside had important ramifications for the movement, one of which was the adoption of protest as a lever for change. Protest, so strongly linked to media, brought new levels of mediation into the movement—on the one side, the protesters, who chose issues to fit the protest model, and on the other side the media, which could choose how to cover issues. For women of the period, however, the perceived success of the early civil rights movement encouraged second-wave feminists to gravitate from the slow-moving national commission to what appeared to be the more immediate changes that could be wrought by protest pressure.

A similar national commission established in Canada in 1967 (the Royal Commission on the Status of Women) used the prestige of the national government to put feminist concerns on the national media agenda. Like the U.S. commission, the Canadian commission was charged with making a report. But its chair, the American-born Florence Bird, nationally known in Canada as a broadcaster under her professional name, Ann Frances, saw the worth of the commission not so much in the final project but the process of gathering information. In the process of information collection, Bird took advantage of the opportunity to establish a public sphere that could be enhanced by media reportage. Women in each region were invited to present "briefs" as the commission traveled to various parts of the country. And Bird, at ease with media herself and generally liked by media practitioners, some of whom she knew, utilized the prestige of the national commission as the "news hook" to engage ongoing coverage. This coverage occurred not only in the regions the commission visited but also nationwide, thanks to the national media institutions that followed the commission's trail. Bird's strategy of taking the commission to the people in a more-or-less unmediated style allowed the hearings to serve as a bully pulpit for subjects that had never before had a national airing. As Barbara M. Freeman writes, the work of the commission "was a watershed for Canadian women, a historical first that allowed issues previously deemed part of the private or domestic sphere to become the focus of intensive discussion in the public sphere" (Freeman, B. 2001: 3).

The Canadian model did not prohibit or challenge the presentation of other views of feminism; rather, it insured feminism a continuing and public presence in the Canadian news media while Bird and her commissioners gathered information for the report. In the end, with the force of government sponsorship at its back, the Canadian media had little choice but to convey the message of a changing place for Canadian women. In the United States, however, the President's Commission on the Status of Women tends to be remembered as a launching pad for NOW rather than as an agent for change on its own merits.

The influence of the civil rights movement clearly encouraged middle-class activists to move to a protest position, reflecting the general American belief that news coverage of the early civil rights movement had been essential in securing passage of the Civil Rights Act of 1964 and the Voting Rights Act of 1965. Moreover, for members of the commission, the connection to the Civil Rights Act was more than relevant, as the commission sought to have women included under Title VII of the act—specifically, the Equal Opportunity Employment Commission, which had been formed as one of Title VII's ramifications. Additionally, the rejection of a government commission may represent a peculiar U.S. sensibility that generally expects the government to react to pressure rather than exert leadership. Finally, Friedan was available to serve as the catalyst.

Thus, the proposal of a name for the organization, scribbled on a luncheon napkin at a concluding commission event (in the oft-told tale) resulted in an announcement in October 1966 of the establishment of the National Organization for Women, to be headquartered in Washington. Friedan was elected president, and Kathryn (Kay) Clarenbach, head of the Wisconsin Commission on the Status of Women, was named chair of the board. Other commission and former commission members also gravitated to NOW leadership roles (Davis, F. 1991; Zelman 1980).

The Commission on the Status of Women had considerable influence on NOW. The prestige of the group's original members, well known on a regional if not national basis, helped in a media world that sought authority figures. Many of the early NOW leaders from the national or state commissions were familiar with the levers of government and business and were often involved in other women's activist organizations. One of the important associated groups was the National Federation of Business and Professional Women's Clubs (BPW), the organization most responsible for shepherding the Equal Rights Amendment through its 1970 congressional approval. Katherine Peden was the BPW's 1961–62 national president and an appointee to the national Commission on the Status of Women. Peden, the 1968 Democratic candidate for the U.S. Senate from Kentucky and later Kentucky's commerce commissioner (among other achievements) is one example of the activist women from the BPW who influenced the commission (Lyne 1992). Margaret Rawalt, a past national president of the BPW and another member of the national commission, was a founding member of NOW and headed NOW's first legal committee. Women attorneys, such as Mary Eastman and Pauli Murray, joined NOW from similar backgrounds of activism on behalf of women. For many commission members, however—and particularly for BPW members— feminism was primarily about equal opportunity in employment. One early press report on the founding of NOW suggested that the organization had an even more narrow concern—equal employment for women in government alone. As the *Christian Science Monitor* summed up the new organization, "Women want policy-making jobs in government now—not tomorrow" (*CSM* 10/31/66: 1).

Powerful women in their own right, familiar with organizational roles and tools, the women on the national commission sought action and change by the levers at hand but generally eschewed the theoretical explorations that were already under way in the American Left. Nonetheless, as much as Friedan, commission members saw women's opportunities limited by the images that were presented to them. In a speaking campaign to clubwomen, Catherine East, executive secretary of the Interdepartmental Committee on the Status of Women and later a member of NOW, explained the disparities in salaries between men and women in terms of a national culture that defined women's expectations by discouraging girls from seeking nontraditional careers. In a statement that would become part of the mantra of the women's movement, East told the audience of the Boston Soroptomist Club, "We can let boys know that a girl's sex attractiveness is not a measure of her worth. We can teach girls that marriage is not necessary to a full life" (Shelton 1966: 132).

Commission members, like Friedan, saw mass media as shaping such perceptions; thus, in keeping both with Friedan's view and with the commission's outlook, an "Image on Women" task force was one of NOW's original groups. But what Friedan brought to NOW that had not been such a concern for the BPW, the federally employed women, or the commission was her tactic of using media for the new organization's goals. As a media professional, Friedan, like Bird in Canada, sought to manipulate the media in ways that would promote coverage of NOW's issues. Thus, for Friedan, the commission's concern for the images of women in media tended to blur with the uses of media for NOW goals. The emphasis on using media was strengthened by the media women Friedan gathered around her in the first sweep for members outside the commission and BPW women. The final piece that cemented the media's role in the organization was Friedan's success in locating NOW's public relations activities in the nexus of mass media, New York City. Friedan was already a public figure because of her book and its promotion, and the founding of NOW gave her the national leadership of the new movement in large part because she took that role to the national media.

Building the Media Engine

In her travels for the promotion of the book, Friedan met excited women to whom the book had been so meaningful that she named her second book with the comment she heard most often, "It changed my life." Her calls to speak did not come from "garden clubs," in Don Fine's dismissive phrase, but from professional women's clubs, such as the National Women's Press Club in Washington and BPW and Zonta chapters. Members of the women's professional organizations, which usually had been established because professional women were barred by professional organizations' men-only policies, were obviously aware of employment barriers against women. For some women, these employment barriers were emblematic of larger forms of discrimination.

Although the accepted narrative of NOW's establishment is one of a spontaneous reaction to the limitations of the commission, it appears that Friedan had been thinking of an organization at least since the publication of the book. The reaction of women she met on tours could only have encouraged her. In November 1963, Friedan addressed the New York chapter of the American Women in Radio and Television and suggested that she was deliberately floating the notion of an organization. The idea fell on fertile ground. In her letter of thanks, the program chairman, Muriel Fox, wrote effusively, "For some time I've been fishing around for a Burning Cause in which to believe—the kind of cause one might perhaps someday espouse on a full-time basis. Some of the old Burning Causes have lost some of their spark through the years. Your talk yesterday convinced me of the great need for a militant, intelligent organization devoted to women's rights—something like a cross between CORE and the Anti-Defamation League, with men as well as women on its staff. My guess is that such an organization will be flourishing in the foreseeable future—with you and Margaret Chase Smith as its prophets" (Fox 11/15/63). The foreseeable future, although without Margaret Chase Smith, arrived three years later when Fox received one of Friedan's exploratory letters asking for five dollars from each recipient to start the new organization. By utilizing the women she had met on her publicity tours, Friedan built a base of support in the new organization.

In that exploratory letter, Friedan used the civil rights motif in her opening line: "Some of us have finally decided to do something about organizing a kind of NAACP for women, a Civil Rights for Women organization, as you will see from the enclosure. The idea, for the moment, is not to set up a big bureaucratic organization with lots of members, but rather to get together women and men who share our purpose, and who can work effectively to stimulate the action that is needed now on a number of problems. There is no organization that now exists to do this. One is very much needed if we are ever to change the stereotyped image of women in America, create some kind of new social institutions that are needed, and break through the silken curtain of prejudice and discrimination that now exists" (Friedan 1966). Of the three goals Friedan set out in her exploratory letter, the "stereotyped image of women in America" shares equal billing with the creation of new social institutions and the breakdown of prejudice.

In the summer of planning between the Washington meeting of the Commission on the Status of Women and the announcement of the formation of NOW, Friedan brought together her friend actress Betty Furness (who, in addition to her own media experience, was married to Leslie Midgley, executive producer at CBS News), ABC reporter and documentary producer Marlene Sanders, and Fox, all of whom had responded favorably to the Friedan letter. The subject was ostensibly image, although Fox remembers the meeting as a social event "in which Betty and Marlene were used to put pressure on me to head the pubic relations. I think that's all that happened at that meeting, not any strategy" (Fox 1998).

Muriel Fox's role in helping to establish NOW as a public presence can hardly be overestimated. Fox was not only connected to an important organization of media professionals, the American Women in Radio and Television, but was prominent—eventually becoming vice president—in the country's most well known public relations firm at the time, Carl Byoir. Fox subsequently became the nation's highest-ranking female public relations professional, and she brought to the founding of NOW the expertise of her profession, the contacts made possible by her employment, and a deep commitment to the organization, including her involvement in the founding and long-standing support of NOW's Legal Education and Defense Fund. From the beginning, NOW had a voice that craft traditions found acceptable.

Like Friedan, Fox had been an activist, if not a leftist, working for the Congress of Racial Equality (CORE) at a time when the organization was considered more radical than the NAACP. Moreover, as a worker during the 1950s Florida senatorial campaign of Claude Pepper, she also had connections with the levers of mainstream politics. A reporter for United Press International when she sought a news career, Fox had also experienced gender discrimination, rejected by NBC "because they already had a woman in the news room." Byoir also originally turned her down on the basis of gender. None of this was surprising for the time. "Of course, *Time* magazine and *Newsweek* wouldn't hire women at this time. They would only use them as researchers, and they could give you all kinds of reasons justifying this, all sounding very silly today. You had to be a feminist, really" (Fox 1998).

Fox is also Jewish, and for the postwar generation the general belief in the efficacy of mass media could only have been heightened in the American Jewish community, with its long history of negative media portrayal and its culmination in German war propaganda. Not surprisingly, Fox specifically mentioned the Anti-Defamation League as a model for a new organization. Bess Myerson has discussed both her pain and her rage when she learned that her ethnicity made some people consider her a less desirable Miss America and how that realization spurred her involvement with the ADL's 1940s antiprejudice campaign (Dworkin 1998: 118). For Jewish women of the era, rejections did not always occur on the basis of gender, and reactions to anti-Semitism cannot be ignored in the anger of women of the time. Fox, not Friedan, inserted the word *militant* into the original NOW release, and nearly forty years later, Fox recalled, "We *were* angry" (Fox 1998).

At the time of her initial NOW involvement, Fox was married to a physician, the mother of a boy and girl, and in financial circumstances that permitted the family to occupy an apartment on New York's East Eighty-third Street, with a retreat in nearby Tappan County. Unlike Friedan, however, Fox was not only skilled but also classically attractive, personable, and conciliatory, factors that were helpful in building relationships with news organizations. Fox's involvement as NOW's first spokeswoman meant that the desire to establish the organization as a public presence would be affected by the standards of corporate public relations. Professionally written news releases, the use of high-placed media contacts, and the understanding of news values would all be part of NOW's early public relations' strategies. "I and Betty were more influenced by corporate and political public relations," Fox recalled in an interview. "The main reason we caught on so fast was because it was so long overdue, but I'd say another reason was because we were very professional" (Fox 1998).

While Friedan's celebrity made her useful for NOW organizing, she and her handlers also were aware of her penchant for negative publicity. According to Fox, Friedan's already established negative public image resulted in the decision to put Friedan forward as the second-in-command of NOW while Kay Clarenbach, the head of the Wisconsin state women's commission and involved in preparing women for career opportunities as director of continuing education at the University of Wisconsin, was named the chair. "Betty Friedan was a New York Jew. She also had an image that was not ladylike, shall we say. Some people called her abrasive. Pauli Murray was a black woman. We were really going after the establishment, so we felt we needed an establishment figure. Kay was tall, dignified, soft-spoken, an academic," Fox said of the decision (Fox 1998).

Other interpretations suggest that the choice of Clarenbach over Friedan was a result of a power struggle between East Coast supporters of Friedan and Midwestern supporters of Clarenbach. Despite her celebrity, early historians of the second wave noted that Friedan's "flamboyant and combative personal style had made her extremely controversial and, in some corners, greatly feared" (Hole and Levine 1971: 84). Before the October national organizing conference, Clarenbach and Friedan were each involved in separate recruiting drives along lines of regional division. Clarenbach may have been tall and elegant, but she was not eager to let the proposed organization fall into East Coast domination. By the time of NOW's organizing meeting, 126 of NOW's 300 charter members were from Wisconsin, Clarenbach's home state (Davis, F. 1991: 57).

Despite her position in the second spot, Friedan came to overshadow Clarenbach almost immediately. By drawing upon the expertise of the circle of media women she had recruited to NOW, Friedan was able to shift attention from NOW's Washington base to New York. While Washington remained the organization's headquarters, New York was the center of feminist activism as it was reflected in the mass media. That shift to New York made Clarenbach secondary to Friedan in terms of the public face of feminism, even though Friedan, as everyone at the time recognized, was herself not a skilled persuader in mass media terms. NOW and later radical women's organizations could not solve this conundrum: the perceived necessity to attract the media while breaking their craft traditions.

Fox's considerable media skills were instrumental in positioning Friedan as the face of NOW. Fox prepared the initial news release announcing the formation of NOW with such professionalism that it was virtually reprinted in Joy Miller's Associated Press story and found publication across the country, including the *Los Angeles Times* and the *Washington Post* but not the *New York Times*. Giving evidence to Fox's connections, the mimeograph machine that produced the release was loaned by the office of U.S. Senator Birch Bayh (D-Ind.) (Fox 1998), who remained a friend to the movement into the campaign for the Equal Rights Amendment.

The New York Bias

Despite the success of the original release, the news conference that came to be remembered was the one that coincided with NOW's first board meeting, held in New York in November 1966 and arranged by Fox to announce NOW's EEOC campaign. Not incidentally, this press conference served as the vehicle to eclipse Clarenbach and established New York as the organization's public face. New York as NOW's virtual headquarters magnified the efforts of NOW's New York chapter and, as a corollary, the actions of the radical Left in stories that were distributed across the United States by the national media headquartered in the city and by virtue of the national agenda set by the *New York Times*.

The news conference was held in Friedan's Victorian red living room in the famous apartment building the Dakota, where the Friedans had moved shortly after the publication of the book (even as Friedan was characterizing herself as an average suburban housewife). Sociologist Gaye Tuchman later blamed the location of the news conference, in living quarters rather than a business office, as one reason media framed the announcement as "novelty" or soft news (Tuchman 1978: 136). For Fox, who certainly had high-ranking boardrooms available, the choice of Friedan's living room was not casual but was considered the best way to get wide coverage: "Since Betty was a celebrity—with an interesting apartment at the Dakota—I knew it would help attract media. I especially wanted TV coverage at all our events" (Fox 1998).

In that respect, Fox was successful. The news release that quoted NOW's letters to the EEOC and President Johnson, coupled with the glamour of the location, served to draw media representatives from eight broadcast outlets as well as three newspapers, two magazines, the Copley News Service, a public relations agency, and several small publications. And Fox was pleased to note that the story found national publication beyond women's sections (Fox 1998).

In terms of the politics of the new organization, Friedan's celebrity, the location of the press conference in her home in New York rather than at the national headquarters in Washington, and the board action that gave her the responsibility "to continue to handle press and publicity" made Friedan the dominant presence in NOW for the rest of the decade. This was emphasized by the agenda-setting *Times*.

The *Times* did not send a representative to the news conference; instead, it devoted a story to NOW but based the piece on an earlier interview with Friedan that Fox had set up by directly writing to the *Times*'s editor, Clifton Daniel—another example of her ability to reach powerful people. The article was published on the day of the press conference in the paper's "Food, Fashion, Family, Furnishing" section, under a piece on how to carve the Thanksgiving turkey, with the slightly ironic headline, "They Meet in Victorian Parlor to Demand 'True Equality'— NOW," a placement that did not please Fox, even if was in the nation's most powerful newspaper (*NYT* 1/22/66: 1–44).

The tone of the story may have been ironic, but the content was all Friedan. Clarenbach, no matter her official position, her numerous supporters, her regional prominence or her WASPish style—with no Muriel Fox behind her— soon dropped out of the public eye. At her death, her public acknowledgement of her feminist activities rested on her niche in the founding of NOW (*NYT* 3/10/94: D21).

Friedan's desire to be the primary name connected to the founding of NOW resulted in an organization whose power rested in New York. This connection to NOW with New York had repercussions for the movement. As home to both con-servative and radical wings of the movement, New York coverage tended to blur the two. Further, the media coverage of the movement was emphasized because so many of the activists based in New York were employed in media professions and looked to media to tell their story. And the existence of a wide range of media in the city, including liberal venues such as the *Village Voice* contributed to coverage that was more extensive than might have occurred in other metropolitan areas. Perhaps most crucial to the movement was that New York was the home of the nation's most important newspaper, the *New York Times*, with its undisputed ability to be the major news agenda-setter—that is, the still-existing tendency for news organi-zations to follow the lead of whatever the *Times* chooses to publish.

Friedan's public orientation was toward an understanding of feminism as a rejection of the cultural conditioning that promoted gender inequities. Her book had spelled out her belief that mass media served as a means of social condition-ing, and her NOW leadership suggested she also believed a corollary—that mass media were powerful enough to undo what they had helped to establish. Friedan's view was reflected in NOW's "Statement of Purpose," which specifically drew attention to the mass media: "In the interests of the human dignity of women, we will protest and endeavor to change the false image of women now prevalent in the mass media." When the Task Force on the Image of Women was established as one of the eight original committees, the New York Committee on Image was targeted as its "nucleus" because of its "geographical location in relation to the center of the communication media" (Carabillo, Meuli, and Csida 1993: 163, 176). The expectation that chapters would regularly interact with media was clear in Fox's 1967 "Public Relations Report," which warned, "Don't let the press lure you into a battle-of-the sexes approach. . . . Don't participate in a discussion that pokes fun at women." Friedan's public announcements as president included urging chapters to promote publicly the national NOW positions: "Local chapters or NOW leaders might use some local action endorsing this program or pinpoint a local target for it, as a leader in issuing this same press release to your own newspapers, radio and TV" (Carabillo, Meuli, and Csida 1993: 215–16, 180). Special media kits were prepared for campaigns. Friedan early warned that to achieve its goals, NOW would use every lever available, including media: "We don't even exclude the possibility of a mass march on Washington," a telling comment in its implication that media attention was the penultimate political tactic (Friedan 1976: 98).

The strategies of corporate public relations clearly assisted in making NOW known. In its first report, the public relations committee chaired by Fox reported its successes: "On the whole, NOW has been treated by the press with respect and fairness. Press conferences have been well attended; and although certain newspapers restrict NOW coverage to the woman's page, most papers carry our stories in the general news sections. Thanks to coverage by Associated Press, NOW has appeared on the front page of many leading American newspapers." The report noted particular successes: Friedan's appearance as part of a two-hour program devoted to the subject by NBC's *Today Show*, an article favorable to NOW in the Sunday newspaper supplement *This Week*, major stories quoting NOW. Friedan also reflected NOW in her ongoing professional writing career in articles that noted her leadership of NOW, as in 1968 column for *Mademoiselle* (Carabillo, Meuli, and Csida 1993: 215). From a distance, Fox reiterated her belief in these strategies: "We just knew if you wanted to succeed, you just had to have public relations and you have to have media support and media attention. This is the way corporations do it. This is how politicians do it. This is how our movement had to do it. We wanted to be big time, and you can't be big time without the media. Betty Friedan certainly understood that" (Fox 1998).

Friedan and Fox soon discovered that their vision of NOW vis-à-vis the media was shared by the women who responded to the call for chapter organization, no single chapter more influential in this regard than the one in New York, many of whose first members were connected to the media. An early chapter president was Ivy Bottini, a graphic artist, who designed the famous NOW logo. Other media-connected members included Dolores Alexander, a reporter for *Newsday* and later NOW's first national executive director; Marlene Sanders, one of a handful of female network correspondents (who later dropped her membership because of conflict-of-interest issues, although she remained a friend to the movement); Lucy Komisar, a freelance writer who became the chapter's first public relations director; Susan Brownmiller, a television reporter, magazine writer, and book author; Florynce Kennedy, an attorney who had long fought civil rights issues using media tools; and Midge Kovacs, a New York advertising professional who later headed up NOW's 1970 image campaign. Singled out by the national organization to spearhead media actions, with members who were part of the nation's most skilled media professional class, and pushed by Friedan to be active, New York NOW helped set a media agenda for the entire country.

The EEOC Campaign

The end of sex-segregated advertising was the first and most successful of NOW campaigns that reflected a partnership of the legal and public relations strains of the new organization. Under the leadership of Washington-based attorney and NOW organizer Mary Eastman, NOW petitioned to have the EEOC find it illegal for newspapers to segregate help-wanted advertisements by gender. Here was a subject related to equal-employment practices that affected many NOW members.

In New York, Dolores Alexander coordinated an elaborate demonstration. Dressed in turn-of-the century costumes, women picketed the *Times* building, chanting, "The *New York Times* is a sex offender," an effort that helped land a spot on television news and a picture in the *Times* itself. Following suit, other NOW chapters picketed EEOC offices in several cities, sometimes dumping piles of newspapers to protest the policy. Friedan threatened to sue the government on the issue at an event to which television crews had been invited, and in February 1968 NOW instituted a suit. On August 9, 1968, an EEOC ruling specifically banned separate listings by sex for help-wanted advertisements. The National American Newspaper Publishers, which wanted no interference in the most profitable area of newspaper advertising, countersued the EEOC, but on December 1, 1968, the *Times* and other major newspapers discontinued the sex-segregated listings. Although the legal action and pressure by NOW officials in personal visits to government officials had been part of the success of the campaign, the visibility of the campaign brought attention to NOW, helped build chapter membership, enlarged Friedan's presence in the public mind, and verified the decision to take public policy concerns into the mass media arena (Davis, F. 1991: 60–61).

Public Accommodations

With the EEOC campaign considered a success, Friedan turned NOW's attention to equality in public accommodations and chose a young acolyte, Karen DeCrow, later a NOW president, to head up its national campaign. In choosing to expand interest to public accommodations, Friedan was clearly following the civil rights model, whose images of young men and women seeking service at southern lunch counters remained fresh in the public mind. By the time this new campaign was launched less than two years after the organization's founding, NOW had received substantial national publicity, including a *New York Times Magazine* article that gave the new movement its name: "What Do These Women *Want?* The Second Feminist Wave" (Lear 1968).

NOW's media activism increased when DeCrow became the founding member of the Syracuse, New York, chapter in 1966. Like others in NOW leadership, she had a media background—a graduate of Northwestern University's Medill School of Journalism who had worked as a textbook editor at Holt Rinehart in New York City before accompanying her husband to his new job in Syracuse. She enrolled in Syracuse University's mass communications program but gave it up to enter law school (DeCrow 1999). DeCrow served NOW in a number of media-related leadership roles and later took her interest in media actions to her NOW presidency. Her media awareness was apparent in a 1968 response to a Chicago woman who was considering a sit-in at Berghoff's Department Store. DeCrow provided a list of suggestions, beginning with the recommendation for an association with the local NOW chapter. "It is good to have an organization behind you. SNCC is composed of about 50 members nationally, but they get their power from being an organization." She also urged dressing conservatively ("the press will try to make you look idiotic"), avoiding joking with reporters, knowing the law, and approaching the business before the picket line was set up "so they can never tell the press that they had no idea that anyone objected to the men's grill, etc." She urged comparison with the civil rights movement: "Stress the black analogy. Can you imagine a restaurant on Adams street for whites only: A shocking thought. This is the same exact thing" (DeCrow 1968).

At its December 1968 meeting in Atlanta, the NOW board adopted three goals for its public accommodations campaign—the inclusion of "sex" in the public accommodations section of the Civil Rights Act of 1964 and in state and local law; a boycott of United Airlines because of its men-only flight between Chicago and New York; and the designation of 9–15 February 1969 as "Public Accommodations Week," aimed at ending "blatant second-class citizenship symbols." As the NOW resolution put it, "All NOW chapters and individual members are urged to protest, demonstrate, sit-in, picket, and otherwise dramatize the situation in each male-only public accommodation" (Carabillo, Meuli, and Csida 1993: 53). Here was a campaign that would seem to have obvious similarities to the highly successful sit-ins of the civil rights movement. NOW's campaign, however, would gain less sympathetic media coverage than the famous civil rights sit-ins and, indeed, would result in some backlash that connected NOW to white middle-class privilege.

Instructions were sent to fifty NOW chapters. Of those, seven chapters partici-pated, a response that pleased DeCrow. "Demonstrating is frightening and difficult and embarrassing, as each of us who has done it knows" (DeCrow, "Memo": 1). As part of its United Airlines campaign, five Chicago NOW members, joined by Friedan, picketed the United Airlines office but received characteristically dis-missive coverage from the *Chicago Tribune*, which quoted a United official as pre-dicting that the policy would not change (*ChicTrib* 2/15/69: 5). In Colchester, Connecticut, some twenty NOW members picketed the Chestnut Lodge, resulting in regional coverage that was likely prompted by the news hook that the leader of the picketers, Diane Fedus, was the daughter of the lodge's owner (DeCrow 1998). In Los Angeles, the chapter's plan for a showdown at the Polo Lounge backfired when the bar served the women who were ready to demonstrate. The action, or intent thereof, received attention in two papers (the *Hollywood Citizen-News* and the *Beverly Hills Citizen*) as well as radio and television coverage, as reported to DeCrow by the Los Angeles chapter president, Sylvia Hartman (DeCrow 1969). In Pittsburgh, the activist chapter had already conducted successful sit-ins at the city's Stouffer's Restaurant and sought to bring attention to its success. In Syracuse, DeCrow and five other NOW members dressed in turn-of-the century costumes to picket a men-only bar, which, on a slow news weekend, gained them TV coverage. In Washington, three women were refused service at the restaurant that had a men-only lunch policy, but they received no coverage or satisfaction from the manage-ment for their trouble.

Given this kind of spotty coverage, the campaign clearly would have sputtered to failure had it not been for the New York NOW chapter activities. Local and national media attention resulted from coverage from the focus in New York on well-known men-only bars—McSorley's Old Ale House, the Biltmore Bar, and the Oak Room in New York's legendary but nonetheless discriminatory Plaza Hotel.

Friedan, Fox, DeCrow, Alexander, and other NOW participants were correct in their judgment that the choice of the Oak Room would draw media attention, for it easily met many of the needs of the news profession—the location was well known, it had visual interest for the television cameras, the event was scheduled at a time that was helpful to deadlines, and the occasion offered an opportunity for conflict. A NOW member simply made a reservation without reference to gender, arrived with the NOW group on 12 February 1969, and was refused entrance in front of the previously alerted reporters. The group seated itself at a large round table. Waiters removed the table, leaving the women, Friedan in fur, sitting in an empty circle. Pictures were taken, although well-dressed women sitting in a circle did not carry the same emotional appeal as young people seeking to be served at lunch counters in the South.

The coverage included a piece in *Time* magazine's most-read section, "People," a classic example of dismissive journalism in its references to "ladies" and "NOW girls" and an emphasis on Friedan "fuming" (*Time* 1969: 33). However, the Sunday supplement *Parade* provided a picture and a straightforward account attached to other issues of wage and employment discrimination (*Parade* 1969: 2). Unlike groups in Syracuse, Colchester, Pittsburgh, or Los Angeles, New York NOW had put public accommodations on the media agenda, even if coverage was problematical.

Nor did the press for public accommodations by public actions stop, although, like the Oak Room, the actions often involved perceived upper-class women denied entrance to men's clubs. In March 1970, a well-known sociologist, Dr. Jessie Bernard, and a biochemist, Dr. Joy Hochstadt, refused to enter Washington's Cosmos Club by the required "Ladies Entrance" (*WP* 2/25/70: B2). As in the civil rights model, there was a certain heroism in taking a public stand that attracted upper-class women as much as any other women, even if lunch was all that was at stake. As chapter 5 will explore, the effort to open up New York's McSorley's Bar to women also took on class issues.

The Limitations of the Civil Rights Model

Both the EEOC and public accommodations campaigns illustrated NOW's allegiance to the civil rights model. Under Fox's direction, the rhetoric of NOW as a civil rights movement for women was reflected in mass media as in the article, "Sex and Civil Rights," appearing in the Sunday newspaper supplement *This Week* (3/19/67: 2). A *New York Times Magazine* story noted that "NOW often makes this analogy between the Negro and the woman in society." One of the picketers in the accompanying art carried a sign that connected the civil rights theme to abortion: "It is a woman's civil right to bear only wanted children" (Lear 1968: 50, 24). Philadelphia's *Evening Bulletin* put it more bluntly: "Rebellion among Women Parallels to Black Revolt to Erase 'Slave Mentality' " (*EvenBull* 3/19/70: 18).

The civil rights motif was serviceable in gaining early attention, but there were obvious limitations. First, this strategy defined the women's movement as a kind of offshoot of the civil rights movement, suggesting that civil rights was an appropriate template for the women's movement and meaning that issues outside of that template—a radical reconstruction of male and female relationships, for example—did not easily fit. Second some people perceived this very public use of the civil rights analogy as another white co-optation of black life—privileged white women riding on the coattails of the civil rights movement for their own aims. Although women of color had been involved in the founding of NOW and a woman of color would be the group's second president, the organization's adoption of the civil rights motif did nothing to lessen tensions between the black community and the women's movement and probably contributed to them. In 1974, Harvard professor Alvin Poussaint reflected a common view in the African-American community when he argued that the attention given to the women's movement was at the expense of black Americans, who were being forced to compete with white women (*NYT* 5/6/74: 35).

NOW was also organized at the time when coverage of the goals of the early civil rights movement was fading in favor of the harsher news emerging from the Black Power movement. Put off by the use of the word *militant* in Fox's press release and connecting it to NOW's use of the civil rights analogy, an editorial in the *Monroe (Louisiana) Morning World* warned, "We are in favor of equal rights for women and don't know anyone who isn't. We are a little afraid, though, that if women follow the path of the integrationists, they'll start saying, 'Women Power' instead of equal rights" (12/30/66: 4A).

Finally, Friedan was obviously not a leader equal in stature to Martin Luther King Jr. a comparison that every reference to the civil rights model could only emphasize. Her demeanor never represented the self-sacrifice, humility, or tacit vow of poverty that accompanied early civil rights leadership. DeCrow remembers Friedan as always "dressing in the height of fashion," even wearing a fur coat to NOW meetings—hardly the image for a social justice movement (DeCrow 1998). Friedan clearly enjoyed her life in the Dakota and, unlike early civil rights leaders, who were supported by their organizations, Friedan supported herself through her writings and appearances as a feminist leader. This fact, alongside her celebrity, gave her an independence from the organization she represented. She did not, for example, hesitate to criticize those who opposed her, offering strongly worded opinions that were sure to be quoted and that helped to maintain her public celebrity while inserting divisiveness into mass media coverage of the movement. Moreover, she offended countless women in the organization, including lesbian women, with a remark she later recanted, calling lesbian activists the "lavender menace." As feminist writer Vivian Gornick observed, "Once Betty Friedan opened her mouth she never shut it" (Gornick 1999). She seemed to thrive on dispute and disorder. "She never learned to chair an orderly meeting small or large,"

Toni Carabillo, a NOW public relations director and no supporter, recalled in her history of the organization (Carabillo, Meuli, and Csida 1993: 30).

It is interesting to contrast Friedan's style to the leadership of other social justice campaigns of the same period. Unlike the women's movement, the influence of the early civil rights movement on other movements was less in direct association with civil rights than in the adoption of its leadership models. In organizing the United Farm Workers, for example, Cesar Chavez's use of fasts established an ascetic, almost religious tone that overcame the tainted image of labor leaders dealing in back rooms. California growers, some of them small and struggling farmers, were characterized as the enemy when faced with Chavez as the transcendent leader. Such leadership was helpful when the UFW established national boycotts of lettuce and grapes, small sacrifices that allowed well-meaning people to play a role in what had been framed as a social justice movement rather than a labor dispute. In the meantime, the UFW also used other well-established labor tactics that were not as transcendent but did not find a place on the national media agenda. The media portrayed Ralph Nader in similarly ascetic ways, a man whose commitment to the consumer movement was above suspicion of personal gain. Nader was seen as a crusader and as earnest rather than threatening.

Historians of the women's suffrage campaigns might note that persuasive techniques based on self-sacrifice and asceticism, a traditional role for women, did not work; indeed, not until Alice Paul instigated an aggressive style did the suffrage movement move forward. It is noteworthy that Fox's first news release announcing the organization used the word *militant*. It was not a casual use, Fox recalled: "We wanted to be militant. We wanted people to be scared of us" (Fox 1998). However, the adoption of public confrontation as a mode of operation, in actions and in speech, jarred with NOW's use of the analogy of the early civil rights movement.

The constant reference to civil rights did nothing to draw black membership to NOW, despite the organization's constant reiteration of its commitment to women of all colors. NOW remained characterized as a white, upper-middle-class organization, and actions such as that at the Oak Room could only promote that notion even though, outside of New York and its suburbs, NOW membership was not necessarily middle class, given that NOW was perceived as "militant." However, Friedan's inability to adopt a style of leadership that fit the civil rights motif, even as the organization used the theme, exacerbated perceptions. Despite the professional manner of NOW's public relations campaigns, NOW's leaders seemed less sophisticated when it came to identifying an alternative to the use of a model that caused so much irritation among black Americans. This irritation turned out to be long-standing and severely damaged not only NOW but the feminist movement as a whole by the general assumption, as personified by Poussaint's comments, that feminism was antithetical to the concerns of African-Americans.

Despite its emphasis on image and its use of professional media managers, NOW was never able to make the press into the carrier of goodwill for feminism, a role the media had served for the civil rights movements, in which, as Nicholas Lemann writes, "much of the press was effectively part of the movement, and an indispensable part." It was not that the press simply recognized the justice of the civil rights cause or acknowledged King's leadership: "it was the staging of events in order to play to the national audience," events that often played out as "a real-life morality play" (Lemann 2003: 89). Rosa Parks was put forward as the example of the hardworking African-American woman who, one day on a Montgomery, Alabama, bus, spontaneously decided she had had enough of living under racist rules and refused to give up her seat. As we now know, however, Parks was a trained civil rights activist whose demeanor and personal history organizers considered appropriate for the action. Television, wire, and magazine photographers transmitted powerful photographs of beaten and bloody nonresisting young people, of children seeking entrance to schools, and of the thousands of peaceful demonstrators on the March on Washington who wanted only to enjoy the promise that the national monuments implied. Such grand events were already part of the panorama of the nation's history when NOW chose to use demonstrations to present its views, mistakenly believing that such a campaign could be transposed to another arena.

The Limitations of Demonstrations

During the early years, NOW and its chapters found few issues inappropriate for public demonstration. The demonstrations tended to be attached to a rhetorical strategy aimed at media attention, including a name for the demonstration and highly quotable placards. In 1971, for example, New York NOW supported a widow who was seeking to deduct child care expenses from her U.S. federal tax return. The demonstration involved women pushing baby carriages and called itself the Baby Carriage Brigade, with the slogan "Are Children as Important as Martinis?" In 1973, in a coordinated national action, NOW chapters presented local Bell System affiliates with a "bill" for four billion dollars in back wages that NOW calculated employees had lost as a result of discrimination. In the same year, NOW members dressed in judicial robes conducted a mock session of the Supreme Court outside the Supreme Court building. The NOW demonstrations were in addition to actions by radical feminists which, in the wider view, may have contributed to a fairly rapid public weariness of the movement. While the subject of each demonstration may have been worthy, multiple demonstrations on multiple subjects did not provide the same kind of clear narratives or powerful events with which the media had been presented at the integration of Little Rock's Central High School, by the beatings of the Freedom Riders, or by the events in Selma, Alabama. In contrast, the use of demonstrations by NOW and many other feminists drew attention to the plethora of areas of feminist activism but did so in what often seemed a nagging litany of demand rather than in the heroic proportions of civil rights.

Nonetheless, by the late 1960s, some of NOW's goals began to be met: the campaign to end newspaper job listings by gender had generally succeeded; public accommodation barriers were failing; and favorable court decisions ruled against the automatic relegation of women into lower-paying jobs. Public actions in most of these areas seemed to have played a necessary if not pivotal role, and feminist leaders, many of them excited by the atmosphere of challenge and change that public actions promoted, could not be blamed if they did not see the long-term consequences.

Friedan stepped down from the NOW presidency in 1970. Under succeeding leadership, the organization continued to experience rifts, challenges for leadership, and sometimes lurching change, not surprising for a maturing organization. In the meantime, the organization was moving toward a professional paid staff, including the hiring in 1973 of a paid public relations specialist, Dian Terry, whose office was located in New York. Terry's files indicate that her strategies were based on accepted public relations practices (NOW-SLRI: 30). But clearly, many NOW members, including some of its leaders, saw public demonstrations as an irresistible siren's song. Even when NOW was not officially involved, NOW members often supported the actions of other feminist groups when word was passed around the feminist community.

By 1970, NOW was only one of a plethora of women's groups, not all of which agreed with NOW policies, even though, for many Americans, NOW's visibility seemed to speak for the whole movement. At the end of 1969, concerns about the splintering movement led Friedan to initiate a series of regional conferences under the rubric of the Congress to Unite Women, a title that recalled that of the 1940s' Congress of Women. After several stormy meetings (at which the press was not allowed), Friedan concluded that the congress had failed to "jell" because of the "shock-tactics and man-hating" strategies of radicals (Friedan 1976: 138). Political radicals, however, saw the congress as the "Congress to Unite White Middle-Class Women," women who did not want to unite along a political ideology: "Women cannot be united if their only common feature is genital structure" ("Congress" 1970: 12). The movement's radical wings clearly were not going to accept NOW leadership, and the media were happy to reflect the split.

3. The Left at Center

For mainstream activist women such as NOW's Muriel Fox, mass media coverage of the women's movement was a desirable goal, to be achieved by methods that melded corporate public relations with the organized protests of the early civil rights movement. But for the radical women who became known as the "politicos," in the jargon of the day, the lessons and culture of the antiwar Left provided the media training ground. In the hands of these radical women, efforts to achieve mass media attention became increasingly dramatic, as they chose to confront symbols of systemic female repression rather than the concrete examples of discrimination that were the focus of NOW's protests. NOW's EEOC demonstrations, for example, were aimed clearly at demonstrable ends, but the demonstrations influenced by the radical women—and the radicals' actions increasingly came to dominate national media coverage—were symbolic expressions of the radical critique of the role of gender throughout American society.

NOW's liberal feminism saw women's oppression as rooted in social and legal constraints based on gender. Once those constraints were removed, women would be "full partners," as NOW's statement of purpose asserted. There would never be a single radical critique, but radical feminists sought major restructuring of society, not simply the opening of doors to benefits that had been previously available to middle-class and generally white males. Some radical feminists sought to construct feminism in Marxist and socialist terms, seeing women's oppression as a tool of capitalistic control; other radicals emphasized that traditional women's values of peace and participation should be central to rather than at the edge of society; others believed that feminism grew from personal experience; yet others sought to build a women's community separate from men.

These strands sometimes blurred and crossed over, as various groups adapted ideas from each other. And despite their ability to catch the mass media eye, no evidence exists to suggest that any of the radical critiques, together or separately, ever dominated feminist thinking, even at the centers of their development in Chicago, New York, Gainesville, and Berkeley, much less nationally. Nonetheless, the radical critiques came to national prominence quickly and for some of the same reasons that had helped NOW get on the media agenda.

Like early NOW activists, significant numbers of radical women sought to cooperate with the media to put the radical critique on their agenda. Kate Millett, after the sudden fame brought by the publication of her *Sexual Politics*, found herself initially flattered by the attention and thought she might be helpful. "For a good while I imagined I was using a diseased system to attack exploitation itself in advocating radical ideas." She concluded the thought: "A tricky proposition" (Millett 1974: 78).

However, in the early days, radical women, as much as their NOW sisters, were fueled by a belief in the efficacy of mass media. Some radicals gave advice that might have been come from NOW's Fox. Karen Kordisch, writing in Denver's alternative women's newspaper, *Big Mama Rag*, argued that formal feminist organizations were necessary because they met a journalistic standard: "The media is more likely to publicize a group function than individual actions and people are more likely to listen to something a group of united individuals recommends than one they've never heard of. It is *crucial* that people hear us and feel our pressure if we hope to accomplish change outside ourselves" (Kordisch 1974: 10). Most important in the history of the radical intersection with mass media was writer and activist Robin Morgan. While charging that media ownership patterns contributed to the distortions media promulgated, she nonetheless believed that mainstream media were crucial to the distribution of the feminist message. "Leafleting on New York's Lower East side for ten years would not reach the housewife in Escanaba, Mich., but thirty seconds on the six o'clock news would" (*NYT* 12/22/70: 33). The belief in the efficacy of the mass media remained with some activists thirty years later. For example, Ellen Willis, a writer for the *Village Voice* weekly and the *New Yorker* magazine during the period, believed radicals' ideas, coupled with mass media, were most responsible for making a place for feminism in the public consciousness: "It was radical feminism that put women's liberation on the map, that got sexual politics recognized as a public issue, that created the vocabulary ('consciousness-raising,' 'the personal is political,' 'sisterhood is powerful,' etc.) which the second wave of feminism entered popular culture" (Willis 1994: 118). "The primary task of the early radical feminist," she said in a later interview, "was public consciousness-raising—getting these new and controversial ideas out to women everywhere. Publicity was not simply a vehicle for the movement; it was at the very center of what the movement needed to accomplish. And our efforts were very successful, despite the fact that the media (by no means always) distorted or were hostile to what we had to say" (Willis 1998).

The Left Press

The ongoing irony, both in NOW and in the Left in general, was that this search for media attention existed alongside the common perception by activist feminists that mass media were damaging to women. The Left press abounded in warnings of the dangers of mass media. In Iowa City, the founders of *Ain't I a Woman* declared, "We have to communicate without the constraints of the pig press. . . . The only thing that appears in the pig media for women is propaganda in its worst form, glorification of the social stereotypes that keep men happy and ridicule, vilification or pity for the women who don't live up (down) to those stereotypes" (*Ain't* 6/26/70: 2). Early on, *Women: A Journal of Liberation* addressed the hegemony of mass media: "The Mass Media plays a crucial role in creating and perpetuating American dominant ideology: racism, imperialism, chauvinism, authoritarianism. We have been brainwashed to believe that the American press is free, that it provides objective coverage of the news, all the news, and that it is a public service. It is time for us to destroy that myth" (Eldowney and Poole 1970: 40). For a journal that claimed to represent the "pro-woman faction"—the belief that women first had to come to an understanding of their oppression by means of consciousness-raising—the role of media in maintaining psychological imprisonment was central.

For many alternative publications, moderate, left, or far left, female portrayal in mass media was an unrelenting theme. "Broadcast television stations decide who they will give coverage to and who they will exclude; they color the image they choose to broadcast to express their own bias" (*BMR* 2/75: 2). *off our backs* similarly warned, "The media always needs an 'angle,' a 'story,' a 'leader,' a 'thread.' For the sake of our movement, we must protect ourselves by rejecting that and forming our own communications" (*oob* 4/25/70: 16). *Fighting Woman News*, a monthly devoted to the martial arts and combative sports, ran a regular column about mainstream media as "The Media–Look What They Wrote about Us This Time!" (*Fighting Woman News* 1/77: 2). Image was a constant theme. *Ain't I a Woman* said that the media created the stereotype of a "liberated woman": "The image of a liberated woman is of a braless, well-endowed middle class naïve looking woman, shouting obscenities as she snips the long hair of every woman she meets whether they want a hair cut or not" (*Ain't* 3/12/70: 5). The New York periodical *Up from Under* asserted, "Contrary to a variety of popular images, Women's Liberation is not a movement of hardened and coldly unfeeling females, shouting slogans, hating men, and scorning 'unliberated' sisters. Nor is it a movement that demands 'instant liberation': women do not have to leave their husbands and lovers, abandon their children, throw away their make-up, burn their bras, quit their jobs, or sleep with each other to be part of the movement" (Lichtman 1970: 23). As an *off our backs* writer put it, "There is a pervasive, insidious, and overt dehumanization of women and girls performed daily before millions of our very eyes and in the sanctity of our own rooms" (Polner 1972: 4). No feminist of the period would have contradicted Florynce Kennedy: "For as we all know from reading the papers and watching TV, feminists are nothing more than child-hating, white middle-class lesbians, who are mainly interested in burning their bras and being called 'Ms.' And beside, they're too homely to get a man. We also know that from reading ladies' page profiles and interviews that all women who have 'made' it, did it by themselves and are 'no women's libbers.' They say so themselves when the reporters ask them. And the reporters always do" (Kennedy 1977: 27).

That general distrust of the media in radical circles encouraged a rush of alternative publications, an explosion prompted not only by the times but also by the availability of cheap offset printing. Like the Left press in general, women's newspapers rejected the values of the mainstream press by taking a partisan view instead of the "objective" reporting of mainstream journalism, utilized personal voices in their editorial matter, and took a collective approach to decision making (Allen, M. 1988). The Liberation News Service, formed as an antiwar vehicle, later carried news of interest to feminists outside of mainstream framing. One alternative publication, Donna Allen's Washington-based *Media Report to Women*, continued to focus on women and media as its central issue many years after the peak of the movement and continues publication even after her death. Thus, alternative publications, word-of-mouth information, essays distributed hand to hand, and conferences provided an informational loop that was considered more reliable than anything the mass media could provide.

Beyond those strategies, the rush for media exposure indicated that, despite misgivings, many radicals were influenced by popular and Marxist beliefs in the "powerful-effects" theory of mass media as much as was their archenemy, Betty Friedan. However, radicals were less attuned to the role of craft traditions than was Friedan, and when reporters, following those traditions, gave coverage that did not please the radicals, the activists were quick to blame bias (which certainly occurred).

In retrospect, the radicals' early decision to seek mass media attention led to the exposure of ideas while they were still undergoing inculcation. Given the general middle-class orientation of the history of the women's movement in the United States, the ideas were startling and revolutionary. But unlike other social change and political groups, where repression made it necessary for ideas to undergo discussion for decades, the radicals of New York, San Francisco, Chicago, Gainesville, Pittsburgh, and other cities found some version of their ideas reflected in the media after conversations of a few months. Moreover, fearing a diminution of their ideas, radicals were not anxious to be connected with mainstream groups; thus, divisiveness—quickly picked up by news coverage as it fit one of the standard definitions of news of conflict—was set in place from the beginning.

The radical women could certainly have looked to the antiwar movement to see the destruction that media could wreak. Todd Gitlin, one of the early leaders of the Students for a Democratic Society (SDS), came to recognize the media's power to damage the organization: "The force of publicity was straining the organization as its weak seams. If access to media was now a source of power, it was also a source of dissension" (Gitlin 1980: 90). Gitlin's warning words did not come until after the protest period was over. For the radicals, the antiwar movement provided other lessons.

The Influence of the Antiwar Movement

Some of the radical ideology began with disaffection within NOW chapters. Ti-Grace Atkinson, for example, came to national attention when she equated marriage with slavery and was a founder of the radical group The Feminists, but she entered feminist circles as the Friedan-anointed leader of the New York NOW chapter. Activist Rita Mae Brown took her energies to other venues when her NOW chapter did not welcome her announcement of her lesbian identity. But second-wave radical feminism is most connected to the 1960s antiwar movement as well as its precursor, the American civil rights movement of the early 1960s. Both had relevance for how radical women chose to intersect with mass media.

As we know from multiple accounts, white women in the antiwar movement, including those who had also been part of the civil rights movement, began drawing comparisons between the role of black Americans and American women as early as 1964. Those discussions were reinforced when the male leadership of the antiwar movement seemed no more ready than men in the wider society to share leadership with women. For women antiwar radicals who were also "red diaper babies"—children of 1930s communists—that discussion returned them to groundwork laid by the Marxist critique of mass media as both a shaper and influence of America society. Moreover, the younger women, coming of age during the heavy newspaper and television coverage of McCarthyism in the 1950s, encouraged a predisposition to suspect the mass media but also to believe in their power to influence. Finally, like the founders of NOW, the young radicals had come to adulthood during the early civil rights movement, with its journalistic images that unequivocally arrayed right against wrong.

When the civil rights movement rejected white activists, they took to the antiwar movement their experience with events that had been mounted to gain the media eye. Those images likely seemed all the more powerful because they had had a role in sparking these people's activism. Adapting the strategies of sit-ins and protest to the antiwar movement led the early SDS to note with a satisfied air, "We have seen antiwar leaflets photostated [*sic*] on the front pages of newspapers with circulations in the millions. We could have been at the mimeograph for ten years, and not reached as many" (Gitlin 1980: 91). The student base of the anti-war movement grew, utilizing young men and women whose middle-class homes had held *Life* magazines on coffee tables and whose television sets had been tuned to civil rights coverage.

The power of public demonstrations in the United States has not arisen from the physical danger that large groups of people pose to those in charge. No U.S. demonstration has resulted in a governmental coup or an exchange of power. The strength of American mass demonstrations has been in the symbolic and dramatic representation of the problem, including the representation of protesters as willing to take risks, although, unlike other countries and with the exception of the deaths at Kent State University, risks to American protesters have been minimal. But because news coverage always seeks expansion on what was last reported—a worse crime, a more terrible disaster, a more tragic accident—movements that rely primarily on demonstrations find themselves having to produce larger and larger numbers of people or more and more dramatic confrontations to retain news attention. When antiwar demonstrators adopted public demonstration as their prime weapon, leaders found themselves caught in a bind of mounting ever-larger demonstrations to provide evidence that a sizable number of Americans opposed the war. By 1969, activists had mobilized 250,000 marchers to converge on Washington for the largest antiwar demonstration ever. But in a country of two hundred million people, no demonstration can ever represent a majority. However, large demonstrations were and remain dramatic, and that characteristic alone was sufficient to make demonstrations sought-after media content. The fact that the mass media seek out dramatic content is quite apart from the question of whether the content is effective in changing public consciousness or in gaining access to political power. Moreover, antiwar activists found that they could become media-recognized leaders on the basis of their ability—as much any other programmer—to come up with product. While news organizations gave these activists the media leadership of the moment, it was a leadership that was not contingent on the usual requirements—that is, political office, organizational office, or the consensus of a particular constituency such as that represented by Cesar Chavez or Martin Luther King Jr.

Faced with the voracious appetite of the nightly news, the discovery that the research activities of major universities were complicit in the nation's defense system provided a new hook for demonstrations, and antiwar activists turned to university protests: "Takeovers" became militant extensions of the civil rights sit-ins. Militant or not, they could only be symbolic takeovers, a fact that the protesters sometimes forgot until police arrived to clear them out. The most famous of the takeovers occurred at Columbia University in 1968. Calling on strategies that had been tested in other university actions, students staged "teach-ins," sit-ins, rallies, pickets, finally shutting down the operation of five university buildings. As one writer described it, "They held a dean hostage, and ransacked university files, uncovering correspondence that belied university officials' claim that there were no institutional ties" to the Institute for Defense Analysis (Morgan, E. 1991: 121). When negotiations failed, two thousand police officers cleared the buildings, on some occasions with violence. Nearly seven hundred protesters were arrested, 30 percent of them women, who received special press coverage. SDS leader Tom Hayden considered it a success: "SDS and its militant vision were suddenly catapulted into a national and international prominence" (Hayden 1988: 272). While the violence of the police action produced some sympathy for the students, sympathy cannot be considered a universal reaction. *Life*'s famous picture of twenty-year-old Mark Rudd with his feet propped up on a vice president's desk may have suggested to readers that the takeover best represented young male arrogance (*Life* 5/10/68: 38).

The Columbia riots in April were followed by another protest benchmark, the Chicago Democratic Convention in August. With Columbia as the precedent, Hayden encouraged escalation. When the violence of the Chicago police caught the attention of the nation's television networks (prompted in part when more than sixty convention journalists were injured in the melee), the news corps, including CBS's Walter Cronkite, criticized the police response, some calling it a "police riot." Again, radical women were involved in the protest: one out of eight of those arrested were women (Babcox 1969: 5).

Perhaps no other demonstration of the period received such sympathetic coverage. Although Hayden had been active in promoting conflict, to many American television viewers the police action appeared unwarranted and spontaneous, promoted by Mayor Richard Daley. However, the propaganda success of the Chicago demonstrations did not please older leaders of SDS, who were calling for an end to "terrorism, sabotage and window-busting for the hell of it" in favor of community organizing. "It is a grave error," an SDS paper said, "to use an essential military tactic in a situation that is not military but social. Here is an excessive fascination with guerrilla war. A military approach to a struggle is useful only when you already have won over large masses of the population" (*NYT* 9/24/68: 25).

It was a call in vain. Under new leadership, antiwar violence on college campuses, now bursting with the Baby Boom generation coming of age, exploded. SDS seemed tame compared to new antiwar groups that now moved from takeovers of university buildings to bombings of them, as at the hotbed of protest at the University of Wisconsin at Madison. After four deaths at Kent State University, two more students were killed and twelve others wounded when police reacted to a Jackson State College protest. The President's Commission on Campus Unrest predicted that if the crisis continued, "the very survival of the nation will be threatened"

(*Report* 1970). By the end of the 1960s, American cities had burned in riot, public figures had been assassinated, universities had been bombed, and the nation's president was abjured by large parts of the population. The sexual revolution was ushering in new standards hardly envisioned a decade before, the unionization of farm workers made the consumption of common foods a political act, and NOW had already called for "militant" action in its first press release. At this moment of escalation and disaffection, the radical women's movement emerged. A product of the time, its supporters were not to retreat from its tools.

The Emergence of the Women's Left

Women activists in the antiwar movement were clearly disillusioned. Despite years of service, the younger leadership seemed no more enlightened than the young man who told Hayden at a 1960 conference, "The first thing you have to understand is that the movement revolves around the end of a prick" (Hayden 1988: 107). Beginning in 1964, antiwar women began discussions that found comparisons in the status of oppressed people and the status of women. By 1967, Shulamith Firestone and Pam Allen, active in Chicago's SDS, moved to New York and established the New York Radical Women. In 1968 Beverly Jones and Judith Brown composed a lengthy pamphlet, *Toward a Female Liberation Movement,* that was passed hand to hand and noted that "people don't get radicalized fighting other people's battles" (Jones and Brown 1968: 20). However, for many other women, the commitment to the antiwar movement remained paramount. To bridge the antiwar movement and the emerging women's movement, the Jeannette Rankin Brigade, named after the World War I pacifist, brought existing women's peace movements together. In January 1968, five thousand brigade members arrived in Washington to demonstrate against the war. The event also attracted women from the emerging radical women's movement, who voiced objections to the brigade's acceptance of women's "tearful and passive" role in the antiwar movements, as Firestone put it (Davis, F. 1991: 78). In an event that called upon the Left's use of political theater, Firestone, Kathie Sarachild, and others staged a mock funeral procession at Arlington National Cemetery to represent the burial of "traditional womanhood." In response, five hundred women left the original convention, aligned with the new movement, and returned to their home bases to form new women's groups. The use of a symbolic event to voice the women's dissatisfaction was an early indicator of the role of symbol in the new women's Left.

The emerging feminists received little respect from the antiwar movement. In a notable episode, Marilyn Saltzman Webb, an SDS veteran and a member of the brigade, was shouted down when she attempted to speak at a National Mobiliza-tion Committee gathering in Chicago: "Take her off the stage and fuck her!" and "Take it off!" (Hole and Levine 1971: 133–34). For many Left women, the January 1968 issue of *Ramparts* magazine, the Left's slickest magazine, was another indica-tion of the male Left's dismissal of women. The issue aimed to profile the women's movement as represented by the Jeannette Rankin Brigade. However, Rankin her-self was dismissed as "an elderly lady banging her umbrella over the head of a man beating his horse" (Hinckle 1969: 24). The magazine's cover featured a headless female torso, a "Jeannette Rankin for President" badge pinned close to the eye-level décolletage, which, as *Voice of the Women's Liberation Movement* put it, "depicted 'political women' as having two tits and no head." *Voice of the Women's Liberation Movement* also gave its "Male Chauvinist of the Month Award" to *Ramparts'* editor, Warren Hinckle (*Voice of the Women's Liberation Movement* 3/68: 2).

This anger at New Left men had ramifications for the media representation of the radical women's movement vis-à-vis men. The specific anger at New Left men came to be represented, by media and the women themselves, as anger at men as a class. For some women, anger was directed toward men as a class. But for all radical women who came to the movement from the Left, the immediate anger was at the men of the Left. "No more, brothers," Robin Morgan wrote in her famous essay, "Goodbye to All That." "No more well-meaning ignorance, no more co-optation, no more assuming that this thing we're all fighting for is the same one: revolution under *man*, with liberty and justice for all. No more" (Morgan 2000: 53).

However, the new women radicals were hardly aligned on all issues. The extent and responsibility of white outreach to black women was argued, as it was in NOW, and radical women were no closer to a solution than were moderate reformers. Disputes broke out between women who became known as the "politicos"— women who sought a dramatic political solution along Marxist lines—and women who wanted a realignment of gender roles. Each of these groups, and the permuta-tions among them, had views toward the use of media. The political feminists saw media manipulation as part of their activism; other feminists on the left, although not the majority, viewed the mass media as a tool that maintained hegemony. For such skeptics, the master's tools were not the way to pull the house down.

Nonetheless, as a whole, the radical women believed in the use of agitprop, but only under established rules to govern behavior with the media. The Redstockings set up a code of behavior: a radical woman alone could not talk to media repre-sentatives; media tasks were to rotate among all members; only women reporters would be tolerated; personal aggrandizement would not be tolerated, including the use of speaking or writing about the movement for livelihood; and women who did not abide by the rules would be ejected from the group. The Feminists argued that the use of spokeswomen led to media stars: "The media uses stars for the very purpose of making ideas seem unimportant, just part of the show. Rather than appealing to reason, the star system nourishes and feeds upon an unfortunate characteristic of oppressed people—the need to look to someone else, to accept things of authority rather than trusting oneself. The result is the 'cult of personality,' hero worship, the dependency of the leader/follower relationship" (*Rat* 6/5/71: 9). Feminists who were seen to use the movement for their own ends ran the risk of being shunned, a practice that became known as "trashing."

These limitations on media interaction frustrated the radical women, who opposed the emergence of feminist leaders such as Gloria Steinem but could not so easily mount an alternative without breaking the rules against stardom. Instead, radical women put their belief in agitprop as a way to put systemic issues on the media agenda in actions in which all women could share equally.

Choosing Agitprop

For both radical and moderate activists, major influences promoted the adoption of protest marches and agitprop actions. What is easily forgotten, however, was how difficult it was to get media attention when it was sought in orderly ways. First-wave feminists had turned to dramatic actions after years of polite petitions, conferences, and legal activities failed. The danger was, of course, that any less-than-orderly behavior was immediately characterized as strident or shrill, and whatever had been the issue instigating the behavior was forgotten in favor of its presentation. This was the case when women who favored the legalization of abortion attempted to have a voice at a 1969 New York state hearing for the Governor's Committee on Abortion Reform—a committee composed of fourteen men and one woman, a nun. After efforts failed to be heard by way of organized channels, the women finally interrupted the hearing with a call for legalization of abortion, not simply reform. However, the committee reacted not to the women's opinions but to their style. The committee chairman chastised the Redstockings' Kathie Amatniek (later Sarachild), "You're only hurting your own case." State Senator Seymour Thaler said that he agreed with the women's position, but added, "I have never met such rude people" (*NYT* 2/14/69: 42). The committee was adjourned into an executive session because of what the chairman termed "the disgraceful conduct of the ladies" (*Nwsday* 2/14/69: 1). Newspapers played up the stridency aspects of the women's objections in headlines as "Invade Abortion Hearings" (*Nwsday* 2/14/69: 1), "Gals KO Abortion Hearing" (*DN* 2/14/69: 1), "Gals Squeal for Repeal, Abort State Hearings" (*DN* 2/14/69: 5), "Women Break Up Abortion

Hearing" (*NYT* 2/24/69: 42), alongside photographs and in text that played up confrontation and the scolding of the committee members.

Nonetheless, the press attention provided an impetus for New York state's passage of an abortion bill in March 1970, the second in the nation after Hawaii. Interestingly, and providing some evidence why the second wave does not remain in popular consciousness, the Redstockings' involvement in the abortion hearings and in the famous related "speakout" (in which women publicly acknowledged that they had undergone abortions) did not get mentioned in the *Times*'s anniversary examination of how the law came into being (*NYT* 4/9/00: Metro 1, 36). Indeed, the lawmakers who favored the issue may have believed themselves as much hindered by the demonstration as otherwise, certainly the view of State Senator Thaler at the time.

Agitprop, even of the mildest kind, turned out to be a double-edged sword. While actions drew news attention, the attention emphasized stridency. Once so characterized, stridency, not the issue, became the story.

Agitprop in Atlantic City

Among the most disaffected of Left women was Robin Morgan, the most influential woman in the radical representation of women's issue in mass media. Beginning as a child star in radio and in television live drama in the 1950s (the character of Dagmar in *I Remember Mama*), she was, by the late sixties, an editor at Grove Press and at the center of antiwar activism. She had participated in Angry Arts Week in 1966, joined the April 1967 peace march on the Pentagon, demonstrated against Secretary of State Dean Rusk at the New York Hilton, demonstrated against the draft, and was part of the demonstrations at Columbia University. She was on the editorial staff at *Rat*, the Left's most vociferous newspaper. As her disillusionment with the Left took hold, she brought to the women's movement lessons from the antiwar movement, which included her belief in the efficacy of building a mass movement by using mass media, and, as most clearly illustrated in the Miss America protest, influences from the Yippie movement.

By the time of the Chicago convention, a handful of protesters who called themselves Yippies (a play on *hippies*) had found less arduous ways of producing content. Abbie Hoffman and Jerry Rubin demonstrated that guerrilla theater, an ironic title, and much braggadocio could similarly bring media attention. As Raymond Mungo, one of the founders of the Liberation News Service, noted, when Rubin "personally announced that 500,000 Yippies would demonstrate in Chicago, only the federal government believed him" (Mungo 1970: 59).

Nonetheless, Morgan was one member of the radical Left who embraced the Yippies. She recalled, "I just walked into the Yippie office one day. There was this hysterical loft with the groovy posters and people sitting around rapping and coffee spilled on the floor, and whenever the phone would ring, whoever picked up would yell, 'Yippie!' It seemed life-affirming, myth-making, just beautiful! It was like the last gasp of the love generation, a real feeling of *communitas*" (Babcox 1969: 8).

Hoffman's biographer argues that the Yippies' emphasis on performance undercut the movement by not involving people in the real-life process of social change (Jezer 1992: 110). Hoffman himself had second thoughts about the Yippies' appeal to "the people" at the expense of more traditional methods of social organization. In his later career as an environmental activist, Hoffman emphasized grassroots organization. Nonetheless, to Morgan at the time, the group was an antidote to her disillusionment with the male leadership of the antiwar movement and led to her decision not to go to the Democratic National Convention in Chicago. Instead, her admiration of the Yippies was to flower a week later when Morgan was among a group of feminists who protested the Miss America Pageant in Atlantic City.

For politicos such as Morgan, the manipulations of craft traditions were useful in gaining attention to the movement at hand. But in at attempt to comply with the movement's rejection of media "stardom," Morgan agreed that no one at the protest was to assume to speak for the demonstration. And while Morgan, a political radical, sought media attention to promote radical political solutions, other radical feminists from the pro-woman faction saw the event as a way to bring attention to the role of women, in the phrase that became part of the later language, as sexual objects.

Representing this point of view was Carol Hanisch, who thought that a demonstration "just might be a way to bring the fledgling Women's Liberation Movement into the public arena—to reach out to other women with outreach and our dreams of a better life." As she recalled, "And here was this American icon—the Miss America Pageant—telling women what to look like, what to wear, how to wear it, how to walk, how to speak, what to say (and what not to say) to be considered attractive" (Hanisch 1998: 197–98). The simple demonstration thus became a representation of various wings of the movement. The call went out to various women's groups, politicos and otherwise, and about hundred women from Florida, Washington, and Detroit arrived with plans to unveil a banner within the convention hall to attract the NBC-TV cameras, to picket the hall, to perform skits on the boardwalk, to crown a sheep as Miss America, and to toss a variety of items aimed at representing women's oppression into a bin, the "Freedom Trash Can"—bras, mass women's magazines, and makeup.

While the women shunned the role of a spokesperson, none of radical women opposed the press release. Unlike the corporate style of releases prepared by Muriel Fox for NOW, Morgan's press release titled "No More Miss America" was filled with the rhetoric typical for Left pronouncements of the time. Its panache was undoubtedly increased by its revolutionary demand that only women reporters cover the demonstration. At the *New York Post*, reporter and later feminist writer Lindsy Van Gelder got the assignment and was told to make it funny—a framing that resulted in long-term consequences for the movement (Brownmiller 1999: 36–37; Van Gelder 1992). Despite the rhetoric of the news release, there was no mention that the contents of the Freedom Trash Can were to be set alight. Rumors of that possibility came from Morgan herself, as she sought to build media interest in the action. Van Gelder, writing a preview under the stricture to make her story bright, used Morgan's idea for her lively lead: "Lighting match to a draft card has become a standard gambit of protest groups in recent years, but something new is due to go up in flames this Saturday. Would you believe a bra burning?" (Brownmiller 1999: 37). The *Post*'s copy desk quickly appreciated the euphony of the *b* words, headlining Van Gelder's story: "Bra Burners & Miss America." So identified, the Van Gelder story and its headline may have done more to bring reporters to the boardwalk for the event than the fiery rhetoric of the press release.

The bin ultimately was not set on fire because organizers, wishing to avoid arrest, agreed to fire officials' prohibition. This decision to forgo unlawful behavior in the Miss America protest helped establish performance as protest in the American second wave of feminism. Although antiwar protests were increasingly violent and lawbreaking, this was one model of Left politics that was notably not followed in the second wave. Risks and costs undoubtedly were associated with second-wave feminist activism in the United States, but arrests and jailing were generally not among them, much less anything akin to the force feedings that had awaited imprisoned American feminists under President Woodrow Wilson. *Militancy*, in the dictionary meaning of taking up arms, was never a characteristic of the second wave, although in press accounts *militancy* was often used interchangeably with *stridency*.

Instead of the promised bra burning, the participants paraded around a roped-off section of the boardwalk, carrying placards and singing, "Ain't she sweet/Making profit off her meat," staged some guerrilla theater, and distributed flyers approved by organizers from the New York Radical Women. As archival footage of the event makes clear, a hostile crowd shouted insults at the picketing women, who appeared unmoved by the taunts. Male reporters were ignored in favor of female reporters, but no one person spoke for the group.

Although the can had not been set alight, Van Gelder's story had put the possibility on the news agenda. In the *New York Times*, Charlotte Curtis's story clearly conveyed that objects were tossed into a Freedom Trash Can but no burning took place. Morgan's meeting with the city's mayor was noted: " 'We told him we wouldn't do anything dangerous—just a symbolic bra-burning' " (Curtis, C. 1968). The tone of Curtis's story was arch but was not one of ridicule. From a later perspective, perhaps most objectionable was that another pageant conducted nearby to select a Miss Black America as a protest to the all-white nature of the original contest was tagged to the final paragraphs of the Miss America story.

The action, however, raised concerns in the radical community. Hanisch, who, according to her own account proposed the action, voiced a common criticism within the pro-woman community: "Miss America and all beautiful women came off as our enemy instead of as our sisters who suffer with us" (Hanisch 1968: 9). Judith Duffett, in her account in *Voice of the Women's Liberation Movement*, found it necessary to defend the action: "Our purpose was *not* to put down Miss America but to attack the male chauvinism, commercialism of beauty, racism and oppression of women symbolized by the Pageant" (Duffett 1968: 4). The discussion went public when Willis, a founding member of the New York Radical Women, limned the pro-woman philosophy in a letter to the *New York Times Magazine*: "It is senseless to blame [a woman] for her oppression. But such distortions are inevitable as long as women are squeamish about naming their oppressors: men" (Willis 1969: 12). In the end, however, Hanisch saw the action as successful. Thanks to mass media coverage, "millions of Americans now know there is a Women's Liberation Movement" (Hanisch 2000: 378). NOW's leadership was not pleased, believing that demonstrations, as in the EEOC picket lines, were best utilized for specific ends, not mass consciousness-raising. "We were annoyed," Muriel Fox said later. "Marguerite Rawalt was horrified" (Fox 1998).

Other feminists of a radical bent found themselves attracted by the boldness of the action but nonetheless sympathetic to the contestants. Karla Jay remembers that for her family, the naming of the first Jewish winner, Bess Myerson in 1945, forever established the contest as a barrier successfully overcome. To denigrate the contest was to dismiss the worth of the effort (Jay 1999). In her memoir, Morgan saw the influence of the action in limited ways. "Possibly the most enduring contribution of that protest was our decision to recognize newswomen only. It was a risky but wise decision that shocked many but soon set a precedent" (Morgan, R. 1992: 22).

Given Morgan's Yippie influence, the interpretation of the protest as the classic example of stridency is surprising. Indeed, the Yippies' humor had initially attracted Morgan to the style: "This may be the only political tactic short of sabotage and terrorism that is left to us now that the day of the mass march has passed. But humor is an extremely potent political tactic because its gives people a sudden and transforming insight into where they're at and where their society is at" (Babcox 1969: 87). However, no one was laughing in the aftermath of the

1968 Democratic convention, which seemed to portend the possibility of a real revolution, and, presented in a less than lighthearted way, the satire of the protest was lost. Bra burning, intended to be a satirical take, instead became an epithet and generally furthered the media stereotype of the angry, strident feminist. As Hanisch wrote in a memoir of the event, " 'Bra-burner' became the put-down term for feminists of my generation. The risqué implication of the term 'bra-burner' made the action more than even many feminists wanted to own. Had the media called us 'girdle-burners,' nearly every woman in the country would have rushed to join us" (Hanisch 1998: 199).

Whatever its shortcomings, the 1968 protest would forever after cause the American public to look at the Miss America Pageant in new ways. And while bra burning became the easy characterization of the movement, the event put the radical agenda before the public as no other action had. The *New York Times Magazine* devoted a lengthy article to the connections between the antiwar and women's movements that were anchored in the protest and included Morgan's unequivocal statement of its purpose: "The Miss America Pageant was chosen as a target for a number of reasons. It has always been a lily-white racist contest; the winner tours Vietnam entertaining the troops as a murder mascot. The whole gimmick is one commercial shell game to sell the sponsors' products. Where else could one find such a perfect combination of American values? Racism, militarism, and capitalism—all packaged in one 'ideal' symbol: a woman" (Babcox 1969: 34). However, at the Miss America Pageant the following year, the *Times* pointedly chose to run a short Associated Press story that noted the ten-hour picket by women only in the final paragraph, another indication that only innovative protests could catch the media eye (*NYT* 9/7/69: 68). Rather quickly, the protest came to occupy almost a fond niche in popular memory. "Is the new Miss America a feminist?" *Newsweek* asked the 1973 honoree, Rebecca Ann King. She was, she said, "probably semi," a response that inhabited the middle ground that media found comfortable (*Nswk* 9/24/73: 58).

Colgate Palmolive

For participants, agitprop actions were an opportunity for a handful of activists to get their view to a national media audience. From 1968 on, various agitprop actions centered in New York and often involved feminists from several organizations: NOW, Columbia Women's Liberation, New York Radical Women, the Redstockings, The Feminists, Media Workshop, and Media Women. One of the advantages for feminist agitprop was the location of the many radicals in what was not only the media center but also the corporate center of the nation and provided well-known and impressive headquarters that could be the focus of demonstrations and helped anchor the story for news media. This intersection often put radicals who sought systemic change and feminists who sought particular goals on the same side of the picket line.

NOW's picketing of the *New York Times* had been closely connected to the *Times*'s refusal to desegregate its help-wanted ads and was part of the larger NOW EEOC campaign. But on the feminist scene in the late 1960s, ideologies and activities blurred, and feminists from various radical wings would periodically flow in and out of New York NOW. One upshot of the fluidity around New York NOW was that actions served several purposes. For Florynce Kennedy, pressuring advertisers was a way to exert pressure on the media. "We're going to have to get at these companies that sponsor talk shows and other programs that treat women's liberation as a joke," she told a New York abortion rally (Goldman 1971: A28). Although the Colgate Palmolive action was ostensibly a call to boycott its products as part of that kind of pressure, the theatricality that accompanied the demonstration and the lack of follow-up on the boycott suggested that it was a way to bring media attention to their representation of Colgate Palmolive products as symbols of women's enslavement to housekeeping. Like the Miss America contest, it was another attempt at public consciousness-raising. Kate Millett donated a toilet from an abandoned art project into which demonstrators poured Colgate Palmolive products. Like the bra burning, the flushing was symbolic.

WITCH

Following Atlantic City, Morgan and others set about the establishment of the Women's International Conspiracy from Hell, an organizational title that was designed as a facade for the acronym WITCH. The name referenced not only the way outsider women have been historically characterized but was a reminder of the McCarthy-era witch hunts that seemed to be revitalized by the 1968 decision of the House Un-American Activities Committee to investigate communist infiltration of the Left. The acronym for the organization had other Left influences: the Yippie take on *hippie*; Valerie Solanus's invention, Society for Cutting up Men (SCUM); and the use of witches in women's Left theater.

WITCH's earliest action occurred in October 1968, a month after Miss America, when members dressed up on Halloween to "hex" Wall Street. In February 1969 a dozen WITCH members took on the "Bridal Fair" at Madison Square Garden, wearing black veils chanting "Here come the slaves/Off to their graves" to the cadences of "Here Comes the Bride" while giving out flyers that urged, "Confront the Whoremakers." Before the police arrived, protesters gathered in a circle to perform an "unwedding ceremony" to represent the "unholy state of American patriarchal oppression" (Hanisch 1998: 215). Finally, they released a handful of white mice to suggest that marriage was mindless. As it turned out, the young women attending the fair became the heroines in the coverage, even from movement-friendly Judy Klemesrud, who represented them—not screaming according to stereotype—but scooping up the pet-store mice in efforts to save them from the short and brutal lives that awaited them in the nether regions of Madison Square Garden: " 'Those people are a pain in the neck' said one young woman. 'I don't see why they have to come in and ruin . . . some thing nice like this' " (Klemesrud 1969: 39). As in the Miss America protest, the Madison Square Garden action also increased dissension in the radical community. Closely following the radical activities, Jay recalled her reaction: "Marriage might be slavery, but we had to offer a positive alternative before we encouraged women to abandon matrimony. And since Robin Morgan was herself married, wasn't her attack on prospective brides rather hypocritical?" (Jay 1999: 38).

WITCH also had chapters—"covens"—that mounted similarly styled actions in their cities. In February 1970, members of Washington WITCH, to a "stunned audience," interrupted a Senate hearing on population control, stopping a speech by Senator Ralph Yarborough of Texas with, "We are witches. We have to come to yell/You population experts/Can go to hell." As described by Alice J. Wolfson, "At a prearranged signal we all took off our coats to reveal witches' outfits, placed witches' hats on our heads, and jumped onto the stage, grabbed the microphones and put on a bit of guerrilla theater. I don't remember the whole skit, but I do remember the recurring refrain: 'You think you can cure all the world's ills, by making poor women take your unhealthy pills.' Each time we chanted it, we threw handfuls of pills at the members of the panel and the audience" (Wolfson 1998: 275). Wolfson's memoir of the demonstration draws attention to the serious purpose behind the actions, the full-time devotion of many activists, and the eventual successes some of the actions produced. Wolfson's efforts in drawing attention to the dangers of the birth control pill led to her full-time commitment to the women's health movement. However, unlike many of WITCH's actions, Wolfson's protests were directed at particular goals.

Institutional affairs were good targets for protesters. In Milwaukee, just five WITCH members interrupted the city's press club Gridiron Dinner meeting in a protest against media. "Media is power, through which you control our life, our spirit, our mind and our soul . . . for American capitalism woman is the home. . . . To sell your product you force us to buy shit" (*oob* 5/16/70: 10). In Washington, radicals and less radical women, some of them reporters from the *Washington Post*, joined forces to protest all-male nature of the National Press Club Gridiron Dinner when the club invited women to be guests at a 1972 event but not to be members. Katharine Graham, publisher of the *Post*, who had planned to attend, chose not to when faced with the formidable picket line and marked the event as a benchmark in her emerging feminist consciousness (Graham, K. 1997: 428).

Morgan's radicalism continued both within and outside of the movement. She was among the cabal of women who took over *Rat* in February 1970 and published the essay "Goodbye to All That," which conveyed the disgust Left women found in the male antiwar movement: "Goodbye to Hip Culture and the so-called Sexual Revolution, which has functioned toward women's freedom as did the Reconstruction toward former slaves—reinstating oppression by another name" (Morgan, R. 1992: 49). The piece was widely republished in the Left press, and a San Diego women's group named its publication *Goodbye to All That*.

Rat was the most well-known of the Left's antiwar publications, routinely publishing sixteen pages of militant rhetoric and illustrations each week. In its first statement, the *Rat* women's collective led with a familiar style:

Death to the bureaucrats, death to the sexists, death to those who care more about egos than they do about change.
   ALL POWER TO THE REVOLUTION (*Rat* 2/6–23/70: 2).

Subsequent issues sought to include the women's movement as part of the larger Left agenda, but within a year the larger agenda had been dropped, and *Rat* became a publication solely concerned with women.

Additionally, as an editor for Grove Press, Morgan became involved in promoting unionism for the activist Fur, Leather, and Machinist Workers Union, which was attempting to organize workers in publishing houses, traditional places that offered low wages for women (in exchange, presumably, for the prestige of working in a glamorous and genteel industry). Morgan was among the sixteen women protesters who barricaded themselves into the sixth-floor executive suites in April 1970 after eight Grove employees had been fired because of union organizing. Morgan was among the nine arrested, a group subsequently referred to in the radical press as the Grove 9.

The success of the agitprop actions in drawing media attention drew imitators as a way to dramatize their points of view. Women in New York and Chicago began to hold "ogle-ins" to dramatize the offensiveness of men making overtures to women in public places. In New York, the ogle-in was prompted by a woman whose breast size had attracted so much attention huge crowds of men gathered daily to watch her get off the subway to go to work (*NYT* 9/20/68: 49). The daily crowd brought its own media coverage. Jay, who had observed the WITCH activities with something of a critical eye, nonetheless chose to use agitprop as a form of public rebuttal. "Feminists needed to proclaim publicly that what we now call harassment happened all the time," she recalled in her memoir. "All sorts of men did it to all sorts of women. It seemed to me that it was high time to protest." Calling on her radical cohorts, the resulting protest received national attention as Jay called on the reliable Marlene Sanders from ABC-TV and other media contacts she knew as an activist and as someone employed in media.

Thus, as brokerage house male employees emerged from the subway exit onto Wall Street, they were greeted by women blowing whistles and loudly remarking on their body parts. "The men were horrified. We were having fun, and in many of the clips I'm laughing (as usual) at my own jokes. Marlene Sanders captured several men on film with gaping jaws, too surprised to comment." The women continued the action at prescreened construction sites. A radio interview on WBAI, covering the event live, followed (Jay 1999: 132–33).

The Feminists

Agitprop was not the only way to attract media to radical ideas. Often the ideas themselves were considered bizarre enough to warrant media attention. Ti-Grace Atkinson was among the first members of NOW and was first set to work as a national fund-raiser as a Friedan protégée. "Her social connections were good, and it may have occurred to some NOW officials that her appearance might help dissipate the traditional image of the feminist as a castrating crow in bloomers" (Lear 1969: 56). But Atkinson was clearly different from the initially genteel image she projected. By 1968, as president of the New York NOW chapter, the ideas that eventually were to part her from the organization were already evident. In a lengthy and generally favorable *New York Times Magazine* article, Atkinson disconnected herself from the NOW EEOC initiatives. "I'm afraid the woman's movement in this country is still pretty low-class, intellectually. Practically all we talk about is equal rights in employment. That's not opportunity: it's opportunism." Instead, she called for the abolition of the nuclear family and the end of one-on-one parent relationships in favor of communal child raising. And she voiced her dismay with marriage: "The institution of marriage has the same effect the institution of slavery had, it separates people in the same category, disperses them, keeps them from identify as a class. The masses of slaves didn't recognize their conditions, either. To say that a woman is really 'happy' with her home and kids is an irrelevant as the saying that the blacks were 'happy' being take care of by Ol 'Massa. She is defined by her maintenance role. Her husband is defined by his productive role. We're saying that human beings should have a productive role in society" (Lear 1968: 55).

The *Times*'s magazine piece may have been the first and last piece of mass media journalism that treated Atkinson's ideas with some degree of respect. Even in generally affirmative context, her comparison of marriage and slavery was viewed as bizarre. On a 1968 visit to Philadelphia (where she had attended the University of Pennsylvania and had been a founder of the Contemporary Arts Museum), still president of New York NOW, Atkinson repeated her famous line, "Marriage as it now exists is a form of slavery" to the Medical Committee for Human Rights. The remark reached a wider audience when it was reprinted in Rose DeWolf's popular Philadelphia newspaper column, although the quote DeWolf chose to use simply skimmed the surface of a speech that had called for the abolition of marriage and family, again comparing it to the abolition of slavery in the previous century. One way the status was maintained, she argued, was through the interpretation of female orgasm only in terms of male penetration. DeWolf recalled, "People didn't say *orgasm* in those days, much less complain that wives did not have enough of them, nor discuss what the male should do to bring such about" (DeWolf 1998).

Atkinson's views led to the formation of The Feminists, whose members agreed that mass media were useful for consciousness-raising and adopted agitprop actions even as they established no-star rules for dealing with it. In September 1969, Atkinson led five Feminists in storming the New York's marriage license bureau. In an article that seemed designed to irritate feminist readers, the *Times* reporter noted the irony of a recording of Tony Bennett singing "I Can't Give You Anything but Love" playing across the street from the bureau, graphically described the protesters' clothing—a "skin-tight, blue-and-red striped T-shirt" for Sheila Cronan and a "run in her stockings" for Atkinson—all in a tone that portrayed the bureaucratic protestations of City Clerk Herman Katz as a sympathetic Everyman contrasted with Atkinson's theoretical onslaught against a system "in which women are being illegally made sex slaves in the unholy state of matrimony" (Clark 1969: 93). Atkinson left The Feminists when it became clear that her attraction to media stardom did not fit with the organization's no-star philosophy.

Taking on *Ladies' Home Journal*

Women's magazines had long been a subject of feminist criticism since Friedan's massive critique of them in her book. Members of Media Women, an organization concerned with promoting professional opportunities for women in that arena, visited Helen Gurley Brown at *Cosmopolitan* to urge that the magazine reduce its emphasis on appearance and sexuality and may have been an influence when *Cosmopolitan* later ran an excerpt from *Sexual Politics*. But the dramatic sit-in at *Ladies' Home Journal* on 19 March 1970 became, like the Miss America contest, one of the classic actions of ambush feminism. This action also came to represent the clash of agendas between radical and not-so-radical groups. Members of Media Women found themselves at odds with radical women concerned with systemic change.

Although the protest was organized primarily by Susan Brownmiller, who represented Media Women, members of radical organizations were nonetheless part of the planning, which included conspiratorial visits to the *Journal* offices, the compilation of demands, and the preparation of a mock-up of the preferred *Journal*. As in the agitprop actions, memoirs of the event give evidence to the excitement of a group of young women united in a sense of doing important work at minor risk. There was even dressing up—"revolutionary disguise" as Jay described it—as the women, usually in jeans, were to wear skirts or dresses so that they could pass into the building without suspicion. A former *Journal* editor provided front door keys and a layout of the floor (Hershey 1983: 84). Serving as recorders and protectors were media, and, thanks to the New York location, the media that the organizers could call upon were major—Grace Lichtenstein, considered movement friendly, of the *New York Times*, Karl Meyer of the *Washington Post* (covering the event despite his gender), and Marlene Sanders of ABC-TV. As Jay recalled, in a rhetoric redolent of the period, "By then, every activist knew that a rolling television camera was the best protection against being beaten up by the pigs" (Jay 1999: 116, 115).

Brownmiller was one of the media professionals active in the New York Radical Women and was already experienced in media—as a reporter for NBC-TV affiliate in Philadelphia in 1965, a network newswriter at ABC-TV, a researcher for *Newsweek*, and staff writer for *Village Voice*. She was successful in her career as a freelance writer even before the publication of her pathbreaking *Against Our Will: Men, Women, and Rape* in 1975, writing one of the first major articles on the women's movement for the *New York Times Magazine*, "Sisterhood Is Powerful," which appeared in 1970.

"I specifically organized the *Ladies' Home Journal* sit-in," Brownmiller said in an interview. "I had by then worked for many years as a journalist. I knew what a story was. I knew this was a great man-bites-dog story—or, in this case, a woman-bites-magazine story—and I knew this would get national and international publicity if we pulled it off. And we did indeed" (Brownmiller 2000).

Shortly after 8 A.M. on 18 March, after having gathered at a church across the street, some two hundred feminist women interrupted John Mack Carter as he was meeting with his second-in-command, Lenore Hershey, in his "opulently masculine" (as Hershey later termed it) corner office at 641 Lexington Avenue. It was a mixed group of radical and moderate women—Shulamith Firestone, Ti-Grace Atkinson, Anne Koedt, Karla Jay, Minda Baxman, and Ros Baxandall from the radical faction, and professional writers including Brownmiller, Sally Kempton, and Alix Kates Shulman. "In they streamed," wrote Hershey, "a noisy, motley procession. They were women of all ages, without makeup, in fashions more *lumpen* than Halston, costumed for revolt. In an office which normally had seating room for a dozen, there suddenly were women everywhere, standing, sitting on the floor, draped over the table and the windowsills, and spilled out into the halls. For the first few moments, they all seemed to shout at once. It was a zoo" (Hershey 1983: 84).

Quickly, the alerted media arrived, including ABC's Sanders with a film crew, Lichtenstein, Meyer with a photographer, and the Associated Press—heavyweights all. Demonstrators hung a banner reading "Women's Liberation Journal" in the office window and read the summaries of stories the protesters believed the *Journal* should carry: "Prostitutes and the Law," "Can Marriage Survive Women's Liberation?" and a column on "How to Have an Orgasm." Proposed cover art was a pregnant woman holding a sign, "Unpaid Labor" (Lichtenstein 1970; Jay 1970).

The women faced Carter and Hershey, wearing a hat, and an unnamed woman of color who had been, in the words of Vivian Leone's amused account, "summoned" by management to represent the *Journal*'s 1.2 million black readers (Leone 1970: 1). Negotiations were interrupted when Firestone, a member of New York Radical Women, said "she had come there not to talk, but to Destroy" and was forcibly removed from Carter's desk when she appeared to lunge toward him as he stood with his back to a plate glass window (Jay 1999: 118). Other demonstrators helped themselves to the cigars on Carter's desk and lit up. A statement was read demanding Carter's resignation and an end to the magazine. "Carter listened in silence," Karla Jay recorded for *Rat*, "puffing away on a ten-inch phallus" (Jay 1970: 4). In his *Post* article, Meyer presented Carter as beleaguered but calm, striving "manfully to be good-humored as the women packed in his office showered him with reproaches like, 'Why hasn't the magazine mentioned how many people die every year from butchery at abortion mills?' " (Meyer, K. "Women Invade": A3). In the meantime, the telephone rang from other executive offices with offers to call the police. Shana Alexander, then the editor at *McCall's*, called to ask if she could bring sandwiches. Hershey, recognizing the moment, refused: "This was *our* sit-in and we weren't about to share it with our chief rival" (Hershey 1983: 85). Hershey's statement is interesting, suggesting a kind of common understanding that such sit-ins were more theatrical than serious business.

For the next eleven hours, Carter and Hershey negotiated with the group. There would be no full issue devoted to the radicals' article ideas, which included, "How to Get an Abortion," "A Prostitute Talks to Her Client's Wife," or "How Women Are Kept Apart." The women rejected a counteroffer, a general article on the movement. Finally, Carter agreed to pay for an eight-page insert, a "Book Bonus," for the August issue in an agreement that, Baxandall, a member of the New York Radical Women and Redstockings, charged primarily benefited women interested in their own careers. She wrote angrily in *Rat*, "It was repulsive in that several professional writers were conducting job interviews and convincing the man they were expert writers, furthering their careers. This turned me off and severed the solidarity" (*Rat* 4/18/70: 4).

Years later, Baxandall was still disaffected by the outcome. "Our idea was to talk to the secretaries, try to get them to organize and confront their bosses about *Ladies' Home Journal*'s lack of relevance to women, including themselves. However, this demonstration was led by some of the new career types, who came armed with their vitae. They didn't want to change *Ladies' Home Journal* in a major way; instead, they wanted to write feminist pieces for the magazine" (Baxandall 1998: 222). Jay was similarly distressed: "Somewhere, all demands, save that of the alternative issue or supplement were gone," she wrote in *Rat*. "What about child-care facilities for the workers? What about hiring Black employees? What about a training program for secretaries so that they too could share in the editorial control of the magazine? What about the minimum wage? What about an end to the ads in the *Journal* insulting women? Sometime in the night, the action had come down with a severe case of anemia" (Jay 1970: 22).

Not all observers agreed. Lichtenstein recalled in an interview that she had been surprised by the "militancy" of the action by women who were "clearly using the student and civil rights movement as their models" (Lichtenstein 1999). As the hours dragged by, some women proposed action. "They began to talk about overturning the file cabinets, burning things," Brownmiller recalled, noting that the women did not understand—until it was pointed out to them—that such actions would mean arrest and probable jail. "They hadn't worked it through to that level. They just knew they were angry, but they didn't know they'd have to spend a night in jail" (Brownmiller 2000).

The action further pointed up the radicals' naïveté, equating their success in taking over *Rat* with the ability to take over a corporate entity. As Baxandall recalled, "Ti-Grace Atkinson, Shulamith Firestone, and I saw that the career types were in the majority, and while they were negotiating with the editors, we walked silently down the backstairs. We had assumed the action would be a real takeover, just like the time we took over the new Left underground newspaper. We assumed that feminists would run the *Ladies' Home Journal* and change every aspect of the magazine. Our demand was for a new order, not for positions in the male hierarchy" (Baxandall 1998: 222).

In *Rat*'s final evaluation, the event's success was limited: "In summary, the Ladies Home Journal action was effective as publicity. As a radical action (that which effects changes in the existing structure) it did not succeed" (*Rat* 4/17/70: 22). However, despite the confusion that surrounded the event, there was an audaciousness and spirit about it that has resulted in a place in second-wave history. It also represented how quickly the movement—even at a time flooded by dramatic events—was able to get important attention.

The action also drew one unlikely convert, Lenore Hershey. Stung by criticism of being a "yes woman," the action awakened her to her years of subservience to Carter. As she worked with the women on the insert, she underwent her own epiphany: "For the first time in my life, I got the feeling of what it was like to have control of a situation, to be in charge." In 1973, when it appeared that Carter was going to be forced from the editor's job, Hershey made a pitch to become editor herself: "I could either wait for another male to whom I could genuflect: Or I could strike out for the job myself." In November she was named editor, the first sole woman to be editor since the magazine's founding female editor a century before (Hershey 1983: 91). Hershey's interpretation of the importance of the second wave in terms of her career provides one example of the acceptance of the second wave primarily in terms of personal career enhancement.

Limiting Agitprop

Not every theatrical statement or action made it to the mainstream media, and it is interesting to examine why Florynce Kennedy's activism did not catch the attention of the media in the same ways as the actions of white feminists. The situation again suggests the difficulties encountered in establishing a viable black presence in the feminist movement. With regard to Kennedy, a black activist whose actions sometimes pushed media-designated boundaries of tastefulness (for example, her "pee-in" action at Harvard Yard), mainstream media seemed less anxious to confer the authority of media leadership.

Although second-wave feminism has long been criticized for failing to bring black women into the framework, that decision was not so much a feminist one as it was made by media personnel. None of the agitprop actions were tasteful, but the decision to draw the lines of taste at Kennedy rather than Morgan had to do with the bias of the profession. Consciously or unconsciously, editors and reporters seemed unable to give leadership to black Americans, feminist or otherwise, outside of the heroic framing of early civil rights and/or sports or the opposing stereotypical view of danger as represented by the Black Panthers. An unrecognized institutional reluctance appeared to exist that mitigated against the promotion of black membership in the women's movement. Reporters certainly noted with some frequency that the women's movement was considered unwelcoming to women of color, despite clear efforts to the contrary.

Kennedy was a media activist who worked outside of NOW but joined with the organization for certain actions. Long an activist attorney, she early attempted to conjoin her battle against American racism with the women's movement. In the 1970s she joined Gloria Steinem on the lecture circuit but had previously established a media criticism group as well as an alternative to NOW, the National Feminist Party, which she used as a platform to bring attention to media shortcomings. "I think we should be kicking ass fairly regularly," she wrote in a 1976 memoir, "and one of my favorite targets is the media. I don't think we should continue to permit the Establishment to feed us only what they think we should have. Marshmallows are not dangerous food—I dig marshmallows myself—but a strictly marshmallow diet for diabetics is what we get from the media. Rhythm and blues, for Black community radio, 'I Love Lucy' for women, jockocracy for men, heroin for junkies. Nielsen says they like it" (Kennedy 1976: 154).

Kennedy, whose politics were entrenched in the 1940s socialism of her Columbia Law School education, established the Media Workshop in 1966, seeking to attack racism in media. When the advertising firm Benton and Bowles refused to give the group information about hiring and programming policies, Kennedy and others picketed in front of its building with signs such as "Is there a bigot in your market basket?" According to Kennedy, "After that they invited us upstairs, and ever since I've been able to say, 'When you want to go the suites, start in the streets.'" The group also picketed New York's WNEW-TV when the station manager refused to see them but did so in ways that indicated Kennedy's concern with media attention. "After we announced the picket line he became available to meet with us, but we went ahead anyway. We were picketing in front of the WNEW Radio, just off Fifth Avenue at 46th Street, and William B. Williams, the disc jockey, came out and asked, 'Why are you picketing over here, Flo? The TV station is up on 67th Street.' 'Because there's more traffic here and it's more convenient to my office,' I said, and they laughed and sent someone down and put us right on the radio. So you see how easy it can be to apply pressure in what I call the testicular area" (Kennedy 1976: 52, 54).

In 1973, at an event billed as the "Hollywood Toilet Bowl Caravan," Kennedy took her style to Los Angeles. Sheets of toilet paper were presented "to pigocrats in media like 'Marcus Welby'" (Kennedy 1976: 79). But she found less press attention given to her than in New York, unable to get *Los Angeles Times* coverage even when she spoke to the Los Angeles Press Club. The *Pasadena Eagle*, however, quoted her at length: "There are very few jobs that actually require a penis or vagina. All other jobs should be open to everyone" (Kennedy 1976: 80). Earlier the same month, Kennedy had organized a "pee-in" at Harvard University's Harvard Yard in an effort to connect bodily waste, as reported in Ellen Frankfort's story in the *Village Voice*, "to the stench of the body politic." A specially written poem by novelist Marge Piercy, "To the Pay Toilet," was read. The pee-in, as Frankfort noted, was really an introduction to a weekend of workshops sponsored by the New England Feminist Party, including critiques of the media's treatment of women involved in the Nixon White House. Frankfort quoted Kennedy at length, more than two columns' worth (*Voice* 6/7/73: 23). Yet Kennedy and her Feminist Party never became more than minor keys in feminist politics, and despite her ongoing use of the media, Kennedy never became well known outside of feminist circles. Even *Ms.* tended to marginalize Kennedy as in Steinem's 1973 article, "The Verbal Karate of Florynce R. Kennedy, Esq.," primarily a collection of her aphorisms. Independent, theatrical, and far from white ideas of media representation, Kennedy's use of the absurd fell mostly on deaf ears.

Trivializing Agitprop

Agitprop was a tool everyone could use in many venues. During the American Psychological Association convention in Miami Beach, a group of women led by Phyllis Chesler, author of *Women and Madness*, demanded that the organization pay a million dollars as reparations for damage to women at the hands of psychotherapy. Moreover, what had begun as agitprop began to be taken up by anyone who had any kind of protest, as in "Women against Consumer Exploitation," which picketed Bonwit Teller in Philadelphia for carrying the midcalf skirt and gathered sixteen hundred signatures calling for the garment's end. In Maryland, a group called Fight against Dictating Designers (FADD) urged women not to buy the style and sold bumper stickers, "If you don't buy, the midi will die" (*Spokes* 8/28/74: 4). In Berkeley, California, members of Women of the Free Future burned academic degrees and academic paraphernalia to dramatize what they saw as the irrelevance of formal education (*Spokes* 6/30/70: 4). The Right began organizing groups with catchy acronyms for names—for example, an organization to support homemakers billed itself as "Happiness of Women," or HOW. Indeed, attention to issues seemed to hinge on the adoption of a catchy title. The establishment of the Society for the Emancipation of the American Male (SEAM) by just two

Michigan couples was sufficient hook for an article by *Times* reporter Marilyn Bender (Bender 1969: 38).

Other women continued to use the tactics of opposition forged by the antiwar movement. In January 1971, a group of women representing the Women's Action Commission occupied a condemned building in the East Village with plans, they said, to open a health clinic, child center, and lesbian collective. After twelve days, they were evicted by police, which led to a demonstration and the arrest of twenty-four people, women who, unlike the war protesters, kicked and punched as they were arrested, causing injuries to at least five policemen (*NYT* 1/14/71: 41).

As in the male Left, the uses of agitprop in the women's Left came to be divisive, as even a small group of women, representing perhaps only the urge of the moment, sought national attention. The fissures had been well established by the Miss America protest and were furthered by the *Ladies' Home Journal* action. In June 1970 two radical women disrupted a taping of the *Dick Cavett Show* after learning that the program would have Susan Brownmiller and Sally Kempton as guests in the same interview with Hugh Hefner. Writing in *Rat*, in a piece that was reprinted in other alternative newspapers, the protesters said they "questioned why the women wanted to appear on a show with Hugh Hefner. It seemed an obvious set up designed to turn debate into entertainment with total disregard for the gut issues of women's oppression." To make their point, the women tried to get on the stage during a commercial break but were kept off by ushers while yelling, "They are using guards and pigs here to drag us off for speaking, for asserting ourselves. This is a fascist country" (*Rat* 6/5/70: 1).

The disruption of Cavett's show, generally considered to be a mass media forum for liberal thought, not only offended Cavett but also appeared to buttress those who dismissed radical ideas on the basis of stridency. Cavett's icy response—"We have two representatives of your side here. Either let them talk or get the hell out"—clearly suggested that the movement should have been more grateful for a friend (*NYT* 4/27/70: 95). Writing in the alternative press, the women argued, "It's obvious we'll never argue our way to freedom on prime time TV. Therefore, we've got to stop the male-dominated media from absorbing Us. If we don't, we run the risk of remaining a dirty joke that elicits the uncertain laughter of defeated wives and girlfriends" (*Rat* 7/6/70: 1).

Agitprop actions were undoubtedly the single most recognized reason for the frequent characterization of the movement as strident. Quickly, however, the word *strident* was used on almost any occasion when female behavior did not meet the norms, and it became a code word for the media-made definitions of the movement that turned on lesbianism (see chapter 6). Activists, however, saw few alternatives for making their messages known, and the charge of stridency, subsequently taken up and repeated by the emerging right wing, may be regarded as the unavoidable result of trying to take the feminist message to the media agenda.

Agitprop was a dangerous tool in many ways—not easy for movement leaders to control and often confusing to laypeople, who were unclear about how to interpret the feminism that the actions represented. Moreover, characterizations leading from agitprop activities served as broad-brush shorthand for media. But even in the women's movement, there was a blur between demonstrations for direct ends and agitprop aimed at broader interpretations. NOW often introduced aspects of agitprop by dressing up in costume, for example, in demonstrations aimed at EEOC concerns. Women in the *Journal* sit-in were themselves not clear on whether they were attempting to take over the magazine, reform its contents, or find jobs for women writers. Women at the 1968 abortion hearings were not mounting an action primarily aimed at media attention or at consciousness-raising but instead sought to get lawmakers' attention, as did members of the Women's Health Collective, but the coverage represented these actions as symbolic-only representations of angry women. For mass media, armed with craft traditions that insisted that confrontation be the lead, there was little attempt to untangle the difference.

Moreover, in part because of prohibition against stars, agitprop did not produce leaders, making it difficult for radical ideas to be presented outside of interpretations of the actions themselves. Radical views of the importance of agitprop did not take into account the difficulty of representing new ideas in a mass media that were committed, as all agreed, to the maintenance of the status quo. Ideas that were part of a fluid discussion thus became poles, as the movement split into ever narrowing factions.

Agitprop and demonstrations were not universally embraced on the women's Left. The socialist feminists of the Hyde Park chapter of the Chicago Women's Liberation Union saw demonstrations as just the initial step in the development of organizations that could exert influence: "It is time to begin to organize for power" (Hyde Park 1972: 1). The founders of *off our backs* called for a moratorium on movement women's involvement in media: "We no longer need to use the mass media to tell people we exist. We now need to develop a practical critique which we can use to guide our future actions and determine how our communications needs can best be met." The danger, according to *off our backs*, was that mass media would insist on a leader, define the movement by that individual, and then discredit the movement by "discrediting her personal life rather than dealing with her politics" (*oob* 4/25/70: 3), a scenario that indeed occurred in the rise and fall of Kate Millett. But the views of the Chicago or *off our backs* women had little influence in the New York circles where media decisions were instigated.

Activist Barbara Epstein, writing from a later perspective, considered that the radicals of the women's movement became "a bit crazed." Like other radicals of the time, these women "not only adopted revolution as their aim, but also thought that revolution was within reach . . . virtually around the corner." Their commitment was genuine, according to Epstein, "but there was something unrealistic about the view that if we did just the right thing, it would happen" (Epstein, B. 2002: 122).

4. The Practice of the Craft

In her "pre-feminist days," as she was to call them, Letty Pogrebin, later a founder of *Ms.* magazine, voiced a common perception. The ideas of the women's liberation movement were "great," she wrote in her 1970 self-help book *How to Make It in a Man's World*. But they were being ignored because "people are offended by the strident attitude assumed by feminists. Men . . . dismiss these demanding ladies as the lunatic fringe and respond to the whole movement only with ridicule" (Pogrebin 1970: 239).

Women activists, whether radical or not, were quick to blame media bias for perceptions that led to an understanding of radical feminism as the "lunatic fringe." There was, indeed, bias in some of the representations, but to many media practitioners—both men and some women—the charges could be baffling, since they believed themselves to be protected by craft traditions that ensured balance and fairness.

The Making of the Craft

Craft traditions in the United States are the profession-specific values on which journalists call in constructing stories. Underlying all the craft traditions is the belief of the necessity of a free press in a democracy and a devotion to the First Amendment as the bedrock not only of the profession but of the nation's democracy. "Craft traditions" are thus considered guides to those ways of making decisions that are considered the best way to serve the intent of a free press. Thus, the craft traditions of balance, fairness, accuracy, and objectivity are considered the basic fundamentals of serious reporting.

Craft traditions are also encumbered by a secondary set of assumptions that have less to do with democracy than with the writing of saleable stories. This secondary set includes an understanding of newsworthiness on the basis of conflict, unusualness, locality (local over global), audience familiarity with participants (such as celebrities), and a broad "human interest" category. This level of craft decisions also includes an understanding of writing different kinds of stories in particular ways: news stories follow an "inverted pyramid" format in which what is considered the most newsworthy item appears in the lead, and what used to be called feature stories have more latitude as the writing is lively and readable.

Underlying how to invoke the craft decision-making process is the idea that reporters are writing for people generally like themselves. And, generally, in most media that is true. Journalism, like teaching, has long been the venue for children of working-class parents, often the first in their families to go to college, who take on white-collar journalism jobs as they move into the middle classes (Weaver and Wilhoit 1991).

Even though this secondary set of characteristics developed out of nineteenth-century mass journalism's need to attract readers, values aimed at readership as much as at truth became ensconced as journalistic values in the new journalism programs at land-grant colleges like the University of Missouri. Here, young men and women were trained like other industrial workers to follow a template that had been proved to be serviceable—providing news, information, and entertainment that was attractive to readers in a context that did not upset the status quo or the advertisers' interest. This training was not considered antithetical to a belief in the First Amendment's authority to protect a free society.

As a result, the state schools provided an ongoing army of entry-level, trained practitioners, as these institutions did to meet the needs of other public concerns in education and health. In the rush toward professional status at the end of the nineteenth century, working journalists formed trade groups, solidifying the craft traditions both in the commitment to First Amendment principles and in the day-to-day practices that directed reportorial and editorial choices.

News broadcasting, at first seeking to adapt newspaper news values to a broadcast format, began to evolve as a separate discipline with its own craft traditions. These included telling a story visually, quickly, and in uncomplicated ways (often running the danger of appealing to stereotypical thinking because of the speed with which information can be processed when those codes are used). However, without the guarantees of the First Amendment (U.S. broadcasting is regulated by the Federal Communication Commission), broadcasters had to be careful about what they aired. Both for reasons of regulation and to maintain relationships with advertisers and audiences, the decision making of broadcast news had another set of constraints.

Herbert Gans, in his study of the CBS news operation in the late 1960s, concluded the acknowledged craft traditions were undergirded by another set of privileged or "enduring" values. He summarized these as journalistic approval of ethnocentrism, altruistic democracy, small-town pastoralism, responsible capitalism, moderatism, and individualism (Gans 1980: 42–52). However, such values, as much as the practitioner traditions, erected further barriers: second-wave activism was centered in the nation's biggest city; radical activists argued for systemic change; and second-wave radicals were not moderate in their approach.

In the 1970s, these journalistic traditions were being challenged by news professionals who questioned why individuals in news stories were always identified by race and marriage status, who found that objectivity was not necessarily served by quoting both "sides" of a story when another side did not exist, and that the unspoken rules of traditional reporting could distort the truth to which the profession was committed. The practice of "new journalism" in magazine writing broke barriers of impartiality and other traditions, in search, writers believed, of a greater truth. And in a time of social change, reporters looked around their own newsrooms and professional organizations and saw little evidence of diversity.

A few female journalists such as Lindsy Van Gelder attempted to ignore stereotypes promoted by craft traditions. But at the same time NOW was mounting events on the basis of what was expected to appeal to craft traditions, an approach that would necessarily entail some use of stereotypes. It was the conundrum of the women's movement: the demand for attention and coping with the result. This discussion finds a complicated answer in which craft traditions both helped and hindered, permitting entry to the mass media from the much despised women's pages, some clear efforts to provide fair reporting, an escalation of opinionated coverage in slick magazines, and an overall disinclination among media professionals to examine how craft traditions can support cultural conditioning.

The First Shot: The Women's Pages

That the Associated Press covered the organizational beginnings of NOW was in part because Muriel Fox's news release signaled the authority of professionalism. It was also because the story was considered to be in the purview of the women's editor of the Associated Press, Joy Miller, one of the organization's few women reporters, and Miller not only stayed true to Fox's story but gave to the story the imprimatur of the AP. For the thousands of customers, the AP imprimatur legitimized the story and thus helped account for the play it received.

The craft traditions made possible much of the early coverage of the women's movement—unusualness, bizarreness, and the always-available canvass for human interest. But the separation of news into broad areas that included women's news first helped NOW get on the news agenda. At most newspapers, from small and midsized publications to major ones, women's page editors made a difference in early coverage. Wire stories that were disregarded by male editors were passed onto women's page editors, who had the discretion to find local angles on the national story.

Columnist Nicolas Hoffman sympathized with women editors who had to operate under management that literally forced editors to put out mediocre sections. "The women's page is a place that ambitious, young reporters want to leave, it's where you don't see the raises passed out, it's low priority, the afterthought of the managing editor who is always saying, 'Oh, on that Nixon visit story, let's get a woman's angle. How 'bout a sidebar on Pat?' In the back of the bus where we ride, that passes for creativity." But at the same time Hoffman saw the sections as freed from journalistic conventions and as the place to experiment with new material (Hoffman 1971: 52). At the *Washington Post*, where he worked, the women's pages did indeed experiment, and the section became a national influence.

The women's movement both influenced and coincided with a movement to upgrade the women's sections in several major newspapers. As early as 1963, in Louisville, Kentucky, a young woman, Carol Sutton, was made editor of the *Courier-Journal*'s Women's World section, which had been routinely filled with society news, household tips, and weddings. She renamed it Today's Living and under her direction, even in this conservative southern town, published articles on abortion, migrant labor, rural poverty, and other social issues (McFadden 1985). That she remained and flourished at the newspaper, eventually becoming its managing editor, speaks not only to her talent and the receptivity of her superiors but also to the readiness of the audience to read about social issues. In 1969 the *Washington Post* introduced its genderless Style section and ordered that news stories about women appear in the sections of the paper that were appropriate to the story (Bradlee 1995). Eugenia Sheppard introduced changes at the *New York Herald Tribune* (Mills 1990: 120). At the *Los Angeles Times*, Jean Taylor took over the women's section and changed its content while upgrading its writing style. As reporter Bella Stumbo said, Taylor "taught me more about writing and journalism than anyone. We sat around and talked about writing. It was the seminars that I never had in graduate school" (Ricchiardi and Young 1991: 87). In 1971, the *New York Times* changed "women's news" in its index to "family/style" and changed the name of the section itself from "Food, Fashion, Family, Furnishings" to "Family, Food, Fashion, and Furnishings," demoting "food" considered "dramatic" at the time (Greenwald 1999: 122). By the end of the decade, enough newspapers were jettisoning the old women's sections that the Associated Press Managing Editors established a Modern Living Committee to examine how many aspects of "modern living" could reasonably be reflected in family newspapers (APME 1979: 248).

Of course, many newspapers did not tamper with the traditional approach to women's news, and "society pages" continued to exist in most small newspapers (APME 1979: 254) while other newspapers took a middle road—printing more leisure-and-life stories yet maintaining some of the old traditions (Marzolf 1977: 201). But even traditional women's sections were likely to be a home for the early "women's lib" stories, sharing pages with recipes and wedding gowns and under the noses of the male editors who had tossed such stories to the women's desk as not being worthy of any other notice. Molly Ivins, who vowed she was never going to work for a women's section because of its low prestige, came to a new appreciation of the sections. "It took me years to notice a remarkable phenomenon. For a long time, the best journalism about women, family issues, and social issues came out of those sections. These reporters were writing about abortion, wife and child abuse, incest—stories far out on the cutting edge. Their stories got into the paper because nobody was paying attention to what they did" (Ricchiardi and Young 1991: 142). The phrase *women's lib* may indeed even have been an invention of a women's section editor who shortened "women's liberation" to fit into an one-column headline while putting an American slang spin on the Marxist phrase.

In a 1974 survey of women's pages in small and midsized papers, Van Gelder was critical that news affecting women was still appearing on pages that emphasized food and social events. "Why do we have to be scrunched into one little newsprint ghetto?" she asked (Van Gelder 1974: 11). Van Gelder's was a familiar complaint. In a letter to her husband, the *Times*'s Charlotte Curtis complained that feminists "are up in arms over my women's pages. They are calling us Aunt Tabbies," a modification of the "Uncle Tom" appellation (Greenwald 1999: 118). However, in the early days, the alternative to the women's pages was the likelihood of no coverage at all. Moreover, when coverage of the women's movement did leave the women's pages and became subject to journalistic conventions, the result was the strident-woman image that would thereafter accompany the movement. Nonetheless, feminists of the time clearly despised the women's section coverage, and one rationale for the confronting actions adopted by early activists was that such actions did not fit the craft traditions of women's pages, which were not geared to breaking news, and thus would have to be used in the regular news columns.

Despite the frequent criticisms of the *Times*'s "Food, Fashion, Family, Furnishings" section, it was nonetheless at the crux of change in the coverage of women. Although Friedan's initial NOW interview appeared in that section, which was cause for derision by NOW feminists, the *Times*'s women's section coverage helped put the second wave on the national agenda, largely because of section editor Charlotte Curtis. Curtis did not join the class-action lawsuit filed by *Times* women in 1974, her own views towards 1970s feminism were mixed, and her female coworkers viewed her suspiciously when she refused to join the lawsuit, yet the coverage of the second wave in her section was immensely helpful to feminism.

Curtis joined the "Four F" section in 1961, with hopes of moving over to the news side (Greenwald 1999: 61). She remained in the section, however, and despite the restrictions imposed by the subject matter of its title had enough latitude to refine her writing style, emphasizing detail, dialogue, and narrative, all part of the New Journalism style of the day. When applied to the subjects she covered—for example, society and parties—the style might even be considered as subversive as it was irreverent. In 1965, she was made editor of the section, and she moved from her role as a talented writer to an imaginative editor and to an influence in women's sections across the country. "No topic was taboo. Abortion, lesbians, unwed fathers and mothers, alcoholism, drug abuse, incest, peace marches, and love-ins all made their appearance—with heavy helpings of radical chic, to be sure—on the women's page in the last half of the decade and into the seventies," according to former *Times* reporter Nan Robertson(Robertson 1992: 122).

What Curtis and other women's page editors were doing was putting on the newspaper agenda stories that had not previously been declared news. As Grace Lichtenstein, a general assignment reporter at the *Times* during the period, described it, "Male editors thought of news in terms of affairs of state and war and everything else as features. All women's news, including health and other issues that we would consider front page today, were on the women's pages" (Lichtenstein 1999). This attitude was nowhere more prevalent than at the *Times*, especially conscious of its role as the nation's newspaper of political record under the direction of executive editor A. M. Rosenthal. Rosenthal had made his reputation in the most traditional of ways—as a foreign correspondent—but he was also a man of widely recognized biases, including ones against the women's movement, the student movement, and the homosexual movement. As Robertson details, Rosenthal's opinionated behavior during the negotiations regarding the Women's Caucus lawsuit against the *Times* made settlement almost impossible (Robertson 1992). Yet Curtis was not deterred from her vision, even in face of Rosenthal's criticisms (Greenwald 1999: 131–38).

Perhaps Curtis's major contribution to second-wave coverage was her hiring of Judy Klemesrud. No reporter was more important to the second wave than Klemesrud, whose byline is attached to more second-wave stories than that of any other *Times* reporter. The child of a small-town editor in Iowa, she began at the *Times* in 1966, at the age of twenty-seven, soon garnering a reputation as "the brightest and most prolific writer on the family/style page" (Robertson 1991: 142). Lichtenstein remembered Klemesrud as a star who "was a good reporter and an incisive interviewer." Klemesrud covered a range of topics, but about one-fifth of her articles in her nineteen years at the paper—she died in 1985 at the age of forty-six—were about the women's movement. What is interesting about Klemesrud is that as a new reporter at the *Times*, she did not hesitate to take on the second wave as a beat at a time when it was not clear that covering the second wave was going to serve her career as positively, as, for example, the coverage of the civil rights movement served the careers of male reporters. Indeed, as a female reporter covering the feminist movement, Klemesrud ran the risk of accusations of favoritism, a situation in which minority reporters can find themselves when covering stories of interest to communities they are seen to "represent." Curtis quickly recognized Klemesrud's talent, saying at her funeral, "She could report as well as write. Uptown pretensions and la-de-dah left her cold" (Greenwald 1999: 205). Protected by Curtis, Klemesrud brought important coverage of the women's movement to the *Times*.

Klemesrud's byline also appeared in the *New York Times Magazine*, a prestigious venue that served to take her reporting from the women's section to the general public. In that setting, she was the first reporter to cover the second wave's emerging lesbian influence in a framing that made it less easy for other venues to be dismissive. And she wrote frequently for other major magazines, including *Esquire*, *Cosmopolitan*, *Ladies' Home Journal*, and *Redbook* (Klemesrud Papers).

Despite institutionalized craft decisions that give little leeway in deciding what is to be designated news, reporters and editors do have roles that can make a difference, at least in the short term. Curtis often was disparaging about some aspects women's movement. She turned her satirical eye on Friedan's efforts to raise money from well-to-do sources to fund the 1970 march (Curtis, C. "Women's Liberation"). After the march, when many women were still euphoric, Curtis was critical of second-wave strategy: "Perhaps what I'm saying is on this anniversary of women's suffrage is that if women want to be taken as seriously as they deserve, they will have to get their message across not just loud and clear but logically and simply. Otherwise, nobody's really going to understand how important this movement is" (Greenwald 1999: 120).

However discomforted she was by various movement tactics, her section contributed to the discussion in ways that were more helpful than otherwise. It is quite possible that had Curtis's predecessor continued in her role, second-wave feminists would have found the *Times* less hospitable. Instead, the *New York Times* became a substantial source of coverage of the second wave. From no coverage in 1965, the *Times*'s coverage peaked in 1975 with seventy stories, plummeting in the following years (Barker-Plummer 2002: 192). Less amenable to feminism in this period were the dominant papers in Los Angeles, the *Times* and the *Herald-Examiner*, where a 1970s communication researcher found a virtual "blackout" on feminist news of the movement in the formative years of 1968 and 1969 (Morris 1973).

The Problem of Conflict

The amount of coverage clearly does not measure how useful this coverage is to a social movement. From the beginning, coverage of the second wave was often spurred by the divisiveness that the movement experienced. Betty Friedan, for one, quickly distanced NOW from the radicals in either-or ways that journalism could not ignore. In her speech to a new NOW chapter in greater Boston that was covered by *Boston Globe* staff writer Ellen Goodman, "Friedan attacked the 'pseudo-radical cop-out.'" "Rap sessions are fine for group therapy, but now we need action," Goodman quoted Friedan as saying. "They say men are the oppressors, love is the oppressor, sex is the oppressor, babies should be born in test tubes. They say, 'Come the revolution, things will change.' Well, what do you do now? Go to bed until the revolution? And go to bed alone?' (Goodman, "How N.O.W.": 38).

This was good, lively copy, calling on the journalistic craft tradition of conflict, all the meatier when the conflict came from within, even for Goodman, one of the journalists of the period who was on the list prepared by NOW's Dian Terry as a friend of the movement. But Goodman could not avoid framing the movement according to craft traditions—division and opposition among the most defining.

Friedan encouraged oppositional framing by bringing to the public's attention, as she had in the Goodman interview, differences within the movement. Friedan's public opposition to the radical critique was ongoing. "I thought it was a joke at first," she wrote in the *New York Times Magazine* long after she had lost leadership of even the moderate wing, "those strangely humorless papers about clitoral orgasms that would liberate women from sexual dependence on a man's penis" (Friedan 1973: 9). Friedan, ever the commercial writer, appeared unable to resist bringing attention to the subjects that would surely result in media interest and, in so doing, setting herself in what she would define as the common sense and comforting middle ground.

The framing by opposites that had been so evident in Friedan's *Girl Talk* appearance became a staple of media coverage as the radicals came to prominence and Friedan spoke against them and they against her. In advancing the story along opposition, there was no difficulty in finding spokeswomen or authorities for either side, and the anger in the split produced lively sound bites or interviews. Moreover, the feminist split fit the traditional stereotype that women could not get along with each other.

News products traditionally provide both guidance and reassurance about an orderly society. This may surprise those who criticize media for encouraging an atmosphere of fear and chaos. But even sensationalism sets out the rules for social order. "Unattended Child Drowns in Bathtub!" "Robber Kills Storekeeper," "Child Molester Sentenced" are all variations of society's rules about parental responsibility, the importance of safekeeping in a civil society, and the limits of tolerance. As Michael Schudson argues, sensationalism is most often content in media products aimed at the working class on the assumption that such people, because of a lack of resources, seek order for their lives, which are characterized mostly by disorder and chaos. By the same token, readers of the *New York Times* do not need the ordering function of sensationalism, presumably because their secure place on the economic ladder gives them the luxury of orderly lives (Schudson 1978).

Like sensationalism, the use of stereotypes can be an ordering device, providing an indication of people's place in society as well as affirming existing beliefs. News organizations have difficulty letting go of stereotypes exactly because they carry meaning quickly and efficiently in ways that can seem to support what the audience considers basic values. Thus, presenting change in a favorable light can jeopardize the reason that consumers may turn to news: reassurance that basic values are still in place.

Covering the Split

The political splits in the second wave were as real as the anger. And, again, feminists, who considered themselves knowledgeable about the media, were not so media savvy that they could control the framing. In 1970, Roxanne Dunbar, a radical activist and founder of Cell 16, was invited to be on a television show along with novelist Rona Jaffe and Friedan. Dunbar had doubts but Ti-Grace Atkinson and Florynce Kennedy encouraged Dunbar to go on the program "to be as united oriented as possible, while raising radical feminist ideas." But by this time, Friedan, still president of NOW, was attempting to impress her view on the mass media by taking on the radical faction in public and demeaning ways. As Dunbar later described it, Friedan "had no desire for friendly gesture toward or united with a radical feminist. She began a verbal assault on me in the dressing room when I refused to have makeup applied, and she did not stop until the show was over. I was dressed in my very best army surplus white cotton sailor trousers and a white man's shirt. She said that I, and 'scruffy feminists' like me, were giving the movement a bad name. . . . The whole experience led me to question the viability of television talking about the movement if it only pitted feminist against feminist." The argument continued on the air—Dunbar accused Friedan of fearing the loss of her celebrity leadership, and then Friedan called Dunbar "an anarchist. I agreed with her that's what I was. She was steaming when she huffed out of studio." Nonetheless, as Dunbar noted, the seduction of media attention was hard to resist. "A week later, I was on another airplane to New York for another television show" (Dunbar 1998: 105–10).

Framing in opposites was enhanced when it came from credible sources. The views of Dr. Edgar F. Berman, Hubert Humphrey's personal physician and confidante as well as a member of the Democratic Party's Committee on National Priorities, gave perceived legitimacy to oppositional views when he pronounced that women's menstrual cycles and menopause disqualified them from leadership. When challenged by U.S. Representative Patsy Mink (D-Hawaii), Berman responded that her attack was an example of her own "raging hormonal imbalance" (Berman 1970: 1B). The introduction of the subject into the public realm also led to innumerable jokes about a female president, menopause, and nuclear war.

The Role of Copy Editors

Copy editors, responsible for headlines as well as cut lines on photographs, may have been most responsible for selecting opportunities for opposition in head-lines. For many readers, who do not get beyond headlines, copy editors set the tone of and shape understanding of the article. The disjointedness that can occur between stories and their headlines becomes clearer when it is considered that copy desks at this time were most often the purview of men who had come up through the reportorial ranks but no longer worked as reporters, which removed them from the day-to-day influences. For these men (there were few women copy editors), an allegiance to traditional news values of opposition and difference identified the most "newsworthy" aspects of the story chosen for the headline. When Philadelphia's *Evening Bulletin* published a series describing the complexi-ties of the movement, parts of the story were headlined, "Revolt against Men," "Men Aren't the Enemy—They Simply Need Education," and "Feminists Declare War for Freedom" (Buckhart 1970). In magazines, "sell lines" on the cover seek to find the few words that bring newsstand sales. In its March 1970 issue, *Atlantic Monthly* provided a substantial collection of essays on the subject of women; how-ever, the writer of the sell lines telescoped the discussion down to three words for the top of the cover—"Women against Men," a message imbibed by any passer-by, whether a purchaser of the magazine or not. Betty Rollin was a feminist herself, but her 1971 *Look* article, intended as an attack on the emerging antifeminist organizations, actually repeated an antifeminist canard in its title, "They're a Bunch of Frustrated Hags" (Rollin 1971: 15). When juxtaposed with the attrac-tive young woman on the cover, naked under her apron and put forward as the example of antifeminism, Rollin's profeminist article did not make feminism the easy choice. Rollin would not have had any role in the cover art, the sell lines, even the article's title, layout, or accompanying illustrations. But, of course, all these editing decisions carried their own messages, and, in this case, no matter the intention of the article, antifeminism came out the winner.

Esquire magazine often presented antifeminist positions, but in 1970 it ran an essay by activist and journalist Sally Kempton. The purpose of the essay was purportedly to clarify for *Esquire* readers why women felt angry toward men. But Kempton was not very politically savvy when she wrote, "I used to lie in beside my husband and wish I had the courage to bash in his head with a frying pan," a quote that *Esquire* chose to use as a pull out (Kempton 1970: 4). From a later perspective, it seems clear there was no benefit to the movement to express such views in the inhospitable setting of *Esquire*; indeed, it suggests naïveté to believe that *Esquire*, of all magazines, was interested in promoting any view other than the notion that feminism was a destroyer of male ego and sexual potency.

Columnists

Column writing has long been a characteristic of the American press, an attempt to insure balance regardless of what appears in news columns. It was adapted to television by permitting commentary, usually by Eric Sevareid and Andy Rooney on CBS and Howard K. Smith on ABC, during the important concluding moments of a program. The conservative nature of these commentaries was certainly on view in the coverage of the 26 August 1970 march. Unlike print, there were no counter voices with the exception of Shana Alexander, a *Newsweek* columnist, herself problematical by feminist standards, who participated in the "Point-Counterpoint" exchange on CBS's *Sixty Minutes*.

However, it was in newspapers where columnists clearly aimed to build a constituency by outrage. Pressed to be readable, even outrageous, to extend their syndication to new markets and protected by the First Amendment, columnists such as Nicolas Hoffman, William F. Buckley Jr., and Harriet Van Horne had few constraints. Indeed, such columnists—and they also existed on local levels—often took on the voice of the perceived "silent majority," the views that columnists considered went unstated. From 1968 throughout the 1970s, Van Horne attacked the movement, which may have been a personal prejudice but just as likely represented the role she took on to reassure her working-class readers that old ways were better. Writing for an elite audience in the *National Review* in a column distributed by the Washington Star Syndicate, Buckley chose an arch and patronizing style, assuring readers of their class (or class desire) prerogatives, which apparently did not include a concern that the issues of women would affect them. Both Van Horne and Buckley, and perhaps all columnists, must be something of actors as they are contracted to present particular points of view in consistent ways. This may insure balance, but it also provides reassurance for readers who seek them out. Not until Ellen Goodman received her syndicated column did a voice challenge the status quo in ways that appealed to the liberals of the time. Friedan was the only recognized feminist who managed to get a column of her own in a mass media product (*McCall's*). Pogrebin had a column on working women in *Ladies' Home Journal* during her prefeminist days. With the exception of Friedan, no activist women were regular columnists in mass media venues, rather a remarkable phenomenon considering the number of media professionals in the movement.

Ironically, the premiere newspaper columnists in the nation during the period were not on the editorial pages but were the twin sisters Abigail Van Doren ("Dear Abby") and Ann Landers. Readership surveys found their columns to be among the best read parts of the newspaper, certainly far exceeding editorials or most of the editorial columnists. Beginning in the 1950s, both columnists brought to their work a sense of fair-minded, considered opinion, responsibility, and service to readers (Pottker and Speziale 1987; Gogol 1987). Even though the trajectories of their columns were shaped by the time, Van Doren and Landers were likely to represent points of view that were in the realm of moderate feminism. They were important in the spread of moderate feminism because one or the other was carried in most of the nation's newspapers in women's sections that aimed to draw working-class and lower-middle-class readers, a group likely to be alienated by the negative coverage of the movement and, like readers in a *McCall's* survey, likely to dismiss the movement as antifamily (*McCall's* 4/76: 91). Landers was among the first group of women inducted into Sigma Delta Chi when the journalism fraternity was opened to women.

The Role of the Radicals

The media professionals who had launched NOW sought to use craft traditions to benefit coverage. The founding of NOW, for example, had been presented relatively evenhandedly in the national media, largely because it fit craft traditions of newsworthiness: it was connected to a newsworthy figure, Friedan; its founding members were figures of authority; and, thanks to Fox, its news releases were prepared in a style that suggested that the organization knew the rules of civil society, including those governing public relations. Less obvious but playing a role in its newsworthiness was the story's appeal to the timely representations of societal tensions (as in the use of the word *militant* in the release), its promise of the bizarre, and the opportunity it provided for the media to provide a new lead to the civil rights movement by playing on NOW's theme of the NAACP for women. For all these reasons, NOW could point to media attention in its first two years. But it was no permanent place. Coverage of the radicals' activities soon came to be the new new lead, much as CORE, then SNCC, then the Black Panthers came to replace the NAACP on the media agenda.

The radicals were first acknowledged in the *New York Times Magazine* in its initial major article on the movement but were characterized benignly: "young, bright-eyed, cheerfully militant" (Lear 1969: 50). Anne Koedt and Ti-Grace Atkinson were quoted generously on positions that were not shared by NOW. Nonetheless, in an article whose tone seemed to be evenhanded, it was clear that, just two years after the establishment of NOW and before the flood of agitprop actions, images of feminists were emerging that would accompany the second wave for its entirety. These media images separated feminists and feminist concerns from those that were perceived to be the characteristics of women in general. This was not new, of course. Populists, anarchists, socialists, labor agitators, Catholics, Jews, homosexuals, racial minorities, and others had found their marginal status empha-sized whenever change in status was sought. That emphasis occurs not entirely because prejudices exist and are easy to tap into but also because prejudices serve to slow down the process of change. Mass media are often given credit (or blamed, depending on the point of view) for promoting rapid change, but change is already well under way when mass media take up an issue. Indeed, American mass media are much more likely to function as a brake on a changing society.

The Problem of "Balance"

"Balance" is theoretically embedded in the structure of American newswriting as a protection against partisan stands. Balance has served to obtain a variety of points of view to help readers/viewers make rational choices, but it often seems rooted in a moralistic pose, implicit or explicit, that seeks to air any opposite point of view. If the women's movement was identified with young, white educated classes, media stories emerged that suggested that the movement was careless about the sensibili-ties of women who did not fit that category. If the movement seemed to be associ-ated with big cities, then stories were published suggesting that feminism was not accepted outside of urban centers. If the movement seemed to emphasize job opportunities for women, there were sure to be implicit criticisms that claimed that the movement denigrated the contributions of women in the home. Such implicit criticisms often meant that feminists who were interviewed were put on the defensive. It also meant that the criticisms could never be put to rest, no matter how much Steinem or various other feminist spokeswomen tried to set the record straight. Once particular images were set—stridency, whiteness, lesbianism, youth—the same questions were repeatedly asked, serving to anchor the oppositional views in the public mind, whether or not those views were credible.

Such a craft tradition provides a ready-made launching pad for the opposite views. The *New York Times Magazine,* for example, which published frequent articles that explained the feminist movement and its goals in a generally favorable light, also provided articles that took the opposite stance. In one piece an expert argued that the current feminist movement had no impact outside educated classes and speculated that the movement was a fad, "one more sociological entertainment," for a self-conscious intelligentsia (*NYTM* 3/19/72: VI26). Any new split provided a news hook for discussion of the state of the women's movement. In the wake of a Friedan–Abzug imbroglio in 1972, when both were eyeing a U.S. Senate seat from New York, Midge Decter was quick to use the split to offer the familiar antifeminist argument that the movement was controlled by a handful of upper-class white women who primarily sought "self fulfillment" (*NYT* 8/5/72: 2). The women's movement was found not to have reached small-town America, as in Hope, Indiana, "where women talk about the movement only very jokingly, if at all," (*NYT* 3/22/72: 54). This latter article, just one of many that Klemesrud wrote on the women's movement, won the Page One Award of the New York Newspaper Guild for 1973, suggesting that reporters have to show the downside on a regular beat lest they be seen as a biased supporter of a social-change movement.

The confrontational framing of American journalism made such stories seem like attacks on the movement as a whole, setting up feminists in a defensive position rather than as part of an ongoing discussion. Because American journalism is established on an either-or continuum, the varying positions of the movement were lumped into the undifferentiated mass that included propaganda from the Far Right that would come to be represented in the name of balance.

Voices in opposition to the movement were in full cry after 1970 and were commercially acceptable and sought out because of the stage set by the women's movement. They were also voices that were as radical on the right as were the movement's most left positions. Their use in the mainstream served to make acceptable ideas that were seen to be eroding before the second wave made it necessary to produce "balance" by bringing them forward. Balance thus came to revitalize ideas that were considered discredited.

Despite the overall aims of craft traditions (as viewed by their practitioners) to protect fairness and prevent prejudices, craft traditions can burden social change movements. The craft tradition of balance is often an excuse to move a story to the next level, a new lead or twist on a continuing story. Ideas come to the mass media agenda because of their newness to the mass media audience, not necessarily their newness to society. They are so introduced by way of the craft tradition of being out of sync—difference makes newsworthiness. Once the idea is introduced, the reformer has a relatively short period of time in which to move the idea from the newness of difference to acceptability. However, if the idea stays on the news agenda, its difference will have to increase to maintain its newsiness—the trajectory taken by the 1960s antiwar movement. In the meantime, depending on the tensions of the time, consumers of mass media have a limited tolerance for difference; when the tolerance level is reached (or is perceived to be at its limit because reporters and editors are tired of a subject), the familiarity of old prejudices is welcomed.

While reporters adopt craft traditions under the philosophy that they insure fairness and give equal voice to all, they can oppose change. Topics about change are introduced on the media agenda because they are different, but difference must constantly be upgraded to stay on the news agenda. However, too much difference, as well as reportorial weariness, leads to the reintroduction of familiar comfort messages. Thus, there is no straight upward trajectory for new ideas into the mass media. The relationship of mass media to new ideas is rather like the stock market, perhaps a seven percent increase over the long haul, with radical rises and drops over the short term.

"Castrating Crow in Bloomers"—The Call to the Past

For the women's movement, the honeymoon from the origination of NOW in the public realm to the introduction of adverse ideas was brief. From the beginning of the second wave, mass media already had at hand an easy cudgel. As Martha Weinman Lear put it in the first *New York Times Magazine* article, "It is the feminist burden that theirs is the only civil-rights movement in history which has been put down consistently, by the cruelest weapon of them all—ridicule." Acknowledging the weapon of choice, however, did not mean that the author was exempt from its use. In noting that Atkinson had been an early NOW fundraiser, Lear commented, "It may have occurred to some NOW officials that her appearance might help dissipate the traditional image of the feminist as a castrating crow in bloomers" (Lear 1969: 24, 56).

What Lear pinpointed (and advanced) was the ridicule that still existed in popular memory of the suffragists from the turn of the century. Indeed, the coverage of the suffragists emphasized what had been the coverage of the women's club movement after the Civil War. As women joined in organizations to advance reform agendas of the late nineteenth century, their efforts were often ridiculed. Even as *Ladies' Home Journal* publisher Cyrus C. K. Curtis utilized clubs to enlarge subscriptions, the magazine's editor, Edward Bok, railed against clubwomen editorially. He was not alone. Even a U.S president found clubwomen an easy target (Gere 1997). What is interesting about the campaign against clubwomen launched in the nineteenth century is the continuance of its images, which moved almost unchanged through the first and then second waves. They were images of women as asexual, marginal, and overbearing, particularly when it came to men. The convention of the milquetoast in terms of a timid man's relationship to his wife was established in the original 1924 comic strip by Harold T. Weber, whose "Caspar Milquetoast" character became part of the nation's antifeminist language and was an easy characterization for male editorial cartoonists.

From its founding, NOW had been concerned with the image of women. In its criticism of media images, however, NOW and the radicals first found themselves confronting images that had been in place for a century. This was emphasized by feminists themselves, who increasingly identified their roots in the first wave. One of Karen DeCrow's 1969 NOW demonstrations sought to have protesters dress up in turn-of the century costumes. The media thus had their hook to reintroduce easily recognized stereotypes from the "Votes for Women" campaign. When the first wave was represented, if at all, it was in terms of the suffragists' public actions—the elaborate marches, the banners, Alice Paul's adoption of the dramatic actions pioneered by the British movement and, always, the grim visage of Susan B. Anthony. The broader ideas expressed in Eleanor Flexner's 1959 book, *Century of Struggle*, an influence on Friedan and other members of the Left, were not in mainstream history books or in popular memory. At best, popular media treated the first wave with amusement. It has been a burden of American feminism's public face that neither in the period of the second wave nor subsequently have women of the first wave ever found a heroic niche in popular culture.

As the second wave came to the fore in the 1970s, the images of the first provided a ready framework, sometimes even without the writer's conscious realization, so embedded were the stereotypes. One of the most pervading stereotypes of first-wave women was their characterization as infertile as part of the belief that study and "brain" work came at the expense of an ability to bear children. This was a canard that had emerged in 1870, when a Harvard physician wrote the pseudo-scientific treatise *Sex in Education*, claiming that to educate young women was to put the nation's white middle class on the road to race suicide (Marsh and Ronner 1996: 29). The book went through eleven printings in its first year and not only became influential in medical circles but quickly moved into popular wisdom during the nineteenth century, when women were encouraged to remain in a separate sphere. Despite the reemergence of the women's movement after the Civil War, the establishment of elite women's colleges and women's "firsts" dotting the landscape, mass media promoted a consumer culture from the 1870s on with a spate of new women's magazines—*Good Housekeeping, Ladies' Home Journal, Women's Home Companion*, and a plethora of others—that indicated that women's brainwork could be best use put to use in making decisions about household purchases. In this sphere, there was no place for the educated single woman. Indeed, she was almost dangerous because she lived too frugally to contribute much to the gross national product, she had no male salary to spend on household goods, and she produced no children to be future consumers—altogether a definition of sterility that could be as alarming in a capitalistic culture as race suicide. The educated woman did not comprise an audience with which the mass media of the time sought to curry favor. Suffragists were thus rendered sterile in their most common representations as old hags, not only beyond childbearing age but bitter. Despite her three children, Friedan was thus seen to fit an image that had been developed at the turn of the century.

However, faced with many young feminist activists in the second wave, sterility could best be represented by a total lack of feminine qualities, a thrust made easier because many feminists shunned traditional appearance. In the second wave, the mass media found a comfortable and familiar place when they could note that feminists lacked qualities that could attract men. Van Horne charged that the demonstrators at the Miss America contest were neurotic because they were unable to attract the kind of men who would make the women feel feminine. They were "sturdy lasses in their sensible shoes." "Most of us," she wrote, "would rather be some dear man's boob girl than nobody's cum laude scholar" (Van Horne 1968: 3). In casting for a way to "balance" the statement made by the Miss America protest, these hoary stereotypes easily came to hand—as if the more radical the proposal, the more reactionary could be the response.

Feminists throughout the period claimed that the mass media went out of their way to focus on activists who eschewed traditional clothing, hairstyles, and makeup. For media makers of the time, such a focus was simply actualizing the craft tradition on the new and different. Thus, surprise was expressed when traditional attractiveness and feminism occurred together. Peter Babcox's account of radical women in the *New York Times Magazine* noted that Bernadine Dohrn, secretary of the Students for a Democratic Society, was both the "attractive and scholarly" (Babcox 1969: 34). A short profile that accompanied an article by Philadelphian Lisa Richette began, "It's hard to pinpoint Lisa Aversa Richette as mentally and spiritually active because she looks so physical and sexy" (*EvenBull* 8/30/70: 8). A 1969 *Washington Post* article on a feminist theatrical group noted, "Anselma Dell'Olio is very beautiful," adding, as if feminism and beauty could not exist together without a canceling factor, "She is also very angry" (Secrest 1969: F1). Vivian Gornick's article on consciousness-raising, which she called a "liberating experience," was nonetheless illustrated with drawings of a woman imagining her various roles—as a physical being, as a mother, and as a worker— all with downturned mouths and unhappy expressions (Gornick 1971: 23).

Given that activist women were angry and that men in general were the frequent target of women activists, mass media established second-wave feminists along lines of asexuality and anger so quickly that in a search for a new lead, feminists who weren't asexual and angry found a quick and prominent place on the news agenda. Germaine Greer built her media niche on being sexy and "a saucy feminist" as *Life*'s cover story had it (*Life* 5/7/71). Beautiful, sexy, and smart, Gloria Steinem provided the ultimate new lead on the old stereotype, as in *Newsweek*'s astonished headline: "A Liberated Woman Despite Beauty, Chic and Success" (*Nswk* 8/16/71: 51).

Thanks to the collective social memory that mass media provides, the images that had been established in the first wave were recalled and refought in the second wave. Whether or not references were specific, the initial characterizations of second-wave feminists clearly were constructed on stereotypes that long had simmered in the public's memory and were familiar benchmarks. To produce first-wave images was not to connect the second wave to a proud history, for indeed that history never had been established in the popular mind. Indeed, as the second-wave unfolded, the history of the first wave was further complicated by representations of first-wave women as upper class and concerned only with white privilege, a charge that was attached to NOW.

Isolation as the Front Line of Attack

References to the first wave initially conjured up caricatures of unsmiling, apparently unfulfilled women. Despite the many organizations and events that were typical of the first wave, the grim visage of the most frequently reproduced picture of Susan B. Anthony conveys an image of isolation. Mass media in the late 1960s and

1970s similarly constructed the women's movement along terms of isolation, first by way of connection with the ridicule associated with the first wave and subsequently by stridency and militancy, which came to be connected to the second wave as logical progressions. Ironically, second-wave activist Anne Koedt identified isolation as the prime characteristic of women in general (Brownmiller 1970: 138). The promise of further isolation by way of commitment to the women's movement made the threat a formidable barrier to the construction of the movement and helps explain why feminists opted for marches of solidarity, joined consciousness-raising sessions, and why the *Ms.* theme of sisterhood spoke to a ready audience.

The theme of isolation was apparent in the early *New York Times Magazine* piece. Photographs accompanying the article show the NOW marchers demure and serious in hats, hose, and handbags. The several images of the illustration apparently have been taken from a single original that has been cropped so that white space separates each marcher from the other marchers as well as from any other context except for the placards they carry. Facing the page is the historical anchor—the "castrating cow in bloomers." The drawing is of an older woman in period dress, turned away from the reader and isolated in white space. She has a "Votes for Women" pennant tucked under her arm, wears pince-nez on her nose, has a downturned mouth, and seems to be peering disagreeably into the article (Lear 1969: 25).

These images of the first wave could only be emphasized as attention focused on the August 1970 march celebrating the fiftieth anniversary of women's suffrage. In a story in the circumspect *Christian Science Monitor*, the second wave is described as women "banding together to pick up where the bloomer brigade left off" (*CSM* 4/24/70: 1). One of the newspaper's copy editors later picked up on this new euphonious *b* phrase with the headline "Indomitable Women of the Bloomer Brigade" for a first-person account by a former suffragist. But the writer herself blended her activity for voting rights with Carry Nation's campaign to prohibit the sale of alcohol (*CSM* 8/24/70: 10). Nation wielding an axe against saloons was one image that history texts of the time tended to recall, and many people saw no difference between Nation's campaign against liquor and votes for women.

In a similar fashion, *Time* referred to the "old crusade" in its coverage of the House passage of the Equal Rights Amendment but did so in a context that made the new crusaders frightening. "A young, assertive Women's Liberation Movement has brought new publicity and fire to the older, more genteel crusade, bewildering and sometimes outraging men in the ways that the black radicals infuriate and frighten whites" (*Time* 8/24/70: 12). The undergirding of the second wave by media images of the first suggests the longevity of media-induced collective memory and the ease which it can be transposed from one period to another, depending on the perceived need of a leavening agent. While stridency and militancy are most considered to be characterizations of the second wave, the images of the first-wave feminists set the stage for these characterizations. One of the second wave's achievements would be rediscovering the history of the first and bringing it back in scholarly ways. But no media consultant would have found the popular memory of the first wave helpful in selling the second.

To Stridency and Beyond

Feminist anger, its reality and its representation, soon came to overshadow first-wave images. Anger in the women's movement was never connected to self-righteousness or even threat, but to aberration, another isolating theme, and eventually to militancy and overtones of lesbianism and deviance—the final separation. Anger was quickly established as the most important media theme of the women's movement, far surpassing in media interest any of the issues that the women wanted to discuss. Until Steinem came forward as an antidote in a new updating of the feminist story, media consumers seldom saw or read a story in which feminism was not portrayed as angry.

Yet many feminists of the period, particularly those in New York who attracted the media eye, were clearly furious. Dohrn told Peter Babcox that "in almost any woman you can unearth an incredible fury. It is often not even conscious, a threshold thing. But it's there, and it's an anger than can be a powerful radicalizing force" (Babcox 1969: 34). Indeed, some activists may have been attracted to the movement because it allowed them to express anger. However, in the strict definition of the word, feminists were never *militant*.

Anger was also a value of emotion and conflict that was easily transferred to craft traditions and served to make feminists good copy, even in surprising venues. In September 1968, feminist anger was utilized as something to promote when David Susskind's syndicated show extended an invitation to four New York feminists—Ros Baxandall, Kate Millett, Anselma Dell'Olio, and Jacqui Ceballos—to participate in a program titled "Four Angry Women." As it turned out, this was no exaggeration. The women were angry before the program, and their anger was intensified by Susskind's lack of preparation. Dell'Olio recalled, "So this was how much we mattered. A man with his own show (and we know how most men feel about their work) had not felt it necessary to go to any trouble at all to talk to four very different, eloquent, highly politicized women for an hour on the air, with his name on it" (Dell'Olio 1998: 160). In fact, Susskind was not very different from many media hosts, who often do not interact with their guests before airtime (or read their books), fearing that doing so will spoil the program's spontaneity. But feminists in the late sixties were quick to take offense, and the Susskind show was one proof that media of the period reflected a rage that clearly existed in the movement.

Indeed, even as radicals criticized Friedan, the ability to express anger publicly—whether genuine or not—also became a requirement for radical leadership. On a 1969 radio show with Shulamith Firestone, Anne Koedt, and Ti-Grace Atkinson, Baxandall recalled, "Ti-Grace Atkinson likened marriage to cancer and Shulie decried pregnancy as barbaric." Baxandall, married at the time, noted. "Stoically I managed to carry on; I counted on my much practiced ability to repress my conflicts and sound militant and right-on no matter what else was happening" (Baxandall 1998: 216).

Leaders such as Shirley Chisholm warned that many women of color and other women perceived feminists as "anti-male, anti-child, and anti-family." In a 1973 speech at the Houston convention of the Women's Political Caucus, she agreed that the media ignored other ways of telling the story in favor of training their "eyes on the young girl shaking her fist and screaming obscenities at an abortion rally." But she also warned there had been "excesses" that did not serve the movement (Chisholm, National Women's).

Anger was an emotion that met craft traditions, at least for a time, but its worth to the movement was problematical when it was reflected in the media at the expense of the issues. Media turned away from the prudish images suggested by the first wave to yet other stereotypes of women—this time the angry women with their roots in the Shakespearean shrew and the Puritan scold. Updated into "militancy," the word of the period, Goodman's coverage of a Boston group served as its flashpoint.

Cell 16

Boston was the location of a feminist group known as Cell 16 that became a symbol for militancy despite its initial aim of avoiding the media. In its statement, in the organization's publication, *A Journal of Liberation: No More Fun and Games*, Roxanne Dunbar was clear: "Our means, other than our education efforts and the formation of communes, will be secret. We shall not fight on the enemy's ground—on its streets, in his courts, legislatures, 'radical' movement, marriage, media" (Echols 1989: 159). But such a statement simply piqued Goodman's curiosity and awakened the reportorial tradition of slipping behind closed doors. She was the first to report on Cell 16 when she secretly attended a 1969 workshop on martial self-help for women. As she recalled, "I sniffed a story" (Goodman 1998). She was surprised, however, that, although she was a young newswriter for what was still called the women's section, her story appeared on page 1 of the Sunday edition under the simple headline, "Women."

The Cell 16 story met too many craft traditions not to be elaborated on in other media. Most important was the 1969 *Time* article on "The Feminists: Revolt against 'Sexism.'" As Carolyn Kitch notes, by 1999, when a *Time* cover asked, "Is Feminism Dead?" *Time* had long participated in coverage of the women's movement that presented a skewed view of the movement despite the magazine's ostensible use of fair-minded craft traditions. It should be noted that American general magazines do not ascribe to the same set of craft traditions as newspapers. There is no call for balance or evenhandedness. American magazines find their niche in the marketplace by reflecting and serving their readers' interests and attitudes. This is as true for the national newsmagazines—*Time, Newsweek,* and *U.S. News and World Report*—as much as for other national magazines. However, while a magazine such as *Esquire* makes clear its point of view by way of illustration and the tone of the article, newsmagazines have sought to build their identities to take advantage of the credibility earned by newspapers by way of craft traditions of balance. In various ways, newsmagazines suggest they are summarizing the news events of the day, not giving opinions on them.

Time, for example, is not easy to recognize as a voice of opinion. Its opportune covers, its readability, its efficient presentation, and its tone of common sense promoted (and still promote) an image of succinct and unbiased coverage. By the second wave, *Time* had long perfected a strategy of writing opinion pieces under a cloak of factuality. Stories were constructed with a large section devoted to a factual summary, often with an array of facts and figures. But the conclusion toward which the factual reporting seemed to be heading was often summarily replaced by an arbitrary conclusion. In the second wave, as in other coverage, reportage for a story might suddenly count for nothing in favor of an unsupported conclusion that barely seemed related to what had gone before. But unsophisticated readers, especially those who might have agreed with the concluding comment, were not likely to notice or care that the appearance of balance was achieved by setting up reportage and comment as cut from the same cloth.

In the 1960s and 1970s *Time* magazine still held the reputation for being among the nation's major forces in shaping public opinion, carrying its moderate Republicanism and probusiness attitude to the nation's smaller cities and towns, where other media choices were limited. As James Baughman notes, for the men and women of small-town America, *Time* offered a "window on a world largely unreported or analyzed in their newspapers" (Baughman 1998: 121). For critics, *Time* was all about carrying forth the Cold War philosophy and domestic status quo of its cofounder, Henry Luce, who told his staff in 1952, "The hell with objectivity" (Swanberg 1972: 163).

Time's role as a magazine of opinion, however, has not meant lack of fact. In its most powerful articles, there is no lack of reporting, a style that makes *Time*'s eventual conclusion seem logical and fact based. In the end, it is not the facts that carry the day but a mortar of opinion. Nonetheless, the belief held by its many readers that *Time* reflected studied thought and unbiased reporting made the magazine a formidable opponent for individuals or groups of which *Time* did not approve.

Time's reporting of the women's movement was shaped by its celebration of the status quo as defined by what Luce wanted to say and what the readers wanted to read. That philosophy was further cemented by the beliefs of the men who ran the magazine. As chapter 6 explores, neither Henry Grunwald, its editor during the second wave, nor Hedley Donovan, its publisher at the same time, had sympathy for women's demands. In its own shop, *Time* did not hire women as reporters (nor did other newsmagazines), a situation that was not rectified until 1970.

Time's first extensive article on feminism appeared in the "Behavior" section, an interesting choice that suggested that feminism was a behavior to be studied. Headlined "The New Feminists: Revolt against 'Sexism,'" the article called attention to the "body of dissidents whose voices, while comparatively muted until now, promise to grow much louder in the months to come: the militant new feminists of the Women's Liberation movement." The word *militant* was used five times in an examination of feminism in terms of fury that did not exclude the possibility that "some feminists" were calling to an end to sexual activity between men and women. However, the magazine also presented a statistical account of the wage disparities between men and women, which was negated by reportage that set out feminist anger as sufficient reason to negate the problem of wage disparities. "Many of the new feminists are surprisingly violent in mood and seem to be trying, in fact, to repel other women rather than attract them. Hundreds of young girls are learning karate, tossing off furious statements about male chauvinists, and distributing threatening handouts ('Watch out! You may meet a real castrating female')" (*Time* 11/21/69: 53). Buttressing the statement was a picture of Dunbar at a karate practice session that she contended was taken when she was unprepared, thereby accounting for her fierce expression (Dunbar 1999). It was used as a companion picture to that of Friedan, although followers of Dunbar's tiny group were hardly equal in number to those who followed the middle road of feminism represented by Friedan. The use of Friedan's picture likely sent a message that feminists were more alike than not. Moreover, it is unclear on what *Time* based its claim regarding the "hundreds of young girls" learning karate.

Time regularly covered the movement into the 1970s but usually did so in ways that reduced the movement's credibility. The emphasis on male dominance of language came in for some ribbing in "Ah, Sweet Ms-ery" (*Time* 3/20/72: 55). A "Time Essay," written by the Sue Kaufman, author of *Diary of a Mad Housewife*, paints a picture of ordinary women who are attracted to feminism but at the price of rejecting the public images of their "more militant sisters" (*Time* 3/20/72: 70). Here was a kind of *Time* doublespeak in action—utilizing a feminist (although admittedly "mad") to give credence to *Time*'s dissatisfaction with women who spoke out too strongly. "Militant sisters" became a barrier to be overcome rather than recognition of the women who put the second wave on the media agenda.

Time's early coverage of the women's movement, peaking with Kate Millett's cover story in 1970, had much to do with the gospel that Kaufman and other well-meaning writers adopted—the belief that it was necessary to distance the movement from the angry radicals so that the movement could gain credibility. That distancing, of course, meant that the ideas the radicals had introduced for discussion by agitprop and outrage disappeared—altogether a successful achievement for a magazine committed to the status quo. "All of *Time*'s reporting on the women's movement," Carolyn Kitch summarizes, "simultaneously acknowledged and dismissed the gains and messages of feminism. Its three decades of coverage of the movement are an example of the media's role in political and cultural hegemony, a system of power in which controversial opinions are aired (rather than suppressed) though in ways that weaken their message" (Kitch 1999: 5).

Newsweek chose to use Shana Alexander as a voice of "reasonable" arguments for women's equality, a voice that could only be expressed by a concomitant distancing from the militant sisters. Alexander saw the second wave as a "No Person's Land" "polluted by hatred, of the self hatred of women and the self-defeating hatred that so many enraged feminists feel for men. Organized sisterhood has always been something of a basket of snakes, chiefly because women have not yet learned or dared to like or trust each other much" (*Nswk* 3/18/74: 43). "Women's Lib Is Foolishness," contended the *Newsweek* headline for her column arguing that women were most concerned with femininity (*Nswk* 11/23/71: 73). These kinds of views were in line with the ongoing war on the movement waged by *Newsweek*, which as much as *Time* framed story after story in negative ways, as is clearly demonstrated by a glance at the headlines of stories of the period. Maureen Maier found that *Newsweek*'s 1970–72 coverage placed second-wave stories primarily in the sections "Life & Leisure," "Medicine," and "Media" (despite the Steinem cover story), that descriptors of women were in terms of attractiveness, and that stories were organized around themes of splinter, disorganization, and difficulty (Maier, "Through"). Like *Time, Newsweek* could sometimes put forth a facade of liberalism.

In 1970, under Helen Dudar's byline, the magazine concluded a story on a conciliatory note: "As I sat with many of the women I have discussed here, I was struck by how distorting the printed word can be. On paper, most of them have sounded cold, remote, surly, tough and sometimes a bit daft. On encounter, they usually turned out to be friendly, helpful and attractive. Meeting the more eccentric theoreticians, I found myself remembering that today's fanatics are sometimes tomorrow's prophets" (*Nswk* 3/23/70: 76). However, Dudar was freelance writer, not a staff member (women staff writers were not employed at *Newsweek* until forced to do by a lawsuit), and her views were expressed in a personal essay rather than reportage.

It was the rare story, in *Time* or other media, in which the subject of divisiveness was not raised, as if to do otherwise was to miss the most obvious point of the story. Attention to factions is a sure way to weaken the perception of the strength of social movements, and the civil rights movement certainly had endured the same kind of coverage of its splits, real and imagined. Many of those leaders quickly learned not to criticize each another in a public forum. This was not a lesson that Friedan would learn. Her outspokenness came at high cost to the movement, exacerbating the imperative of a craft tradition that embraced conflict.

Rage in Isolation

Time was the most apparent example of a doublespeak that pervaded the mass media at the end of the decade. By the end of 1969 the second wave had moved into nation's written media in ways that often appeared to be sympathetic but nonetheless promoted stereotypes under the guise of balanced reporting, as in an article by Sara Davidson that appeared in *Time*'s sister publication, *Life*. Davidson anchors the article with her reaction to the Miss America contest—already the benchmark event—but quickly routes the reader through what was becoming an explanation of various feminist divisions—notably The Feminists and Atkinson, whose comment "Marriage means lifelong slavery" was accompanied by a picture of a training session in karate. Davidson's journey included a lengthy stop to describe the session. "In their journal *No More Fun and Games*, Female Liberation members urge women to leave their husbands and children and to avoid pregnancy. Women should dress plainly, chop their hair short, and begin to 'declaim themselves' by dropping their husbands' or fathers' names. They should live alone and abstain from sexual relationships." The photograph illustrating the piece, of women wearing grotesque false breasts, did not suggest a critique of the U.S. breast fetish as much as suggest that women who dressed in displeasing ways were separatists and antimale. For its full-page introductory picture (when *Life* was still in large format), the magazine chose to forefront a sad young woman, the sign "woman" hanging around her neck like a sentence, alone on a New York street (the urban background sending its own message) except for a group of men eyeing her suspiciously. The photograph is mournful rather than strident, a spoiler contrast to the celebratory nature of the issue's cover story on Apollo 12.

The article's tourlike approach has much in common with a *Time* article that appeared a month earlier—the same emphasis on the radical groups, on fury, and on the rising fear that rights for women would result in lack of sexuality between men and women. These themes would be carried forth by other media, and while the agenda-setting function of *Time* and *Life* is not to be dismissed, nor are the prejudices of its male editors. Moreover, the construction of fear is a long-standing craft tradition that would be complicated after 1970 when the discussion of lesbianism in the movement became common.

"These Chicks Are Our Natural Enemies!"

Outside of the newsmagazines that sought to put forward an image of balance, most magazines were clear about their focus and, indeed, may have been easier for feminists to deal with than the mushy ground of mainstream "balance." The disruption of the *Dick Cavett Show* encouraged the development of a highly advertised *Playboy* piece. Accompanied by a Jekyll-to-Hyde illustration and titled "Up against the Wall, Male Chauvinist Pig!" the article was subtitled, "Militant Man Haters Do Their Level Worst to Distort the Distinctions between Male and Female and to Discredit the Legitimate Grievances of American Women" (Hunt 1970).

Despite its timely release, the *Playboy* article had been in the making before the Cavett episode, when Susan Braudy was commissioned for the piece. However, her draft was not focused enough on the militants for Hugh Hefner's taste. As reported by feminist activist Claudia Dreifus, writing for the Liberation News Service, Hefner circulated a memo that overruled the initial judgment of one of his editors:

> It sounds like we we re way off in our upcoming feminist piece. . . . Jack indicates that what we have is a well balanced "objective" article, but what I want is a devastating piece that takes the militant feminists apart. . . . Jack seems to think that the more moderate members of the feminist movement are coming to the fore. I don't know what he's been reading that brings him to this curious conclusion, but I couldn't

disagree more. What I am interested in is the highly irrational, emotional, kookie trend that feminism has taken in the past couple of years. These chicks are our natural enemies! The only subject to [*sic*] feminism that is worth doing is on this new militant phenomena and the proper *Playboy* approach is to devastate it. (Dreifus 1970: 11)

Esquire magazine was hardly to be outdone, in January 1971 publishing Helen Lawrenson's screed, "The Feminine Mistake," accompanied by a full-page, full-color illustration of a portly, booted woman brandishing the most easily recognizable symbol of radical feminism—a flaming brassiere.

Harper's Magazine, considered to have an elite readership, also had a peculiar relationship with women's issues, most having to do with gender roles and the sexual anxiety of the period. Its editor at the time was a southerner, Willie Morris, but its executive editor was Midge Decter, an outspoken antifeminist. Of all of its cover stories, perhaps the most angry was one of a woman's thighs with the upper edge of a miniskirt level with the reader's eye. Its "sell" line was famous quote from Sigmund Freud, "What does a woman want? For God's sake, what does a woman want?" (*Harper's* 2/70).

The emphasis on "militant feminists" never ceased and came to represent the undergirding fear of the period that heterosexual sex was dead while limiting that possibility to women that men would not want anyway. Steinem put the language in perspective. In a 1972 *Meet the Press* interview, Shana Alexander, then at *Newsweek,* asked Steinem to identify movement opponents "since it is a militant movement" (although the connection was unclear). Steinem demurred: "I would more likely call the Pentagon a militant movement" (NBC 1972).

5. August 1970

As the end of her term as president of the National Organization for Women, Betty Friedan was beset by criticism from the radical women, beset by criticism from within her own organization, and beset by criticism from the lesbians within and outside of activist circles. The Congress to Unite Women had failed. Seeking to conclude her term in a memorable way, she proposed a women's "strike for equality," a twenty-four-hour period when women would walk off their jobs on the fiftieth anniversary of the passage of the Nineteenth Amendment, 26 August 1970. In a stirring moment, the announcement was made at the last NOW convention at which she would preside: "I propose that the women who are doing menial chores in the office cover their typewriters and close their notebooks, that the telephone operators unplug their switchboards, the waitress stop waiting, cleaning women stop cleaning, and everyone who is doing a job for which a man would be paid more—stop—and every women pegged forever as assistant, doing jobs for which men get credit—stop!" (Friedan 1976: 145)

The NOW leadership was not as stirred. Friedan had not discussed the proposal with any members of the board—even Muriel Fox was stunned—and the responsibility for Friedan's massive plan would fall on the new president, Aileen Hernandez, and the young organization's small resources. Nonetheless, the public nature of the pronouncement, Friedan's commitment to the strike, and the public relations buzz that it produced brought to the task not only NOW leaders but supporters from every strand of feminism. On the strike day, an estimated fifty thousand women marched down New York's Fifth Avenue while other demonstrations occurred across the country. Historian Susan Douglas said it was "probably the most important public action of the movement" (Douglas 1994: 77). Another historian of the second wave interpreted it as "such a publicity coup that it triggered further growth spurt in the movement" (Davis, F. 1991: 115). Thirty years later, Friedan called it "the high point of my political life" (Friedan 2000: 241).

Despite a collective memory in which the march is most represented by Fifth Avenue filled with exuberant women, the events of the day were not uniformly successful across the nation. In places that fell short of the New York march, local media interpreted a lack of participants as a failure of the movement as a whole. What also has been forgotten is that the 26 August march coincided with the campaign to pass the Equal Rights Amendment in the U.S. Congress. Indeed, on 10 August 1970 the House did indeed approve the amendment. The 26 August event, however, just two weeks later, made no official connection with the ERA, which was to face the much more difficult task of Senate confirmation and state-by-state ratification. This disconnect between the 26 August event and the upcoming battle to ratify the ERA removed the obvious political agenda from the march activities in favor of three "demands" of the day—twenty-four-hour child care, abortion on demand, and, in a general clumping, equal opportunity for women in education and employment—none of which were tied to particular pieces of legislation.

The loss of the event as a political lever for the ERA campaign was one of the compromises made to radical Left women, who had little interest in political reform. Nonetheless, the coverage of the House passage of the proposed amendment did in fact set the stage for the march activities, as did a change in New York's public accommodations law, permitting women to be served at previously men-only bars. When the march is coupled to those two stories—as well as to the coverage that preceded the march—the march seems less the apex event of the period. And if it was, as women's historians remember the event, the public high point of the second wave, it also revealed the deep-seated animosities against women.

True to her labor past, Friedan's first call was for a female work stoppage to promote passage of the ERA. She testified before a U.S. House subcommittee that if Congress did not provide equal rights to women, it would suffer the consequences of a women's general strike. As United Press International reported, " 'I warn you,' she said, 'if you have not sent this amendment to the states by Aug. 26 [for ratification] we are going to track you down—in your offices, on the beaches, in the mountains, wherever you are. And we're going to stay with you until you do" (NYT 5/8/70: 34).

Despite her reach for the cadence of leadership, Friedan was hardly in a position to warn anyone, much less the U.S. Congress, given the lack of regard for her in both NOW and the general feminist community. As the reality of the march to provide a united front became clear, the rhetoric of dire warnings subsided, along with references to the ERA. The resulting compromises led to the construction of the march along lines of universality, a celebratory rite in which all women could find meaning. In one of her first interviews as NOW president, Hernandez remained true to Friedan's initial plan. "Our aim is to try to prove that we could shut down the country" (Goodman, "Aileen Hernandez"). This was an obviously ambitious and perhaps impossible goal as well as a departure from NOW's tactics of confrontation tied to specific goals, as in the EEOC campaign and public pressure for the passage of public accommodations laws. The strike aspects of the 26 August events came under criticism from both conservative and radical quarters. For the pro-woman faction, the call for women to stay off their jobs was risky for those who needed the day's wages; other radical women were not about to follow anything that Friedan said, particularly at a time when she was attempting to rid NOW leadership of its lesbian members. The essential New York NOW, with lesbian leadership, not only censured Friedan for her antilesbian statements but also refused until the last minute to participate in organizing the New York rally. As strike day approached, there was confusion about the strike itself in all quarters. Was it indeed a "strike," as Friedan had originally called for, with women refusing to go to work or to do household chores? Was it to be a boycott of certain products considered detrimental to women? Was it to promote the upcoming Senate vote for the ERA, as Friedan had indicated back in May but not addressed in any of the ERA publicity? Despite the three demands, the purpose of the strike became muddy as leaders tried to shift the focus from labor strike to the symbolic mass demonstration. On the eve of the event, Friedan described the purpose of the strike to the *Times*'s Judy Klemesrud: "to make women aware of their power, and the fact that they can use this power to make changes in the world." But Friedan could not resist adding, darkly, "And if changes aren't made . . . I'm afraid that what could happen with women might make the race riots in Detroit look like child's play" (Klemesrud, "Coming Wednesday": 14). It was a farfetched threat that still gave some credence to the ongoing media descriptions of the movement as militant. By this time, Friedan had also backed away from her earlier announcement of a sexual strike, but this, like the announced labor strike aspects of the day, remained in the public sphere and confused coverage and public understanding.

Friedan continued to receive most mass media attention for planning the August march, as in a *New York Times Magazine* profile that focused on her efforts to raise money in East Hampton. At the time, the article pleased no one (although Friedan noted it favorably in her 2000 book), featuring a picture of Friedan with the strap of her dress falling and bringing attention to Jill Johnston, a lesbian writer for the *Village Voice*, who chose to strip off her T-shirt to take a dip in the pool as Friedan was about to introduce Gloria Steinem. Altogether, the event appeared to associate the movement with the kind of "radical chic" supporters of the Black Panther Party. Friedan also participated in writing the lyrics of a special song to celebrate the day, another action that did not please women of the Left, who suspected Friedan of trying to make money off the song because she had applied for a copyright. "We're going to reprint your song, and we're going to give it away free!" "Some Red Witches" wrote in an open letter. "We refuse to allow the women's movement to become a commodity" (Some Red Witches 1970).

Despite Friedan's marketing of the song to women's groups at the special price of ninety-five cents, it was not destined for widespread adoption.

Friedan soldiered on as the official national coordinator of the strike day but had so little support from the women's community that she could not lead a meeting on the subject without Left women talking over her. In the meantime, organizers from the Socialist Workers Party seemed to be taking on leadership roles that tended to make the march too conservative for radical women, as in the defeat of Friedan's plan to begin the march at 110th Street, thereby including Harlem, in favor of a march that ran from 59th to 42nd Street, expected to draw more mainstream women and at a time that women could march after work (Klemesrud, "Coming Wednesday"). Friedan turned to Karen DeCrow, who had come of age coordinating NOW's Public Accommodation Week activities and who moved from her home in Syracuse into Fox's city apartment for six weeks to be close to the strike headquarters. But DeCrow, as a Friedan protégée, represented a leader who was persona non grata to many New York–based feminists. Mediating the gap between NOW and the radicals was Jacqui Ceballos, a member of New York NOW with ties to the radical feminist community. As an independent coordinator of strike-day activities, Ceballos served as a conciliatory influence (as she does today as coordinator of the Veteran Feminists of America), seeking to bridge the gaps among the angry NOW members, independent feminists, and radical feminist groups, including the Socialist Workers Party women, who, Ceballos noted, were "good at organizing" (Ceballos 1998) but who were also suspected by NOW as well as Left groups as seeking to take over the movement entirely. A writer for the alternative publication *off our backs* was among those suspicious of the Young Socialist Alliance. "YSA showed an immediate interest in the Publicity Committee, virtually attempting to control the relationship with the media." The *off our backs* writer objected to the lack of welfare demands: "Their willingness to accept a minimum position (which excluded our poor and black sisters) in the interest of 'keeping the coalition together' was obvious" (*oob* 9/30/70: 3, 2). Ironically, Friedan, the early socialist, found her original ideas for the march compromised by another generation of socialists that sought to build the movement's base by setting out what was considered an agenda on which most women could agree.

Ceballos's task was thus mammoth, and to encompass the wide variety of feminists, the New York march could focus only on size: "My committee concentrated on attracting the thousands we'd boast would march," Ceballos recalled in a memoir of the event. "The 1,500 or so card-carrying feminists would show, but how could we attract others? A poor showing would increase the ridicule we were constantly subject to, and hurt the movement. A dramatic action would do it. But what? We'd demonstrated at the Ms. America Pageant, sat in at the

Ladies Home Journal, demonstrated at the White House and the Capitol, thrown Ajax down a toilet at Colgate-Palmolive's Park Avenue office, released white mice at a bridal fair—what could we do that had not been done?" (Ceballos 1996: 3).

As it turned out, all kinds of things had not been done, and many of the actions would be left for the day itself. One prelude was to be an "invasion" of the Statue of Liberty, scheduled for the day of the House vote. It is perhaps one of Ceballos's unheralded successes that she was able to turn a promotional event for the march into a political statement. "We wanted to send a message to Congress, and at the same time publicize the march and strike" (Ceballos 1998).

The March and the ERA

The Equal Rights Amendment was championed by Representative Martha Griffiths (D-Mich.), who by 1970 had been a member of the House of Representatives for sixteen years. Griffiths's stewardship helped make possible the adoption of an amendment to the 1964 Civil Rights Act prohibiting sex discrimination. By 1970, the forty-seven-year-old ERA proposal remained in the Judiciary Committee, which was chaired by the measure's major opponent, Representative Emanuel Celler (D-N.Y.). In a long shot, Griffiths agreed to sponsor a petition to bring the amendment to the floor, although the petition would require more than two hundred signatures. Thanks to her own legislative skill and the pressure exerted on legislators by the members of the Business and Professional Women, the petition received the necessary signatures. Although the second wave was well launched by this time, the BPW's efforts, led by Marguerite Rawalt, resulted in success in the House.

Despite her leadership on the ERA, Griffiths is an interesting and almost forgotten figure of the second wave. Indeed, some of her legislative success with the ERA may have been because she was not considered part of the new wave of feminists, a distancing that for some reporters seemed to legitimize the proposal. Writing for the *New York Times*, one reporter framed her as "disdaining the militant overkill of many leaders of the women's liberation movement." Moreover, "Unlike some militant feminists, Mrs. Griffiths is no man-hater" (Hunter 1970: 23). In its coverage of the House passage, *Time* gave special attention to Griffiths along the same lines, heading its boxed article, "Martha Griffiths: Graceful Feminist." Accompanied by a smiling picture, the article noted that Griffiths was a "cheery woman" who "happily concedes" that her career "has been more advanced than hindered by men." Her "powers of friendly persuasion" were credited as equally contributing to her success, and the list of her accomplishments concluded with her assignment as chair of the

"House Beauty Shop," an assignment at which "most militant liberationists would scoff" (*Time* 8/24/70: 30–31). As in all its coverage of the women's movement, *Time* established a framework of narrow acceptability, and Griffiths, no matter the legislative skill put to use in the revitalization of the amendment, was made to fit it. Notably, Griffiths tended to be paraphrased rather than quoted directly in this and other articles, so it was unclear whether she held strong views that had led to her leadership on the ERA. For a woman who held legislative position, that characterization may well have reduced the power of her leadership.

That characterization did not help in feminist groups either. Her name seldom appeared in feminist literature, she was not a speaker in feminist circles, and although feminists eventually united in the ERA campaign, Griffiths was notably absent from the drive, not even one of the "sponsoring sisters" (Klemesrud, "Coming Wednesday": 16). Griffiths never captured the public imagination. This disassociation between the legislator who achieved the House passage of the ERA and feminist activist women involved in the march was made clear when she was given no role in the 26 August events.

Griffiths's lack of presence in the movement may also have resulted from several of her personal characteristics that were out of sync with the times. She was older than most of the activists—the age of many of the young feminists' mothers—and she was Midwestern and Protestant at a time when the leaders were from cities and Jewish. Neither she nor the ERA was radical enough for many women activists of the time. Radical feminists saw the ERA as a nonissue because it did not seek revolutionary change for all women in society, and such feminists resisted efforts to turn the march into a promotional effort on behalf of the ERA. When the radical D.C. Women's Liberation group began planning with the Washington NOW chapter (or, as the radicals called it, "the National Organization for White Middle-Class Straight Women with Professional Status"), the representative for the radical group noted despairingly, "It soon became clear that NOW viewed passage of the Equal Rights Amendment as their most important goal to the exclusion of anything that, in their minds, might jeopardize this goal" (*oob* 9/30/70: 2).

For march organizers such as Ceballos, this lack of unity on the issue of the ERA was another barrier to be overcome. Passage of the ERA was not one of the "demands" of the march. Instead, Ceballos and her workers found a way to promote the ERA as a lead-in to the strike day.

Ceballos came to feminism not out of mass media but from the theatrical world. Before she came to New York and took up the feminist cause, she had been director of an opera company in Bogotá, Columbia. In 1969 she joined a feminist theatrical troupe, the New Feminists, organized by Anselma Dell'Olio. When Patricia Lawrence suggested the Statue of Liberty action, influenced by a similar action by a Puerto Rican group the year before, Ceballos brought to the event a theatrical even celebratory sense that moved the news frame from the usual confrontational mode and wrapped support for the ERA within it. The idea was to place banners on the top two balconies of the monument. Surreptitious visits were made for measurements of wind velocity. News media were alerted. On the day of the event, several women smuggled in forty-foot banners furled on broomsticks inside the legs of their jeans. Nearly thirty years later, Ceballos recalled the event in a style that captured the spirit:

> But suddenly the chopping was above us. CBS, NBC and ABC helicopters were circling Ms. Liberty! We dashed madly up the winding staircase, the guards in close chase and barely reached the balcony ahead of them. Fending them off was not easy but someone up there was helping and in spurt of a heavy wind the first banner was secured. **Women of the World Unite.** Cheers came from below. The cameras captured it all. Our message would go out, but we worried that we'd not get the second banner up before being arrested. But in the flash of a second the guards halted. The mayor had sent a message, *Leave the women alone.* Up went the second banner. **Strike for Equality August 26.**
>
> At Ms. Liberty's base the women whipped out their signs and began chanting
>
> What do we want? Freedom!
>
> When do we want it? Now?
>
> ERA! ERA! ERA! Today
>
> We are your tired, your poor, yearning to be free.
>
> We are the women. We demand equal rights. (Ceballos 1996)

The McSorley's Incident

Despite the whirring of the helicopters, the Statue of Liberty action was not the only New York feminist story of the day. NOW long had sought legal public accommodations guarantees for women. The city of New York had passed such a law, which was scheduled to go into effect on 10 August. But feminist attention was on the Statue of Liberty activity rather than on the law, so it was perhaps not surprising when a *New York Times* reporter, Grace Lichtenstein, called Lucy Komisar, the public relations director for the New York NOW chapter, seeking a hook for the public accommodations story (Komisar 1998). Lichtenstein, who recalls that many of the movement stories were volunteered by reporters rather than assigned, does not remember if this was a desk assignment or one she chose to pursue on her own (Lichtenstein 1999).

Komisar, a professional freelance writer, was working at home. She agreed to meet Lichtenstein at 4 P.M. at McSorley's Old Ale House, a formerly men-only bar that had long been the focus of feminist disgruntlement. By the time Komisar arrived, the bar, already opened, had complied with the new law, and women had been served. But Komisar was refused entry because she could not prove her age with a birth certificate. Angry, Komisar tussled with the guard, a moment caught by the *New York Times* photographer, well positioned at the bar's entrance. Once inside, Komisar, with Lichtenstein at her elbow, became involved in a verbal confrontation with a male patron, who subsequently poured his stein of beer on her head. Protesting, she was escorted out of the bar, where the *Times*'s photographer took more photographs, including one that appeared in the *Times*—Komisar with arms akimbo and drenched with beer, a group of patrons laughing in the background.

Coverage of House Passage of the ERA

When the House gave its approval to what had long been considered the doomed ERA, the news media had at hand two ready-made sidebars and dramatic art to accompany the story—the jubilant and celebratory Statue of Liberty demonstration and the *Times*'s pictures of Komisar, tussling at the door of McSorley's or wet and ejected out from the bar. The Statue of Liberty demonstration had been covered by the Associated Press and United Press International; and the *Times*'s version of the McSorley's incident was distributed by the Times News Service; however, a subsequent Associated Press story seemed to be drawn entirely from the *Times*'s account and may be considered its incarnation.

The House passage made the front page in all the newspapers—from the *Chicago Tribune*'s black banner "O.K. Women's Rights Bid" to the *New York Times*'s decorous one-column head—such differences arising more from the newspapers' styles than from differences in news judgment. The use of the two related stories, however, points to the questionable concept of balance.

Despite the heavy coverage of the Statue of Liberty demonstration by broadcast media, the *Times* chose not to publish the dramatic pictures of the banner-festooned Statue, tagging news of the demonstration to the final paragraphs of the McSorley's story, a choice that may have been predicated on privileging what seemed a legitimate news story over a manipulated one. What are problematical are the choice of art to accompany the story and the tone of the story, which served to present Komisar as bizarre and indeed deserving of both refusal at the door and her later ejection. There was no acknowledgment that Komisar had been unfairly refused entry in what, in hindsight, seems like a newspaper setup, nor was there sympathy for her ejection, when she was the victim of another customer.

While the *Times*'s front-page art featured an attractive young women having a convivial drink at the center of a group of seemingly admiring men, two inside photographs showed the solitary Komisar fighting to get into the bar next to the second photograph of her ejection. Even the placement of the three pictures—the approved woman on the front page and the angry feminist marginalized to a less-important spot—suggests a metaphor of approval and disapproval. The placement of the pictures carried out the narrative tone of the story: A male patron had showed Komisar an obscene poem, which she attempted to snatch out of his hand.

"Why you little . . ." he shouted, dumping a stein of ale over her head.

"You can't do that," she shrieked, lunging at him. The two exchanged a few weak blows before she was escorted, protesting, outside.

"They're really boorish, horrible men and I don't think I'd want to have anything to do with them," Miss Komisar, drenched but smiling, said as she sipped an ale at the bar [presumably after she reentered; this is not clear]. "They're lower-class men who have a lot of problems with their masculinity."

The *Times*'s story offers opportunity for a wealth of interpretations. The language of the story, as in Komisar's "shrieking," represents not righteous anger—she had, after all, had to wrestle her way in—but hysteria. Even her attire was mentioned, "purple pants suit and sandals," as if, in August, that was not appropriate. But perhaps the most insidious interpretation is its invitation to use lower-class men to condemn assertive feminism. The *Times*'s account emphasized the offenders in terms of class, quoting Komisar with an arch tone: "They're lower-class men who have a lot of problems with their masculinity." In contrast, the young woman who had arrived earlier with her husband predicted in the story's summing up that some "militant feminists" might drop by in the next few weeks to be "abused and called names." " 'Yes, it will be like slumming,' sniffed Miss Komisar" (*NYT* 8/11/70: A10).

Interestingly, New York's *Daily News*, the newspaper that served a working-class population, played the McSorley's incident positively—a front page picture of a female *News* reporter and the son of the owner having a comfortable beer together, and a pair of inside stories, including a first-person account by the female reporter (Kramer 1970: 5). The *News* used the McSorley's coverage as part of a page given over to related stories—the Statue of Liberty demonstration, with an accompanying picture of the House vote, and a Brooklyn legislator who had announced intended legislation for pensions for housewives. And on the following day, the

News's editorial cartoon ("The Lib Takeover") portrayed a jubilant Statue of Liberty arrayed in a jump suit and sunglasses that were not terribly different from those belonging to Komisar.

In the nation's newspapers outside of New York, the *Times*'s version of the story, distributed by the Times News Service and an Associated Press account that drew its style and information from the *Times*'s story, dominated and provided the context for the House vote story that it accompanied in a side-by-side layout. The story comprised page 1 news in most mainstream newspapers except for the *Rocky Mountain News*, where it appeared on page 3. The *Chicago Tribune* in particular called on a number of familiar stereotypes by the use of juxtaposition. The *Tribune* used the story under an Associated Press photograph of Martha Griffiths, an interesting choice. Rather than a photograph of celebration and congratulation, as would be expected to illustrate such a victory, Griffiths's face has been cropped so that all that is apparent is that she was powdering her nose; the caption read, "Equal but Feminine." The *Tribune* edited Griffiths to a picture in isolation, a small unimpressive square that drew the reader's eye from the banner headline to the McSorley's account.

The *Tribune* was not alone in its use of the Griffiths's nose-powdering picture. The *Washington Post* also used the image to illustrate the House vote, although on the jump page. The *Sacramento Bee* used the picture of Komisar outside the bar, accompanied by the Associated Press story based on the *Times*'s account. The picture appeared on the second page next to the jump story on the House vote. Philadelphia's *Evening Bulletin* used the same picture of Komisar on the front page, next to a UPI photograph of women raising their fists in front of the statue. The *Milwaukee Journal* showcased an arresting two-column AP Wirephoto of the Statue of Liberty and its banner, "Women of the World Unite" next to the House story. But a two-column head on the McSorley's story, taken from "press dispatches—that is, the *New York Times*—undercut the glorious image of the Statue of Liberty.

One newspaper ignored the McSorley's story. The *Los Angeles Times* provided a one-column cut of the Statue of Liberty and its banner over the House story— no McSorley's in sight. But the *Times* simply missed the boat. One of its writers would do his own McSorley's story, which appeared on the same day as the 26 August march coverage. The *Rocky Mountain News* provided what would have undoubtedly pleased the feminist organizers—the UPI picture of demonstrating women in front of the statue placed over the story of the House vote.

The *Rocky Mountain News* also carried New York's accommodations story but omitted any mention of the Komisar incident. Instead, the Denver paper ran a first-person account written by the Associated Press writer, Susan Everly, the first woman to drink in what had been another New York men-only bar, the Biltmore (Everly 1970). It was the only use of that story in the sample studied here, leading to the question of why newspapers would choose the McSorley's incident over a story on a similar subject by an AP writer. The journalistic tradition of playing up conflict clearly made the *Times*'s version the preferred choice.

The McSorley's incident captured the attention of the national press in ways that the historic House vote did not. In his column, William F. Buckley Jr. saw the incident in terms of "women's lib types," invading a male sanctuary, although Komisar had come by herself (Buckley 1970). Harriet Van Horne interpreted the McSorley's incident in terms of Komisar's entrance: "Any woman who shoves her way into this murky dank sawdust-filled dog hole deserves not an egg in her beer but a mickey." She echoed what was by this time a familiar refrain: "A funny thing happened to them on their way to McSorley's Saloon. They've lost their femininity." The *San Francisco Sunday Examiner and Chronicle* emphasized the theme when it headlined her column, "Militants' Mistake" and used a quotation from the article, "So many of the liberators are filled with contempt for their own sex" as part of its headline (Horne 1970). *Time* magazine used the incident jocularly. "When the women appeared [one woman had been involved], rowdies booed and cursed ostentatiously, exhaling the fumes of onions and Limburger cheese. One fellow confronted a vice president of NOW and poured a stein of ale on her head" (*Time* 8/24/70: 12).

The McSorley's story was also grist for editorial cartoonists. The *Los Angeles Times* editorial cartoon was self-righteous in its rendering of two black women, who, noting a demonstration mounted by two cranky and elderly women (the first-wave stereotypes again) outside a men-only bar, exclaim, "Now what's their beef about?" (*Los Angeles Times* 10/17/70: 11–17).

The McSorley's story appears almost to have been seized by a press eager to ridicule the movement by using stereotypes at hand and certainly provides an example of how the mainstream failed to give to the women's movement the sympathetic or heroic treatment given to the early civil rights movement. It would have been unimaginable, for example, for the mainstream press to offer "balance" to sit-ins by way of personal "sidebar" views from reporters who decried not the strategy but the cause. By contrast, the use of the McSorley's story countered the celebratory nature of the Statue of Liberty demonstration and the success of the House passage.

The McSorley's story might be interpreted as an expression of what were considered male fears—the invasion of sanctuary, the loss of masculinity, a dislocation of tried-and-true roles—although how much of this was manufactured by such coverage is, of course, difficult to ascertain. But there was certainly white fear of black advance that the mainstream press chose not to illustrate under the guise of balance.

Coverage of the House passage of the ERA and its various editorial accoutrements whetted media appetite for the 26 August events. As the day of the march approached, there was no guarantee that the various marches planned in New York City and around the country would draw sufficient numbers to suggest the strength of the women's movement. This was particularly true for areas outside of New York City, where NOW chapters varied in strength. Some chapters avoided taking the chance of mounting a demonstration that could fail so easily. The Denver chapter, for example, urged women to adopt a one-day, no-buy program, a less easily quantifiable campaign than either a march or a labor stoppage, accompanied by a news conference that made awards to area women (*Rocky Mountain News* 8/26/70: 3). Among those concerned that the day would fail because of its media framing was Griffiths herself: "The editors of the papers are treating this thing as a joke. They're laughing. And if it's not an absolutely fabulous success, then they will say that women don't want rights . . . they're happy where they are. . . . This stuff was said about Negroes for years" (Meyer, K., "Boycott": A10).

Role of Women's Pages

The nation's newspapers provided plenty of premarch space, most of it thanks to writers on what had been the women's pages. The *New York Times*'s coverage included a full-page spread in Charlotte Curtis's 4-Fs section that limned the history of women's rights in America and was repeated, under different headlines, in other papers as a result of syndication (Bender 1970). This was a safe historic peg that many women's sections of newspapers chose to take and was both appropriate to the anniversary as well as safe, generally avoiding the demands of the march. The *Washington Post*'s Myra MacPherson interviewed Alice Paul (MacPherson 1970). In the *Boston Globe*, illustrated with first-wave images, Ellen Goodman wrote a sympathetic article that stressed the unity theme of the "moderate" NOW and the "radical" Bread and Roses coming together (Goodman, "Feminists"). The *Globe* previously had experience with Bread and Roses when fifty members demanded a meeting with the paper's editors to protest it as "an actively racist, sexist institution" (Evans, L. 1970: 300).

News Coverage

U.S. News and World Report summed up the demonstrations as "generally, good-humored, colorful and orderly—but not massive," reminding its readers that 26 August had been called as a national "strike day" and had implicitly failed in that call (*USNWR* 26). Coverage in the metropolitan areas where activities existed was, in the word so favored by headline writers, "mixed." At the locus of march activity, New York City, the *Times* gave it a front-page story, a four-column headline, an eye-level photograph of exuberant marchers, and a continuation of the story with a banner headline and a picture of the Washington march. The story, written by Linda Charlton, stressed the inclusive nature of the march, although one of the speakers remained inexcusably nameless as "a black speaker from the Third Woman's Alliance" (Charlton, "Women March").

Coverage also included several sidebars, one concerning Friedan's trip to the hairdresser: " 'I don't want people to think Women's Lib girls don't care about how they look,' she said as she paid the cashier $10. 'We should try to be as pretty as we can. It's good for our self-image and it's good for politics' " (*NYT* 8/27/70: 30). Lichtenstein, the McSorley's reporter, weighed in by noting that the original aim of the strike—quitting work for the day—had not been accomplished (Lichtenstein, "For Most Women"), a theme that was mitigated by the three-column photograph of women massed in the Bryant Park rally that was used to illustrate the story. Susan Douglas has argued that the coverage in the *Times* was less than fair because the *Times* chose not to interview any of the women marchers or to discuss the issues involved in favor of "balancing" the march with interviews with women who were not supporters, thus turning what had attempted to be an inclusive event into one of win and loss (Douglas 1994: 163–91). Nonetheless, the success of the New York march in terms of the number of participants, with photographs to prove it, minimized the negativity.

Local media in other metropolitan areas where the activities were less than overwhelming viewed the events as failures. "Women's Strike Day Gets Mixed Support," headlined the *Milwaukee Journal* with the sidebar, "Slip of the Lib: Some Women Show Little Enthusiasm for the Strike," stories that were carried to inside jump pages with similarly gloomy headlines, "Liberation Backers Stay at Home, Rally" and "Strike Gains Very Little Momentum." Tucked away inside was a positive story about windup activities, "Liberation Spirit Still Strong as Strike Day Ends" (*Milwaukee Journal* 8/26/70: 1, 12, 6).

Such mixed messages were the norm for several newspapers. The *Boston Evening Globe* interspersed fairly straightforward news coverage with jocular sidebars, as in its story of the integration of two of Boston's formerly men-only saloons, yet another echo of the McSorley's story: "Militant women, thirsting for equal rights yesterday, violated two of Boston's oldest strongholds of mas-culinity. And civilized drinking many never be the same again" (Botwright 1970). Strong front page art was countered by the use of inside pictures that paired an informal shot of Friedan with a studio shot of a representative of a tiny counter organization known by the acronym HOW, as if it represented an organizations equal in size or influence. Another *Globe* picture showed local construction workers posing with a sign that read, "Female Steamfitter Wanted Must Be 38-23-38" (*BG* 8/27/70: 3). For the *Philadelphia Inquirer*, "caterwauling" characterized the event (*Philadelphia Inquirer* 8/27/70: 7).

In Atlanta, the *Constitution* chose to run a front-page AP Wirephoto of an intense and angry demonstration in San Francisco, although there were numerous marches around the country to choose from. The inside story framed the local activities as insignificant and slightly ridiculous: "The scene was less than sobering for those sitting on the concrete benches in Plaza Park Wednesday sharing bottles of cheap wine. They hardly noticed the approximately 25 feminists who, with banners and placards, gathered in the park at noon to celebrate the 50th anniversary of woman suffrage" (*Atlanta Constitution* 8/27/70: 10). The *Constitution* also chose to use a column by Dr. Edgar F. Berman, whose previous claims that women's "raging hormonal imbalance" made them poor choices for leadership roles had resulted in his ouster from the Democratic Party's Committee on National Priorities.

Headlines and photo captions were sometimes at discord with the stories. "Libs on the March to 'Demand Equality,' " according to the *San Francisco Examiner*, the quotation marks apparently used to represent readers who thought the state of women was fine as it was. The *Examiner* editors captioned a UPI Wirephoto of the Washington march as "Angry-looking young women militants grimly march up Connecticut Avenue in Washington" (*San Francisco Examiner* 8/27/70: 1). In Los Angeles, the *Times* chose to feature as its front-page art a city councilman, head in hands, obviously bored with the strike-day presentation. "Not Exactly a Triumph," the *Times* headline writer noted, adding, "L.A. 'Women's Lib' Marchers Greeted by Cheers and Jeers" (*Los Angeles Times* 8/27/70: 1). An Associated Press story about the national activities received the headline, "It's Women's Day Today—Watch It, Bub!" In Philadelphia, headlines were bland, but leads were not, even when written by a female reporter. The *Evening Bulletin*'s account of the Philadelphia rally noted that spectators gathered "to watch militant women's liberation groups in action," a characterization that was the work of a female reporter who regularly covered the subject (*EvenBull* 8/26/70: 1).

Because of apparent deadline difficulties on the day of the march, the *Chicago Tribune* gave the march two full days of front-page coverage. Coverage on 26 August included plans for that day, including the de rigueur picture of Friedan with her mouth open. The following day, the coverage was vitriolic: Michael Kilian's story of local events adopted a tone of male camaraderie, beginning, "If yesterday's 'Women's Strike for Women' was a taste of female revolution to come, the male establishment can rest easy. In Chicago, at least, the event was a flop." The piece continued in the same tone on the inside jump, which was headlined, "Strike Flops, Women in City Keep Working" (Kilian 1970).

The previously pristine *Rocky Mountain News* gave notice to the "No Buy Day" campaign chosen by the Denver NOW, but the paper's editorial cartoon nonetheless presented a stereotype. An overbearing and unattractive woman arrayed in a "Women's Lib" shirt, wags a finger over her Milquetoast husband, who is caring for the squalling children: "I'm going out with the gals and don't wait up for me!" (*Rocky Mountain News* 8/26/70: 50). Another editorial cartoon rendition by Bill Mauldin, the nationally syndicated *Chicago Sun-Times* cartoonist, marked a similar theme: yet another Milquetoast husband says, "Yes, Dear" to a large-busted woman with "Women's Liberation" on her chest.

Coverage by the *Washington Post* may have been most successful in avoiding insidious sidebars that trivialized the day, possibly prompted by the newspaper's settlement on the same day of the women's suit against the Post-owned *Newsweek*. Notably, the *Post* also gave first-page play to a call for boycott of several products, a thrust of the equality-day activities that was often overlooked or underplayed. And the *Post* caught something of Friedan's single-mindedness. When the *Post* reporter asked her about the possible snarling of traffic predicted for the New York march, Friedan answered in her typical style: "I'm sorry. This is our hour of history. We're going to take it" (Meyer, K. "Women's Lib").

It is also interesting to note the response of the black press, which was generally uninterested in the woman's movement and in August 1970 was devoting much of its national coverage to the Black Panther courthouse shootings in California and the subsequent FBI hunt for Angela Davis, who was believed to have supplied the gun used in the attack. Chicago's *Daily Defender*, for example, did not mention the House passage of the ERA. The movement's emphasis on self-defense, as in Cell 16's demonstrations of karate, was reflected in a July *Defender* editorial cartoon: a large woman says to a surprised and seated male, "Mister, would you mind getting fresh with me? I've got a couple of new judo chops I'm just dying to try out." The *Defender* broke no new ground in terms of women's coverage. Traditional women's club stories, cosmetics, and beauty pageant news were in a clearly designated women's section, classified advertising was still divided by gender, and the only direct reference to the feminist movement during the period was in a story taken from a *Redbook* magazine promotional release that was headlined by the *Defender*, "Dr. Margaret Mead Has Called Feminist 'Movement Superficial' " (*Defender* 7/17/70: 18). The movement's influences could be found in other ways, however—for example, in a regular series that profiled both contemporary and historical black women. Thus, it was not altogether surprising when the newspaper gave over its cover photo to the rally on the Northwestern University campus on 26 August as it was being addressed by an African-American student leader, Eve Jefferson. Inside, the story written by a female reporter carried the problematical headline, "No Bra Burning in Rally," reminding *Defender* readers, as in the white press, of the most popular characterization of feminists (Nesbitt 1970).

Finally, New York's *Daily News*, the supporter of Komisar, provided the least mean-spirited coverage—a front-page photo of the march under the headline "Gals Unbutton Their Lib," a centerfold of more pictures, related stories, and—perhaps the litmus test—a flattering photograph of Friedan (*DN* 8/27/70).

Finally, the professional magazine *Editor and Publisher* summed up the most prevalent attitudes of the news coverage, printing a collection of editorial cartoons resulting from the march, all of them drawing on the stereotypes of the day (*E&P* 9/5/70: 14–15).

Television

Premarch attention from national television news had not been sympathetic. Douglas summarized the 25 August editorial offered by Howard K. Smith on ABC-TV: "While sympathetic to 'Indians and Negroes,' who had been 'genuinely mistreated,' Smith confessed to a 'modified unsympathy' with women's liberation. He found a 'few of their demands,' such as equal pay, equal access to 'some jobs' and child-care centers 'good.' He suggested women were already more than equal, since they constituted 53 percent of the population and 'they get the most money, inherited from worn-out husbands' " (Douglas 1994: 179). By the strike day, there could be no doubt that the nation's eyes would be upon the women's movement, but just as clear was a cluster of expectations that had been largely set by the intersection of media craft traditions and organizational change.

On the day of the march, the television networks' focus on New York suggests that television overall reflected similar biases to those in the print media. Most critics agreed that television carried out the presentation of the strike in ways of conflict. Marchers were shown in angry scenes, their critics in tranquil settings. ABC concluded its multipart coverage by abutting President Richard Nixon's comment that that women should play a larger role in American life with a statement from Senator Jennings Randolph (D-W.Va.) that the women's movement was composed of "a small band of braless bubble heads," a quote that was as irresistible to CBS and NBC as it was to wire reporters, although none of those services would have permitted a racist remark to balance the story of a civil rights event.

Several reporter stand-ups—the on-camera comments concluding their pieces—as well as comments by anchors offered final statements. Eric Sevareid predicted that the movement would splinter like other movements (CBS 1970). On NBC, Frank McGee said that while women should have equal rights, some demands of feminists were "nonsense" (NBC 1970). Commentators failed to recognize the irony that just two of the reporters on the three networks that day were women. In assessing the television coverage, Douglas writes, "The network's pattern of framing the story, especially [Richard] Threlkel's segment, suggesting that most women were quite content with their lot, were well treated financially and emotionally, simply could not comprehend a series of complaints that seemed exaggerated and irrelevant to their lives" (1994: 184).

Anger at the network coverage was profound. Midge Kovacs, an advertising executive and NOW activist, recalled her reaction for the professional magazine *Advertising Age*. "That evening, seated in front of the television set, switching dials to catch the news coverage of the march on three networks, I received my first taste of media distortion of the women's rights movement. Cameras moved in for tight shots of stringy haired, braless women in T-shirt, with angry signs. With my own eyes, I had seen a cross-section of women at the march, including establishment types, career women and many older citizens, but none of these women were represented that evening on TV" (Kovacs 1972: 73). In its review of the New York event four years later, the New York–based Media Women noted, "The August 26, 1970 strike—the biggest political demonstration by women in the history of the United States—was covered in a haphazard and thoughtless manner" (Strainchamps 1974: 10). The strike also received notice in November's *Glamour* magazine in which a photograph of two marchers—one in a "mod" outfit, another in a suffragist costume—were characterized as being united on the issue that "fashion must be fun."

Still, because of the New York turnout, the 26 August march was considered successful. It brought new membership to feminist groups, including NOW. Eleanor Smeal, later its president, joined the organization on that day (Smeal 1983). Criticisms, like that of Kovacs at the time or Douglas in her later assessment, have focused on feminist images in the march. The 1963 civil rights March on Washington—the icon that the 26 August march sought to emulate—had also been criticized on the basis of media images, but with the opposite charge that the images were so placid that they flattened out the concerns that had instigated the march. Media stories portrayed the earlier march, as John Lewis saw it, as a big picnic, a hootenanny combined with the spirit of a revival prayer meeting: "It was revealing that the quotes they gathered from most of the congressional leaders on Capitol Hill dealt not with each legislator's stand on the civil rights bill, but instead focused on praising the 'behavior' and 'peacefulness' of the mass marchers" (Lewis, J. 1998: 226). Whether peaceful or not, the lesson may have been that televised mass marches are marginally important in getting particular issues before the public but serve instead as a general agenda-setting technique.

The 26 August march doubtless put additional spotlight on the women's movement. The day after the march, the *Times* provided a lengthy analysis of the movement in a generally favorable light, although its editorial column on the subject of "The Liberated Woman" the same day was cautionary. The *News* addressed appropriate "lib" dressing styles, the role of cosmetics in the liberated women's arsenal, and assessments of the movement—not all favorable—by prominent women. A week later *Life* magazine produced a cover story with the blurb, "The revolution that will affect everybody" in an account that emphasized both exuberance and the national scope of the movement. "Women's liberation is the liveliest conversational topic around," the text burbled in a change of tone from Sara Davidson's earlier article, "and last week the new feminists took their argument for sexual equality into the streets" (*Life* 9/4/70: 2). *Ladies' Home Journal* produced the promised "The New Feminism" in its August edition, although the piece was separated from the rest of the magazine by its insert nature as a "book bonus."

Friedan, meanwhile, was claiming that the time for protest had passed and been replaced by positive action; nonetheless, under the banner of the Women's Strike Coalition, she was shortly found among three hundred women marching to the New York mayor's residence to reiterate demands for free abortions and child care. Media attention was insured by the inclusion of Bella Abzug, Shirley Chisholm, and entertainers Shirley MacLaine and Joan Rivers (Friedan 2000: 249; *NYT* 12/13/70: 66). However, that march resulted in further movement division because Friedan was infuriated by the wearing of lavender armbands meant to convey support for lesbians after Kate Millett had told *Time* she was "bisexual" (Friedan 1976: 158).

Friedan's fury might have also resulted in part because it had become clear that she had been replaced as the public face of feminism and was acknowledged primarily as a second-wave founder, as in Paul Wilkes's November 1970 *New York Times Magazine* profile, "Mother Superior to Women's Lib" (Wilkes 1970). Of the many feminist leaders emerging after the 26 August event, the media's first choice was Millett, whose *Sexual Politics* was now a best-seller and who received sidebars in the march coverage in both the *Times* and *Life*, the latter calling her "the furious young philosopher who got it down on paper" in a two-page spread (*Life* 8/31/70: 65).

It was one of the shortest media moments on record. Five days after the march, in its 31 August edition, *Time* came out with its cover story, "The Politics of Sex," featuring what was widely interpreted as an angry portrait of Millett. And on 14 December, in the magazine's "Behavior" section, another article concluded *Time*'s "second look" by pointing to Millett as a negative force: "Kate Millett herself contributed to the growing skepticism about the movement by acknowledging at a recent meeting that she is a bisexual. This disclosure is bound to discredit her as a spokesman for the cause, cast further doubt on her theories, and reinforce the views of those skeptics who routinely dismiss all liberationists as lesbians" (*Time* 12/14/70: 19).

A few days later, Gloria Steinem—at one point holding hands with Millett— was the focus of a news conference to voice solidarity with lesbians and male homosexuals (*NYT* 12/18/70: 47). The women's movement had arrived at full center on the nation's media agenda, and at the same moment, beginning with the *Time* story, was already beginning its skid.

6. Media and Mitigation

Soothing Sexual Angst

For organizers of the 1970 march, its New York success lay in the notable achievement of bringing together thousands of women of difference into one symbol of unity, not so different from the famous March on Washington that was such a strong memory for women of the era.

There were important differences from the civil rights march. The feminist march did not get flattering coverage in all venues, particularly network television, whose commentators tended to counter its visual messages of solidarity with critical commentary. And events in the rest of the country were not as successful in media terms as the march in New York; nor did news media outside of New York automatically give the New York event favorable coverage.

Of course, what was considered favorable was in the eyes of the beholder. For most feminists of the day, what was to be celebrated was that the majority of women—ordinary women—agreed on the major issues. Thus, feminist critics decried it when reporters and photographers selected, as Midge Kovacs had put it, the "stringy haired" and the "braless." Feminist critics saw bias in the coverage, as if the television camera had focused on a Black Panther during the penultimate speech by Martin Luther King Jr. at the March on Washington. While defenders of media could call on the craft decision of difference as reason for coverage, the coverage of the day often had a note of delight at events that were less than successful and was quick to portray activists along lines of stridency.

For mainstream feminists, the emphasis on solidarity and its corollary, the rejection of images of the "braless" and the "stringy haired," was one attempt to keep at bay their great fear that the second wave would be dismissed if it came to be viewed as promoted and populated by lesbians. However, the 26 August march forced the issue: Kate Millett was outed in the aftermath of the strike coverage. Soon after the march, lesbians were acknowledged to be involved in the women's movement—Judy Klemesrud led the way with a story for the *New York Times* followed by a lengthy piece in the paper's Sunday magazine (Klemesrud, "Lesbian Issue"; Klemesrud, "Disciples").

The subject of lesbians in the movement stretched the envelope of subject matter suitable for mass media at the time. However, it was new, interesting, and cheap content that could be presented in ways that appeared progressive, whether or not progressive attitudes were as responsible for coverage as the enticement of new and enticing subject matter. For media, however, the subject also resonated with the long-standing theme of danger—in this case, the danger to the sexual potency of men. Lesbians in the women's movement and by default the movement itself became one of the strands entangled in the warnings from the noir films in the 1940s to the attacks of "momism" in the 1950s. In 1962, the author of an *Esquire* article warned that American women were becoming "entrenched witches" because young women had been told by their mothers to get everything they could from a man and not give anything back. The consequence of this "essentially selfish" behavior was tantamount to "Lesbianism" (Frazier 1962: 103).

The angst of the era might be illustrated by the advertising history of Marlboro cigarettes. The Marlboro Man campaign began in 1955, originally represented by a variety of men in traditional manly occupations. By 1963, the Marlboro Man was portrayed by the solitary cowboy (Flaherty and Minnick, "Marlboro"). The campaign came at a time when manly occupations for white working-class men, in steel, coal and heavy industry, were being lost overseas and American jobs turned to those in a service economy and the employment of women. The loss of manly occupations, the rise of women's employment, the civil rights movement, and the recognition of black men in the culture, with the associated memory of black potency, conjoined with a new threat—the acknowledgment of the homosexual in American society, verified by *Time* in a 1969 cover story (*Time* 10/31/69). Here was a confluence of changes that complicated and even mystified the new permissions for sexual freedom. For mass media, lifting the gates of sexual prohibitions came at a time when it was not so clear, at least for men, that permissions were the same as their actualization.

As we know, issues of sexual freedom of the 1960s had been quickly translated from counterculture into the commercial vein of popular books, movies, and music. "All Americans seem to be engaged in one vast, all-pervading, all-permissive, Sexological Spree," William Nichols, publisher of the Sunday supplement *This Week*, complained to a business club in 1967 (William Nichols 1966–67). By the end of the decade, *Time* called it "The Sex Explosion," but its cover art was hardly intimate: a couple clearly apart despite the partially open (or closed) zipper between them (*Time* 7/11/69). By that year, emerging feminists, including the young women who rejected the sexual assumptions of the men of the antiwar movement, were forming consciousness-raising sessions in which women examined the sexuality of gender roles. One undertone of the 26 August strike was the question of "sleeping with the enemy." But radical and lesbian women took the theme into new worlds of redefining sexuality. Writing in *Rat*, lesbian activist Rita Mae Brown charged, "Sexuality is the key to our oppression. We are continually seen in sexual terms, we are defined by our genitals as brutally as a non-white is defined by pigment be it red, yellow, black or brown" (Brown 1970: 8). Those discussions led to intimations that barriers between heterosexual and homosexuality would blur. An essay, "The Woman Identified Woman," passed hand to hand through much of the radical community, arguing that sex roles served only to dehumanize women and that there would be no need of sexual categories if sexual expression were allowed to follow feeling (Radicalesbians 1970).

However, Anne Koedt's short article, "The Myth of the Vaginal Organism," made a particular impact in popular media as it moved from its 1968 publication in the New York Radical Women's *Notes from the First Year* to the 1970 anthology *Notes from the Second Year: Women's Liberation* and then was further anthologized in *Radical Feminism*, of which Koedt was an editor. By 1973 the article was recognized in an advertisement for *Radical Feminism* as "famous" (*Ms.* 3/73: 1). From the anthologies, the essence of Koedt's article permeated into a mass media encouraged by the media openness to issues of sexuality in the decade of the 1970s. *Ladies' Home Journal* warned its readers not to be intimidated by the emphasis on sexual technique and assured its readers that "a woman can adjust herself to have an orgasm in a very short time" (*LHJ* 8/71: 52).

However, for most mass media, the issue of clitoral versus vaginal orgasm was viewed not as an enhancement to sexuality but as representative of a women's movement that rejected male sexuality and indeed even as endangering men's ability to perform sexually. *Esquire* magazine devoted a cover story (a naked man staring downward in distress) to the issue of impotence, as expressed by the cover line "The Impotence Boom (Has It Hit You Yet?)." The writer agreed that while there were no hard facts to substantiate this conclusion, there surely seemed to be an epidemic of impotence in the country (Nobile 1972: 95). The *Esquire* writer was not the only one to see impotence as a trend, even if there were no statistics to support it. The cover art for Midge Decter's article in *Atlantic Monthly* put the fear at its bottom line: a cartoon of a screaming man, legs akimbo, being pushed toward a guillotine by two burly female executioners. If there could be any doubt, the "sell line" removed it: "The Movement to Stamp Out Sex" (Decter 1972).

Decter, no friend to the movement, used Koedt as the starting point for arguing that the women's liberation movement was about the rejection of sexual partnerships with men because of the privileging of the clitoral orgasm over any other kind. Women liberationists sought to "repeal the sexual revolution altogether" and thus would lose their "womanly power" to control the terms of the relationship with men, receiving "nothing of truly central value in return." Decter suggested that lesbian ideology was driving women back to what she called a "new chastity." "It is difficult to say just how large a contingent of lesbians has been exerting influence on and through Women's Liberation. One's impression is that it is quite large" (Decter 1972: 54).

Even if male impotence was not the problem, as mass magazines would have it, Decter nonetheless had identified and encouraged the sexual fear that existed just below any discussion of the women's movement in the mass media. In so doing, Decter helped give credence to one of the ongoing canards of the antifeminists—that the women's movement would open the floodgates to the legalization as well as societal approval of homosexuality. Phyllis Schlafly, in her influential *Phyllis Schlafly Report* and in her speeches and interviews during her anti-ERA campaign, played on the fears of homosexual marriage, homosexual teachers, homosexuals in college dormitories, and homosexual public servants (Schlafly 1974).

Ironically, these twin fears of impotence and homosexuality existed in a mass media world of ever-expanding heterosexual boundaries. By 1970 *Playboy* still flourished, now joined by *Penthouse* and other sexually explicit men's magazines. Spurred by the competition, *Playboy* published its first full-frontal nude in January 1972. But women, it seemed, were to move even into the male preserve of lust: *Cosmopolitan* appeared in April of that year with an almost full-frontal nude centerpiece of actor Burt Reynolds. The magazine *Playgirl* debuted the following spring, crossing into new mass-magazine territory when male frontal nudity became its hallmark (Nourie and Nourie 1990: 369). The pornographic film *Deep Throat* moved into the popular culture by way of comedy routines (and later became the pseudonym for the *Washington Post*'s Watergate source). Marlon Brando's film *Last Tango in Paris* introduced what had been once considered sexual perversion into the broader culture. John Updike turned away from the subject matter of his *New Yorker* stories to make a bid for best seller status in the sexually explicit *Couples*.

A 1970 issue of *The Writer* asked, with a hint of plaint, "Does It Have to Be Dirty to Sell?" It was a complicated question. The 1969 best-seller *Everything You Wanted to Know About Sex but Were Afraid to Ask* suggested the theme of uneasiness that existed below the surface of the high interest in sexuality. "Little Dr. Reuben and His Big Sex Book" as the headline writer to Betty Rollin's article put it in a *Life* article, made the author a new celebrity on the talk shows, almost toppling Dr. Joyce Brothers from her throne as the nation's public therapist (Rollin 1970). Brothers increased the quotient of sexual discussion on her radio program and published her own sexually oriented 1972 book, *The Brothers' System for Liberated Love and Marriage*. While the Reuben book promised information as guidelines to the new sexual world, the title of Brothers's book suggested that information alone was not enough: a "system" was necessary. Paperback publishers eagerly joined the discussion with two 1973 titles, *Combat in the Erogenous Zone* by Ingrid Bennis and the more precisely named *Vaginal Politics*, by Ellen Frankfort, a *Village Voice* writer who covered the movement and raises the issue of how beat reporters can influence the wider discussion when they take content instigated by their beats into the wider world of book publication. In the meantime, Dell's number-one 1971 best-seller was *The Sensuous Woman*, a book whose title evoked a simplicity that could no longer be assured. A reviewer in *Commonweal* welcomed the publication of yet another sexual aid book as "tackling the complex web of anxiety-creating myths" (Haughton 1972: 482).

When the various threads are taken together, the sexual revolution of the 1970s as expressed in mass media had less to with the sexual freedom of the 1960s than with a new kind of sexual angst that seemed most to impact the middle class and was most connected with a threat to male sexual hegemony. The 1970 film *Diary of a Mad Housewife* had as its heroine an upper-class young woman who took a lover rather than suffer the insensitivities of a self-aggrandizing husband. *How to Survive Marriage* was the title of a documentary presentation of middle-class family problems in an NBC series in the 1974–75 season. The female lead in *A Woman under the Influence* chose incarceration in a mental hospital (another theme of the decade) over what once would have been considered the protection offered by the family. Novelist Charles Webb, whose *The Graduate* had limned the 1960s so well, portrayed his subjects in *The Marriage of a Young Stock Broker* as unfulfilled, unhappy, and passionless. Indeed, heterosexual passion seemed a thing of the past, and it was fitting but ironic that the film adaptation of D. H. Lawrence's novel *Women in Love* ensconced Lawrentian passion in a period piece. Even Julie Andrews, transparently clear in her previous films, was cast as a femme fatale in *Darling Lily*, a movie about a World War I British music-hall entertainer who was also a German spy. Passion was not to be trusted. Interestingly, the blockbuster hits of the 1970s came from the hands of the young male directors of the "New Hollywood," whose films—sci-fi, adventure, or the nostalgia of *American Graffiti*—established worlds where men clearly dominated. *American Graffiti*, directed by George Lucas, looked back to the 1950s, when questions of sexual identity were as removed as they were in sci-fi adventure. However, even this film was not free of the suspicions of the time: the young man who remains in his limited hometown of Modesto, California, and becomes an insurance broker does so because of the manipulation of his girlfriend. The other young hero, with fantasies of women but without a real girlfriend, is free to go to Canada and becomes a writer (and avoids the Vietnam War).

Television situation comedy also addressed the displacement of traditional and implicitly sexual roles. On the heels of the 1970 march, CBS—betting that entertainment and social issues could be married for new profitability—introduced the *Mary Tyler Moore Show.* Despite the tumult of the seventies, the radicalism of the women's movement was lost forever with the first episode of the program. For millions of watchers, the *Mary Tyler Moore Show* put the movement in the most sensible perspective—feminism as new job opportunities for women without the loss of any of the traditional values. The classic show drew millions of viewers to its 8 P.M. Saturday-night time slot, anchoring the week, much like a Sunday sermon, in commonly shared values on which most Americans could agree.

But for all its apparent embodiment of traditional values, the *Mary Tyler Moore Show* also embodied the anxiety of the decade by introducing a young woman about to embark on a new life without a male partner. As the famous title song put it, she "could make it on her own." That seemed to extend to sexuality as well, as the attractive Mary Richards never had a regular boyfriend for the run of the show, which put into high relief the unacceptability of the other male characters, all inappropriate for one reason or the another: too old (Mr. Grant), married (Murray), too selfish (Ted), or too unthinkable (Gordy—the only attractive male but black). Here was the perfect young woman, but no male was in readiness. Although the program seemed to present an acceptable feminism—Mary was everyone's sister— it nonetheless brought its own discomforts, not the least of which was no clear place for a male partner, no sense of future (Mary's job never changes), and a narrow world peopled with characters who, like family, must be tolerated for the whole to exist. Mary must negotiate many small insults that come about because of her people-pleasing personality, and her success is based on how well she can achieve a measure of compatibility. From the famous first episode (in which Mary responds to the interview questions out of sequence), Mary accommodates, despite her discomfort. The program admits to discomforts but provides an unchanging landscape far from systemic solutions.

The *Mary Tyler Moore Show* was not an immediate ratings success and did not become so until it was clear that the program did not break with the genre of situation comedy, which, by virtue of the routine of its form and the familiarity and affection that viewers come to hold for the characters, held at bay the same discomforting themes it had introduced. The show represented talented escapist fare, an enclosed, self-sufficient world to the side of the main event, even to its Saturday-night time period, which suggested that its viewers were not in the fray of the sexual revolution.

The situation comedy that was considered to be most directly feminist, *Maude,* presented its audiences with a mature, tall, angular, and deep-voiced woman who was married to a classic Caspar Milquetoast husband. The machinations of the plot hardly mattered—the program's messages were in the mannish, directive, and overweening style of the title character. Indeed, the feminism of *Maude* might be thought of as a cover to introduce a related concern represented in the media of the decade, transsexuals. The character of Maude was not so far from a male in drag. The abortion episodes that caused so much furor survived perhaps because Maude's pregnancy never seemed quite real—one can only imagine the bigger furor that would have accompanied the same plot device for Mary Richards. In variety programming, African-American comedian Flip Wilson introduced the female character Geraldine Jones, whose irreverence and black skin, for white viewers anyway, served as a distancing device, as Milton Berle's exaggerations had served for his many female characterizations a decade or more before.

Outside of television, issues of transsexuality were addressed more directly in a spate of articles in the first half of the decade. In a 1970 article, "Transsexuals: Male or Female?" *Look* magazine saw no middle ground (*Look* 1/27/70: 28–31). A novel by homosexual author Gore Vidal, *Myra Breckenridge*, was premised on a sex-change operation and reached new audiences as a film. Transsexuality is not the same, of course, as homosexuality, but for media of the time, transsexuality seemed to speak to the impending blurring, then disappearance, of gender sureties. In the 1970 film *Dog Day Afternoon*, the audience only slowly comes to realize that the bank robber, played by the surely uneffeminate Al Pacino, has two "wives," his female companion and his male lover; the latter's desire for money to pay for a sex-change operation provides the motivation for the robbery.

Male homosexuality became a mass media theme following the emergence of the male homosexual liberation movement after the 1969 Stonewall riot. After the American Psychiatric Association removed homosexuality from its mental illness category in 1973, the subject increased in mass media visibility. As media scholar Alex Toogood noted the following year, homosexual characters were regularly appearing in entertainment shows: "The homosexual has become this year's resident freak" (Toogood 1974: 22).

The "freakishness" often resulted from confusion of homosexuality with transgender in an underlying fear of sexual merge. In *Harper's Magazine*, Joseph Epstein's "The Struggle of Sexual Identity" (1970) was represented on the magazine's cover by a muscled forearm emerging from a women's dress. The title itself suggested an implicit value that homosexuals "struggled" before "giving in" to the call and was not so much about homosexuals as about Epstein's frequently proclaimed homophobia. The centerpiece of the film version of James Dickey's novel *Deliverance* is a compelling scene of homosexual rape. The four suburban men of the film, entering a new and fearsome terrain, seemed most unprotected by the lack of women to assure them of who they were. Writing in *Harper's Magazine*, Norman Mailer called himself a "prisoner of sex" (Mailer 1971). For many male readers, to be imprisoned in sexual sureties was a condition devoutly to be wished.

Mailer's article infuriated feminists like no other. Writing in the third person, Mailer reprised the writings of radical women (although not Steinem, whom he knew), spending much of the article excoriating Millett's *Sexual Politics* and concluding that women had the right to explore as long as female fecundity (with a male partner) was not jeopardized. The article brought a change in the editorial direction of *Harper*'s. Using the sexually explicit language of the article as a pressure point (although profit was the issue), the magazine's owners forced the resignation of editor Willie Morris (*NYT* 3/5/71: 37) followed by that of Midge Decter, the executive editor (Decter 2003: 63). Morris returned to the South, but Decter remained a public antifeminist voice in other venues.

NOW and Gender Merge

Throughout her leadership, Friedan maintained that women's liberation was liberation for men and women. NOW pointedly included men on its board of directors, opened membership to men, and emphasized from the beginning that the title of the organization indicated that it was dedicated to women but was not necessarily comprised only of women. "Many people think men are the enemy," Friedan was quoted in a headline in a *New York Times Magazine* article, but "man is not the enemy; he is the fellow victim" (Wilkes 1970: 29), a phrase she often repeated on lecture tours. At the time, Friedan's acceptance of men tended to be seen as another example of her reformist, middle-class nature. But in retrospect, given what we know about her Left past, her initial resistance to lesbian goals (not a Marxist concern), and the importance she placed on organization and the identification of power, this position seems much more related to her socialist past. A call by a socialist feminist group, the Chicago Women's Liberation Union, for the women's movement to adopt a set of clear strategies echoed Friedan in these areas. In rejecting separatism, the group argued, "Sexism, not men, is our political enemy" (Hyde Park 1972). But with Friedan out of leadership, NOW began to reflect themes on the women's Left, including the notion that differences between men and women were socially constructed. Wilma Scott Heide, NOW president in 1972, used the phrase "human liberation." As Heide put it, men and women were not so different: "Individual differences are far greater than gender differences" (Heide 1971–72: 408). This was not the same as calling for men and women to be "full partners," NOW's original statement of purpose, but rather claimed that differences did not exist. It was probably less than comforting for men to consider that there were few innate differences between the sexes, particularly middle-class males, already in occupations that did not require physical strength (in a recessionary period that jeopardized even that job security) and under increasing awareness that women, economically or sexually, could make it on their own. If there was any doubt about the need for masculine strengths, Lucy Komisar put them at rest: "The caveman mentality has outlived its usefulness when technology made the hunter obsolete," she wrote in the *Washington Monthly* (Komisar, "Violence"). No wonder the jokes that sought to make menstruation into a mental illness began to be heard. The fairly rapid acceptability of premenstrual syndrome as a legal defense may have affirmed sexual difference at a time when it was under attack.

While the emergence of the gay movement is generally connected to this time, for millions of American mass media consumers the recognition of lesbian women in the United States had to do with discussion of lesbians in the women's movement that occurred at a time of perceived attack on heterosexual men. Moreover, adding to male uneasiness, was the difficulty of identifying lesbians, one emphasis perhaps for the use of labels of bralessness and stringy hair. Some feminists such as Gloria Steinem refused to identify their sexual preferences (chapter 7) as a way to claim solidarity with lesbians in the movement. Janet Guthrie, breaking into auto racing and in 1976 the first woman qualify for time trials at the Indianapolis 500, was called "lesbian libber" by those who saw no place for women in the sport. She refused to identify herself as the heterosexual that she is: "I didn't because that was the time that gay issues were starting to come to the forefront, and I didn't want to put down gays," a position that did not help her gain corporate sponsorship for her racing career (*Philadelphia Inquirer* 5/20/01: B20).

Mass Media Response: *Time* and Kate Millett

It is a theme in this book that mass media fan the flames of discontent as they find newer and newer takes on a story and then, before the flames destroy the structure, banks them. In this period of sexual merge, when lesbianism was an easy target, *Time* magazine stands out as one of the decade's flamethrowers. Kate Millett had been active in New York radical circles since their beginnings. She was also a sculptor, writer, and part-time college teacher as she pursued her Ph.D. at Columbia University. In contrast to Friedan's deliberate shaping of *The Feminine Mystique* for commercial publication, Millett's *Sexual Politics* came to publication almost by accident. Millett was contacted by a representative from Doubleday, Betty Prashker, who had had a tip from a friend that Millett was working on a writing project. Prashker chose not to pursue the original project, but when she asked if Millett had something else, Millett offered her Columbia University dissertation, "Sexual Politics." The dissertation was a work of literary criticism and examined, amid dense sections on the rise of patriarchy, the sexual imagery of D. H. Lawrence, Henry Miller, and Norman Mailer as representative of male dominance in overall society.

Prashker was more than taken with the work, not only seeing in it commercial possibilities but also responding personally: "I read it and was really excited. It looked at these writers in an entirely different way and it made me understand what the term 'sexism' meant. I loved the title, too." When she presented the book at the sales meeting, her presentation was so enthusiastic that it was greeted with applause. A chapter was sold to the *American Review,* foreign rights were sold, and the publisher of Avon Books bought the paperback rights from his hospital bed, all before the book was published (Prashker 1998). Its success seemed assured when the *Times*'s book reviewer devoted two columns on separate days to his review, the first particularly favorable (Lehman-Haupt 1970). The *Washington Post* provided two reviews, a male and female view, printed side by side (MacPherson 1970; McPherson 1970).

At the time of publication, Millett's bisexuality was not known in the publishing world. Prashker believes that had it been, "I would have had a harder time in the early stages of the publishing process" (Prashker 1998). Millett herself, living with a male sculptor, seemed not exactly clear about her sexuality but, unlike Friedan on the question of Left associations, had made no clear preparations for a media response as she was taken into the world of celebrity, which included her portrait on a *Time* cover.

Time had a self-serving reason to provide a cover story on the movement. On 3 May 1970, a group of 107 editorial workers at Time Inc. announced plans to file a formal complaint of discrimination with the New York State Human Rights Division. By the time of the suit, the magazine was already a symbol of employment discrimination because of its policy of hiring women only as researchers. Steinem was not shy about how she had been offered a researcher's job but not a reporter or writer's job at *Time.* Moreover, the influence of the magazine, its role as an opinion magazine, and its long connection with Cold War politics gave to its newsroom culture an unmistakable sense of self-satisfaction. *Time* did not admit to discrimination, and twenty years after the fact, Hedley Donovan, editor-in-chief, remained defensive. "I thought Time Inc.—even under the old caste system, which included very well-paid women chiefs of research—was offering women a remarkable number of attractive professional-level jobs" (Donovan 1989: 254). Despite the lack of enthusiasm by editor Henry Grunwald and Donovan, the lawsuit was settled with the organization's promise to promote women and recruit women of talent. By July, Joan Manley, formerly director of sales for Time-Life Books, was appointed publisher for sales for all of Time Inc. At *Time* itself, women researchers began to be promoted, and the magazine hired its first woman reporter, B. J. Phillips, from the *Washington Post.*

The choice of Phillips indicates that *Time* searched among the top talent. At the *Post*, Phillips had been the major writing influence that reshaped the newspaper's old "For and about Women" to the renowned "Style" section that had been pioneered by Carol Sutton and Charlotte Curtis. The *Post*'s editor, Ben Bradlee, described Phillips as someone "who looked like a waif and wrote like some tough new kind of angel" (Bradlee 1995: 300). In the white-male sanctum of *Time*, Phillips survived what Grunwald rather gently called "hazing," although she returned it in kind when she arrived topless for one editorial meeting (Grunwald 1997: 300).

One of her first jobs was to cowrite the cover story "The Politics of Sex," an occasion when *Time* could show the world, and the New York State Human Rights Division, the magazine's new leaf. The existing *Time* women were brought together to report the cover article from a national perspective; the sole male on the project was Bob McCade, Phillips's coauthor. Writers do not have the final word in mass media products in general, particularly at *Time*, which not only adhered to a rigid style but also set the tone of any cover story by its choice of cover art, the editor's prerogative.

Grunwald had spent his entire career in *Time*'s atmosphere of partisanship and had little sympathy for the women's movement in general and none at all for Millett. Almost thirty years after the publication of the Millett cover, Grunwald's tone remained dismissive as he repeated the canards of the original *Time* article: "Among the fiercest of these militants was Kate Millett, a sculptor and college instructor who had published an explosive book, *Sexual Politics*, of which her former thesis adviser at Columbia University remarked: 'Reading it is like sitting with your testicles in a nutcracker.' In it she argued that 'patriarchy,' including the family, must be destroyed. She claimed that there was little biological difference between men and women with the exception of the specific genital characteristics. That, I thought, was quite an exception. We put her on *Time*'s cover, and she sternly looked out at the reader from under unruly dark hair" (Grunwald 1997: 407).

His decision to summarize the Millett episode in terms of the stereotypes of the original article gives evidence to the strength of the stereotypes *Time* presented even when the stereotype was embedded in what appeared to be even-handed coverage. However, American readers, used to the journalistic tradition of balance, can easily read between the lines to dismiss whatever information is included to meet the craft tradition and instead fix on whatever stereotypes are comfortable (one explanation for the success of the *All in the Family* television show, which drew a wide spectrum of liberal and not-so-liberal viewers). Despite its ostensible nod to balance, the *Time* article provided plenty of opportunities for readers to fix on stereotypes, beginning with Alice Neel's cover portrait.

Grunwald's comment also suggests that the Neel portrait was a rendering taken from life, when in fact the portrait was an interpretation by an artist of highly stylized works. Although Neel painted the portrait from a photograph (Millett refused to sit on the basis that the movement should not encourage stars), Neel's interpretation differed from other pictures that had appeared in the mass media. The *Life* article had shown Millett smiling; she was laughing in a photograph that accompanied a favorable article distributed by the Washington Post Service; and the 27 August profile shot of her in the *Times*, long hair held back by a headband, was demure—almost a reference to stereotypical view of her Catholic girlhood. The *Washington Post* reviews of *Sexual Politics* were accompanied by a dramatic drawing that emphasized her long hair as unruly and theatrical but not off-putting. However, the Neel portrait was the first public portrayal of her in the grip of what many saw as the stereotype, the grim "militant" on which the media had fixed. But while unflattering by traditional standards and in the context of the time sensitized by the media emphasis on militancy, the portrait in retrospect can be also seen to be arresting and powerful and as having caught the movement's intent and seriousness as no other work did. In the portrait, an angular Millett seems to be leaning into the reader's space, as if tipping off balance the observer's world, which indeed she was. Neel was a painter whose work had long been overlooked, and *Time*'s choice of her for the cover helped to rejuvenate her reputation. Her blunt style was reminiscent of the 1930s social protest movement but was suited to the 1970s: "Collectively, her portraits produce a disquieting experience," an art scholar has written. "None of her sitters is without ambiguity; even if the pose is relaxed, tension exists" (Fine 1978: 205). In 1974, in part because of the new exposure as a result of the *Time* cover, Neel had her first one-woman show in eight years and—a point of some irony considering feminist response to her Millett portrait—became a new icon for the second-wave. Writing in *Art in America*, critic Pat Mainardi called Neel's work a "symbol of both the discrimination and neglect woman artists have had to endure, and artistic integrity and courage in the face of official hostility" (Mainardi 1974: 107).

The choice of a female painter whose career had never reached the heights some thought she deserved because of her gender was appropriate for the magazine's cover subject. And perhaps the ambiguity that Neel brought to her portraits was also appropriate for Millett, whose memoirs have provided painful accounts of her struggles with the fame brought by the movement. To the media watchers of the women's movement, however, the Neel portrait seemed another opportunity for media in general to show the movement to the world as stringy-haired and braless. And if the Neel portrait had not already soured many of *Time*'s readers, the 14 December issue would finish the job. *Time* disclosed its scoop—Millett had admitted she was a lesbian.

Lesbianism in the movement was the subject of public discussion, already raised by the Luce-owned *Life* magazine in its earlier profile, in which Millett was quoted as saying "I'm not into that" when asked about radical lesbianism. Primarily, however, Millett had been goaded into her statement by lesbian feminists at a public forum. For feminists who shared Friedan's view that attention to the "lesbian issue" was a strategic mistake, the story compounded the problem. "They set you up for this," Millett's sister told her, "*Time* magazine, that cover job" (Millett 1974: 77, 17).

Lesbian activists saw the *Time* story in terms of opportunity. Shortly after the publication of the issue, a news conference was organized by lesbian feminists Ruth Simpson and Barbara Love to give public support for Millett and, not incidentally, to place lesbians unequivocally on the reform agenda. It was attended by its two organizers, Millett, Steinem, and—reluctantly—Ti-Grace Atkinson, who hesitated because she thought the press conference was not making enough radical points. According to Susan Brownmiller's later account, Atkinson wandered off so that the press corps would interview her alone (Brownmiller 2000). The news conference was covered for the *New York Times* by the movement's faithful friend, Judy Klemesrud. Lesbianism, she wrote, "had been hidden away like a demented child ever since the women's movement came into being in 1966, was brought out of the closet yesterday" (Klemesrud, "Lesbian Issue": 47).

Friedan did not attend the news conference, her position well known, but she nonetheless reiterated it with her usual gusto for Klemesrud's story: "I think it was a terrible mistake," she said of the news conference. "The C.I.A. couldn't have thought of anything worse. It did not represent the majority of women in the movement. I think everyone's sex life is their private business. I'm opposed to sexual politics, and I don't think we should have a sexual red herring diverting us. Trying to equate lesbians with the women's liberation movement is playing into the hands of the enemy" (Klemesrud, "Lesbian Issue": 50).

The news conference not only brought lesbianism out of the feminist closet but put it clearly on the news agenda with Klemesrud's article in the *New York Times Magazine*, "The Disciples of Sappho, Updated." Timely in its connection to the opening of a lesbian club in New York, Klemesrud portrayed the lifestyle in terms of its variety rather than in the usual stereotypes. Two years before the American Psychiatric Association was to take homosexuality off its list of mental illnesses, Klemesrud's comment was wry: "Although the medical profession still largely maintains the 'sick theory' regarding homosexuality, it is hard to find a lesbian who considers herself sick" (Klemesrud, "Disciples": 40).

Klemesrud's attention to lesbianism should not go unheralded, coming at a time when a sympathetic portrayal of lesbianism was enough to raise suspicions about the writer's orientations, and it is not surprising that Klemesrud found it necessary to include a comment about her own heterosexuality. Klemesrud's article, however, signaled that lesbianism, like male homosexuality, was part of the media agenda.

Mitigating the Monster

Whatever individuals may have believed privately, the introduction of lesbianism into the mass media did not open the floodgates to the subject in general or set out a campaign of media-spawned hate. Homosexuality did not return to the mass media agenda in significant ways until the AIDS campaign. At a certain point—a kind of "no return" position—the mass media find a new take in permitting a new position to take ground rather than exacerbating what has already been done. In the classic thesis-antithesis approach of the American Hegelianism prevalent at the founding of the mass media during the nineteenth century, mass media do not go to the death challenging their enemy. In this most pragmatic of philosophical underpinnings, mass media take on some of the enemy's position—the resulting Hegelian synthesis. Such a functioning helps maintain national stability and can provide a window to reform if not revolution.

In that mode, the mainstream media took over themes, in some form, that had first appeared in the radical lesbian Left. The interest in female sexuality spurred by Koedt's article led to Bantam's republication of Helene Deutsch's 1944 tome, *The Psychology of Women*, which reoffered Freudian theory as one escape from the new challenges. But the best-seller that challenged the male view of Reuben's book was Barbara Seaman's *Free and Female: The Sex Life of the Contemporary Woman*. Despite its sweeping title, the book concerned itself with the sexual life of the heterosexual contemporary woman and thus provided some surcease from the worry that lesbians were going to take over what had been a male role; nonetheless, this work provided the most up-to-date account of women's sexuality and was both easily available and accessible without condescension. Seaman's book is one of the notable achievements of mass media in the period, well documented and responsible, bringing to a spectrum of readers the reemphasis on women's sexual pleasure and the biology that made it possible, one of the issues to which the radicals had brought attention.

Like Friedan and so many of the activist feminists, Seaman was a mass media specialist in her position as child care and education editor of *Family Circle* magazine. Her book was personable and anecdotal in the women's magazine style, but it was also well documented. But lesbian sex was not mentioned at all, and the book is an example of how mass media mitigates culture's dangerous ideas, in this case the notion that the clitoral orgasm marginalized the necessity of men. However, it would be Germaine Greer, who would most be Kate Millett's media antithesis, providing assurance that the nation would stand.

Germaine Greer

Arriving in the United States amid the maelstrom of sexual anxiety came an Australian writer, academic, and follower of popular culture, Germaine Greer, who combined intellectuality, feminism, humor, and—the most important element in mass media terms—thoroughgoing heterosexuality. The title of Greer's best-seller, *The Female Eunuch*, speaks to the emphasis on sexual anxiety of the decade as much as Friedan's title, *The Feminine Mystique*, spoke to the Cold War threat hovering over the fifties. Unlike Friedan, however, Greer offered more surcease than sorrow. In an eclectic, amusing style that confidently bundled Shakespearean references with personal anecdote, grand and unsupported statements about all women, and insightful, instinctive observations, Greer's conclusion called for a rekindling of passion between men and women, a partnership in which men and women were sexual equals. She had little patience for American women's libera-tion organizations, left or right, and noted the role of media in good Marxist fashion: "In fact, despite the generally derisive attitudes of the press, female liber-ation movements have so been very much a phenomenon of the media. The gar-gantuan appetite of the newspapers for novelty has led to the anomaly of women's liberation stories appearing alongside the advertisements for emulsified fats to grease the skin, scented douches to render the vagina more agreeable, and all the rest of the marketing for and by the feminine stereotype. Female liberation movements are good for news stories because of their atmosphere of perversion, female depravity, sensation and solemn absurdity" (Greer, *Female Eunuch*: 306). Although her book dealt with various aspects of Western women's role, readers were likely to remember her concluding emphasis on sexuality. As further evi-dence of the mainstream attention to Koedt's article, Greer took it on for partic-ular attack—"At all events a clitoral orgasm with a full cunt is nicer than a clitoral orgasm with an empty one, as far as I can tell" (Greer, *Female Eunuch*: 307).

The book was first published in 1970 by a British firm and sold well enough for it to be published by the U.S. publisher McGraw-Hill, which paid $29,000 for the rights and then sold them to Bantam for $135,000. By that time, Greer had already become a celebrity on the basis of the European sale of the book, her writ-ings on popular culture, and her position as an editor of *Suck*, a European sex paper. She gave every evidence of enjoying celebrity.

In contrast to Friedan's initial publicity in the women's magazines, Greer's introduction to American readers came in *Rolling Stone* magazine, where she was included, apparently, on the rationale that she was a musicians' "groupie." *Rolling Stone* was an interesting choice, the only U.S. mass magazine that was open to language that included the words *fuck*, *cock*, and *masturbation* and references to drug use and casual sex (Greenfield 1971).

The *Rolling Stone* article was the first wave of the book publicity campaign. Greer was paired with another European writer, Hildegard Knef, on the cover of *Publisher's Weekly*, but the money was surely on Greer. The first printing of *The Female Eunuch* was set at fifty thousand, double that of Knef's *The Gift Horse*, and the initial publicity budget was advertised at twenty-five thousand dollars, ten thousand dollars more than that for Knef's book (*PW* 3/15/71: 1). The campaign also included the talk show circuit, where Greer's radicalism—the call for an end to marriage, for example—was not as important as her assurances that feminism did not mean the end of sex between men and women. *Life* greeted her with alacrity in a cover story, "Saucy Feminist That Even Men Like." She was clearly the antidote to Millett, and the *Life* article quoted a book reviewer expressing regret that Greer's book "had not appeared early enough to catch some of attention lavished on Kate Millett's *Sexual Politics*," a sentence that was immediately followed by: "Sensuous and attractive to men, Germaine Greer makes no secret of the fact that she enjoys their company too." In a flattering article and pictures, Greer's feminism was framed as a choice to stridency. "The tendency in women's liberation to explain the whole phenomenon as unilateral oppression of women by men is terribly misleading and leads nowhere. It is important women should see they have connived in the situation. . . . If you go about shrieking, 'Men must give us freedom!' then you endorse their mastery. What you have to shriek is: 'Your time is up' " (Bonfante 1971: 32).

In the context of *Life* and its array of pictures, including a full-page one with her boyfriend in an intimate setting, Greer's radicalism was reduced to a half dozen points in a separate box. In the end, radicalism for the mass media pivoted on the role of men. And there was no danger here. As the outtake quote had it: "I don't go for that whole pants and battle dress routine. It just puts men off." The article concludes on an odd note. Greer had been briefly married, the author discovers, until "she ran away" (Bonfante 1971: 30, 32).

Unlike Millett at *Time*, Greer had obviously participated in the *Life* article, even to posing with a bundle of wood in her arms outside of the city background of most feminist action. Her pleasure and pursuit of celebrity further provided solace that her radicalism was not very dangerous. One of her most famous appearances was on a panel of feminists that pitted—and the verb is apt—feminist viewpoints against those represented by Norman Mailer, the feminist apotheosis (as if it took three women to equal one Mailer), at a New York event that was formally named the Dialogue on Women's Liberation but quickly became known simply by its location, Town Hall. Greer was joined by Jacqui Ceballos, organizer of the Statue of Liberty action and president of New York NOW (who surprised Grunwald because her "reputation for militancy was belied by her Junior League appearance"); critic Diana Trilling—"easily the most learned," as the *Times* had it; and Jill Johnston, a "Proselytizing Lesbian" (Grunwald 1997: 410; Shenker 1971: 19). Greer had agreed to participate after Millett (whose book had included Mailer as an example of a patriarchal writer), Gloria Steinem, and Robin Morgan had turned down the opportunity, an offer, Greer later said, that surprised her because of the newness of her celebrity. She nonetheless chose to participate even when other feminists asked her to step down (Greer, *Female Eunuch*).

The event itself echoed the "radical chic" events of Black Panther days in its emphasis on the celebrities. Gail Sheehy called it "this year's Truman Capote party, a fashion show of by-lines. Planets of thought were contained within several rows: Jacqueline Susann breathing on Susan Sontag, Lionel Tiger in suedes and Steve Smith in a tight pageboy, the duchess of *Vogue*, Diana Vreeland, behind the liberator of McSorley's saloon, Lucy Komisar. A large helping of men came with apparently serious intentions" (Sheehy 1971: 3). Few reporters could resist naming the attendees, as if for the old "society" sections: "The place was festooned with literary personages and subcelebrities. Clusters of the New York Review of Books people; a pride of New York magazine stars; many important feminists. And Philip Roth, Lionel Tyger [*sic*]; Ned Rorum, Robert Brustein, Marya Mannes, Mr. and Mrs. Stephen Smith, representing the Kennedy family, and Arthur Schlesinger representing American history. It was one of those nights when New York turns out to be a glittering elite assembled in the first five rows of the orchestra and blowing kisses to one another" (Dudar 1971: 191). Other accounts noted the presence of Jules Feiffer, Norman Podhoretz, Midge Decter, Philip Roth, and, minimally, Friedan (Drexler 1971: 28). Altogether, the event represented a significant gathering considering, as one writer noted, that an Andy Warhol opening took place on the same night (Morton 1971: 28). Not attending were radical feminists such as Morgan and Atkinson, who objected to Mailer's presence. Nor was Steinem among the glitterati, not wanting perhaps to confuse her growing role in the women's movement with her former support for Mailer in the New York mayoralty contest. Grunwald, *Time* magazine's managing editor, was in the audience too: "I rooted for Norman but fully expected him to be mauled if not dismembered" (Grunwald 1997: 410). Indeed, Mailer's appearance accounted for the success of the event in drawing the crowd, as suggested by in the *Times's* headline, "Norman Mailer v. Women's Lib"

(*NYT* 5/1/71: 19). Greer was chosen as the heavy hitter, equal in weight to Mailer. Despite the rest of the panel, Mailer and Greer were paired as theatrical opposites in a story line that moviemakers had found to be tremendously powerful in the comedies of the thirties—intimations that Greer and Mailer would turn the electricity of the evening into a personal realm and prove, as in the films, that independent women needed only to be "tamed" by powerful men. *Playboy* offered a fledgling dominatrix scenario. "Was it true, as had been rumored, that she had amorous designs on the embattled Norman'?" (*Playboy* 7/71: 27).

The framing of Mailer and Greer in these ways was to emphasize Greer's sexuality, as personified by her clothing, which was the focus of the reportage. "Draped in black with a crazy fox fur dribbling off one shoulder," Greer looked to columnist Sheehy like "Gypsy Rose Lee with a Cambridge brain and an English accent" (Sheehy 1971: 8). To the *Playboy* columnist, Greer was "leggy, alluring and formidably intelligent" (*Playboy* 7/71: 27). However, the female reporter for the *New York Post* saw Greer in an unconscious Garden snake metaphor. She "slithered up to the lectern in a fluffy little silver fox and a slithery black gown" (Dudar 1971: 4). A female *Village Voice* reporter asked, "Would Norman, Germaine, and Jill pose for modern sexual tableaus, each taking the sexual position which suited them (or their cause) best?" (Drexler 1971: 28). A male *Village Voice* writer was more typically admiring: "Splendid in jewelry and décolletage, bringing unheard-of-Catabrigian vowel values and consonant crispnesses to the humble word 'fuck'" (Morton 1971: 28). For male observers, Greer's intelligence, when suitably encased, clearly emphasized her heterosexuality.

Given this focus, it is not surprising that Johnston became an aside even after she told the audience, "All women are lesbians." In what had been a prearranged "action," two women appeared onstage and, as the *Post* put it, "the three of them rolled affectionately about on the floor while Mailer snapped peevishly: 'Come on Jill, be a lady'" (Dudar 1971: 28). To an audience most interested in Mailer and Greer, Johnston's theatrics were not compelling, and Johnston and her entourage disappeared from the stage, quite literally giving up the forum.

Despite the billing of the event as a dialogue, the subject of interest was what seemed to be the uncertainty of intersection for male and female sexuality. The last question of the evening, from Anatole Broyand, a new book critic for the *New York Times*, seemed to emerge from a frustration that it was an impossible passage. Broyand asked how liberated women could be expected to act in a sexual context. But the sense of the question—an extraordinarily basic one that was on everyone's minds—was lost when he finished up his elaborate introduction with the exasperated "What do you women want?" "'Whatever it is we women want,' Miss Greer lashed, 'it isn't you honey'" (Sheehy 1971: 8).

No matter how electric the evening; the bursts of applause; the shock, amusement, or squirming at Johnston's stage performance, the evening served as a willing media event that reiterated positions, even on the issue of heterosexuality. No
matter the promises of coresponsibility for passion made by her book, Greer's sexual persona, when coupled with her withering intellectualism, her foreign exoticism, and her overweening confidence, hardly negated anxiety for men or women.
What woman could compare to Greer? What man could meet the challenge?
Greer and Mailer were indeed "gladiators," the description given by both Sheehy
and Grunwald, but such a public pairing on those grounds emphasized distance
and the media view that feminism was tantamount to sexual rejection.

Greer's celebrity was to increase after Town Hall, when *Esquire* assigned her to
write about the event. In another indication of how New York activities and New
York media drove so much of national media agenda, the story was considered of
broad enough appeal to warrant an *Esquire* cover: a coy Greer, posed with her
hands crossed over her genitals, cradled by Mailer in a gorilla suit. In "My Mailer
Problem," readers learned that the original proposal for the event was made by
Mailer in an effort, according to Greer, to maintain his celebrity, provide grist for
future writing assignments, and, most important, make money. Greer later discovered that the proceeds of the gate for the Town Hall event were to go primarily
to Mailer, with some undeclared proportion going to the women involved. She
declined to go on a David Susskind program when she learned that Mailer had
acquired the rights to the program, and, new to celebrity or not, Greer hired attorneys to protect her monetary interests. She did not again meet Mailer in a public
forum but found his name repeatedly coming up in her ongoing interviews, and
the event served to maintain her celebrity as well (Greer, "Mailer Problem").

Greer brought an independent perspective to the women's movement. Hired
by *Harper's Magazine* (in the wake of Mailer's article and Morris's departure) to
cover the Democratic National Convention in 1972, she pinpointed feminists'
lack of real influence in George McGovern's candidacy. Despite his support by
the stars of the feminist community, he was, as the title of her article put it in a
sexual innuendo, "McGovern, the Big Tease." The article concluded with a reference to her sexual attraction to a male McGovern supporter (Greer 1972).

In the end, Greer's role in the American women's movement was relegated to
the short period of time that served to ameliorate the sexual tensions that the
second wave had played a role in generating. But taking on that role also eliminated
her, in American media terms as well as those of the women's movement, from
any other serious leadership role. She founded and directed a women's study
center in Tulsa, Oklahoma, but generally remained out of the national discussion
of feminism. In 1982 she returned to her academic roots in England, where she

retains a celebrity status. Her U.S. tour in 1999 to promote her book, *The Whole Woman*, engendered little of the interest that had accompanied her first tour. Greer's exoticism never made her a serious candidate to carry the flag of U.S. feminist heterosexuality. If heterosexuality was to be embodied only in wonder women such as Germaine Greer, new anxiety was to be raised.

In the outer world, the concern continued that feminism was tantamount to the end of male-female sex: "Men who are threatened by the women's liberation are always dredging up the question of whether there is sex after liberation," Nora Ephron commented in her *Esquire* column. "The answer is, nobody knows what happens to sex after liberation. It's a big mystery" (*Esq.* 7/72: 42; Ephron 1991: 18–19).

Not for Friedan, who was out of power but still retained the role of mother of the movement. The *New York Times Magazine* did the movement no favor when it published in March 1973 "Up from the Kitchen Floor," in which Friedan attacked the "disrupters," the NOW members who "continually try to push lesbianism or hatred of men." And then there were the FBI and CIA infiltrators (Friedan 1973: 33). As if to confront Friedan, in another part of the *Times* that Sunday was a Klemesrud interview with Steinem, but the topic was fashion, with Steinem explaining that she did indeed streak her hair and that she bought her famous aviator sunglasses from an expensive shop (Klemesrud, "Now a Word"). And, there were, of course, accompanying photographs. The choice was not difficult.

7. Gloria Steinem

The year Friedan published *The Feminine Mystique*, Gloria Steinem also published her first book, *The Beach Book*, a frivolous and elaborate coffee-table production that celebrated the urban, educated, white adult. Published by Viking, one of the new firms that Michael Korda describes as not askance to marketing books as product for particular audiences, *The Beach Book* ensconced an ephemeral and satirical style in the permanency of a coffee-table format—a kind of satire on the format itself. Steinem's ability to attract the rich and famous even in this venue was already apparent. The amusing introduction to the paean to the beach, "tolerable only to the inert," was none other than the economist, John Kenneth Galbraith, one of Steinem's lifelong friends. He had agreed to do the piece, he noted, because he liked the book "and the girl who put it together" (Steinem, *Beach Book*: ix).

By 1963, the "girl"—that is, Gloria Steinem—was already well on her way to celebrity, a path that was paved by an understanding of the currents of the time and her use of connections developed by her cool but powerful personality. But as observers then and now have often noted, her attractiveness was not passive. An acquaintance from the 1960s recalled, "She had the uncanny ability of adapting herself to the romantic image most appropriate for the boyfriend of the moment" as recorded by Leonard Levitt in his 1971 profile. "Gloria is—or was—a mirror that gave a man back the image of himself he wanted to see" (Levitt, Leonard 1971: 89). These were characterizations that Steinem herself has supported to an extent. On a 1993 television show, Steinem told Oprah Winfrey, "I had learned in Toledo, growing up, how to get a man to fall in love with me. Now, this is an important survival skill and we should recognize it. It's a survival skill because if you make much less than men, if you need one man to protect you from the violence of other men, if you need marriage, society says, in order to enjoy sexuality or to have a child, you learn as a survival skill, in a deep sense, how to get men to fall in love with you" (Winfrey 1993).

Steinem was able to use that ability with regard to the nation by manipulating messages in a mass media environment. Chief among those abilities was her inclusion of herself in the messages she carried. In mass media, this involved the use of her celebrity (and her photograph) as part of the package and a writing style that emphasized the broad, uncomplicated ideas of universality in which all generous-minded people could become involved. In television, her most important medium, she became a spokeswoman for the women's movement along the same broad ideals and by the presentation of herself in the limited context that insisted viewers participate. She was indeed a McLuhanesque heroine, adapting herself to the medium as she had adapted herself to the visions of the young men in Toledo, Ohio. Her ability to use the medium on its own terms gave profound strength to her message but would also shape the message according to the tenets of the medium that carried it—broad ideas that required right feelings rather than intellectual understanding or hard choices. Steinem became the expression of a feminist reform agenda, the "liberal takeover," as radical feminists saw it. As the nation's most famous, most influential, and subsequently most enduring feminist, Steinem came to represent the only ground on which Americans were ready to consider feminism. It was the same ground that fit with mass media standards, as it must be for any content that is to be embraced by mass media. This examination seeks to explain her media elevation as the convergence of her style, her experience as a media practitioner, and the stage in the news coverage of the movement that looked for equilibrium. As Germaine Greer had been the antithesis to Kate Millett, Gloria Steinem was media's agreement to an acceptable feminism.

Although she was a successful freelance writer during the 1960s, her success seemed predicated on a cluster of factors. Indeed, Steinem in her early career seemed to be a model Helen Gurley Brown had proposed in *Sex and the Single Girl*, the career woman who had as much right to pursue a career seriously and the same time take pleasure in her sexual self as any man ascending the ladder of urban success. Steinem views herself in those years as writing nonserious articles because doing so was the only way to support herself and her prefeminist social activism (Steinem 1994: 268). One does not negate the other, and her inculcation of the Brown system of success carried out what one of Steinem's biographer notes was a lifelong ability to fashion herself, even as a child and a young woman, to the style of the moment, perhaps as a result of an early life of dislocation (Stern 1997).

As Steinem herself has often chronicled, her early life was one of edges: a child of a Jewish-Christian marriage, a mentally unstable mother, a largely absent father, and a youth spent in a working-class environment that represented the family's decline from better times (although it would not prevent her from attending a Seven Sisters college). The upshot of the neglect she says she experienced as a child was to give to her a sense of invisibility, of being "not as real as other people," as she told Oprah Winfrey in the 1993 television show (Winfrey 1993). This sense of invisibility offers some explanation for the role of fashioning of self that Steinem's career represents.

As is now well known, Steinem began her career as an organizer for a CIA-funded organization, the International Research Service, which sought American youth participation in overseas communist youth festivals (Stern 1997; Franks 1975). Tom Hayden recalls that he met twice with Steinem during that period and that "she explained how an American delegation including outspoken Liberals like myself could defend the United States against Soviet-sponsored delegations to the 1962 Helsinki youth festival eager to exploit American racism." She was sophisticated and appealing, and her name, Hayden says obliquely, "kept coming up in conversation among eager young men" (Hayden 1988: 37).

She continued to work part time for the organization even after she moved to New York to establish her writing career, but she soon made connections in the city's magazine and publishing circles. In the 1960s, in a city of millions, the publishing circles were still small—the major magazine editorial offices were clustered along Madison Avenue, and writers and editors mixed with political, corporate, and café society. As in other businesses, circles may not have immediately opened up, but in the late 1950s and 1960s, the postwar boom offered opportunities for the ambitious and attractive. Steinem, already experienced in the usefulness of connections made in college and government venues, was well suited to the time.

Thanks to an introduction offered by Susan Hayes, whom Steinem had met while working for the International Research Service in Cambridge, Massachusetts, where Hayes's husband was on a Neiman Fellowship at Harvard University, Steinem became the assistant editor of a satirical magazine founded by Harvey Kurtzman, later the creator of *Mad* magazine. Her job was to find celebrities willing to pose for cover art, a position that allowed her to exercise her considerable charm while building her social and professional contacts, which, not surprisingly for an ambitious young woman moving in media circles, often blurred (Heilbrun 1995: 87–93). By 1962 Steinem had published four articles, three in *Show*, a slick magazine, and a fourth in *Esquire* (an examination of the influence of the birth control pill on sexual activity on college campuses) (Steinem 1962). To be published in a prestigious national magazine when she had been involved in freelance writing for barely a year or two is noteworthy and points to her use of the tools at hand—from her personal connections to her ability to identify social trends.

Steinem debuted in *Esquire* when the magazine was seeking to reach urbane, educated males in the eighteen-to-thirty-four age group, perhaps an odd choice for a magazine begun in 1933 in the Great Depression at the remarkable price of fifty cents a copy. The men who founded the magazine had been involved in publications promoting the menswear trade, and the new magazine was aimed at young men on the success track who wanted guidance in achieving the right look. From the beginning, its publisher and a founder, Arnold Gingrich, sought prestigious freelance articles on the manly arts—Ernest Hemingway on fishing, for example—"to deodorize the lavender whiff coming from the mere presence of fashion pages" (Gingrich 1971: 81). As late as 1959, on the cusp of its new journalism phase, Gingrich viewed the magazine as "at its heart, a fashion magazine" (Gingrich 1959: 6). *Esquire* also was grappling with new competition for the magazine leisure market segment, which now included *Playboy, Holiday*, and *Sports Illustrated*. Giving over the sexual arena to *Playboy*, Gingrich brought in a new group of ambitious editors, his "Young Turks," whose work had a major influence on magazine writing in general and played an early role in Steinem's career specifically.

The young men included Steinem's friend from Cambridge, Harold Hayes, subsequently *Esquire*'s articles editor and managing editor. Hayes emphasized writing quality, attractive men and women, raciness, clothing, and examples of life that readers might envy. Much as the women's magazines sought to guide their readers, *Esquire* served as a guide for the urban postwar male. Despite its stated purpose to attract well-educated male readers who could think for themselves, *Esquire*'s articles and celebrity profiles were strongly directive; even its amusing pieces provided satirical guides to what was "in" and "out" as in columnist Dwight Macdonald's discussion of "high" and "low" culture. Steinem drew considerably from Macdonald when she wrote a guide to "The Ins and Outs of Pop Culture" for *Life* in 1965. In seeking to appeal to the young male readers, however, *Esquire*'s editors, like Friedan, caught and expanded on the uneasiness of prosperity. *Esquire*'s tradition of cartoons was one way of maintaining an equilibrium—serving as a kind of grounding amid all the glossy ads and articles about success. The emphasis on full-page color cartoons with juxtapositions of a buxom young woman and an "old toff" represented traditional makings of vaudevillian and burlesque humor. Notably, *Town & Country, Country Life*, and other magazines that seek to serve an established class of readers have never felt the need to introduce the leveling aspects of humor, while the *New Yorker*, like *Esquire* serving an up-and-coming audience, extensively uses cartoon humor. Interestingly, *Esquire*'s signature artwork, full-page, color cartoons, was provided on freelance basis by an African-American artist, E. Simms Campbell, whose work appeared in every issue of *Esquire* from its debut until his death in 1971. *Esquire*, which sought to represent the embodiment of the confident young male at the epicenter of his world, was actually the work of men on the margins, from Gingrich himself, from Pennsylvania Mennonite stock, to Campbell, whose work—but not his face—was integral to the magazine's success (Harvey 1999).

In the early 1960s, Steinem was dating the art director of the magazine, Robert Benton, who was responsible for much of the satirical attitude aimed at attracting the demographically desirable males. Benton also provided Steinem with a protector in the *Esquire* world. Possibly because Steinem clearly preferred the friendship of Susan Hayes during this period, Hayes became one of the few men in Steinem's life who did not become one of her loyal supporters, a situation that had consequences for her magazine career. However, thanks to her connection with Benton, Steinem was close to the changes at *Esquire*, and when the magazine was planning its 1962 college issue, Steinem was invited by Clay Felker, one of the Young Turks competing for the editor's job, to write an article on the use of the birth control pill on college campuses. The article, noting that the birth control pill was likely to sexually liberate women without enough sexually liberated men to go around, was, as a biographer noted, an illustration of "perspicacity" as Steinem's most important attribute (Stern 1997: 131). Steinem's byline occurred alongside Benton's in another article in the same issue, a satirical illustrated guide to "The Student Prince." But Steinem was not mentioned by name in Hayes's editorial column, which seemed to mention all other contributors that month.

Felker reemerged in Steinem's life a few years later, when he established *New York*, the magazine that launched her as a political columnist. He was later helpful to the launch of *Ms.* But shortly after Steinem's article on the birth control pill appeared, Felker left *Esquire*, having lost the battle for the managing editor's position, and Steinem was denied an important ally at a magazine that was already helping fashion the careers of its writers. Although she wrote an article on Jacqueline Kennedy in 1964, Steinem's place at *Esquire* was as a minor writer. She later complained that male editors refused to give her important stories. Hayes certainly did not nurture her talent, and later, when she had achieved celebrity in the women's movement, he commissioned and published an article about her that she considered so negative that she tried to prevent its publication.

Although biographers may point to various personal motives for Hayes's refusal to attend to Steinem as much as his other writers, it may have been that Hayes did not recognize Steinem as being as talented as other writers in his stable, men who were pioneering what came to be called the New Journalism. New Journalism was in the mode of 1960s radicalism in that it rejected traditional feature writing, with its web of unwritten rules with which Friedan had had to contend, in favor of personal observation in a model that utilized fictional narrative techniques. Here was a mode of writing that included the reportorial eye as a conscious part of the story and could include anecdote as reportage, as Left periodicals had pioneered. Whether or not Steinem practiced New Journalism at the same level of expertise as her *Esquire* colleagues, she was nonetheless influenced by the style, clearly seen in her use of personal anecdote and reportorial involvement. However, Steinem's use of the freedoms allowed by New Journalism was selective. She enlarged on the New Journalism permissions for the use of *I* in her reportage to the point that much of her writing over the years has seemed most rooted in the traditions of the personal essay. Such writing may seem self-revelatory, but in fact her writing, as in her responses to interviews, has relied on a selected number of stories from her childhood. Even in the 1990s, she was still relating well-known stories about growing up in Ohio, one of the factors that has contributed to the stability of her image. The reliance on the personal to make political points has also included her expansion of herself into a universal *I* in which her reaction is seen as representative of all women. These aspects of her writing did not fit so easily into *Esquire*'s model but would find audiences that were used to the accessible style of the women's magazines.

Despite her appeal as a subject of biography, her many years as a writer, and her own characterization of herself as a writer, there have been no examinations of Steinem as a writing professional. She is a writer who does not bring attention to her writing, believing that her message can best be delivered in ways that are familiar to readers, emphasized by her use of anecdote and an aversion to complication. These initial characteristics of her writing became more prominent when her writing reached the audience provided by *Ms.* When she did not become a regular contributor to *Esquire*, Steinem lost important editorial mentoring, although it would clearly have been at a cost to her feminist message. Her role as a social movement leader was not one that encouraged complication and experimentation in writing. Thus, to remain in the role of public spokeswoman, her writing has had to be essentially pedantic, not the stuff of artistic adventurers. Steinem's sacrifices to the women's movement include the limitations placed on the development of her writing by her public position.

But even if Steinem had been as an adventuresome a writer as others who published in *Esquire*, it was clear, as in the birth control article, that Steinem's emerging feminist consciousness would not find a place in a magazine whose most utilized female writer up to that time was Helen Lawrenson. From Lawrenson's first appearance in the magazine in 1936 and through succeeding editorial changes, including Hayes's elevation to managing editor, Lawrenson regularly contributed articles aimed at maintaining chauvinistic stereotypes of women. In 1959, in "How Women Feel about Other Women," during Hayes's period as articles editor, she claimed, "Women's dislike of each other has seemed to increase with their financial political and social emancipation" (Lawrenson 1959: 74). In 1970, when the women's movement's was in full voice, Hayes, now managing editor, published Lawrenson's article on the women's movement, "The Feminist Mistake," featuring a full-page, four-color illustration of an angry, portly woman in boots waving a flaming brassiere above her head. The illustration, even giving it the most generous reading of humor, may be the pinnacle of stereotypical portraiture of the second wave (Lawrenson 1971).

Hayes may have viewed his reliance on Lawrenson as a way to speak for the anxieties of his readers, but personal bias should not be excluded as a reason for his editorial decisions. Like Henry Grunwald and Hedley Donovan at *Time*, Warren Hinckle at *Ramparts*, and Willie Morris at *Harper's Magazine*, male editors and publishers of the time were not recognized for their progressive attitudes toward women. In some cases their biases were passed along to readers under the rationale that the views represented those of readers when these editors may in fact simply have been passing on their own prejudices.

While *Esquire* was not to play a major role in her writing career, Steinem's relationship with Benton was considered interesting enough for Steinem to be included among a pyramid of young women in a photo layout of the "Girlfriends of the Editors" (Heilbrun 1995: 166). As *Playboy* used Hugh Hefner as its example of the ideal man, the clubbishness represented by the "girlfriends" article was similarly part of a marketing strategy that sought to illustrate the kind of life that *Esquire* readers might enjoy. Barbara Nessim, Steinem's roommate in the early 1960s, was featured in the article as "A Bachelor's Choice of Marriageable Girls," described as a painter, designer, and "swinger" (*Esq* 5/62: 87).

The marketing of *Esquire* by turning its editors into representations of young men readers might admire may have been an influence on *Ms.*, as when its staff was given the public face of an inclusive happy family for which readers might wish in their own lives. The *Ms.* "family" was also a counter to *Esquire's* male domain, suffused by a know-it-all tone that Rust Hills, one of the Young Turk editors, acknowledged "many found obnoxious." He characterized his time at *Esquire* as working at "the exact center of the world . . . the red-hot center of 1960s' sensibility" (Hills 1995: 30). Radical feminists often came to the women's movement after rejecting the antiwar movement's male-only leadership style; Steinem's experiences at *Esquire* seemed to have many of the same qualities. Accepted as a "girlfriend" but not as one of *Esquire's* hot young writers, Steinem turned her attention elsewhere. The following year she wrote the article for *Show* magazine that gave her instant celebrity and is still remembered—"The Bunny's Tale," her account of the undercover job she took as a waitress at a Playboy Club. While the assignment was in line with the long tradition of using women as stunt reporters, "The Bunny's Tale" indicated Steinem's ability to catch the tide of the moment, the use of her beauty as a selling point for her magazine pieces, and a New Journalism approach that relied on personal narrative. Pointedly, though, while these qualities served to make the article famous, "The Bunny's Tale" has never become famous as a piece of writing comparable to the *Esquire* pieces by Tom Wolfe and others.

The Beach Book emerged from collaboration with Benton, who brought the manuscript to the attention of his friend, Viking Press's young publisher,

Tom Guinzberg (whom Steinem later dated). Steinem's name appears alone on the spine of *The Beach Book*, but the work had an iconoclastic and independent air that Benton brought to *Esquire* and may have reflected his influence. The biblical account of the Flood, D-Day, Ian Fleming, the Peanuts cartoon strip, and the ship of Ulysses in the straits between Scylla and Charybdis were all gathered together under gossamer, irreverent connection to a beach. In the upscale audience it sought to attract, its sophistication, deft touch, and coolness were surely light years away from Friedan's writing.

However, no one claimed that *The Beach Book* changed her life; nor, despite Steinem's commercial sense, did it find a second printing. Like Friedan, Steinem was no stranger to the role of marketing, and Viking—if for no other reason than she was the publisher's girlfriend—sought to promote it. *The Beach Book* got a plug in the *New York Times Magazine* when Steinem supplied an amusing counterpart to the essay "American Women Are Rude" by writing "Visiting Englishmen Are No Bed of Roses," an article that gave no indication of Steinem's future feminism. "Some residue of our frontier tradition," she wrote, suggesting that Englishmen tended toward the effete, "makes us feel the difference between men and women should be accentuated" (*NYTM* 3/28/64: V164). She wrote frequently for *Glamour*—ten articles in 1964—and her role in the magazine began to shift from freelancer to subject matter. In that year, she was the featured subject of a six-page spread in an article that was the first to note that there was a Steinem "look" (*Glamour* 1964). In the same year she was considered celebrity enough to be given equal billing with Saul Bellow in "Gloria Steinem Spends a Day in Chicago with Saul Bellow." In October, involved in freelance writing for just three years, she wrote, "How I Became a Writer" for the magazine. In November, she contributed to the *Harper's* series "Why I Write" with the article, "What's in It for Me?" By that time, in August, *Life* published "The Ins and Outs of Pop Culture," which was accompanied by a game board illustration with various photographs of Steinem posed along its route (Heilbrun 1995: 416–23). In 1965, she was well known enough to get the attention of *Newsweek* as "News Girl," in which she was identified as the "world's most beautiful byline" in an article focused on her attractiveness and the men she dated, all rather extraordinary content for a middle-of-the-road newsmagazine. More extraordinary still was the photograph that accompanied the article—Steinem in a miniskirt with the subhead, "Gloria Steinem: Easier Than You Think" (*Nswk* 5/10/65: 9).

Biographer Carolyn G. Heilbrun notes Steinem's unhappiness with the headline (Heilbrun 1995: 127), but the copy editor clearly was responding to Steinem's self-commercialization, easy to spot in a city filled with up-and-comers. The consciousness of her "look"—from her clothes, designer glasses, and salon-styled hair to her trim figure—was discernible to those familiar with the signposts of ambition. Packaging not only denoted but was part of content, she appeared to recognize.

Not surprisingly, the consciousness of her presentation continued when she adopted and adapted the jeans and T-shirt dress of the feminist movement. The sense that Steinem's look suggested she was a poseur was the cause of much of Friedan's anger toward Steinem (despite the fact that Friedan was as much a lover of fashion as Steinem), and Friedan regularly brought attention to the fact that Steinem's hair was professionally "streaked." Nor did Steinem's adoption of jeans and simple tops, introduced by the radical community as a rejection of consumption-oriented femininity, ever serve to embrace her to that community any more than did her reference to herself as a "revolutionary" on a New York City cable program when comparing herself to Friedan, the "reformer" (Watson 1981). Women who were not Steinem's supporters were often put in a position that made them seem envious—another easy characterization for media. However, there was irony in the fact that the woman who was most identified with the second wave represented herself, by her own hand, along standards that feminists were seeking to overturn. What rankled with radicals and others may well have been that consciousness of appearance in ways that do not break standards of acceptance suggests a similar view of the world. Steinem signaled that she accepted the rules of society, and this aspect of her appearance that made her a safe choice for media celebrity.

Oblivious to the women's movement for most of the decade, Steinem assiduously pursued her freelance career and its handmaiden, her own celebrity. Her articles appeared in *Show, Esquire, Glamour, Ladies' Home Journal, Vogue,* the *New York Times Magazine, Life, Look, Harper's, Queen, McCall's,* and, beginning in 1968, *New York,* the publication that gave her the opportunity to be a political reporter. By that time, she was prolific and successful in the competitive world of national magazine-article writing, publishing four articles in 1962, seven in 1963, seventeen in 1964, thirteen in 1965, twelve in 1966, six in 1967, seventeen in 1968, and twenty-two in 1969, the majority of those in *New York* after becoming a regular contributor (Heilbrun 1995: 416–23). Up until her *New York* connection, her articles were written on a freelance basis, each one a separate endeavor, and the regularity of their appearance speaks to the ambition and hard work that belied her cool exterior. By 1965 her income on the basis of freelance work was estimated at thirty-five thousand dollars, considerable for the time. Altogether, her freelance career was more financially rewarding and encompassed a larger variety of magazines than Friedan's had a decade earlier, and the use of personal glamour had been a conscious part of Steinem's career development. Her life in the decade before she became the most well known representative of the women's movement gave evidence to the qualities she would exhibit as a feminist leader—her commercial sense, her grasp of the moment, the role of personal appearance, and a writing style that made its point on the basis of anecdotal experience that was nonetheless—unlike Millett—far short of confessional. Steinem was a controlled presence, a considerable contributing factor to her later television fame.

By the end of the decade, Steinem's political interests and writing led her into the arena of women's politics. Most famously, because she has often referred to the occasion, Steinem attended a hearing on abortion in February 1969 for "The City Politic" column and the subsequent abortion "speak out" organized by the Redstockings. As a woman who had undergone an illegal abortion, the realization that other women had shared the same experience was, as she recounts, her first step into feminism. At the time of her feminist awakening, she was already a local celebrity, and, at the first breath of her connection to what was now becoming a hot media issue, she was immediately transfigured into a timely celebrity. After her *New York* column on abortion, for example, she was invited to speak to the Washington's Women's National Democratic Club. At the same occasion, Sally Howar, a celebrity journalist herself, threw a party at which Steinem's picture was taken with Henry Kissinger and George McGovern and published alongside Howar's article, with McGovern cropped out. The appearance of Steinem and Kissinger in the same photograph led to ongoing speculation that she was Kissinger's girlfriend, a subject she repudiated with, "I am not now and never have been a girlfriend of Henry Kissinger." This quote was considered smart enough to appear in the *New York Times*'s "Quote of the Day," and her supposed connection to Kissinger was of some use to both of them (Stern 1997: 210–12). Despite her interest in farm worker unionization and her emerging feminism, she was clearly part of what might be called "café society," famous for being famous rather than for her career achievements. The names of freelance writers, no matter how prolific, are seldom known outside their circle of editors.

Her celebrity and its basis would impact on the public face of feminism. Steinem rather than a political or intellectual leader was chosen to write, "Why We Need a Woman President in 1976" for *Look* magazine. The article had little to do with political realities in favor of the broad generalities and universalities that marked her writing about women. In the idealized nation she postulated, a female president would end the waste of female potential: the woman president "could free the talent and human aspirations of half the population." Like Friedan, the vision included and was useful to men: "Men and women progress together, or not at all" (Steinem, "Why We Need" 58). She continued to participate in press attention in an article in *Harper's Bazaar* the following month (Sheppard 1970). Then, in July, a month before the 26 August march, Steinem wrote about her newly decorated apartment for *House and Garden*—useful, perhaps, in keeping her in the public eye but hardly the kind of article that one would associate with an emerging national leader (Steinem, "After Too Much"). In August, she published the *Time* essay, "What It Would Be Like if Women Win" as part of *Time*'s march coverage. Later in the year, *McCall's* published her "What *Playboy* Doesn't Know about Women Could Fill a Book," another article picking up on the themes of the day but clearly a step down from a discussion on the presidency. From a later perspective, Steinem's interest in "growing" her celebrity by the tools at hand counters traditional notions that view leadership as an answer to a higher call, as demonstrated during this period by Martin Luther King Jr., Cesar Chavez, and Robert F. Kennedy. Because Steinem's leadership was largely based on media's decision to allow her to take that position, she was at the mercy of media to show interest in her as an ongoing content provider. This was not a position of leadership in any traditional way that can call on a body of organized supporters or levers of power, as she would find out when women's concerns were dismissed during the 1972 McGovern presidential campaign, which she had strongly and publicly supported. It is not surprising that when she established *Ms.* magazine, she was seeking a tangible base from which to operate.

The promotions for *New York* included television appearances. Fan mail began to arrive in such bulk that it was answered with routine notes (Levitt, Leonard 1971: 201). Even before the strike day, her image was well enough known to be co-opted by advertisers. The Rice Council of America used a Steinem-like model—long hair and large sunglasses—over the caption "No man wants the same thing every night. Be creative with rice." It speaks to perception of women's power that an advertiser could commercialize a feminist image without a second thought (and would continue to do in the promotion of products such as Virginia Slims cigarettes, Charlie cologne, and many others).

Nonetheless, her renown was useful as a drawing card to the 26 August activities. Jacqui Ceballos called Steinem one of "the jet set, the beautiful people with connections to the Hollywood set," a configuration useful in attracting reporters to the march (Ceballos 1998). She became one of the event's "sponsoring sisters," as the *New York Times Magazine* article put it, along with Joan Rivers, Bella Abzug, and Shirley Chisholm (Klemesrud, "Coming Wednesday" 1970: 15). Steinem was not the star of the march, but New York's *Daily News* nonetheless found room for a picture of her at the microphone (*DN* 8/27/70: 3).

Still, her recognition as the premiere mass media spokeswoman for the movement remained a moment away. Kate Millett received the special sidebar article in the *Times*. But Steinem was more than waiting in the wings. Her two-page *Time* essay that accompanied the *Time* magazine cover story was accompanied by a photograph of Steinem in profile, hair richly cascading. Here clearly was the

Time version of choice—the angry Millett (or perceived to be angry) countered by the reasonable and beautiful Steinem, who predicted an idealistic society in which "sexual relationships become partnerships of equal adults" (Steinem, "What It Would").

Still, had it not been for her work for *New York* magazine, her career would have been different. Felker not only gave Steinem the opportunity to become a political reporter but further helped groom her as a media personality. As unusual as it was to hire a publicist for specific books at the time *The Feminine Mystique* was published, Felker was similarly ahead of his time for having on staff a publicist for his magazine. One aspect of the publicist's work was to book staff members, particularly the cool and attractive Steinem, on local radio and television shows (Steinem used the same strategy a few years later in the promotion of *Ms*). At the same time, she became active in liberal Left politics—from Norman Mailer's bid to become mayor of New York to work in California as a supporter of Cesar Chavez and the United Farm Workers Union.

During this period the exercise of a liberal ideology was the common currency in the circles in which she moved. However, involvement in liberal politics was ridiculed by the *Times*'s Charlotte Curtis (herself a liberal) when support for liberal causes moved onto the celebrity cocktail circuit—for example, when she skewered the party given by Leonard Bernstein for the Black Panther Party (Curtis, C., "Black Panther"). Earlier, a fund-raiser for the United Farm Workers at the home of George Plimpton skirted the radical chic image when it was covered in Curtis's section. Attended by "Norman Mailer and his political entourage" (presumably including Steinem), the article compared the gathering to the "real" society event occurring at the same time, with neither coming off well (*NYT* 4/19/69: 23). After the Black Panther party, one of *Esquire*'s hot young writers, Tom Wolfe, prepared his own satire for *New York* magazine, a piece that initially included a reference to Steinem as the planner of the farm workers' event, Steinem was persuasive enough to have herself removed from the published article, even as it retained a reference to the event (Stern 1997: 170–71; Wolfe, T. 1970).

Controlling the Image

Steinem's ability to have herself removed from Wolfe's article was emblematic of her ability to control her image. As she emerged into the national spotlight on the basis of her media accessibility, it was clear that she also ran the risk, if not the likelihood, of destruction by the same monster. In April 1971, Steinem turned down a request from Rex Reed to interview her for a profile in *Esquire*. The reason, she wrote to Hayes, was that enough people had told her that Hayes disliked her to make her suspicious (Polsgrove 1995). Those suspicions would likely have been furthered by the assignment of Reed, a writer who had so much challenged old precepts of flattering celebrities that the resulting articles, as in his Barbra Streisand profile, often seemed cruel. Moreover, there was no reason to believe that *Esquire* would give feminism a fairer shake by way of Steinem than it had in the publication of Lawrenson's account of feminism earlier in the year.

Hayes wanted an article on Steinem that reflected his own focus. "Please bear in mind we don't want yet another testimonial to the canon of her greatness," he wrote in a memo, "but rather an article on her *manufactured* greatness. . . . On record is her acuity, charm, and intelligence, but what is not on record is how she uses this equipment to further her own ends. Apart from the background information on her rise to prominence—which is absolutely fascinating stuff and central to the piece—there is a real challenge in trying to decipher her subterranean art in spotlighting a trend early enough to get cozy with the driver of the wagon" (Polsgrove 1995: 252–53).

Hayes got exactly what he wanted when *Esquire* acquired an article that had been rejected by the *New York Times Magazine,* a publication that had been largely supportive of feminism. The manuscript that the magazine turned down could not have been more closely written to Hayes's specifications, addressing Steinem's beginnings with the CIA front and the usefulness of her various lovers in her climb to prominence. In retrospect, it also seems fair, bringing attention to Steinem's complications and independence. Less fair—indeed overkill—were the article's title, "She," and the three-page color comic illustration, in which Steinem was portrayed as a cartoon superwoman.

As it became clear that Hayes was going to publish the article with or without her cooperation, Steinem continued to object, telling Hayes that to visit her painful childhood would be hurtful to her mother, just now regaining her mental stability. The argument continued through the fact-checking process (during which a former lover wrote to the magazine on her behalf), and she finally turned to attorneys, not the last time she sought legal control over her public image (Polsgrove 1995: 250–56). Its final publication, however, did almost nothing to damage Steinem's reputation, much less to dislodge her from her growing leadership position. Steinem's many women supporters did not read *Esquire,* and those who did could interpret the article as another example of press bias against the women's movement. Most importantly, Steinem was proactive on her own behalf. In January 1972, on the heels of the *Esquire* story, *Redbook* published a major interview with her by her friend Liz Smith, who had already published a Steinem profile (Smith, Liz 1972). The article, the magazine trumpeted, was the introduction of a new magazine policy of covering the movement for the liberation of women, a phrase it used without quotes or rancor, given that Sey Chassler, the magazine's editor, was one of the few men on NOW's Board of Directors. Yet Chassler was not unaware of Steinem's attraction. "We thought talking about Gloria was a sound way of talking about the renaissance of the women's movement, rather than talking about hairy legs" (Stern 1997: 226).

The *Redbook* piece followed a question-and-answer format, a somewhat unusual style that gave the advantage to Steinem with her legendary ability to handle interviews in any form. Smith's questions skirted the subject of former lovers, insisting on the use of the word *friends*. True to its stated purpose, however, the article dealt primarily with feminism. To Smith's question, "Well, who is Women's Lib for? Whom can it benefit?" Steinem provided a two-column answer that was as much a platform as any of those on her speaking tours. Moreover, Steinem's role as the new torch carrier in the long history of the women's movement was emphasized by inset pictures of famous predecessors—as if Steinem was appropriate to take her place beside Mary Wollstonecraft, Sarah Grimké, Lucretia Mott, Elizabeth Cady Stanton, Susan B. Anthony, Carrie Chapman Catt, Charlotte Perkins Gilman, and Eleanor Roosevelt. Steinem's picture, a full page in profile complete with cascading hair, faced the introductory page. Whether feminists regarded her as equal to the gathering in which she was placed, it was, nonetheless, an important article in taking feminism away from the snippets of television images to a national audience of responsive American women whom Steinem knew from her speaking tours.

At the time *Redbook* was still a major player in the women's magazine field, with some four million readers, and it exercised an editorial policy that was less traditional than some of its sister publications. In its aim to reach to women between ages eighteen and thirty-five, *Redbook* not only published fiction that broke ranks with the kind of fiction published in women's magazines but also offered a wider range of articles than appeared in *McCall's* (owned by the same corporation). In November 1971, for example, before the creation of *Ms.*, *Redbook* published "When Women Love Other Women: A Frank Discussion of Female Homosexuality," a lengthy compilation of views about lesbians. Many of *Redbook's* articles reflected issues that had been introduced by the feminist community. The magazine also included articles about African-American women, rape, vasectomy, and even a *Redbook* "Guide to Backpacking," not the usual fare for women's magazines. But *Redbook* was not about to let go of traditional content, and its pioneering articles appeared next to recipes and cosmetics care. Chassler was quoted as saying, "No matter what happened women are still responsible for their families in major ways that men are not sharing" (Nourie and Nourie 1990: 433). The new content was surely introduced as a way for the magazine to find its own niche, and *Redbook* would later face its own problems as interest in magazine fiction, a longtime stalwart of the publication, waned. In the 1980s, the magazine reinvented itself as a magazine for married women. However, in the early 1970s, *Redbook*, with its emphasis on new content and its stylish use of graphics, like *New York*, may have influenced Steinem's idea of founding a magazine of her own.

The various impulses that led to the founding of *Ms.* will be explored in Chapter 8, but here it is appropriate to mention that another attraction for Steinem in founding a magazine undoubtedly was the control over her own image. Over the years, Steinem's control over her image has been substantial—from her presentation of herself to the encouragement of writers favorable to her and the occasional use of attorneys and more insistent means. She offered herself to Carolyn G. Heilbrun for a 1995 biography that portrayed Steinem in the rise-and-succeed narrative that Steinem had long established for herself. Steinem cooperated in the book's marketing, even providing interviews on its behalf (Feldman 1995: 25). Another biographer, Sydney Stern, notes that although Steinem cooperated in the researching of the book, she sought to excise sections that did not fit with the narrative thrust that she has long put forward (Stern 1997: 448–49).

Even at times when Steinem was in less control—photographs at news events, for example—she seemed to do well. One interesting picture in *Life* shows her casually picking at her nails, cigarette smoke drifting in front of her face, while next to her Barbara Feigen Fasteau makes a point with one arm raised like a Roman senator. Betty Friedan and Wilma Scott Heide, NOW president, have their eyes turned to Fasteau (although both appear equally bored). Yet Steinem's momentary lack of attention may have carried some weight for the *Life* readers who found Fasteau's lecturing gesture off-putting (*Life* 6/9/72: 50).

One exception to the overall media view of Steinem was Judy Klemesrud, the *New York Times* reporter who had covered the unfolding of the movement but profiled Steinem only as a fashion icon. In an odd chapter, and an atypical action for a reporter that suggested some personal angst, Klemesrud responded to a 1974 *People* cover story in which Steinem said that she wished to move out of the public eye (*People* 1974). In a letter to the editor, Klemesrud wrote, "So Gloria Steinem is trying to 'lower' her famed profile. Is that why her face is on the cover of *People*, one of the nation's largest circulation magazines? And is that why she agreed to be interviewed for a two-page spread that included three additional photographs? Good luck, Gloria, I hope you succeed." More typical of reportorial response was that of the writer of the *People* article, Patricia Burstein, who came to Steinem's defense (Heilbrun 1995: 273). Although Steinem's effect on men long has been chronicled, she was equally effective with women reporters for reasons that included not only agreement with Steinem's feminist principles but also the charm that did not differentiate on the basis of gender. Thus, it is not surprising that in 1976, when the Redstockings attempted to resurrect the CIA story, its initial press conference was generally ignored in the mass media—by male and female reporters alike.

Mass media's decision to appoint Steinem as a feminist leader occurred quickly. By the second mass march to celebrate the anniversary of the vote, the *New York Times* chose to use on its opinion page part of a speech Steinem had made at a *Harvard Law Review* banquet and used the lead from her article, "The first problem for all of us, men and women, is not to learn, but to unlearn" as a headline for the three articles connected to the march (one by Bella Abzug, another by Paul Hemphill giving a male point of view) (*NYT* 8/26/71: 37). In October the *Times*, which had published Steinem's "A New Egalitarian Lifestyle" on the first anniversary of the 26 August march, published an article in which she claimed that culture, not biology, shaped women, a familiar stance of the time that was espoused by Millett and radical feminists. (Steinem, "Machismo"). By that time, *McCall's* magazine, whose editor, Patricia Carbine, would shortly become the first editor of *Ms.*, had designated Steinem "Woman of the Year" for the January issue, a remarkable accolade considering that Steinem's connections with feminism had existed for less than three years, that she had no organizational base, and that she could point to no concrete feminist achievement. The major contributing influence to her receiving that title apparently was her nonconfrontational style. She was cited for "bridging the gap between early militants whose vehemence frightened away people they wanted most to reach, and thoughtful, dedicated women who understood woman's status must change," suggesting again how Steinem was a media-designated solution for a public seen to be wearying of confrontation (*McCall's* 1972: 67).

Her choice as woman of the year eclipsed several other women who had received national publicity by this time, including radical thinkers who had done much to put the feminist agenda in the media spotlight, political leaders like Martha Griffiths, and organizers for feminist concerns, as well as another of the media's rising stars, Germaine Greer. Indeed, next to Greer, Steinem seemed down-to-earth and homegrown, and her personification of traditional American qualities rather than her beauty helps explain Steinem as a choice. Steinem's open looks, independence, and sense of humor reverberated in a nation whose advertising and entertainment industries had long had a special niche for the indigenous "American girl." From the "Christy girl" of early American advertisements to the 1930s screwball comedies, mass media has had a special place for young women who can express what is thought to be quintessential American style in their optimism, humor, and belief that fair play will win out. Steinem was able to call on this American icon—one of the few images available to women—by adapting it to the needs of television. Her persona was further emphasized by an unflappable and witty speaking style, a contrast to what many viewers saw as the argumentative approach of other feminist personalities. Heilbrun suggests that Steinem's media style was a result of a personal history that rejected confrontation and the burning of bridges, the characteristic that enabled her to turn aside male attentions while retaining male friendships. That certainly may have been the case, but however her style was developed, the result fit the television medium, which, as Marshall McLuhan argued many years ago, projected coolness as authority and passion as disorder. At a time when feminist fury was often the focus of news attention, Steinem's distinctive voice and flat accent provided a level line and gave to whatever she was saying, even when it was controversial, a sense of order. Moreover, her accent was not easy to identify, although to some it may have sounded high class. In any case, it carried none of the encumbrances of the accents of Friedan or Abzug.

What was most important about Steinem's style that made it ideal for television was that it provided not only controlled but limited information. One of the medium's characteristics in the United States is its seeming lack of willingness to accommodate complicated messages, and American broadcast messages, in entertainment or news, are reduced to their common denominators. Some of this has to do with the broad audiences that American television seeks and the necessity of making messages strong and simple because of the placement of the television at the confusing center of the American home, at least during the period discussed here. More importantly, we might consider that television has functioned in the United States like tabloid newspapers, whose limited agendas have been interpreted as ordering information for lower-class media consumers (Schudson 1978). If television is considered as a way to provide order, the regularity of television becomes important, news and information presented on schedules according to clock time, unchanging kinds of personalities sit at anchor desks, and entertainment programs support rather than challenge existing ways of thinking. Television audiences have required order on several fronts, from the disinclination to tolerate the rescheduling of a popular show to a similar disinclination to see program characters change. Audiences appear to want novelty only when it is encased in a larger construct of predictability.

Television during the 1970s functioned as a mode to simplify the confusing messages of the time in a number of ways: in the limited visual information on the basis of just 525 lines on the television screen (rather than the more than 600 lines of other national systems) to the long and lingering close-ups of the one-dimensional faces on soap operas that insisted on the full attention of viewers. Because of Roone Arledge's influence at ABC-TV, televised sports events focused on significant plays that moved along an orderly narrative. Large and confusing events could be ordered by a retreating camera and sweeping views. Civil rights marches, gatherings in convention halls, even antiwar marches could lend themselves to the transmittal of an orderly view when they were attached to broad generalization, whether or not the gathering was intended to be orderly. That clearly could not happen with the 1968 riots at the Chicago Democratic Convention, in which disruptions occurred in dozens of different locations, or in the coverage of the war in Vietnam, where reporting was up close and personal.

In another era—a peaceful one until the attacks on the World Trade Center—television reflected the confidence that is possible when a serious enemy is not thought to exist. The television screen reflected half a dozen pieces of information simultaneously: a reporter in one portion of the screen; pictures of an unfolding event in another corner, above several lines of information, stock and weather news, and upcoming promotions. After the 2001 attacks, it is not surprising that initial television coverage returned to a mode that was not very different from coverage of the Kennedy assassination of forty years earlier: the security of single anchors over long periods of time, the lack of diversionary commercials or other programming, and a handful of images that soon represented the event in symbolic terms.

Given the pressures of the time, the television world of the 1970s sought simplification, at least in its visual images. The women's movement as much as any other topic was affected by this preference. For the 1970 television screen, the overarching characterization emerging from the welter of detail that Friedan offered the camera was confusion, which the viewer rejected as "homeliness." For television purposes, Friedan had too much content—a face that was a compendium of competing heavy eyebrows, lines, and a prominent nose—all awash in a torrent of words that hardly simplified the visual message. Even newspaper writers referred to Friedan's looks, and descriptions of her, no matter how kindly meant, were usually in terms of confusion: "gray-haired combination of Hermione Gingold and Bette Davis" (Klemesrud, "Coming Wednesday": 14); "her clothing is in disarray (baggy white panty hose, two buttons undone on her dress)" (Wilkes 1970: 27). This way of viewing Friedan became so universal that it is a surprise to see her in the 1963 special *The World of the Girls* as a svelte young matron or to hear Karen DeCrow recall that Friedan dressed at the "height of style" (DeCrow 1998). For other reasons, although primarily because of her bisexuality, Millett also offered confusion. Moreover, she was an artist, a writer, a filmmaker, a scholar, a memoirist—but not in ways that were interpreted as many parts of a whole, as in the way a multitalented male might be characterized as an avuncular "Renaissance man." Notable women often receive that accolade for a single achievement; more talents seem to dissipate public regard for the original.

In contrast to Friedan's and Millett's images of confusion was Bella Abzug, no traditional beauty but whose big hats with their sweeping lines provided not only easy ways of identification but a visual simplification, even a thinning down of her bulk for the camera. Added was a clear, direct style, confidence, and humor. Indeed, Abzug was easily identifiable as an East Coast personality to those in other parts of the country—unlike Friedan, whose upbringing in Peoria, Illinois, further confused viewers' attempts to place her. Abzug also benefited not only from the unwavering political support she received from Steinem but also from appearing with Steinem in many of photographs. More than any other public figure of the period, Steinem appeared to understand, consciously or instinctively, that television of the time worked best with an uncomplicated narrative, both visually and in its messages. This would have ramifications for the kind of feminist ideology that she presented. Her initial presentation of her message was herself, however, one that gave highly organized information and limited personal information. The lack of public information about her personal life, even as she wrote about much of it in the anecdotal style she had brought from the magazines, served to further the authority of the cool Steinem personality. While she often referred to her growing up to illustrate aspects of her status as Everywoman, much about her seemed to remain unsaid, and, as Stern writes, even the biographical information she presents has always downplayed the well-to-do nature of her father's family and her mother's moderate family wealth. In Levitt's *Esquire* article, a former roommate, Barbara Nessim, characterized Steinem as someone who "was always very closed with her life. She never got involved where she could get hurt. She always spoke in the same tone to everyone and I only remember her crying three times in all the time we lived together: when John Kennedy died, when Robert Kennedy died and when our furniture didn't arrive on time" (Levitt, Leonard 1971: 210). In a sympathetic profile, Nora Ephron described Steinem at the time of the 1972 Democratic Convention as someone who had transformed herself from one of the "radical chic beautiful people" to a person who was unequivocally dedicated to the cause: "She projects a calm, peaceful, subdued quality; her humor is gentle, understated" (Ephron 1991: 44). These qualities transferred easily to the television medium.

Steinem is well known for her refusal to divulge information on anything but her own terms, which has meant that any personal revelation references a political point, as a young interviewer discovered in the 1990s: "I found it almost impossible in my interviews to keep Steinem on the topic of herself" (Pearson 1994: 3). As she became a nationally known figure in the 1970s, what was most mysterious about her was her sexual partnering. Despite her lively 1960s social life, one of the characteristics of her metamorphosis into a feminist leader of the 1970s was her refusal to encourage reportorial curiously about her relationships with men. The reportorial curiosity was there early on, as noted in a 1965 *Newsweek* "Newsgirl" article. Six years later, Steinem appeared again in *Newsweek*, this time on the cover with a head shot that was as enlarged as any that appeared on the covers of women's magazines. *Newsweek*'s reportorial interest was again apparent. In that story, *Newsweek* not only listed former male companions but printed a picture of her with Rafer Johnson, an African-American athlete and former intimate (*Nswk* 8/16/71: 51–54).

What is interesting and again demonstrates Steinem's understanding of media messages in more subtle ways than NOW or Friedan demonstrated was how she was able to quash the interest in her personal affairs. The *Esquire* story contained much of the information that would not be generally known until the 1990s, suggesting how one arm of mass media can smother another. In a *Vogue* profile, Steinem's friend Liz Smith told the Steinem story as a classic American narrative of overcoming difficult circumstances. Moreover, in both Smith accounts, the sexually active woman of the 1960s had mostly disappeared (Smith, Liz 1971, 1972). Unlike Friedan, whose flirtatious behaviors were often noted; Greer, who celebrated her heterosexuality; or Millett, whose name could hardly appear without a reference to bisexuality, Steinem's image in the 1970s came to be one of a woman who had no ongoing intimate relationships. Her relationship with another African-American, Franklin Thomas, which existed from about 1971 to 1975, at the height of the movement, was not known outside her own circle (Heilbrun 1995: 244). As Ephron noted in her column, Steinem "has managed to keep whatever private life she still has out of the papers" (Ephron 1991: 43). Indeed, despite their curiosity, reporters seldom seemed to gain much information about her personal life. As Friedan downplayed her role as a radical labor writer, Steinem downplayed her life as a heterosexually active woman, a subject that had not been a matter of particular privacy before her involvement with the women's movement. However, although she is a frequently photographed woman in her role as a feminist spokesman, there are few pictures that show her accompanied by a male during the height of the second wave, and she did not address her experiences with male companions in the many articles and speeches that otherwise relied heavily on personal anecdote. For media purposes, narratives about her life stopped with her adolescence. There remains, even in her 1992 book, *Revolution from Within*, a veil over large portions of her private life. Personal references are always in service to a larger point: her cancer scare, for example, led her to adopt a more healthful lifestyle, as should all women (Steinem 1992: 245). During the second wave, Steinem's lack of publicly understood sexuality played an ameliorating role at a time when lesbians were characterized as a deviant political group. When Steinem came to public attention as a feminist leader, she brought with her a strategy that included attention to lesbian concerns. In her *Time* essay, she pointedly included a recognized place for lesbians and homosexuality in her idealized world. "Lesbians or homo-sexuals will no longer be denied legally binding marriages, complete with mutual-support agreements and inheritance rights," she wrote, although the statement was followed by a kind of disclaimer that suggested that homosexuality was a personal-ity disorder: "Paradoxically, the number of homosexuals may get smaller. With fewer possessive mothers and fewer fathers who hold up an impossible cruel or perfectionist idea of manhood, boys will be less likely to be denied or reject their identity as males" (Steinem, "What It Would" 23). She was not to repeat these notions about the formation of homosexuality again (assuming they were her views, not those inserted by a *Time* editor). More typically, when *Ms.* was estab-lished, the magazine gave coverage to lesbians, the first mass magazine to do so on a regular basis. Steinem's acceptance of lesbians in the women's movement helped build support among the segment of the women's movement that Friedan eschewed. Part of that strategy was served by Steinem's decision not to declare her heterosexuality in the media and to allow to stand rumors that she was a lesbian; if asked directly, she answered, "Not yet" (Heilbrun 1995: 255).

Indeed, as the interviewer in a 1981 New York cable channel program pointed out, reporters who interviewed Steinem during this period were well aware of her heterosexuality. "It was generally known you were not a lesbian," Patrick Watson commented, "but you were often asked, 'Were you or were you not a lesbian?' and you never gave a straight reply." Steinem agreed that for the mainstream media, her strategy had been to obfuscate. "They seemed to wish I was a lesbian because it would explain it [her feminism]," she responded. "And I discovered a great reply, 'Are you my alternative?'" (Watson 1981).

Media obfuscation regarding Steinem's sexuality might be considered an exchange. For the journalists, the often used "Are you my alternative?" answer, delivered with a smile, provided the quick sound bite mainstream journalists sought while allowing them to maintain the bête noir that the movement was essentially a movement for lesbian rights. Steinem saw the exchange as allowing her to exert some control over the interview by not providing information she saw as designed to marginalize the movement or lesbians. It was not a strategy, she said in the 1981 interview, that she used in the women's community, "when I was asked honestly, when the question came from more hospitable questioners" (Watson 1981).

Nonetheless, outside of New York, in provincial feminist circles, her sexual ori-entation remained unclear, possibly supported by the knowledge that she had for six years shared an apartment with Nessim, an artist. In Denver's *Big Mama Rag*, lesbian writer Chocolate Waters found herself overcome by Steinem's celebrity and her sexual attractiveness, but had to note: "Applications for the next interview with Gloria Steinem are now being taken. No dykes need apply" (Waters 1972: 22).

One of Steinem's less recognized stands might be her public refusal to reject lesbianism as a choice for her life. In terms of the women's movement, the association of lesbians with the cool and collected Steinem might have retained lesbians in the overall women's movement at the same time that it eroded some stereotypical thinking about the lesbian community in general. Her ambiguity also served to make Steinem acceptable to a women's movement that included both straight and gay women; Steinem, in a foreshadowing of the editorial inclusiveness that would mark *Ms.* magazine, represented a blending of lines, including sexuality, that had been emerging in popular culture. As even critics credited, Steinem quickly recognized the shape of the culture, allowing her to take the risk that her ambiguity was acceptable to the mass audience.

On a practical level, in positioning herself as someone acceptable to the lesbian community, Steinem was not only filling a vacuum in the women's movement but also finding a constituency that was likely to follow her into the liberal feminism as later espoused by *Ms.* magazine. NOW clearly had tapped into the long-dormant activism of lesbians who were not part of the radical women's Left. Lesbians, despite a lifestyle that remained illegal in some parts of the nation, were not necessarily anti-capitalist or New Left activists. Younger lesbians did play a role in the radical Left for a time before moving—like Karla Jay and Rita Mae Brown—into gay activism. But for other lesbians in the women's movement, lesbianism was a matter of sexual preference, not a call for the total reorientation of society or a rejection of men. Lesbians may have clustered into NOW chapters precisely because NOW was a middle-class organization. While Friedan saw the clustering as the "lavender menace," Steinem saw the clustering as an indication of women who had few representatives, either in the women's movement overall or in society at large. Middle-class lesbians who were members of the women's movement likely appreciated that Steinem could define herself as a feminist without a defensive attachment to heterosexuality.

The upshot of the Steinem style was that it permitted the viewer to invest in whatever point of view was meaningful to the viewer: the lesbian could define Steinem as a possible sister lesbian; the heterosexual woman could view Steinem as an independent woman who did not need male identification but could get it if she so chose; and the male viewer who admired her beauty might have found Steinem's seeming asexuality a subject of personal fantasy. Because the image she projected provided limited and controlled information, consumers of media had the possibility to construct for themselves that part of her that was not in the public eye, an imaginary place that, as biographers have noted, had long been part of her attraction to male companions. Even those men and women who did not find Steinem's message compelling might have found it difficult to resist the various levels of attractions she offered. Like Marilyn Monroe, whom Steinem admired and wrote about, Steinem appealed to both sexes because her image beckoned viewer involvement. "That feeling of connection to Marilyn's loneliness felt by so many strangers," she wrote of Monroe, was so compelling "that we fantasized our ability to save her, if only we had been there" (Steinem 1972: 35).

Vulnerability may not have been the reason that strangers connected with Steinem, but not every dot in the photo or line on the screen of Steinem's public face was completed, leaving it to the media consumer to complete the details. In his discussion of the rise of the underground media, David Armstrong draws attention to the different roles that film and video play in carrying radical messages. Film tends to be sharply critical, while video, which came about during the early 1960s, was ameliorating. Instead of viewing media as a tool with which one class would overthrow another, video activists saw media as means of bringing people together (Armstrong 1981: 70). The development of video as a reform tool may have resulted from the tradition of alternative film and the lack of a similar tradition in video, but it also may have resulted from the medium itself. To return to McLuhan, the incomplete information provided by television in contrast to film results in a different reaction to the television medium than to film. The viewer necessarily must invest something of her/himself in the television presentation in ways that forge bonds, but not so much as to lead to active participation, as in the "hot" medium of radio.

But Steinem clearly fit with electronic media. In the 1970s, the period of her greatest influence, Steinem personally was responsible for much of the dispersal of the feminist message over the mass media landscape. She may have been the prime feminist influence for many American women because of her appearances on local and national television; the numerous articles that appeared about her; the publication of *Ms.* magazine, which often seemed another incarnation of her; and her perpetual speaking tours, which were sure to be accompanied by interviews in local media.

Despite the affection that many women across the nation held for her, she was not embraced by all feminists. In 1972, Steinem was referenced critically in terms in a general work meant to be a primer for the movement: "She is highly photogenic, she associates with the people the media likes to photograph, and she is careful to push for the liberation of women in unstructured, non-philosophical ways that Americans like" (White 1972: 122). In Judith Hole and Ellen Levine's 1971 work, *Rebirth of Feminism*, Steinem is mentioned only in passing—twice in footnotes, once in an appendix, and once as Gloria Steinem, "the writer" (Hole and Levine 1971: 169n, 215n, 427, 229). She was seldom mentioned at all in the Left press, and never seriously. Like Friedan, who remained a public feminist presence without organizational power, Steinem was a media spokeswoman for the second wave. As her ongoing and widespread speaking engagements indicated, Steinem was the most popular of all feminist speakers. Steinem is now the media symbol of the second wave to the exclusion of Friedan or anyone else, as in the Barbara Walters's 1999

ABC-TV program on the twentieth century's most memorable women: Friedan was reduced to a ten-second sound clip while Steinem was a program commentator. Mass media has subsumed the complications of second-wave feminism into Steinem's unruffled lines. She continued as the voice of 1970s feminism into the new century, and at the age of sixty-six wrote a short article for *Time* on her new marriage. Marriage, she wrote, no longer "takes away a woman's civil rights." *Time*'s copy editor was less esoteric, heading the piece, "Finally Real." For *Time*, at least, her mystery had been put to rest. Marriage had made her "real" (Steinem 2001: G8).

Steinem quickly eclipsed Friedan in the media spotlight, seeming to represent everything Friedan did not. Friedan, in her frustration, struck back and encouraged media representations of the women's movement as divided. Friedan attacked Steinem and Abzug as "female chauvinists," women who were endangering the movement by "an anti-male agenda" (*NYT* 7/9/70: 43). The comments extended what Friedan had written in an article in *McCall's* magazine. Friedan also probably hoped to damage Abzug's ambitions for Jacob Javits's seat in the U.S. Senate while Friedan considered a challenge. Neither Steinem or Abzug was associated with groups that sought to maintain female exclusivity. In fact, Steinem, seeking to establish her own base, had in 1971 cofounded the Women's Action Alliance, which sought to assist women in practical local actions. The board included not only her political friends, Abzug and Chisholm, but two old male friends, Nat Hentoff and John Kenneth Galbraith. The Women's Action Alliance represented Steinem's philosophy of an idealized woman's community based not on the rejection of males but on the strength that might come by way of many lateral connections between women. Unlike many women's organizations, which were small and focused, Steinem's vision was broad and encompassing. The Women's Action Alliance aimed to avoid a hierarchal structure but to serve as an "information house." Its newsletter provided up-to-date information about feminism around the world and often predated articles on the same subjects that appeared in *Ms.*

But even with Steinem as a founder, the Women's Action Alliance, although in existence thirty years later, never gained the same kind of public attention that the press gave to NOW, although the goal of organizing on the local level was far more consistent with traditional social change methods than was NOW's structure. The Women's Action Alliance had not been in existence for very long when Steinem and her colleagues realized the mission of the envisioned "information house" could be served more directly by a magazine. *Ms.* was about to be born, and Steinem would have a platform that would maintain her as a national spokeswoman for the next decade in ways that would permanently imprint liberal feminism on the media agenda.

8. *Ms.* and the Success of Liberal Feminism

In 1969, Shana Alexander, who was the first woman staff writer and columnist for *Life* magazine and who achieved additional celebrity through her weekly appearances on CBS's *Sixty Minutes*, was offered the job of editor of the nation's largest women's magazine, *McCall's*. Friends urged caution: the magazine was in difficulty and needed a figurehead. Like most of the mass magazines of the time, the circulation of *McCall's* was dropping—a loss of a million readers during the second half of the 1960s. For Alexander, who as a writer had never had to be concerned with the business side, the twenty months of her editorship were, she said, the "worst in my life." The realities of mass media magazine publishing came as a shock. "The underlying reason for ladies' magazines, I learned, was never ladies' needs but advertisers' needs. Manufacturers of soap powder and diapers and Tampax assumed an all-female readership. But the average family income of our subscribers was $13,000; fewer than one in four had gone beyond high school. The magazine we were trying to sell them, more accurately, to give them—the price being only fraction of what it actually cost to produce it—was aimed not at serving their needs but exciting their fantasies. The editorial pages showed readers an impossible never-never land of furs and jewels and designer clothes. Our Christmas dinner menu featured roast suckling pig, fantasy food not even moderately rich readers could afford, and certainly could not find at the supermarket; even if they did, it would not fit into any known home oven" (Alexander 1995: 276).

McCall's, in fact, was not so much ignoring the world around it as trying to accommodate it in the well-worn format of the service magazines. Alexander as a choice to head up the magazine was one of its attempts to find a middle ground between women's activism and concerns for traditional readers, as it had in 1968, when the magazine established "Womanpower-in-Action," a clearinghouse for female volunteers who were concerned about violence in American life. "Women must find positive alternatives to the extremes of apathy and vigilantism and especially to the current wave of destructive violence," said the public relations release that accompanied the campaign (*CSM* 11/1/68: 16). Although activists, from Friedan to members of the Left, constantly criticized women's service magazines for their homogeneity and the narrow role they espoused for women, it would be wrong to say that the magazines ignored the issues of the time. *Ladies' Home Journal* had built its reputation in the 1900s on its fight for unadulterated foods and other campaigns that fit with the moral housekeeping mode of the time. In the 1960s and 1970s, women's magazines tended to reflect in some manner the drift of the time in an inclusive approach. When Patricia Carbine took over *McCall's* following Alexander's tenure, she was not breaking tradition in bringing Betty Friedan and Gloria Steinem into the editorial pages any more than her predecessor had in running a disquieting selection from Germaine Greer's *The Female Eunuch*. Women's service magazines, as much as women's sections in newspapers, provided readers—alongside stories of Thanksgiving turkeys and suckling pigs—with articles that addressed many of the issues of the day (as *Charm* did with Friedan's 1955 article) in ways that may have been limited but were hardly as hostile as the articles that appeared in general interest magazines such as *Time*. The messages in the women's service magazines could be contradictory, but they were contradictions that readers generally were able to accommodate when presented under the brand images of service magazines that had been on the American scene for a hundred years.

The problem that faced women's service magazines at the time was not accommodating new content. Alexander's major problem, like other magazines of the time, was the loss of advertising, which was at its lowest level in seven years (*Nswk* 1/18/71: 55). While magazine professionals blamed television, adding to the problems were the rising costs of labor, production, and second-class postage. Mailing became impossibly expensive for the big-format magazines, whose size and glossy paper were part and parcel of the lush life the magazines promised. Indeed, the heft, sophisticated design, four-color illustrations, quality photographic reproductions, even the sweet smell of good paper stock in the delicious moment of the turning of the first page—all longtime characteristics of American mass magazines— made their consumption as much a sensuous experience as shopping in the fantasy world provided by great department stores, which, like the magazines, were on the decline.

But critics wondered if mass magazines had lived beyond their time. Advertising professionals turned away from *Look* and *Life*, saying the magazines had lost their purpose. "Both magazines are having a great deal of trouble defining their place in the world," one media director told a 1971 interviewer (Welles 1971: 8), yet no magazine fought more to be recognized as relevant than the American icon, *Life. Life* gave up its fashion department in favor of an expansion to grittier subjects: one single issue was devoted to a week of American dead in Vietnam.

For publishers, perhaps, the single-issue approach was one way to meet the challenge of the emerging specialty magazines, but to the editors the issue reflected the dissident nature of the time: "The magazine dropped its life-long posture as the earnest, cheerful broker of the high-mindedness and the good intentions of the American establishment and declared itself on the side of the growing mass of dissidents, ready for profound change" (Wainwright 1986: 363).

After a torturous stewardship marked by her inability to attract the necessary advertisers, Alexander was unceremoniously replaced by her second-in-command, Carbine. Given the period, Carbine had had a remarkable career. Rising from her start as a researcher at *Look* magazine, she became its managing editor, then its executive editor. Carbine remained at *McCall's* from January 1971 through April 1972, long enough to give a regular column to Betty Friedan and to anoint Gloria Steinem, not Friedan, as *McCall's* "Woman of the Year." Primarily, however, Carbine moved *McCall's* back to its traditional track as a service magazine. "She had turned the magazine back toward homemaking but she has continued to offer carefully structured glimpses of the world beyond the home. Madison Avenue is skeptical that she can successfully involve both older conventional readers and young, more 'liberated' ones" (Welles 1991: 13). However, Carbine's decision to return *McCall's* to what were considered traditional roots was not because readers did not accept the new editorial content—they had already chosen to accept the new content—but because advertisers would not accept it. In the competitive world of print advertising, advertisers of traditional products have no reason to take chances.

Before final judgment came on the success of Carbine's strategy, she was gone, giving up her position as vice president of McCall's Publishing to join the triumvirate of founders of *Ms.* Although Steinem would be most connected to *Ms.* as its public face, Carbine was arguably as important because of her understanding of the business side. A woman who had seen *Look* flounder because of its lack of identity and who had returned *McCall's* to profitability, Carbine was to undertake management of a magazine that aimed to have only real content, not fluff; to permit entry only to those advertisers that lived up to the magazine's code; and to have as its name a new word that most people could not pronounce. It would also be a mass-market magazine but would appeal to what was considered the specialty interest audience of women's rights. Nonetheless, the publication would be expected to attract enough readers so that advertisers carried the cost of production.

This all sounded at odds with the tenets of traditional magazine publishing, but *Ms.* in fact was on the cutting edge of business thinking. By 1970 the most financially successful magazines—that is, those that attracted advertisers—were closely targeted at specialized audiences. The trend had begun in the postwar period with the 1944 launch of *Seventeen* magazine, which defined young girls as an economically viable market thanks to the work of Estelle Ellis, a pioneer in the new field of demographics. In 1950, Ellis's work contributed to the launch of another groundbreaking publication, *Charm*, which defined working women as a separate market (Ellis 1994–99). By 1973, a judge at the National Magazine Awards found that the dominant trend was "specialization and sub-specialization." The most successful publications were "those having an aura of indispensability to readers with special interests" (Barrett, E. 1973: 24). Advertisers found such magazines—*Cosmopolitan*, *New York*, *Psychology Today*, *Rolling Stone*, and others— different from television audiences, which featured large numbers but not necessarily from among the demographically desirable groups advertisers sought. Clay Felker, publisher of the glossy *New York*, where Gloria Steinem had come of age as a political writer, was among the new publishers who recognized and profited from the trend, which he would call "service journalism" (MacDougal 1974). While Felker had lost the battle with Harold Hayes for the editorial top seat at *Esquire*, the success of *New York* had proved the viability of a journalism that eschewed fantasy to meet the particular needs of the audience when wrapped in an attractive package with good writing, attractive layout, and a sense of being in tune with the times. *New York*'s influence on *Ms.* went beyond its role in carrying the *Ms.* preview edition enfolded in the 20 December 1971, issue. *New York* was described by its design director as a "magazine not designed to look beautiful but to carry a sense of energy, compression, density and information" (MacDougal 1974: 42). It was distinguished by bold graphics and strong cover art. Coming from this graphic tradition, Sam Antupit, a former art director of *Esquire*, designed *Ms.* and helped set in place the magazine's typographical characteristics. *Ms.* became famous for covers that are now classics and for a typographical layout that utilized a light type and narrow columns on the assumption that its readers would not have to be beguiled into reading by lavish (and wasteful) use of white space. With an overall size smaller than the big format magazines (which postal rates made prohibitively expensive to mail), the *Ms.* design principles rejected many of those developed by women's service magazines while retaining sufficient numbers of its traditions—the use of departments and an anecdotal narrative style—to provide readers with comfortable moorings. And from the beginning, *Ms.* retained and expanded on another strength of the women's magazines—close connections with readers.

What advertisers particularly liked about the new specialty magazines and their service journalism was the involvement they promoted with their readers. "This involvement," an observer of the journalistic scene at the time wrote, "advertisers are certain, 'rubs off' on their ads, which are better read and more readily believed and acted upon" (Welles 1971: 12). Here was truly middle ground between the old and the new that *Ms.* could inhabit, pleasing advertisers by an involvement with readers that service magazines had long promoted.

Mitigating the Medium

Ms., once it had evolved from a modest newsletter idea between Steinem and Brenda Feigen of the Women's Action Alliance, was in tune with changes in the magazine field. Its audience certainly was to be as defined and targeted as the readers of *Cosmopolitan*. Readers were likely to be of a high enough demographic profile not only to respond to radically different content without offense but also to draw advertisers. Finally, one of the *Ms.* hallmarks was the active participation of readers to such a point that they often seemed to consider themselves part of the ownership.

Given the changes in the magazine industry and the success that feminist-oriented books had achieved in the mass market, *Ms.* was not an outlandish proposal. Nonetheless, it was an ambitious endeavor that, despite the connections of Steinem and her circle of founders, lacked access to sufficient capital. The connection to start-up capital came by way of a West Coast acquaintance, Elizabeth Forsling Harris, whose association resulted in so much grief for Steinem and her compatriots that Harris was subsequently bought out (Thom 1997). What gave them the sense of mission that overcame the major obstacle of financial backing speaks not only to the sense of accomplishment that the movement had achieved in less than a decade but also to the belief that the moment was now; nothing was impossible. That permeating optimism was surely evident among the women who came together to make *Ms.* a reality. Letty Pogrebin described those first meetings as "intoxicating"; Mary Peacock spoke of the "infectious malaria of start up" (Thom 1997: 12, 17).

Despite the excitement, the women who launched *Ms.* were not neophytes. The magazine's leadership was drawn from a base in New York, a city that provided the nation's largest pool of professional women writers and editors. Suzanne Braun Levine, the magazine's executive editor, had been an associate editor at *McCall's*, features editor at *Mademoiselle*, and a reporter–writer for *Seattle Magazine*; Pogrebin was a freelance magazine writer, a publicist for Bernard Geis Associates, author of *How to Make It In a Man's World*, and a columnist for *Ladies' Home Journal*; JoAnne Edgar and Mary Thom had been researchers at *Facts on File*; Catherine O'Haire, later copy editor, had worked for *Life*, *Show*, and the Reader's Digest Book Division; Mary Peacock had launched a magazine of her own; Susan Braudy was one of the first female writers for *Newsweek*. B. J. Phillips, the first woman writer for *Time*, later joined the staff, as did Ellen Willis, a radical feminist and music critic for the *New Yorker* magazine.

One study notes that the original *Ms.* editors, half of whom were graduates of Seven Sisters colleges, were not representative of the women that the magazine saw as its readers and were out of touch with the women they wanted as subscribers (Farrell 1998: 41). But although the founders of *Ms.* were unlike most of their readers, as are all journalists by the fact of their professional association, these women nonetheless were closer to the readers than a simple reading of educational background suggests. As professional journalists, they shared a belief in the efficacy of mass media and the adoption of at least some of the craft traditions. And, despite their college backgrounds, they were more likely to come from nonelite backgrounds, another characteristic of the men and women who choose mass media as careers. Attendance at elite colleges may be seen less as a signifier of their class than as a signifier of their class ambitions. The inability of the *Ms.* founders, including Steinem, to access major funding early on surely suggests that they had few intimate contacts with wealth.

Instead of being labeled *elite*, the founding women of *Ms.* might better be considered "liminars," individuals who were not clearly of one class or another, neither insiders nor outsiders, and that status played a role in the direction of the magazine. This kind of betwixt-and-betweenness is not unusual for mass media practitioners. As the research of David Weaver and G. C. Wilhoit (1991) demonstrates, media practitioners are often the offspring of lower-middle- or working-class parents, likely members of ethnic or religious minorities (although not African-American until recently), and often attend public rather than private colleges. From those beginnings, media workers take on jobs that are considered middle class or at least that bring about middle-class associations as the career ladder is mounted. The less-than-affluent backgrounds, however, allow practitioners to be close to the interest levels of the constituency that mass media serves, which is, as Alexander identified and scholars verify, lower middle class. Meanwhile, the mass media industry has served as a ladder of success for its workers, who generally view media work as valuable in its ability to give voice to those without advocates.

Further, the employment of men and women from lower-middle-class or marginal-group backgrounds funnels the explosiveness that can accompany liminar status. Believing in the efficacy of mass media and attracted by the possibilities of upward mobility, such liminars might turn to mass media for the changes they seek to make rather than take their energies into organizing. It is not surprising, then, that the women involved in launching *Ms.* had backgrounds connected to liminar status or that they would be drawn to a media product aimed at seeking solutions while building their careers.

Steinem's childhood, with its intersection between the lower-middle-class neighborhood in which she grew up and the middle-class status of her family background, provides the prime example of a liminar status. The facts of Steinem's background are well known and need not be repeated. However, many of the same characteristics are seen in the backgrounds of other founding staff members.

Carbine most notably represents the status of betwixt and between when one goes beyond the immediate facts of her biography. She was indeed the product of private schools on the Philadelphia Main Line. Her father, James T. Carbine, was an executive with the Pennsylvania Railroad, and the family lived in comfort in a Main Line suburb—altogether the epitome, it would seem, of insider status. That status is not so clear in view of other aspects of her life. Carbine was one of six children in what she described as a traditional Irish-Catholic family headed by a strong-willed mother who was sent to work after the sixth grade. Although Carbine's father rose to be the railroad's general manager for coal traffic and was a member of many exclusive clubs, he started out at the age of sixteen as a railroad elevator operator. The slippery slope of status could only have been emphasized to his daughter at his death in 1947, when she was fourteen (*NYT* 6/15/47: 15). Carbine's mother subsequently made another middle-class marriage, thus enabling the six children from her first marriage to be the first generation from either side of the family to be raised in financial comfort (St. George).

Despite private schools, Carbine did not follow the marriage-and-family path of childhood friends in the Main Line of the 1950s. Indeed, her choice of a mass media career in magazines (rather than book publishing, the usual career track for graduates of the Seven Sisters colleges) was more typical of the upwardly mobile career path of a first-generation South Philadelphian. Nor was her decision to pursue a media career at the expense of husband and children typical of Irish-Catholic families of the era, well to do or not, much less her unwavering support of abortion. They seemed decisions made possible by her sense of herself that was not bound by obligations to any particular status.

Suzanne Braun Levine and Letty Cottin Pogrebin were among several Jewish women drawn to the new venture. While to be Jewish in New York is hardly to be of outsider status, it is interesting to speculate on the reasons for the number of Jewish women drawn to feminism, a subject of recent scholarship (Levitt, Laura 1997). Pogrebin, who has written on the subject, said in an interview, "We should consider that to women of Jewish and immigrant-family backgrounds, mass media careers offer the opportunity to serve an ethnic group that likely has been ill served by media at one time or another. The barriers to women in mass media careers might be new expressions of the same kinds of barriers that had already been overcome by their families" (Pogrebin 1998).

However, up until her *Ms.* association, Pogrebin had demonstrated a careerist mode of thinking. She had learned under the master—Bernard Geis, a book publisher who launched books on the basis of their ability to engender mass media publicity. Pogrebin worked as director of publicity, advertising, and subsidiary rights for ten years until close to the firm's bankruptcy in 1971. Like *Sex and the Single Girl*, Pogrebin's 1970 book, *How to Make It in a Man's World*, sought to capture working women for its audience, exhorting women to seek executive-level positions and providing advice on necessary fibbing, dealing with amorous attentions, and dressing and speaking appropriately to reach that goal. She later disassociated herself from the book as "pre-feminist," and the book indeed seemed out of its time, given that by 1970 feminism had been on the media agenda for a half dozen years. This was not a background that would seem to propel her toward *Ms.*

By the time Pogrebin was involved in the planning of *Ms.*, however, she had turned to a new career as a freelance writer. By that time, she had also shed some of the beliefs expressed in *How to Make It*. But her road to feminism was probably not very different from that of many of the readers of *Ms.* whose commitment also had been delayed by the issue of stridency and who may have believed in the power of individual women to negotiate gender inequities. On a practical level, Pogrebin brought to *Ms.* her experience as a publicist. She had been active in the Publishers Publicity Association, knew the New York publishing world, and was experienced and knowledgeable in the role of launch in putting a media product on the public agenda. She would periodically put her publicity skills in service to *Ms.*, and even in her later career, as president of the Authors Guild, her emphasis on marketing remained, as in her advice to authors on book tours: "Be animated and charming. Be funny if you can. Do it for your book's sake. Don't hang back. Don't let yourself get eclipsed" (Pogrebin 1999: 37). Pogrebin's sensibilities would be represented at *Ms.* with the hire of Karen Lippert as publicity director.

JoAnne Edgar is one of the most interesting members of the founding group as she brought to the mix the most traditional American liminar status—the southerner. Born in Jackson, Mississippi, to a full-time homemaker mother from a long-settled Jackson family who held traditional white views on race, her father's rise to middle management took the family from Jackson to Canada to California and provided the contrasts that challenged the early lessons of her upbringing. Indeed, by college, Edgar, unknown to her family, had become a civil rights activist at her racially segregated college in Jackson. At one point in her activities to integrate the school, Edgar's name was listed in a public announcement that fell into her grandmother's hands and resulted in family contretemps (Edgar 1999).

Edgar subsequently moved to New York and continued her civil rights activism but found, as had many other white women at the time, a diminished place for her in the movement, and her efforts turned to job activism when she and her female colleagues at the *Facts on File* publication discovered "thousands of dollars" in wage differentials between the female and male workers. She eventually was introduced to Steinem while she was helping to establish the National Women's Political Caucus, and, beginning with the typing of the caucus's bylaws, Edgar quickly found herself in a position as Steinem's reliable administrative assistant, a role that would segue into a place on the magazine. Edgar's involvement with *Ms.* lasted for seventeen years, during which time she was unswervingly committed to feminism, Steinem, and the magazine; like the other founding women, however, Edgar had neither capital nor connections to capital to offer for the magazine's financial well-being. And she shared with other members of the group, including Steinem, a commitment to feminism that had developed not by way of early radical meetings but through the ether of the time, as feminism percolated through popular culture.

Nor was insider status typical of other long-term *Ms.* associates. Mary Thom was a midwesterner from Cleveland, Ohio, who had attended Bryn Mawr College. Levine was born in New York to middle-class parents and was a 1963 graduate of Radcliffe College who had worked her way back to New York after graduation and a job at *Seattle* magazine.

What is clear about the founding members of the magazine is that all their careers up to their association with *Ms.* had been all affected by their gender. Although job discrimination had been the most obvious elucidation of gender status, each woman had rejected a complicated set of gender expectations created by regional, ethnic, and religious upbringings. What made gender discrimination unpalatable to these woman while other women simply put up with it was that it emphasized the dislocation that the women were already experiencing. No dilettantes, already risk takers, unwilling to accept the secondary status that could seem to echo what once had been their family status, such women responded in activist ways when they found themselves stymied by the same profession that was supposed to represent the people's voice.

These women's concern with the here and now was reflected in an editorial product that seldom called on its readers for sacrifice—one hallmark of most social movements. As in the founding of NOW, the editorial outlook of *Ms.* was to reflect the career tensions of its founders, their outsider status, their impatience as part of the youth of the period, and the media environment of immediacy. The *Ms.* founders did not engage in the kind of audience research that sought to prove the existence of a national audience with the same concerns. Limited by the lack of funds that under ordinary circumstances would accompany the launch of a national media product, *Ms.* magazine depended on the return of interest cards from the preview edition. These were most utilized as a subscription base rather than a way to determine the magazine's focus.

Ms. was conceived as a national publication with an appeal to women across lines of class, color, and ethnicity and attempting to offer diverse editorial content. It was not so much that the magazine sought a diverse audience—*Ladies' Home Journal* long had had a substantial African-American audience—but that it was going to reflect interests of all its diverse readers in the belief that what was shared was womanhood: despite various permutations of class, race, and ethnicity, all woman shared commonalities. These communalities were not those of house and home, as the women's service magazines would have it, but those of an exclusion from the American table of opportunity. Although the founders were aligned with New York, Steinem's constant lecture tours certainly had made her believe that all women were alike in that they all shared outsider status. She frequently articulated the notion that outsider status could be overcome by understanding women in terms of commonality. As ethnic groups had concentrated on the similarities of the concerns facing all members of the group, the so-called group politics of the time, *Ms.* established kinship on basis of gender. Women were women before they were members of a radical group, religion, or class. Under the universal umbrella of kinship, all women, all of them outsiders in one way or another, were to be embraced.

Ms. and Values of Kinship

Protected by an overarching theme of kinship, *Ms.* was to introduce subject matter that had heretofore never found the light of day in mass magazines. However, in introducing these contents, *Ms.* called on some familiar traditions of the women's magazines. Much of the magazine—from its format, its cover sell lines, and its use of celebrity covers—seemed to have much in common with *McCall's* and other women's magazines. Even *Ms.*'s dramatic preview cover—a many-armed re-creation of a Hindu goddess—sounded the familiar women's magazine theme that women at home had to be mistresses of many arts. In an illustration in the Betty Crocker cookbook of the era, a woman holds aloft the many dishes she has prepared before noon. But the cover illustration was open to other readings and established from the beginning the way the magazine merged old forms with new content, a subterfuge that recognized that mass media meanings could exist beyond their surfaces. The woman of the illustration was, as a reflection of another culture and religion, an exotic, outsider image for Americans; as such, it constituted a revolutionary choice for the launch of an American mass magazine. Moreover, the multiple arms of the illustration suggested not so much one woman representing many arts but many arts practiced by many women, all of whom were related by their gender. A sell line in the upper left corner gave clue to that notion: "Gloria Steinem on Sisterhood." *Ms.* was on the way to its grand experiment. If women were to be outsiders by the fact of their gender, that fact also offered surcease. Kinship between women could salve the outsider status that the gender implied.

Steinem's emphasis was the great dread of the politico segment, which feared that an emphasis on personal change would take the place of efforts to transform society. Nonetheless, *Ms.* attracted the cultural feminists who had played a role in the development of the second wave of feminism—radical women such as Jo Freeman, Kathie Sarachild, Ellen Willis, and Robin Morgan would all write for the magazine (and Morgan later served as its editor).

The content of *Ms.*, while much of it was new to mass media, was presented in ways that were consonant with the strains of American liberalism that believed that fairness was accomplished primarily by overcoming prejudicial thinking—a familiar theme to those who had come of age in the civil rights movement. It was a theme that did not call for expulsion (except for prejudicial thinking) but rather expanded to include what had previously been left out. *Ms.* did not call for the reorientation of the U.S. market economy but called for feminism to take its place as a logical extension of American life and culture. Because the achievement of this goal was based on the acceptance of all women in a network of women's kinship, alternative ways of addressing feminism based on the restructuring of political power or social class and ethnic issues could not be adopted unless kinship was included. Thus, many of the goals and beliefs of the decade as promulgated by *Ms.* were premised on the values of support for the empowerment of all women in whatever realm, as in support of any woman running for office; the sharing of power regardless of talent or efficiency; class-action suits on behalf of all women; the establishment of social services for all women; and a belief that all women had more in common than not, regardless of individual culture. These were expressions of an idealized family, all for one and one for all, and it is not surprising that in Freeman's article on "trashing," *Ms.* often countered its female critics with black sheep characterizations and admonitions of appropriate behavior for sisterhood.

Given this view, it is not surprising that the original choice for the name of the magazine was *Sisters*, a title that was discarded, according to *Ms.* legend, only after Catholic activists objected, claiming that the name reminded them of convent days. The final choice of *Ms.*, however, did everything *Sisters* did—and more. The name claimed for its readers the right of self-identification as women and advanced a systemic change in which courtesy titles for women would not be defined by marital status but by gender alone. All women were included under "Ms." The magazine's name also indicated the nature of the magazine's editorial policy of the primacy of gender. Steinem's "Sisterhood" article in the premiere issue could be taken as the statement of the policy as much as the official editorial statement. Her article noted that the "deep and personal connections that women made" occurred across "barriers of age, economics, worldly experience, race, culture—all the barriers that, in male or mixed society, seem so impossible to cross" (Steinem 1972: 46).

Moreover, the magazine presented itself as an endeavor shared with its readers. Editorial policies were periodically explained in its "A Personal Report from *Ms.*" Although Steinem would be the most recognizable name on the masthead, other members of the staff were also promoted. An article on advertising policies included a group photo of the advertising saleswomen. Staff softball games seemed like family events. The pool of writers became familiar names. *Ms.* encouraged readers to write, with the result that the magazine was swamped with letters indicating that readers indeed believed they had a stake in the magazine's ownership (Thom 1987). Although women's magazines had always sought to build readers' sense of involvement with the product, *Ms.* developed a sense of kinship with its readers in ways that had never before existed in American mass magazines— a long-standing affection that offers one explanation for the magazine's survival.

In its concern with female universality, there seemed no one who was not included in the pages of *Ms.*—housewives, mothers, radical politicos, lesbians, women of color, and varied ethnicities and ranks of women were seen to share similar problems and outlook, as if the divisive strands of the women's movement could, once gathered under the single roof of *Ms.*, work together in the common cause. Steinem emphasized inclusivity in her speaking tours, continuing to include a companion woman of color. Her support of Kate Millett was consistent with the *Ms.* policy as well as with Steinem's personal politics.

This approach introduced subjects that had never before had regular mass media attention. *Redbook*'s 1971 article on lesbians was not the start of a new policy. In the mass media, lesbians had been most often represented in terms of their connection to feminism as in the attention given to Millett and Friedan's comments. *Ms.*, largely at the insistence of Steinem, who had designated Anne Koedt's article "Can Women Love Women?" to appear in the premiere issue, included the subject on regular basis by assigning a column to a lesbian couple, Del Martin and Phyllis Lyon. The column was criticized in the lesbian community as serving more as a tool for the education of nonlesbian women than as a forum for lesbian interests. In an "indykement" of the magazine, *Lesbian Tide* counted that just 5 of 505 articles and 9 of 531 letters to the magazine were clearly lesbian identified. "Until *Ms.* reevaluates and begins to adequately represent the politics and lifestyle of Lesbian radical Feminists, we the Lesbian Nation cancel our subscriptions and support of a magazine whose pages have canceled our reality" (*BMR* 7/72: 1). By that time, *Ms.* was considered too conservative for the lesbian writer Chocolate Waters: "I ran around frantically gathering up past issues of *Ms.*—which I'd long since stopped reading" (Waters, "Non-Interview": 2). From a later perspective, such lesbian readers appeared not to recognize that *Ms.* was including a subject that had previously received little positive mass media coverage.

Economic diversity was also represented in continuing representations of women and welfare benefits. In June 1973, *Ms.* published a special issue, "Women and Money," that further invoked the editorial policy that women shared more commonalities than not, in this case because women had been oppressed by a caste system that relegated them to economic lower rungs. Here was an opportunity for a larger critique, but Steinem's solution was a call for women to alter their views on money and to demand adequate compensation. "It will be a long road. The first step is believing in ourselves; understanding that we are indeed smart, even if we aren't rich. And the second is giving up the myths of power, so that we can see our economic plight as it really is" (Steinem, "If We're So Smart": 37, 127). Other articles supported these themes in the personal, anecdotal style of self-help articles that was so familiar to women's service magazines—"How I Learned to Stop Being Grateful" and "People's Money Hang-Ups."

Steinem referred to herself as a "revolutionary" rather than a reformer (Watson 1981). Critics, however, tended to judge her on the basis of her *Ms.* articles focused on consciousness-raising for women who were not at the point of challenging systemic power structure. The *Ms.* umbrella did include a place for the radicals. Jane Alpert was involved in several bombings of military and war-related corporate buildings in New York City in late 1969, went underground, and resurfaced in *Ms.* magazine with a cultural feminist classic, "Mother Right" in 1973. To the opponents of liberal feminism, "Mother Right" further disengaged feminism from Left politics. "For a radical feminist analysis of women's concrete, material oppression, they substitute fantasies of lost matriarchies, female superiority and 'mother right.' They defend themselves against criticism with an appeal to a phony concept of sisterhood that stigmatizes disagreement as 'divisive' or 'anti-woman' or 'self-hating' " (Willis 1975: 171).

With this editorial policy that emphasized that all women shared common problems, *Ms.* sought inclusion of all at the same table, whether or not all wanted a place at the same table or at the table offered. Individuals of the majority culture simply had to shift slightly to make room for the recently disadvantaged. What would accomplish this shuffling of chairs was the act of personal transformation when each woman would understand, one at a time, how all women were disadvantaged. One of *Ms.*'s popular columns was "Click," in which readers wrote to the magazine (sometimes with an accompanying copy of an advertisement) describing an event that made them come to a realization of a feminist truth in a sudden, personal epiphany—the turning on of a light. The notion that conversion to feminism could come without great conflict or study is not out of step for a nation whose inhabitants could change night into day by a click or a nation whose Puritan ancestors came to religion by way of an emotional rendition of godly intervention. While "Click" was not intended to be more than supporting documentation for feminism, it represents the magazine's emphasis on right feeling and common sense. What the magazine did not reflect, despite Steinem's own definition of herself as a revolutionary, was the real struggle for some women to come to feminist beliefs beyond equal pay for equal work. As Elizabeth Spelman writes, some women require more than turning a switch to reject a home culture (Spelman 1988). *Ms.* generally ignored that for many women, adoption of feminist principles would likely put them at odds with the world in which they moved, including the possibility of never finding a male partner who would meet feminist standards. Nor, to some critics, did *Ms.* convey the enormity of adopting an ideology that was also at odds with most of the history and religions of the world. *Ms.* made a limited kind of feminism possible for ordinary women but in so doing could not help but define feminism in terms of diminution.

One upshot of the *Ms.* decision to represent all women was that all women expected to be represented in particular ways and frequently disapproved. As letters to the editor indicated, many readers had a sense of communal ownership of *Ms.* Despite all its efforts for inclusivity, criticism of *Ms.* came from women of color. Feminist scholar bell hooks, for example, provided a caution: "Divisions will not be eliminated by wishful thinking or romantic reverie about common oppression despite the value of highlighting experiences all women share" (hooks 1984: 144). Alice Walker, an African-American staff writer, quit in 1986, citing alienation caused by magazine covers that generally featured white subjects (Thom 1987). Another writer for the magazine, Lindsy Van Gelder, said that editors believed a nonwhite cover would depress sales. Van Gelder herself was among the disaffected and has written that one article with a lesbian theme was held in inventory for nearly four years as *Ms.* downplayed lesbian issues after *Cosmopolitan* identified previous lesbian references to persuade Chevrolet not to advertise with *Ms.* (Van Gelder 1997). Pressure from advertisers clearly was unremitting. Robin Morgan said that if the magazine wanted to retain substantial advertising from Procter and Gamble, the company had to be informed when any of four particular phrases were to appear in the magazine: *lesbianism, witchcraft, abortion,* and *gun control* (Calvacca 1993: 25).

For other feminists, *Ms.* represented co-option—women of different race and classes being wrenched from their authentic cultures in favor of the world of the middle class. For some critics, Steinem and *Ms.* represented an undue emphasis on individual success. Indeed, to Marxist feminists, Steinem's celebrity was a way of maintaining hierarchal expectations. *Ms.* brought women of color into its pages but usually did so by way of articles on successful women (although *Ms.* primarily defined success as leadership), much as the women's service magazines had put forward particular reformers as leaders.

Revolutions in Media Time

Perhaps the most tension between the magazine world of mass medium and the real world of political action exists because of the promise of change. As the "Click" articles suggest, an important characteristic *Ms.* shared with mass media was the foreshortening of time. This characteristic is particularly relevant when a media product seeks political changes.

To get to the essence of any story, media reports necessarily reorder time to emphasize newness and change. The pyramid style of the traditional news story is the most obvious example in which information is presented according to its craft-designated importance. The rise of television as a serious news competitor increased the role of timeliness as a news value, emphasized by the development of the "action news" format in the 1970s, which suggested events piling up one on top of another. Anchors in the action news format developed a style that downplayed even pauses between stories, as if to cover the news was not to allow time for full breaths. Meantime, the new video technology allowed television producers to edit "sound bites" into a few seconds while satellite and live reporting were incorporated into television news programming often just for an instantaneous effect.

The technology that speeded up new reportage of the 1970s clearly reflected a generation that had experienced enormous changes and immense events at a breakneck pace. The founders of *Ms.*, most of whom were not even forty, had grown up during the 1950s and had come of age during the explosive 1960s. When *Ms.* was founded in 1972, there was no reason to believe that the pace of events, like a bullish stock market, would falter—and, indeed, the pace of events did not. Feminism was a product of the fast-paced society of the time in which change seemed to be happening with the speed of light—or a light switch. Not surprisingly, the *Ms.* editorial policy suggested that overturning tradition could be accomplished speedily, by personal transformation that mimicked the speed of change of the times.

The magazine's belief in the possibilities of speedy change reflected a particular kind of American optimism and egocentricity that was not surprising for women who had grown up with the American global presence. Thus, it seemed appropriate that the national convention for the International Women's Year should be celebrated in Houston, Texas. Although Texas was hardly on the cusp of female emancipation, the booming city represented newness, prosperity, and the promises empowerment could bring. Steinem, like thousands of other women who attended the conference, reflected in the pages of *Ms.* on these dawning days of glory. The "contagion of feminism," like the "contagion of liberty" of the American Revolution, seemed unstoppable: "There are many, many such recent proofs that the contagion of feminism is crossing boundaries of space and language; that women on every continent are beginning to question their status as, in Yoko Ono's famous phrase, 'the niggers of the world.' At its most global, there is a conviction that feminism is itself a natural and antinationalist force. As its most personal, there is an unexpected, exhilarating, and intimate sense of true connections with other women's lives—unknown women living many worlds away" (Steinem 1975: 45).

The Houston convention embodied the *Ms.* concept of universality under feminism as defined by the magazine. There was nothing that the power of feminism could not accomplish if women would join together, an easy enough task on the face of it. Underlying this philosophy was that *Ms.*—as much as any other mainstream product of mass media—represented the belief in mass media as a lever to power. The difference between *Ms.* and other mass media vehicles was that its editors fully believed in the efficacy lever. *Ms.* was part of the tradition of mass media that sought to bring its readers to an understanding of shared values, with the implication that solidarity is the most effective lever of power.

The Influence of *Ms.*

At its height, *Ms.* reached a circulation of 550,000. "Ms. Makes It," *Time* announced in December 1972. The profitability of *Ms.* in 1972 was such that it established the Ms. Foundation to fund feminist activities. But its early success occurred not only because it clearly did touch a nerve in American consciousness but also because of the attention brought to it by Steinem and the conscious marketing of the magazine by Steinem and through references to her.

Despite the democracy of its editorial organization, *Ms.* was most shaped by and associated with Gloria Steinem. Not until the founding of *George* by John F. Kennedy Jr. in 1995 would a mass magazine be so clearly associated with a publicly recognizable figure. From the premiere issue onward, the magazine took advantage of the connection. Steinem's name was conspicuous on many of its cover sell lines, and the tenth anniversary edition had a classic Steinem shot on its cover.

The fact that the double-page cover folded out to represent a range of other women only emphasized the hierarchal nature of the magazine, as Steinem seemed to be speaking for all the women. In the fifteenth anniversary edition, published in August 1987, Steinem's picture appears in the upper left corner promoting her article, "Gloria Steinem Looks to the Future." Steinem was indeed the ace in the hole that the magazine used regularly to bolster advertising and circulation. Taking a page from Felker's *New York* magazine, *Ms.* brought on board a publicity director in 1971, even before the magazine was available. "Whenever possible," Mary Thom writes, "publicity director Karen Lippert linked the magazine's media promotions with feminist groups working on the issue at hand" (Thom 1976: 196). The recognition of the *Ms.* name was often put in service to local women's groups, who would receive media attention as long as the *Ms.* connection lasted.

Lippert also saw her role as protecting Steinem's image. Steinem was not put in situations that could backfire—thus, for example, she was not booked for debates and opportunities to debate the Equal Rights Amendment and abortion were turned down. Lippert recognized Steinem's value: "For Gloria to be dealing with these issues one person at a time, making stars out of all of them—it would have been a media circus. But we used the media smarter than that" (Thom 1997: 199). The magazine was unabashedly self-promotional, conscious of its role as a groundbreaker. One aspect of its use of celebrity covers was that the magazine could thus get further exposure. Cover subjects Katharine Graham, Sally Ride, and others became connected to related press functions. Ride took a copy of the *Ms.* in which she was the cover story into outer space, and it became a part of the Smithsonian collection, events that garnered further press coverage and furthered a sense that *Ms.* was historic and was a national resource.

Because of its stature and celebrity, the magazine's public relations staff periodically mounted issue briefings that attracted media attention. There was a necessary blurring of lines in such briefings scheduled by Lippert in her role as publicity director, even as they were presented in terms of a service forum. When *Ms.* took on a particular issue, Lippert set up television and press appearances. As Thom notes, "Arranging television appearances and organizing events around such issues as wife battering, or incest, or sexual harassment was an important part of her job" (Thom 1987: 199).

The upshot was that Steinem as well as Carbine, Levine, Edgar, and Pogrebin and other staff members who became the focus of media attention and who were highly skilled in media craft traditions, maintained an aura around *Ms.* Despite ongoing criticisms about *Ms.* from a variety of sources, the strategic use of Steinem and the emphasis on *Ms.* as a organization that aimed to serve women rather than make a profit from them played a role when *Ms.* successfully sought nonprofit status in one of its many chapters of its struggle to remain viable. There was also a media fondness for Steinem that translated into a protective stance around the magazine she represented. This was no better illustrated when the radical feminist Redstockings group attempted to discredit her.

The Challenge of the Redstockings

In 1976, at the height of its fame, the *Ms.* approach to feminism was challenged by the Redstockings, the branch of the New York Radical Women that had broken off as a result of the Redstockings' point of view. Ellen Willis, one of the group's founders, was a writer for the magazine, and the Redstockings shared with *Ms.* the idea that female oppression was rooted in gender, not classic Marxist economic criticism. They also shared a belief in the women's movement as a mass movement. That belief turned the Redstockings' attention to mass media. They had been the subject of a Mary Ellen Mark photograph in *Life* that accompanied an article wherein they noted that it was time "to build a mass movement" (*Life* 12/12/70: 66–78). While the core group may never have numbered more than a few dozen women, Redstockings was one of the most influential groups of women in the second wave of feminism. The group challenged abortion rules, introduced consciousness-raising into the movement, and, coming from a leftist perspective, retained the Left's belief in a dramatic reorientation of society. Indeed, they early put on the table ideas that had barely been discussed in the public realm, such as the call for women's right to choose abortion at a time when the word was hardly spoken out loud. Critical of the mass media, the Redstockings nonetheless believed that the mass media could spread ideas if constrained by guidelines that would provide some control over the final product. The Redstockings' desire to spread their ideas was conjoined with the Left's penchant for action, leading to dramatic challenges to the media itself. Ros Baxandall, for example, a "red-diaper baby," was at the forefront of demonstrations, including the 1970 sit-in at the *Journal*.

Finally, the Redstockings' attention to media also represented the career focus of some of their members as much as NOW represented the media employment of some of its leading members. Willis came to the movement as a professional writer. Shulamith Firestone, in addition to her Left experience with SDS, published the scholarly *The Dialectic of Sex* in 1970, subsequently released in paperback by mass media publisher Bantam. Kathie Sarachild, a former editor of Harvard University's student newspaper, *The Crimson*, had been editor of a Left publication, *Woman's World.* Alix Kates Shulman was a novelist. Barbara Leon published the 1970 book *Brainwashing and Women: The Psychological Attack*. Other members wrote for alternative papers. In 1975 Random House republished many of these writings in *Feminist Revolution: An Abridged Edition with Additional Writings* (Redstockings 1975).

Given their goal of building a mass movement and their connections to the world of mass media, the Redstockings would have seemed to be logical supporters of *Ms.*, and, indeed, as the connection with Willis suggests, there was some cautious optimism. Two years after its founding, when she quit the magazine, Willis wrote, "I did not expect such a magazine, of necessity an expensive commercial venture, to be a spearhead of radicalism. I envisioned it, ideally, as a genuinely liberal forum for women writers who cannot express themselves freely in male-controlled publications. I hoped *Ms.* would change and grow, that it would be open to new ideas, criticism and suggestions—including mine" (Willis 1975: 170).

But to many members of the Redstockings, as they attempted to revitalize the group in the mid-1970s, *Ms.* represented a decline into the despised liberal feminism. Writing in the Redstockings' collection, Carol Hanisch, another former journalist, represented the collective's view, "Today the women's liberation movement is in the hands of a group of liberal opportunists, and therefore in the hands of the Left liberal male establishment. These women—some of the *Village Voice* writers, and the 'women's lib ladies' in communities all over the country—are scrambling frantically after the few crumbs that men have thrown out when we radicals began to explore the truth and demand some changes." The liberal takeover had been made possible, Hanisch wrote, because of an emphasis on lack of structure (although Hanisch had formulated the policy in the late 1960s), particularly the stricture that there be no leadership, including no designated media spokeswomen. "The major effect of the no leadership line was to stop the pro-woman faction from continuing to take their politics to the masses of women. It simultaneously served the personal ambitions of some" (Hanisch 1975: 163).

What served to cloud discussion of their position was the Redstockings' 1975 public attack on Steinem in which she was connected to the Central Intelligence Agency because she had at one time been involved with an organization that was considered a CIA front. The implication was that Steinem and *Ms.* were agent provocateurs, part of a conscious ploy to destroy the radicalism of the movement (Heilbrun 1995: 285–87). Steinem and her handlers at *Ms.* erected a curtain of silence. "Steinem was angry at the nature of the Redstockings' attack, and she did not want to appear to legitimize the accusations with a response, especially since the regular media seemed barely interested in the story," Thom recalled (1997: 76). Despite Steinem's celebrity, the silence was generally respected by reporters and reflected the number of friends she held in the media, including women reporters, many of whom believed that the radicals' confrontational tactics were no longer newsworthy and damaged the movement as a whole. However, the issue began to brew in the women's movement: the feminist institute Sagaris rejected funding from the Ms. Foundation (followed by Steinem's six-page response), and a lengthy account appeared in the *New York Times*, unsurprisingly headlined "Dissension among the Feminists: The Rift Widens." The article noted that the FBI had designated Steinem a security risk and advised a government agency not to hire her for a consulting position because of her leftist associations (Franks 1975: 19). What the *Times* did not examine was that the FBI and perhaps the CIA did indeed infiltrate the women's movement. This fact would not come to public attention until June 1977, when a *Ms.* cover story detailed the FBI surveillance (Pogrebin 1977).

To Betty Friedan, the Redstockings' charges were not paranoid. Friedan—her own radical past perhaps an influence—had never been shy in talking about the potential threat of the CIA. Her original opposition to the public acknowledgment of lesbians in the movement suggested that nothing "could have pleased the CIA more" than this method of defining the movement (Klemesrud, "Lesbian": 47). It may have been too much to expect Friedan not to comment on the subject, given her animosity to Steinem, the infiltrations into the movement that had occurred, and her own suspicions of the CIA's role. Thus, in an interview with a United Press International wire service in Mexico City, where she was attending the International Women's Year Conference, Friedan called for Steinem to "react" to the charges. There was a "paralysis of leadership" in the movement, she said, quite possibly because of the CIA. The story appeared in the *New York Times* as "Betty Friedan Fears C.I.A. Movement Role" (*NYT* 6/23/75: 23) and thence made its way into the heartland by way of the *Times*'s news service. The public nature of the controversy encouraged Random House to publish the Redstockings' *Feminist Revolution*, which was intended to include the original Redstockings' charges against Steinem but did not because of the intervention of Steinem's lawyer. The story continued to circulate with the 1976 publication of Friedan's *It Changed My Life*, described as "a monument to innuendo" by Steinem's biographer, Carolyn G. Heilbrun. (Heilbrun also contends that the *Times* treated Steinem unfavorably because of the friendship between managing editor Abe Rosenthal and Friedan, a protection that included the reassignment of a reporter who unfavorably reviewed Friedan's *The Second Stage* [Heilbrun 1995: 301–2].) If Rosenthal had special regard for Friedan, he did not extend it to the women who worked for the newspaper, who instituted a lawsuit for equal pay and opportunity that was not settled until the 1980s (Robertson 1993).

Inside the movement, the question of Steinem's culpability boiled. Steinem was not popular in the alternative press, but the Redstockings' attack was not automatically greeted with enthusiasm. As a writer in Denver's *Big Mama Rag* put it, "While we agree with the Redstockings that 'the *Ms.* editors should come forward with more information about their unusual stockholder,' we feel that their method of combining attacks on *Ms.*' finances with attacks on the magazine's and Steinem's politics comes dangerously close to smear tactics." Fellow radicals were not above suspicion of self-promotion. Was the attack on Steinem a marketing ploy for their publication? (*BMR* 7/75: 5).

Ms. staffers closed ranks, with the exception of Willis, who made her public departure with an open letter that suggested that the Redstockings' charge should be taken more seriously. She also used the occasion to call the magazine a "propaganda organ" for the kind of politics that did not challenge the power structure. The "party line," Willis charged, "was an obsession with electoral politics, self-help, a presentation of sisterhood as sentimental papering over of divisions, an emphasis on attacking sexual roles rather than male power, and class bias reflected in the avoidance of basic economic issues" (Willis 1975: 171). (But true to the *Ms.* mission, Willis, like Morgan, who had also criticized the magazine, later returned to *Ms.*)

The episode did little to take either *Ms.* or the movement back to its leftist roots. Willis could have predicted how *Ms.* would react to an attack by one sister on another: the magazine republished Jo Freeman's article on "trashing" in the April 1976 issue (Joreen 1976). "Trashing" was described as a technique of character assassination to disparage and destroy alternative ways of thinking. But there was a kind of doublethink at work when Steinem, the most well known feminist in the country, with mass media practitioners virtually at her beck and call, was viewed as a victim of trashing at the hands of a small group that the media found no difficulty in marginalizing as wild-eyed fanatics. The episode also marked the final skirmish of radical feminism and the ascendancy of liberal feminism. For many new feminists, eagerly reading *Ms.* every month, mounting NOW actions on local levels was "radical" enough.

Stretching the Envelope of Mass Media

Ms. continued to articulate and publish articles on major issues of interest to women that had heretofore gone unrecognized. Many of its issues—with startling and compelling cover art—brought mass media attention to new subjects such as battered wives, teen sex, international women, lesbian issues, and sexual harassment. Such issues offered new content to mass media and in some permutation became part of the mass media agenda. Advertisers began to recognize that such topics appealed to a certain segment of women. In 1979, advertising researchers examined the reading habits of a new category, "feminists," compared to "moderates" and "traditionalists." "Feminists" were found to be more educated and younger than women in other categories, more likely to read newsmagazines and the *New York Times*, more likely to be Jewish, and in general to uphold the perception that feminism was "an elitist-intellectual affair." The researchers did not suggest, however, that advertisers flock to *Ms.* to reach this desirable audience; instead, the study suggested that advertisers support national and international newsmagazines (which the feminists were likely to read) to achieve "effective segmentation" (Venkatesh and Tankersley 1970: 37).

Ms. put new content on the mass media agenda, but that content was picked over by other mass media vehicles for their own benefit. Struggling to present its universal agenda, *Ms.* nonetheless was to be associated with those issues that other parts of the mass media spectrum were not so quick to address.

Ms. and Abortion

Abortion was the *Ms.* bottom line. Mass media outlets generally have few bottom lines, and those that exist are so broadly acceptable as not to draw dispute. However, *Ms.*'s unequivocal and front-page position on this confrontational topic represents an important exception. The continued legalization of abortion was on the *Ms.* agenda from the beginning. The premiere issue included a list of prominent women who had undergone abortions, and the final issue before it was taken over by Lang Communications showcased a cover with "It's War" in giant, blood-red letters (*Ms.* 8/89).

The women's movement assumed that the acceptance of legalized abortion was the initial threshold to becoming a feminist. The belief in abortion in *Ms.* functioned as the kinship belief under which all women could unite. Although *Ms.* went to great lengths to indicate that it was not antichildren—child care was often covered, a sweet baby graced an early cover, and *Ms.* staff members sometimes brought their children to the office—abortion as an issue that raised doubts among some women was not addressed in the pages of *Ms.* In her account of the magazine, Thom does not include coverage of abortion as a subject of discussion among the staff. *Ms.* appeared to reflect an initial assumption in the feminist community that to be a feminist assumed a prochoice position. In 1970, for example, the mass march in New York included as one of its three demands abortion on demand. Women who considered themselves to be feminist yet viewed acceptance of abortion with difficulty eventually were forced into splinter groups. Abortion was one subject that to *Ms.* was not debatable. Although Willis and critics of *Ms.* claimed that the magazine papered over feminist differences, coverage of abortion was always in a battle mode—the line from which feminists would never retreat. In the history of *Ms.* magazine, it was advertisers' last straw.

The Limits of Advertising

Ms.'s aim was to bring new content to a mass audience, believing that change could be accelerated when sufficient numbers of women were reached by the broad distribution that mass media allowed. But from the beginning, getting advertiser support made that goal a challenge that finally could not be overcome. Advertisers often objected to the editorial stance of the magazine, and major advertisers, such as Clairol hair coloring, pulled their advertisements when *Ms.* would not buckle to pressure. Moreover, the magazine turned down advertising that it considered detrimental to women and chose to drop the Virginia Slims cigarette account. Furthermore, some advertisers simply would not advertise in a feminist magazine that they, if not the women's Left, considered radical. The *Ms.* advertising policy was shared with readers in a 1974 article that is something of a primer on the consumer nature of women's magazines: "It wasn't women's potential as readers and opinion-makers that inspired big publishers to begin directing magazines our way—or got newspaper publishers to start women's pages, for that matter. It was our potential as consumers." But in 1974 the magazine hoped that advertisers would accept the policies of selectivity. "In general, advertisers have to show a willingness to change" (*Ms.* 1974: 56). Later, in a less sanguine article, "Sex, Lies and Advertising," Steinem expressed her bitterness that advertisers did not change (Steinem 1990). What is perhaps surprising is that Steinem, an experienced media person, had not initially understood the enormity of the advertising divide.

As *Ms.* struggled on financial shoals, media watchers at the time said they were not surprised. Even Felker, who had been instrumental in helping establish *Ms.*, eventually came to believe that the idea of a commercially sponsored, ideologically driven magazine was impossible: "I can't think of one ideological magazine that has ever made money, whether it's *Ms.* or the *New Republic* or *Nation.* The simple fact of the matter is advertisers never want to get in the middle of a fight." *Ladies' Home Journal* editor John Mack Carter noted that women's magazines survived on advertising from cosmetics, fashion, personal-care products, and packaged-food companies: "Feminist ideology is simply antithetical to those kinds of advertisers" (Farhi 1989: D1). Pogrebin put it most succinctly: the magazine "never had a problem with readers. It always had a problem with advertisers" (Kuntz 1989: E7).

In 1979 the Internal Revenue Service gave *Ms.* nonprofit status so that it could operate as an educational entity under the Ms. Foundation, saving significant postal costs and allowing fund-raising but prohibiting support of particular political candidates. Advertisers still did not rally in sufficient numbers to make the magazine financially viable, leading the foundation in 1987 to sell a controlling interest to an Australian publisher, John Fairfax, which in turn sold it to the two women who had been sent from Australia to run it. The magazine was redesigned and, critics said, became too much like any other women's magazine. In 1989 it was sold again to Lang Communications. In a final hurrah before it was sold to Lang, the same August 1989 issue that had the cover article on abortion carried the least advertising in the magazine's history. "You didn't want to position your advertisement adjacent to editorial that was loud and took strong positions," Joel Kushins, media director at the Bozell advertising agency, said at the time. "Advertisers didn't want to be in that issue" (Kuntz 1989: E17).

In 1990, Lang turned it into a subscriber-only magazine, bringing Morgan on board as its editor-in-chief. There was hope that Morgan would emphasize radical feminism. "I have not mellowed," Morgan commented in *Folio*, the magazine of the magazine industry. "There's a whole new resurgence of energy and quite justifiable rage as we enter the nineties." The strident-woman theme was emphasized when *Folio* chose to use "She's Still Angry" on its cover, although there is nothing angry in the accompanying picture (Hovey 1990). Moreover, during Morgan's three-year editorship, anger was not a particular theme, as she emphasized literature, poetry, and women on the international scene. By 1993, when Morgan left the magazine, it reportedly had two hundred thousand subscribers. Then in December 1998, after more permutations and threats of closure, a dozen investors led by Steinem and including the magazine's editor-in-chief since 1993, Marcia Ann Gillespie, operating under the name Liberty Media for Women, purchased the magazine from MacDonald Communications. In 2001 the Feminist Majority Foundation assumed ownership. Editorial and business functions of the magazine were transferred from New York to the foundation's Los Angeles offices. Steinem remains connected as a magazine figurehead.

Ms. magazine introduced new content to the mass magazine marketplace and influenced the agenda of other mass media vehicles. New content was disguised by the media traditions that had long been associated with mass women's magazines and thus served to ease *Ms.*'s way into mainstream American culture. Domestic violence, sexual harassment, and equal pay for equal work certainly soon became issues that were accepted in the broad society without a feminist framing. Some issues quickly separated from their second-wave beginnings, as even the political Right could find no argument to oppose them. As many of the issues *Ms.* had introduced became acceptable and taken on by other media outlets, *Ms.* lost—or was perceived to have lost—its edge.

As the place of *Ms.* is evaluated in second-wave American feminism, what emerges is its success in normalizing for other mass media vehicles what had been outside of mass media attention. "Sexual harassment" did not even have a name when *Ms.* introduced the subject with an issue that featured a compelling cover that used the usually comforting image of a doll to make its point (a male hand thrust into the top of the doll's dress). Similarly, the traditional enlarged head shot of an anonymous woman that graced service magazine covers was subverted when *Ms.* introduced the subject of domestic violence by using a head shot of a woman with a blackened eye.

These subversions of traditional mass media forms were in line with the techniques that had added oppositional subtext to film noir and to some of the movies and television programs of the 1950s. *Ms.* turned this process around, putting subversive content up front but normalizing or mitigating it by framing the content in ways that called on familiar mass media traditions—glossy cover art, sell lines, and the comforting familiarity of Steinem's association with the magazine. It was a seductive challenge to the charges of stridency and thus was an appropriate magazine incarnation for Steinem, whose traditional use of image seemed to give a sense of common sense to whatever she said.

Swept into this river of normalization were all the outsiders that *Ms.* chose to represent. No portion of womanhood failed to come under the umbrella of the *Ms.* inclusive view. No one was an outsider—whether or not she wanted to be. Women could be insiders, the magazine promised, by accepting the inclusive view. For readers of *Ms.*, the gender flag offered the same kind of insider status that newspaper-generated patriotism had provided for new immigrants years before.

The Limits of Inclusivity

The financial turmoil of the magazine's history has been blamed on advertisers who turned away from the magazine despite its message of broad-based sisterhood. Its high-point circulation was certainly large enough to support many magazines, but the fact that the magazine had to finally accept its role as a niche publication suggests that its editorial policy, despite its inclusivity, did not speak to or for all women. The commonalities of gender that Steinem's writing so often addressed turned out less easy to make part of the national agenda than the subjects that the magazine had introduced, and in the end, inclusivity turned out not to be an editorial policy that expanded circulation base. Radicals, for example, viewed their identity in terms of marginality, saw benefit in remaining on the edges as the way to articulate options, and found something lost when, for example, Willis was included as one voice of many under the *Ms.* umbrella.

As in the early civil rights movement, striving for integration of black and white, the *Ms.* inclusivity did not differ greatly from the American melting pot. In this universal context, difference was not essential, merely a color on the rainbow, as long as everyone agreed on the rainbow and its role as a common goal. *Ms.* assumed that all feminists agreed on the common goal of liberal feminism. Most *Ms.* readers may have done so, and to these readers, the magazine's stories on abortion, sexual harassment, domestic violence, and lesbians were radical enough. From a later distance, however, these topics seem logical pegs on the American progressive agenda.

In its time, however, especially to those outside feminism, *Ms.* represented Left politics and would continue to do so, even after some of its positions had become mainstream, because of the magazine's unshakable position on abortion. By other standards, including those of members of the Left (who might periodically appear on *Ms.* pages as house radicals), the open arms of sisterhood were not enough to make a revolution. And it might be considered that *Ms.*'s insistence that there was room at the table of sisterhood for everyone in some sense robbed marginal groups of power. The benefits of marginality evaporate when thinkers on the edge of a society are forced to come in out of the cold. Lost are the freedom to explore and to experiment, to enjoy a sense of danger, to be special, and to fail, all in relative privacy. Attention can stifle creativity, as marginal groups, now fearing its loss, turn their efforts to the defense and extension of points of view that otherwise would be fluid. Creative and intellectual freedom best occur in marginal territory, as it had in the late 1960s, when new ideas exploded from angry young women crowded into small apartments. Given a small part of a larger stage, however, radical thought after 1970 seemed to shrivel. In 1970, Robin Morgan had written "Goodbye to All That," the benchmark essay that claimed Left territory for women's issues. By 1972, when *Ms.* appeared, the leftist agenda was subsumed or dispersed.

Finally, the *Ms.* push toward inclusivity did not take into account that large numbers of American women never regarded themselves as outsiders and thus had nothing to gain from putting their foot into a feminist circle on that basis. Many strongly religious women see women as the center of family life and do not equate economic or even legal discrimination with outsider status. Ethnic and other minorities do not necessarily see themselves as marginal, however the world views them. The view of the majority culture is not necessarily mirrored in how the minority group views itself. Nor were some women quick to risk the assured security of their insider status—whether achieved through class, race, religion, ethnicity, or neighborhood—on the basis of a magazine that may have been perceived as a call to exchange traditional institutions of cultural and religious significance for the nebulous state of sisterhood. As an emphasis on multiculturalism grew and became reflected in mass media through narrowcasting and a segmented marketplace, the *Ms.* view of the world based on the commonalities of gender became less compelling. Feminism often seemed a choice to be made at the expense of any other identity, as in Shirley Chisholm's 1972 presidential candidacy, when her remark that she had been discriminated against more because of her gender than her race cost her the support of a large part of the black constituency.

Ms. was clearly a magazine of complaint. There was never any attempt to sugarcoat gender status to make problems more livable—long a function of women's mass magazines that sought to elevate the influence of home. However, the long-term maintenance of outsider status for those who want to be inside is a discomforting one. Advertising research has long indicated that consumers tire of constantly repeated messages. We may consider that such fatigue does not exclude messages from and about social movements, even those aimed at activists. For the generation of original *Ms.* readers, the fatigue may have been accelerated when juxtaposed with the successes that many of the women achieved because of growing opportunities. Some *Ms.* readers surely fell by the wayside as new chapters of their lives unfolded. It is not surprising that in its latest incarnation, *Ms.* is seeking young women readers. Like *Seventeen* magazine, *Ms.* may have to constantly court new generations of readers if it is to remain viable. Nonetheless, *Ms.* continues, with Steinem still prominent in efforts to build circulation. "I also promise you," she wrote in the 2001 letter to bring in new subscriptions, "that *Ms.* will always look at the world *as if women mattered*—all women, not just one group or another."

For most American feminists who came of age during the 1970s, *Ms.* occupies an affectionate and important place. At the time of its greatest influence, however, critics viewed the magazine as taking an opportunity for institutional change and replacing it with the traditional reform of American liberalism. Opportunity for the kind of change that radicals of the time envisioned may never have existed, but *Ms.* clearly helped to usher in a reform agenda with the media at the top of the list.

9. Efforts to Reform the Media
Print

Ms. magazine not only was an instrument calling for reform but also sought to prove that new content, new management style, new demands on advertisers, and new employment opportunities for women could exist in a mass media setting. In its first years, its success could only encourage the goal of media reform.

Most women activists considered reform of media essential to the success of the women's movement. Some women radicals believed that mass media, the "tools of the master," could neither be an instrument for reform nor be reformed. *off our backs* devoted its statement of purpose to the impossibility of the mass media ever presenting an accurate picture of women and to the corollary that the mass media could not be a lever for change: "The mass media are our enemy; no matter how seriously they may approach, no matter how enlightened they may seem, women's liberation threatens the power base of the mass media" (Ferro, Holcomb, and Saltzman-Webb 1970: 1). Such women often turned to separatist activities and established a skein of alternative newspapers and what were called "woman-identified" media businesses such as the Feminist Press and Daughters Inc. (publishing houses that aimed to give women control over publication of their works), women-owned bookstores, feminist speaking bureaus, video companies, and entertainment businesses. Olivia Records signed and promoted a considerable number of women composers and singers who played almost exclusively to female audiences. In the meantime, women's bookstores served as meeting places for feminist women and carried lesbian texts that were not easy to find in mainstream bookstores.

However, the largest group of feminists, from radical to middle of the road, looked on mass media as important to reform because of what was perceived as mass media's influence in the culture. As in demonstrations, some of the efforts to reform mass media brought various groups of women together to pursue a common objective—the assumption that to have more women in the media industries would mean that such women would work to change the antifeminist attitudes that emanated from mass media. "Newsrooms were honeycombed with closet feminists who understood that this burgeoning movement was speaking to us,

and who eventually went on to transmit the message to the world," reporter
Lindsy Van Gelder wrote in a common understanding (Van Gelder 1992: 80).

From the beginning, NOW sought media reform in tangible ways, eschewing
the radicals' consciousness-raising approach. The NOW thrusts emphasized three
areas: employment of women in media; the reform of content; and the image of
women in media. What were not challenged—and could not be through the levers
that were available—were the ownership patterns of media industries, advertising
as the base of the industry, the limitations of craft traditions, the move toward an
entertainment-based news business, or the influences of the coming new technology. In fact, media reformers seldom took the long view in their efforts to solve the
problems of the moment. From a later perspective it can be seen that the reforms
that were being instituted were occurring in a volatile, converging environment—
for example, the development of cable—that would limit their impact.

The reform of mass media had long been on the liberal agenda, in part a result
of the Adorno-Horkeimer theories of the 1940s, which had been adopted by
a range of media critics who otherwise had little in common with the socialist
outlook of that school of thought. In its 1968 examination of the causes of urban
disorder, for example, the National Advisory Commission on Civil Disorders
(the Kerner Commission) criticized the media's negative portrayal of African-
Americans and the lack of media attention to concerns of the African-American
community. Women academics, notably Gaye Tuchman, adopted the same model,
claiming that the media's stereotyped portrayal of women resulted in employment
discrimination (Tuchman 1974). NOW, of course, had held such a position from
the time of Betty Friedan's founding of the organization. Further reinforcement
came in a strong statement that was likely written or influenced by Friedan and
was made at a concurrent conference with the 1975 International Women's Year
Conference in Mexico City. The statement called on the mass media to hire and
train more women in management and as content producers, to remove stereotyping, to portray women in dynamic ways, and to insist all media employees go
through nonsexist-language training programs: "The mass communications media
have great potential as a force for social change and must exercise their significant
influence" (*Press Woman* 1/76: 10). That call for social change included the reform
of mass media, most particularly the employment of women. This thrust was in
some part because many of the activist women in the New York base were media
professionals and sought benefit for themselves; it was conjoined with the notion
that the gatekeeper holds the key to the media landscape and that, once in power,
women could reform media from the inside.

Ben Bagdikian, an editor at the *Washington Post* during these years, described
the difficulty of changing a newsroom culture in which, for example, the Associated

Press and United Press International routinely sent cheesecake photographs of women over the wire circuits simply to entertain male staffers. Bagdikian noted the response of one typical editor when UPI queried its members on the practice: "We all enjoy a good cheesecake shot. And the ones I get make the rounds and end up on bulletin boards, rarely in the paper" (*WP* 4/17/72: A22). The Associated Press Managing Editors conducted a similar poll on the same issue, finding a "wide gulf of opinion" on whether the girlie pictures should be distributed. As in the UPI poll, many editors saw the photographs as morale boosters: "One a day keeps old age away" (*E&P* 4/21/73: 16).

Reforming Employment

In 1995 Helen Thomas was asked by a *San Francisco Chronicle* reporter, "When you first started out, did you face obstacles as a woman that you might not have faced if you were a man?" Thomas answer was pithy: "Where did you come from, Mars?" (Thomas 1999: 39).

Even as news managers began to notice the white-only nature of their news-rooms in the 1960s, they were slow to recognize the gender disparities in hiring, in deployment, in promotion, and in wages. Traditionally, women in news had tended to work within the limits defined for them, replicating when they could the men-only professional organizations from which they were excluded and seeking ways to be influential in the women's news spheres they could dominate. Female journalists who sought careers outside of women's news came to believe that they could best pursue their objectives by remaining aloof from other women journal-ists, and, like foreign correspondent Georgie Ann Geyer, found that they could operate as an asexual "little sister" or be embraced as one of the boys by unques-tioningly accepting craft choices. In some cases, women reporters took on what were considered masculine traits—that is, not showing emotion to receive the ultimate compliment of being a "first-rate newspaperman" (Lumsden 1995). Anna Quindlen, beginning her career in the 1970s, said she would have "ripped my tear ducts out rather than cry" (Ricchiardi and Young 1991: 128). CBS corre-spondent Lesley Stahl was dismayed when U.S. Representative Patricia Schroeder (D-Colo.) wept as she announced that she would not run for U.S. president: "This was seen as evidence she was unfit: women are too emotional, too unstable" (Stahl 1999: 284). Women responded with stoicism and sacrifice. Charlotte Curtis did not reveal to the *New York Times* management that she had breast cancer lest it hinder chances for promotion (Greenwald 1999). The *Times*'s metro editor, Joyce Purnick, doubted that she would have been promoted if she had had a family (Dowd 1998).

Pressure for feminist action in employment was certainly coming from members of the profession whose careers were already stymied, although radicals were quick to charge "careerism," as at the *Ladies' Home Journal* action. This charge was not entirely false, for the action had been sparked by Susan Brownmiller of Media Women, an organization established by media professionals for their own advancement. Members of Media Women saw no reason why they should not be concerned with their own careers as well as no reason why this concern should preclude their involvement in other aspects of the movement. Yet some women were interested in the movement primarily for its impact on their careers. Since such women sought the destruction of barriers—standards of beauty and myths of competence, for example—that stood in the way of employment, they were not interested in changing media beyond correction of obvious concerns of image and bias. Business could continue as usual (once the most grievous prejudices had been eliminated), if it included a full complement of women.

That thrust was exemplified in 1974 when the organization Media Women (of *Ladies' Home Journal* fame) published a collection of essays, *Rooms with No View: A Woman's Guide to the Man's World of the Media* (Strainchamps 1974). The sixty-five mostly anonymous contributors offered compelling voices from within, telling how it was for women across a swath of media industries—stories of similarities in entry-level difficulties, in barriers to promotion, and in salary discrepancies. However, unlike the writings of Left women on media, none of the short essays addressed issues beyond employment. In that focus, a similar collection of essays could have been published for just about any of the nation's industries. The fact that a book aimed to a general audience from a major publisher (Harper and Row) was considered appropriate for the media industry and not for other industries or institutions speaks to the glamour of media in the United States (as well as the natural tendency of media workers to express themselves by way of media). The book pointed up that reform of media along employment lines carried with it the implicit promise of media reforms that would affect all women.

The publicity brought to the hiring disparities in media clearly helped to bring about change. In its coverage of the *Ladies' Home Journal* sit-in, even *Advertising Age* pointed out that the *Journal* did not have a woman among its thirty-two sales representatives, nor did the other service magazines (*AA* 3/26/70: 1). Advertising directors were not apologetic about the lack, explaining that their male clients were not eager to deal with female salespersons. (Cathleen Black, in her job as a saleswoman for *Ms.* magazine, has frequently said that she was able to get into many offices simply because the clients wanted to see what a woman salesperson looked like.) In print, using the major tool of the EEOC, and in broadcast, using the lever of the license renewal process, legal suits and complaint and petition procedures became the name of change.

Time magazine came in for particular attention, since the magazine's policy of refusing to allow women writers was well known and since more than one of those rejected women had become active in the movement. In May 1970, 102 editorial employees at Time Inc.—mostly women who worked as researchers at *Time, Fortune, Sports Illustrated,* and Time-Life Books—filed a complaint with New York state's Division of Human Rights. By July, as noted earlier, B. J. Phillips led the way as the magazine quietly reformed its hiring practices.

One of the unintended consequences of passing off women's movement stories to women reporters was that the women reporters, who may have been reluctant to take on the assignment, nonetheless began to recognize their situations in the stories they covered. Lynn Povich, once a *Newsweek* researcher, recalled, "The news-magazines were traditionally all-female researchers, and all the writers were men and certainly all the editors were men. And we sort of, those of us who covered the women's movement, got religion when the women's movement happened. And we were reading about it and covering it and saying, 'Hey you know, this is us.' I mean here we are, many of our women are as well-educated as the men who are hired as writers" (O'Brien 1999). Nan Robertson's account of the women's activism at the *New York Times* describes Grace Glueck's experience in 1969 as a kind of epiphany. When the publisher committed the paper to the increased hiring of minorities, Glueck asked, "What about us women? We're half the population. We've got the education, there isn't any cultural gap, and still we aren't getting anywhere on this newspaper either—it is totally dominated by white men" (Robertson 1992: 134). At the sight of another memo later in the year announcing the promotion of four men to high positions, Glueck was moved to question the publisher in writing about women's careers at the *Times.* The timing of Glueck's epiphany speaks to the place the women's movement had made for itself in the national culture by 1969.

Glueck's experience was the start of a long road at the *Times,* culminating in a suit against the newspaper by a women's caucus led by the Timeswoman Betsy Wade. After being fired by the *New York Tribune* when her pregnancy became known, Wade was hired by the *Times* in 1957 as the paper's first female copy editor. When she arrived to take her place at the copy editor's rim of the traditional horseshoe desk, "a whimsical assistant put a ruffle around the paste pot near me." She was posed for a photograph for the *Times*'s in-house magazine (Wade 2002).

More than ten years later, when a 1972 complaint to the EEOC had produced no changes, Wade, now chief of the copy desk, became the lead of the seven named plaintiffs in a suit against the newspaper. As the suit progressed, the *Times* made some efforts to address some of the concerns, one result being the 1977 hiring of Anna Quindlen (Ricchiardi and Young 1991: 125). However, the paper refused any official agreement until a 6 October 1978 federal court order required it.

The *Times* was notably unapologetic. Wade later served as the first woman president of the New York local of the Newspaper Guild and was a popular travel columnist at the paper until her retirement.

At *Newsweek,* Povich and other women affected by the movement they covered approached the American Civil Liberties Union in New York, which was headed by Eleanor Holmes Norton, who agreed to take the case on the basis that the *Newsweek* masthead clearly indicated that the men were at the top and the women were at the bottom. "And *Newsweek,* of course, was shocked and horrified that its women hadn't come to them and said, 'We have this problem, what's the matter,' so and so forth," Povich recalled. "And we said, you know, we've seen the men here who are your most valuable writers and most valuable editors, and if they complain about something, nothing happens. Why would you even listen to the most, the bottommost, disenfranchised numbers of your thing? So they settled. They are a very liberal organization; they obviously didn't want any trouble" (O'Brien 1999).

The women at *Newsweek* had chosen to be very public about their discontent in order to embarrass Katharine Graham's magazine. Using the tactics of the second wave as their example, the women timed the release of their complaint to the Equal Employment Opportunity Commission to coincide with the Monday morning newsstand appearance of the *Newsweek* cover story, "Women in Revolt." To make sure the irony would not to go unnoticed, the women called a news conference and telephoned their contacts at other organizations. "The editor may justifiably grumble that the women should have come to his office first, but the women believed it was the public nature of their action that produced results," according to one assessment (Diamond 1970: 17). However, *Newsweek's* sister publication, the *Washington Post*, gave the announcement short shrift (and failed to mention the newspaper's connection to the magazine) but quoted *Newsweek's* response that the women were demanding "the establishment of quotas"—a hot-button phrase if ever there was one (*WP* 5/28/72: A4). Nonetheless, the next month the *Post* management pledged to increase "as fast as possible" women in middle and upper management (*WP* 6/2/72: C4). Changes were not fast enough for the *Post* women. In 1974, the EEOC upheld the Newspaper Guild's charges that *Post* women were paid less, were promoted less, and were discriminated against on the basis of marriage and child status.

The premiere wire service, the Associated Press, had been closed to most women reporters despite the existence of one major female reporter, Frances Lewine, who had covered the White House women's beat since the days of Eisenhower. However, a changing culture and a new emphasis on lifestyle issues encouraged the AP to establish a special bureau that included four women and one man (Sherr 1972). These changes were not sufficient to deter the Wire Service Guild from preparing a statistical analysis of thousands of personnel documents subpoenaed from the AP. But it took ten years of litigation for the suit, beginning in 1973, to be concluded. At its 1983 settlement the consent decree, in which the AP did not admit any violation of nondiscrimination laws, set a goal of 37 percent women for entry-level reporting and editing jobs as well as goals for female promotion. A fifty-thousand-dollar fund for the training of women was set aside. However, the same decree provided nearly half a million dollars for black reporters, with most of the money earmarked for an affirmative action plan specifically designed to bring black reporters and editors to the AP.

Publishing

Robin Morgan, at the 1968 Grove Press sit-in, was an early activist in seeking to open employment practices in the publishing industry. It was widely known that the industry routinely hired female graduates of the Seven Sisters colleges as clerical help at appallingly low wages while young men out of college were immediately put on the editorial track. "The young men would be made associate editors straight out of Yale, but the women were the handmaidens of the male editors," according to Nan Talese of Random House (Feldman 1997: 84).

Some women rose to prominence under the difficult circumstances and needs of the time, including Helen Meyer, the president of Dell when that company purchased the paperback rights to *The Feminine Mystique*, and Phyllis Grann, who rose to be chief executive officer of Penguin Putnam. But not until 1973 was Meyer admitted to the exclusive Publishers' Lunch Club (limited to 125 company officer members). By 1984, there were 10 female members; in 1997, 29 of the 103 active members were women (Feldman 1997: 83).

As NOW's EEOC campaign began to bring attention to gender disparities, a few women began to rise in the publishing ranks. Doubleday hired Betty Prashker after the federal government indicated that it would not give business to the company unless it had a better female hiring record. Five years later, Prashker had purchased what would become a best-seller, Kate Millett's *Sexual Politics*, one proof that women in the right positions could make a difference. But like other women, Prashker found herself at a professional disadvantage when she was not allowed to join New York's Century Association, "founded by gentlemen for the pleasure of gentlemen" (Feldman 1997: 85).

As in other spheres of media, women in publishing sought legal redress. Group and class-action suits were brought by female employees against *Reader's Digest*; Houghton Mifflin; Addison-Wesley; Allyn and Bacon; Little, Brown; and Macmillan. As in the newspaper media, suits were not settled for years after they were instituted. In 1986 Macmillan agreed to pay $1.9 million as a result of a 1978 suit that had been brought by four women but came to cover fifteen hundred women.

Not all women sought redress of grievances by legal means. In San Francisco women took several direct actions aimed at reform of print and broadcast. Nine women from the Women's Liberation Front disrupted the annual meeting of CBS stockholders, claiming that the network was presenting derogatory images of women, or, as *Advertising Age* put it, "Militant Femmes Shake Up CBS' Annual Meeting" (*AA* 4/27/70: 8). In July 1970 women smashed two front windows of the *San Francisco Chronicle* and left a letter to the editor demanding an end to "chauvinistic news coverage" (*Spokes* 8/28/70: 5). Another fifty women marched into the publisher's office of the *Chronicle* and presented a list of demands (Davis, F. 1991: 114). While such real militancy anchored the theme of stridency, quieter means did not always work. Twenty-five female editorial employees of Atlanta Newspapers, publisher of the city's two major dailies, signed a petition questioning story assignments, hiring practices, and salary discrimination, to no avail. The organization hired two women in 1970—a copy editor and a dictationist—while adding twelve male reporters. As one of the women told an interviewer for a professional magazine, "Three of the women on the *Journal* city desk are doing junk work, and when they ask for full-fledged reporting jobs, they are told more experience is necessary and the paper will be happy to find them a job on a weekly. Meanwhile, the paper blithely hires male interns right out of college." Moreover, when the women posted a petition seeking supporting signatures of male reporters, the jovial responses included "Donald Duck" and "Tiny Tim" (*CJR* 7/71: 37).

Nonetheless, one by one, managers in the nation's media centers found themselves facing, at a minimum women's caucuses and increasingly the Newspaper Guild, demanding equal opportunities for male and female members. Because suits were settled slowly, with settlements often not finally agreed upon until the 1980s, a more conservative era, managers were slow to instigate changes and negotiations were reinstituted at *Newsweek*, ABC-TV, and the *New York Times*. At the same time, new women coming into media businesses without the experience of second-wave activism were less likely to carry the burden of leadership (Robertson 1992).

Reform of Professional Institutions

Accompanying the claims of women for hiring and promotion was a similar call that women be included in journalists' professional organizations. Women sought to integrate them for the same reasons NOW had sought to integrate previously all-male organizations—access to industry gossip, business connections, sociability with people of shared values, and support in the drive for equal opportunity. Journalistic organizations share these characteristics, and like all professional organizations, they play a role in shaping the product as it comes to the public. In publishing circles, networking was often accomplished by means of private clubs to which women were refused membership. The city of New York eventually sued the Century Association, which had rejected Prashker, and the similarly discriminatory University Club.

Sigma Delta Chi, the major professional organization for working journalists, did not accept women members until November 1969, sixty years after its founding. (Ann Landers was in the first group of ten women who joined the Chicago chapter.) The following year, three women—Ann Landers, Charlayne Hunter, and Katharine Graham—integrated the previously all-male convention program. In Washington, Helen Thomas led the charge to integrate the professional organizations that served reporters covering the national beat, including the handful of ambitious women—Bonnie Angelo of *Time*, Sarah McClendon for a group of southwestern newspapers and broadcast outlets, and Frances Lewine of the Associated Press—all of whom strongly resented being kept away from the newsworthy functions of the male-only National Press Club. Called "the Witches of Washington" by a visiting British journalist, "harpies" by Jacqueline Kennedy, and "formidable" by Barbara Walters (Healey 1970: 3), these women gained stories under difficult circumstances but were likely to be viewed as eccentric. This was particularly true for McClendon, whose humorous treatment by John F. Kennedy in news conferences set the style that allowed women reporters to be affectionately tolerated but not seriously considered. Thomas, who did not escape that same amused tolerance in press conferences, subsequently integrated the White House Correspondents Association and the Gridiron Club.

In the meantime, the women's movement energized the generally conservative regional women's press associations that heretofore had demonstrated little leadership in changing women's position in the journalistic professions. By the mid-1970s the National Federation of Press Women devoted an issue of its national publication to the struggle for women in broadcasting (*Press Woman* 4/76).

Changes in Content

The National Conference of Editorial Writers lacked a prohibition against women members but had few simply because there were few female editorial writers in the country. One of them, Dorothy Nordyke of the *Amarillo (Texas) Globe Times*, found herself the only female participant at the group's 1968 conference. When she queried her colleagues about why there were so few women editorial writers, the replies give some understanding to why the second wave got some short shrift in editorial columns. John J. Kerrigan of the *Trenton Times* told her, "Men reach conclusions on logical progression. Women jump to conclusions using intuition rather than logic. And it could be the public finds it hard to accept opinions of women as being as strong as those of men." An unidentified editorial writer responded, "A woman editorial writer wouldn't know what she was thinking until she typed it out" (Nordyke 1969: 30). By 1971, David Gillespie of the *Charlotte (North Carolina) Observer* found himself impressed when a panel of feminists, including NOW founder Pauli Murray, spoke to the group: "There wasn't a 'kook' on the panel. Editorial writers who were prepared to poke fun at the subject found themselves sitting up and listening. This wasn't a group of bra-burners or a contingent interested only in standing at the bar of McSorley's Ale House" (Gillespie 1970–71: 13). In the same year, Desmond Stone, a judge in editorial writing for the Pennsylvania Women's Press Association contest, was so impressed with the winners that he had the entries reprinted for the national organization: "Frankly, I was not prepared either for the excellence of some of the writing or for the number of women writing editorials in Pennsylvania. Both discoveries were vastly encouraging" (Stone, D. 1971: 41). This surprise at basic competencies is disturbing when it is considered that these were men whose editorials were expected to exert leadership in their communities.

The decision to permit female membership in Sigma Delta Chi led the organization, by way of its magazine, *The Quill*, to examine gender in reporting practices. A woman sports reporter who had not been allowed in the press box at Yale University presented her views on discrimination by male reporters (*E&P* 8/23/69: 60). Another woman reporter described as "a 27-year-old housewife and full-time consumer reporter," called for hiring women for all beats, not just the women's pages (Janensch 1970: 31). By 1972, *The Quill* published Pam Sebastian Kohler's article that moved discussion from basic hiring concerns to issues of content. Kohler decried the framing of stories about women in terms of body images. "Whether she is a princess or a waitress, a congressman or a secretary, a woman cannot escape the stigma of her body in the news columns" (Kohler 1972: 26). Respondents to the Kohler article were positive, but all were quick to note that the editors had chosen to illustrate the article with a photograph of Kohler when they had not used photographs of the other male reporters in the series.

Lynn Sherr had also written about her new expanded job at the Associated Press in *The Quill*. In the spring of 1970, AP, with fanfare at its annual meeting, introduced its "Living Today" department, whose five women and one man

(Jurate Kazickas, Ann Blackman, Dee Wedemeyer, Ann Hencken, Sherr, and Dick Blystone) covered youth and lifestyle issues in a dramatic expansion of what had been Joy Miller's women's beat. In her *Quill* article, Sherr described her role as the "Chief Cause Watcher," which included the women's movement, and it was on that beat that she covered the 1970 march. Sherr's coverage of the march serves as an example of a reporter seeking to represent the women's movement without bias but within the parameters of an appeal to a perceived construct of traditional women. As she later wrote in another professional magazine, the *Columbia Journalism Review*, Sherr chose to frame her march story in terms of its affect on a housewife-observer. "I abandoned the radicals and found a Queens housewife— daughter of a longshoreman, niece of a policeman, wife of an architect and mother of two—to follow around. It was an enlightening day. Especially when we went for drinks at the Men's Bar at the Biltmore Hotel. The bartender asked if we were over 18. The gentlemen applauded" (Sherr 1972: 37).

By avoiding the radicals as her story focus, Sherr clearly sought to avoid the long shadow of stridency considered so harmful to the movement. However, in telling the movement story in terms of its acceptability to a working-class women, she rubbed off what she considered the rough edges of the movement. The price of that acceptability was dropping those ideas that had been accompanied by radicals and, indeed, stridency. Like the writers of *Ms.* and the many feminists who espoused liberal feminism, Sherr sought to expand the number of places at the table without upsetting it, indicating the mass media's tendency, when faced with social-change stories, to search for the middle ground that does not endanger structures already in place. Sherr was not unlike many women in media who agreed with the principles of the movement and often found themselves shaping movement stories in ways that downplayed what they considered the destructive elements of stridency. Nora Ephron recalled the pull at the time: "I am a writer and I am a feminist, and the two seem to be constantly in conflict" (Ephron 1991: 98).

Stylistic Changes

Concern for image became the most common change of content, including image as carried by the framing of language. Feminist critics of newspapers had long decried the use of *girls* to identify women; the use of *housewife* or *homemaker* as the prime adjective for a woman, no matter how extraordinary her exploits; and the use of the phrase *women's lib*. When the American Symphony Orchestra named a female executive director, the *Philadelphia Evening Bulletin* was in line with the traditions of the time when it headlined the story "Girl, 23, Named Executive of

Stokowski's Symphony" (*Evening Bulletin* 3/5/70: 38). In 1971, the editor and women staff members of Stanford University's student newspaper challenged a set of guidelines published by the Associated Press Managing Editors Association, saying that they maintained stereotypes that promoted women's secondary view of themselves. These objections reached a professional audience when they were reprinted in the *Columbia Journalism Review* (Durham 1971). Interestingly, the battle for image was fought on two fronts: that women should not be framed as secondary to men, and that stereotypes affected women's sense of self.

As style changes were just being considered at most newspapers, two editors of the *Washington Post*, Ben Bradlee and Charles Seib, wrote unambiguous memos to their editorial staffs: "Words like divorcee, grandmother, blonde, or housewife should be avoided in all stories where, if a man were involved, the words divorce, grandfather, blonde or householder would be inapplicable," Bradlee wrote. He warned of the pitfalls of "first women" stories: "Stories involving the achievement of women are often implicitly condescending. They imply 'pretty good for a woman.' There always will be a place in a good newspaper for stories of achievement, but they should be written without a trace of condescension." Seib warned of phrases such as "leggy blondes" (*E&P* 7/25/70: 13). These edicts did not change long-ingrained practices overnight. A reader complained that the *Post* headline writers continued to refer to women as *girls*, in one case using the word to describe a forty-five-year-old nun (*WP* 6/19/72: A21). And the *Post*, in an area outside of Bradlee's authority, continued to divide its lucrative help-wanted advertisements by gender, while the company's newsmagazine, *Newsweek*, was slow to retreat from its hoary stereotypes.

However, many media companies adopted updated guidelines. In 1974, McGraw-Hill produced "Guidelines for Equal Treatment of the Sexes in McGraw-Hill Company Publications." Scott, Foresman issued a similar policy in "Guidelines for Improving the Image of Girls in Textbooks" (*PW* 4/74: 5). The news media often lagged. In 1977, Patricia Carbine of *Ms.* magazine told a group of national newspaper editors that women were still underreported and reported inaccurately, noting that the *New York Times* resisted the use of *Ms.* as an honorific (*NYT* 4/1/77: 28). In that year AP and UPI finally adopted stylebooks that called for equal treatment of gender and warned against sexist references, condescending phrases, and stereotyping. Not until 1987 would the *Times* permit the use of *Ms.* Judged by its reporting textbooks, journalism education was most resistant of all (Steiner 1992).

Although the *Times* came late to the use of *Ms.*, Max Frankel instituted an examination of the newspaper's traditions. Frankel dropped engagement notices on the rationale that these were self-proclaimed positions. Men and women began to appear in the pictures of married couples, along with note of their ages and the bride's career. These practices are not as trivial as they first might appear, as the *Times*'s new policy meant it had to provide rationales for its choices beyond the social prominence of the families. Merit on the part of both members of the couple became a new value, although the merit itself was measured by traditional standards. But the *Times*'s acceptance of the new measures nonetheless gave the paper's imprimatur to the acceptance and importance of careers for women, the acceptability of women over thirty as brides, and the acceptability of marriages of couples of mixed race and religion. These changes were arguably more influential to society as a whole than other newspapers' practice of dropping wedding and engagement notices in favor of paid classified advertisements (Van Gelder 1978: 116). Of course, many smaller newspapers, knowing the nature of their readership and seeing no benefit in forcing their judgments of success on newly married couples, clung to traditional ways, including full-length photographs of brides and lengthy descriptions of bridal wear.

Women's section editors were not unified about change in their pages. At a 1973 conference at the University of Missouri, one women's page editor thought her readers were getting tired of "stories about liberation, abortions, amid all their concerns about getting kids to school and the price of beef and other foods." The women's editor of the *Seattle Times* called for moderation: "In their quest for 'new' subjects to write about, [women's sections] went overboard on social issues and attention grabbers. They became filled with articles on rape, poverty, prostitution, venereal disease, alcoholism, sterilization, illegitimacy, homosexuality, malnutrition" (Almquist 1973: 28). An academic pushed for change: "Women are no longer expected to just write three or four graf engagement announcements. They are expected to do in-depth reporting" (Williamson, L. 1973: 14). The writer for the *Holyoke (Massachusetts) Transcript* seemed to fit the new bill, describing her stories on news that concerned women—why men composed the majority of jurors at rape trials and the connection between welfare and the status of women (Corea 1971).

Clearly, however, coverage of the women's movement did not necessarily mean increased coverage of issues that involved women. For some editors, coverage of the movement was enough. And for careerist women reporters, covering women's issues still brought the risk of being labeled and confined. A few reporters, such as Ellen Goodman, wrote about the women's issues that had been raised by the movement, including the widening wage gap between men and women (Goodman, "Wage Gap"). Vivian Gornick, a staff writer at the *Village Voice* from 1969 to 1977, covered both the movement and issues that involved women. Interestingly, while the *Times*'s Judy Klemesrud covered the women's movement—a fifth of her total work—most of her other stories were not related to women, and many were celebrity profiles. Goodman, Gornick, and Ephron were among a handful of reporters who went to the next step, actually covering women's issues without a hook to the movement itself.

Other journalistic conventions have been slow to change and in a 1989 report, Kathy Bonk's Communications Consortium reported that three major papers (the *Chicago Tribune*, the *Houston Chronicle*, and *USA Today*) referenced women an average of 50 percent of the time, while the nation's most important newspaper, the redoubtable *New York Times*, referenced women just 5 percent of the time. *USA Today*, owned by Gannett, which had made female hiring a priority, had 41 percent of its bylined stories written by women, correlating the claim that an increased number of women reporters would result in more women finding their way onto the news agenda. The *New York Times*, the newspaper that had the fewest female bylines, also had the fewest references to women (WMM 1989). Friedan, founder of a new organization, Women, Men, and Media, said that women in media were coming up against "a glass ceiling, women only going so far" (*USA Today* 4/10/89: 11A).

Women in Management

By 1975, the call for more women in management was high on the agenda of media reform, encouraged by the activities of the United Nations World Conference on International Women's Year. An accompanying conference adopted a platform for media reform premised on the idea that a reformed portrayal of women would speed their integration into the mainstream and that this could best be accomplished by women in management who "encourage the critical review within the media of the image of women projected" (*Press Woman* 1/76: 10).

In 1974, Carol Sutton became the first woman to be made managing editor of a major U.S. daily, the *Louisville Courier-Journal*, a position she attained by taking a secretarial job as her first step. Her rise had also come through the women's section of the newspaper, which she had revised into the coverage of wide-ranging social issues. In 1979, she became a senior editor, overseeing both the *Courier-Journal* and the *Louisville Times*, and in that position recruited journalists from minority groups. At Sutton's death in 1985, Irene Nolan, the assistant managing editor of the *Courier-Journal*, described Sutton as "a role model and an inspiration for a generation of young journalists, especially women" (McFadden 1985: B8). In 1980, Mary Ann Dolan, then thirty-two, was made managing editor of the *Los Angeles Herald-Examiner*, another meteoric rise considering her start writing engagement notices for the *Washington Star*. At that time, Jean Shirley Taylor, assistant editor at the *Los Angeles Times*, was on the track that led her to the city editor and managing editor positions. Cathleen Black was made publisher of *USA Today* in 1983, then became president of the American Newspaper Publishers Association, and in the 1990s became president of Hearst Magazines. In 1988, Valerie Salembier, who had begun her work life as a receptionist at Time-Life and in 1970 was the first female sales representative at *Newsweek,* was named publisher of *TV Guide,* an organization that had never had a woman above the ranks of middle management. By some hand of feminist justice, she later became publisher of that opponent of feminism, *Esquire.* By 1985, Geneva Overholser, who had begun as a general assignment reporter on the *Colorado Springs Sun* in 1971, was writing about foreign affairs on the editorial board of the *New York Times,* a post she left to become editor of the *Des Moines Register* and subsequently a columnist with the Washington Post Writers Group.

Some achievements of these and other women were helped by a commitment to the hiring and promotion of women made by media companies. Gannett, the nation's largest newspaper owner then and now, was the prime company in establishing routes to management, thanks to its chief executive, Al Neuharth. In 1974, Neuharth hired the first woman publisher for a Gannett newspaper. In 1982, when *USA Today* was launched, three of its six managing editors were women. Cathleen Black, who had begun as a saleswoman at *Ms.* magazine, was soon hired as president of the national newspaper and then was made its publisher. Black had the highest profile of Gannett's eighty-eight publishers, and by 1989 22 percent of them were women. Four women sat on Gannett's board. But Neuharth was disappointed that his lead was not followed: "Journalists and editorialists generally are much better at preaching than practicing proper behavior" (Neuharth 1989: 246). By the end of the 1980s, a study for Women, Men, and Media indicated that women accounted for just 6 percent of top positions in media management (WMM 1989). In the *Wall Street Journal's* view, progress for women in media industries was "paltry" (*WSJ* 4/10/89: B1).

David Lawrence Jr. executive editor of the *Detroit Free Press,* put some blame on women themselves, saying that they did not put themselves forward lest they be considered strident and demanding. He suggested that "women need to do a little bit of consciousness-raising themselves" (LaRocque 1983: 9). Sally Quinn, a well-known reporter for the *Washington Post's* "Style" section (and briefly a CBS morning television anchor) also blamed women for their own problems. "There are so many jealous bitches," she said in an interview in the trade magazine *Editor and Publisher.* "Just let one woman rise from the crowd and other women delight in tearing her down. Those Libbers who make the most noise get nowhere. And those of us who rise above them are the quietest. We don't like to rock the boat" (Scott 1974: 22).

The changes in hiring in the print media were spurred by a variety of sources: the industry's concern with avoiding lawsuits, the belief among some companies that such hiring was the right thing to do, and, not least, the pressures brought by a time of declining newspaper readership. Indeed, by the 1980s, newspaper managers had begun looking for ways to meet the challenges of readership decline. Newspapers initiated readership surveys, underwent redesigns, introduced computer graphics, and provided zoned editions so as not to lose readers who moved from the cities to the suburbs. The concept of news moved beyond the political world and, as storytelling and consumer news began to take on a larger role, the hiring of women reporters was not far behind (Haiman 1982). As Al Neuharth put it, women reporters and women managers made good business sense: "A company in the information business will not long be successful if it ignores or neglects any segment of its audience" (LaRocque 1983: 5).

One bastion that finally began to change was the women's service magazines, routinely headed by male editors. On the rocket trail of celebrity after her best-selling book, Helen Gurley Brown had early on convinced Hearst to allow her to put in place a *Sex and the Single Girl* magazine version of the book. Brown's imprint on *Cosmopolitan*, and perhaps on the culture, is legendary, and the success of the magazine served to encourage the establishment of *Playgirl*, which took readers to places at which *Cosmopolitan*'s cover sell lines (however broadly) only hinted. But most affected by the movement was Lenore Hershey, who pushed to become the new editor of *Ladies' Home Journal* after the sit-in awakened her to her own ambitions (Hershey 1983). Hershey was followed by other women in other magazines. The number of women executive editors and editorial department heads grew substantially in the "seven sisters" magazines from three top female executives in 1965 to fifteen in 1985. On the second tier, departmental heads, male employment dropped from twenty to just four, while female employment in those positions grew from thirty-eight to fifty-five during this period (Joliffe and Catlett 1994: 803). The new women editorial managers arrived at a time when the women's service magazines were trying to fit their traditional roles into the changing world of women in the 1970s. This represented an effort not only to keep editorial content current but also to please advertisers, with their traditionally strong influence on the service magazines.

Reforming Images

From the activist feminist standpoint, reform of media employment was one way to reach a goal of the reform of women's images in media, a reform that was seen to affect women's perceptions of themselves. As Germaine Greer told *off our backs*, "The first move any women's movement must make is to raise the self-image of women the same way that the black movement found it could accomplish nothing without raising the self-image of the black people" (*oob* 6/24/71: 4). In the concern for raising self-image, feminists turned to the images of women in advertising in the belief that demeaning advertising images were powerful not only in the way men thought of women but also in how women came to view themselves. *Ms.* recognized the general second-wave disgust with advertising images by insisting on a rigorous review of advertisements submitted to the magazine, a policy that resulted in the rejection of the substantial Virginia Slims account. Meantime, the *Ms.* "Click" column brought attention to advertisements that women found objectionable and served as a consciousness-raising tool.

Florynce Kennedy saw an attack on advertisers as the lever (the "testicular lever," as she called it) that would work to end media-promulgated misinformation about the movement. Kennedy and five men carrying signs disrupted the New York Advertising Club's Andy Awards in 1970, holding up the program for some twenty minutes (as police were called) while Kennedy "harangued" the audience (*AA* 2/16/70: 2, 16). At an abortion rally in Washington, she called for a boycott of companies "that sponsor talk shows and other programs that treat women's liberation as a joke" (*WP* 5/16/71: A28). However, the approach to advertising as a lever of overall media reform did not have as much broad interest as the reform of the advertising message itself. For women of the second wave, the images of women in advertising hit a nerve like no other. NOW's early campaign aimed at the airline slogan "Fly me, I'm Cheryl" was deconstructed into multiple meanings.

The campaign against negative advertising was affected by the same belief in the efficacy of mass media that underlay other reforms of media. "The real-life mirrors are the media," Lucy Komisar wrote, "and for women the invidious mirror of all is advertising." The ubiquity of advertising, the skill of its practitioners, and the male influences on the industry made it, Komisar said, a "propaganda machine for a male supremacist society. It spews out images of women as sex mates, housekeepers, mothers and menial workers—images that perhaps reflect the truest status of most women in society, but which also make it increasingly difficult for women to break out of the sexist stereotypes that imprison them" (Komisar 1971: 207). Columnist Ellen Goodman looked specifically at pharmaceutical advertising for tranquilizers targeted at male physicians: "The woman here is portrayed as a passive dependent victim, bringing her problems, typically, to a man to solve. This is a pervasive view of women, the weaker sex, training to lean on a man's shoulder" (Goodman, "Keep Her Chained"). Academic researchers made similar conclusions, first in a 1971 survey (Courtney and Lockertz 1971). In 1974, after examining two decades of women's images in women's magazines, researchers found fewer examples than of women portrayed as housewives than in 1971 but nonetheless concluded, "The overall results would appear to corroborate feminist charges that the images of women reflected in ads are quite narrow" (Sexton and Haberman 1974: 46).

Protests against demeaning images had been part of the early protests, as in the Miss America contest. At the June 1970 Special House Subcommittee hearings on discrimination against women, Komisar cited a diverse list of products whose advertising she declared to be demeaning to women and indicated that NOW would be boycotting some of the products (Komisar, "Advertising"). In August, the Women's Strike for Equality called for the boycott of Silva Thins cigarettes, Ivory Liquid soap, Pristine (a feminine hygiene product), and *Cosmopolitan* magazine, but calls for boycott faded in the day's activities. Unlike the United Farm Workers, NOW, in 1970 or later, was never able to mount a successful national boycott, even of products that crossed interest groups. Feminists sought to build on the already existing objections that toys were too violent, unsafe, or militaristic by protesting the passive stereotypical nature of toys for girls, with some success (*NYT* 5/12/71: 38). Turning away from boycotts, NOW returned to its tried-and-true system of publicity tactics. At its 1970 national convention, the organization devised the campaign "Barefoot and Pregnant Awards for Advertising Degrading for Women." Chapters were urged to select local advertisers for the designation and to send press releases to local media.

The New York NOW chapter, however, eschewed the barefoot and pregnant designation in favor of the less off-putting "Old Hat Award," which went not to the manufacturers of the designated products but to their advertising agencies, a difference that pointed to the professional media membership of the New York chapter. Thus, the Leo Burnett agency rather than American Tobacco was considered responsible for the Virginia Slims campaign, which was seen as distorting women's liberation for commercial purposes (Sloane 1971). This most famous campaign was launched in 1968 by a company that had pioneered advertising as dramatic stories. The cigarette campaign, filmed in sepia, featured a series of satiric fictional historical events in the early suffrage movement. In the first commercial an announcer intoned that a "Pamela Benjamin" was caught smoking in a gazebo. "She got a severe scolding and no supper than night." The voice continued, "In 1915, Mrs. Cynthia Robinson was caught smoking in the cellar behind the preserves. Although she was thirty-four, her husband sent her straight to her room. Then, in 1920, women won their rights." The ad concluded in color, with a model smoking a cigarette against the jingle, "You've come a long way." Print followed the same format. By all accounts, the campaign succeeded in attracting new female smokers, who may have considered that responding to the campaign was a way of declaring some kind of symbolic allegiance to issues in the women's movement.

In 1971, New York NOW continued the professional thrust with a "Dialogue with Women Program" that included representatives of seventeen agencies on the issues of advertising and women. "I was much more impressed than I thought I would be," Reva Korda, a senior vice president of Ogilvie and Mather told the *New York Times* (*NYT* 1/18/71: A52). In this workshop and in other dealings with the profession, the NOW chapter took pride in following the craft traditions for professional presentations. As Midge Kovacs commented, "You know we're the most conservative of the women's groups and we're working within the society. All we want to do is effect change in advertising through a reasonable approach" (*NYT* 8/26/71: A63). In addition to its picket lines, the NOW group also met with the offending agencies, including the Willie Free agency responsible for the "Fly Me" campaign. "It was very nasty," Kovacs recalled. "They were annoyed at us for putting the spotlight on them. They thought we were frivolous." (By contrast, she noted, the Olivetti people set up a breakfast for the picketers.) Kovacs's group also set up slide presentations for most branches of the media (Kovacs 1998). In four articles in *Advertising Age* from 1970 to 1972, Kovacs, who led the NOW assault on advertising images, bombarded professional decision makers with reasons why they should change their images (Kovacs, "Are Your Ads"; Kovacs, "Where Is Woman's Place?" Kovacs, "Women Simply"; Kovacs, "Women's Rights Drive").

Feminists of the period could offer hundreds of examples of images, as Komisar put it, that "legitimize the idealized, stereotyped roles of woman as temptress, wife, mother, and sex object, and portray women as less intelligent and more dependent than men" (Komisar 1971: 211). Komisar initiated a personal effort that caught the national eye. At her own expense, Komisar had stickers made that read "This Ad Exploits Women" and began to affix them to offensive subway posters (Komisar 1998). The sticker idea was soon picked up by NOW chapters as a guerrilla action that individual women could accomplish. In 1970 the *New York Times Magazine* used the sticker motif as the illustration accompanying one of the major articles on the movement, Susan Brownmiller's "Sisterhood Is Powerful."

Push from the Inside

Of all media business, none had more barriers to women in positions of authority than advertising. As in publishing, college advertising majors who were women began as clerical workers in agencies, while male counterparts entered on the career track. Once in the business, women were allowed to work only on those accounts that sought to attract women purchasers. A few women nonetheless managed to rise to prominence: Franchelle Cadwell was president of the Cadwell Davis and received awards from the Art Directors Club and the Copy Club;

Diane Gartner, was vice president for research at Dunkel and Charlies and a member of NOW; Jane Trahey was president of Trahey-Wolf; Ann Tolstoi Foster was vice president of J. Walter Thompson, the largest agency in the world at the time; Amelia Kaufman Bassin, was creative services director and vice president of Faberge. In 1963 Carolyn Jones was hired at J. Walter Thompson on the usual secretary track. By 1968 she helped form Zebra Associates, a full-service agency composed of African-American principals, and she later helped to found the Black Creative Group (*NYT* 7/8/01: 28).

The most well known woman in advertising of the late 1960s and 1970s was Mary Wells, who founded her own firm, Wells, Rich, Greene, in 1966, when she was offered the presidential salary, but not the title, of the company for which she worked (Wells Lawrence 2002: 44). By 1970, her firm ranked thirteenth in the nation in terms of billing (*AA* 2/23/70: 36), and she was the highest-paid female executive in the world (*AA* 1/19/70: 3). She was a public figure because of her success, her traditional blonde attractiveness, her power marriage to the president of Braniff Airlines, and a client list including Braniff and Benson and Hedges for whom she mounted what are now considered classic campaigns. *Advertising Age* said she had a "mystique" and described her as both "brainy and calculating" (*AA* 1/19/70: 3). But she took no public position on feminism, took no particular interest (judging by her memoir) in promoting professional women's careers at her agency, and was not involved in the push to change women's images in advertising.

Wells contrasted with other advertising women—and a few men—who called for more women in the profession and for a reassessment of the images of women. A Los Angeles advertising woman, Muriel Sparkman, argued that the use of idealized sexual imagery in advertising was a projection of male fantasy and made women resentful. "In short, she resents being used as a *commodity*" (*AA* 1/12/70: 42), a statement that would not have been out of place in an alternative publication. Trahey took the industry to account for selling products to women by putting "female brain power back in the dark ages" (*AA* 3/16/70: 92). But Cadwell purchased an arresting, two-page ad in *Advertising Age* to rebut an advertising survey that suggested that women had limited interests. Headlined "The Lady of the House Is Dead," the copy read in part, "The notion that women are hysterical creatures with inferior intellects that best respond to tales of Aladdin-like giants and magical clowns is horrendously insulting. When over 55 percent of the women in the country are high school graduates and 25 percent have attended colleges, aren't they beyond 'house-itosis'? At the very least women deserve recognition as being in full possession of their faculties" (*AA* 4/27/70: 86–87).

In the rising consciousness of the time, even in the conservative advertising business, two female researchers at Batten, Barton, Durstine, and Osborne persuaded their firm to conduct focus groups to discover what women considered degrading in advertising. The results, according to Komisar, "summed up everything feminists here and elsewhere have been saying: Women do not like ads that are either blatantly exploitive and insult them or reinforce the sex role stereotype" (Komisar 1971: 236). By that time, the concern was reaching a wider audience, as when *TV Guide* published the guest editorial "Is That Really Me? Today's Woman Has a Tough Time Recognizing Herself in Those TV Commercials," by Ann Tolstoi Foster (Foster 1971). The article carried some weight in professional circles because Foster was a well-known professional woman in advertising who also took her message to *Advertising Age* (Foster 1972). Indeed, *Advertising Age* reflected the discussion of feminism and advertising in more than one article, but by 1971 the publication also reflected the industry's frustration at trying to please multiple audiences: "When, for example, an advertiser bows to a suggestion by one of the women's lib factions that his advertising is in some ways demeaning, he is only too likely to be whapped by another faction claiming that his new advertising is patronizing" (*AA* 8/8/71: 12).

Additional exposure was given to the new NOW campaign that focused on TV commercials when two NOW members, also professional writers, had a piece on the subject published in the *New York Times Magazine* (Hennessee and Nicholson 1972). Judy Klemesrud followed the campaign for the *Times* (Klemesrud, "Madison Avenue"). In 1975, the National Advertising Review Board (NARB), an oversight group made up of advertising industry representatives, reported that prejudices were demonstrated in the images of women in advertising. The report included a "checklist" of questions that advertisers were supposed to ask themselves when creating ads, including, "Do my ads portray women as more neurotic than men?" (NARB 1975: 76).

The advertising industry had its own concerns about images, less about reform as concern that traditional approaches would lose women as consumers. New approaches were considered as a way to take advantage of an expected "new society" in which women would make as much money as men (by 1980, according to one account), have more money to spend, have more education, and wield more power in the home and in the nation.

The advertising business thus began to redirect advertising aimed at women, especially after the debacle of the National Airlines "Fly Me" campaign. AT&T's decision to permit women to take on linesmen's duties was promoted by its advertising campaign, which showed a woman high on a pole with the line, "The Phone Company Wants More Installers Like Alaine MacFarlane." A pharmaceutical company advised that "New Birth Control Is Easy as a Tampon." Moreover, Quaker Oats and Hunt-Wesson, were turning away from advertising household products as performers of magical feats to more straightforward presentations.

While some companies could adjust their advertising fairly easily, it was more difficult for makers of beauty products, given a movement ideology that eschewed makeup and hair products as symbols of female oppression. To wear makeup became a political statement, and women, even those who were far from radical, found themselves moving away from the heavy cosmetics look of the 1950s to a middle ground that sought an idealized natural look as represented by Steinem. Following the lead of other advertisers, the beauty product business came to embrace the movement as a marketing strategy. In 1973, Revlon introduced Charlie, a fragrance that was advertised by a campaign featuring a model in a pantsuit, a new mode of clothing, in a lively, city environment supposed to represent the life of a young working woman. The advertising campaign was successful enough that it was considered the major reason for making the product the best-selling fragrance within the year. Other companies embraced advertising that celebrated independence and empowerment, even though they did so to sell the same products that had been sold to a previous generation by opposite paradigms. The manufacturer of Peter Pan brassieres, concerned about the "anti-bra movement," shifted its focus to a new-style bra "that makes you feel like you're not wearing one" (*AA* 2/2/70: 26).

For feminist women activists, this shift in advertising would seem to have achieved their goals for positive images of women. But Naomi Wolf argues that the marketing and advertising of beauty products co-opted the movement while helping to move the nation into a new conservative period because essential framings had not changed. According to Wolf, "Elizabeth Arden's is 'the most advanced treatment system of the century' as if aging required chemotherapy" (Wolf 1991: 226). In an earlier era, the Charlie girl, no matter her independence and bon vivant attitude, was still as slim and lovely as any model in a previous period and thus promoted not only the desire to be as slim and lovely but also the connection to a successful career. If advertising largely succeeds because it must always present its products as strategies to fill hardly understood desires, Charlie kept the tradition alive.

Advertising as Mitigation

It should be no surprise that advertising—of all the media industries—seeks to serve American consumerism by the means at hand. In the 1970s, the means at hand were interpretations of the movement itself, presented with all the persuasive skills of the industry. That the industry succeeded cannot be considered simply the success of a well-practiced craft but must be seen as the willingness of the population to be so moved. The industry is not so skilled, as advertising professionals will be the first to say, that it can move mountains. What the advertising industry was able to do in embracing the movement was to take advantages of the vulnerable spaces that had already been identified by the media coverage of the movement. Most damaging of these was the image of stridency—interpreted as male hating and humorless—that women refused to accept either as true or as a badge of honor. Perhaps every social change movement has characteristics that cannot be borne, and stridency—with all its meanings that have to do with male/female sexuality—was the bête noir of the women's movement. Advertising messages that used liberation themes, in one way or another—the humor of the Virginia Slims campaign or the Charlie campaign that offered the possibility that independence and attractiveness could go hand in hand—served to mitigate a characteristic that the movement was never to shake but clearly did so at a price.

Tools of the Master

As NOW and other activists challenged traditional advertising images of women, another thrust of the reform was to use advertising as a proactive tool for the promotion of the movement itself. Kovacs was so appalled at the coverage of the 26 August 1970 demonstration that she became an activist to change the image of women in advertising. As a member of NOW's national Image of Women Committee, she launched a major public service campaign with the help of Anne Tolstoi Foster and Mary Jean Tully, NOW's unofficial fund-raiser.

In February 1971, Kovacs asked the Advertising Council to consider a campaign emphasizing equal opportunities for women. Foster's team at J. Walter Thompson produced a series of five print ads and two television commercials, each of which included a pithy copy line: "This healthy normal baby has a handicap. She was born female" was the most popular of the series, which also included "Womanpower. It's much too good to waste." Another ad showed a group of men seated around a board table and asked, "What's wrong with this picture?" Another image featured a knobby-kneed cartoon figure with rolled-up pants legs and a whimsical copy line, "Hire him, he's got great legs." The council agreed to accept the campaign only if it was disassociated from NOW sponsorship on the basis of a council policy that prevented it from promoting groups that sought to influence legislation. The council suggested a "dummy" group—a phony organization made up of well-known people, a long-sanctioned approach in similar situations. But under the leadership of Wilma Scott Heide, NOW rejected the idea, instead choosing to launch the campaign under the auspices of the organization's Legal Defense and Education Fund and thus, in some cases, limiting the placement of the ads because of the connection to NOW. This also meant that the considerable resources of the Ad Council would not be used, and Kovacs would have to devote her own energies, over several years, to the placement of the television and print ads. After *Ms.* agreed to run the series, the campaign was picked up by national, regional, and specialty magazines, including *Time*, *Newsweek*, *The Statesman*, *The Progressive*, *Management Adviser*, the *Saturday Review*, *Business Week*, *Lady Golfer*, and others. Kovacs believed part of the success of finding these venues was because public service departments in media companies, one of the lowest rungs, were usually in the realm of women employees. In retrospect, her regret is that not one of the ads in the series was devoted to women of color (Kovacs 1998).

It might also be considered that, as other products and services had utilized or co-opted the movement ideology for their own ends, little courage was involved in using any of the NOW ads that were familiar in their professional preparation, argued for equal employment, and could give the media vehicles in which they appeared to have the cachet of being on the leading edge. Indeed, media vehicles that use public service advertising are usually in a winning situation, donating time and space that otherwise would not be sold, alleviated from the responsibility of taking a position by the separate nature of an advertisement, and protected by media consumers who can be resistant to those messages with which they do not agree. For all of these reasons, the campaign received many awards and was considered one of the most successful of all grassroots efforts (Fallon 1975).

Did Reforms Make a Difference?

In 1970, the *Columbia Journalism Review* devoted an issue to "The Coming Newsroom Revolution." Edwin Diamond predicted an emerging "reporter power." News reporters, he said, had been affected by the social change movements of the time and would bring that sensibility into the newsrooms. He saw evidence of reporters organizing beyond wage concerns to demands for a say in the editorial direction of their newsroom products. He believed that the reporter-activists might succeed because owners feared the loss of the talent pool and were adverse to unpleasant publicity (Diamond 1970). In a continuing articulation of the power of women in the media, Cathleen Black told the National Federation of Press Women in 1988 that women were changing the face of the media. The growing female presence, she said, meant that women were helping to set the national agenda for news coverage (*Press Woman* 8/88: 2). This was a belief held by feminists of the time, and there were indications that women in pivotal positions could make a difference, beginning with the paperback publication of *The Feminine Mystique* at a house headed up by the powerful Helen Meyer, the later publication of *Sexual Politics* by Betty Prashker, hired by Doubleday as a way to avoid sexual discrimination litigation, and the involvement of Robin Morgan in the publication of radical Left thought in the mainstream press. In other reflections of success of the rationale, Bella Stumbo, a *Los Angeles Times* reporter who had written a series about a victim of rape humiliated in the court process, saw her work instigate a television show. Shortly thereafter a state law was passed to protect the rights of the victim (Ricchiardi and Young 1991: 87). And even in cases where the connection was not as direct, reformers could look at the changing attitudes that allowed other reform measures to go forward.

Although journalism often seeks a reform agenda, the direct relationship between reform efforts and a journalistic representation is not easy to assess, although writer Kay Mills believes that changes have been significant although, even thirty years later, not sufficient (Mills 1997). However, one fairly discrete area that lends itself to an initial examination of the question is that of women's service magazines.

The editorial direction of magazines, women's magazines as well as general interest magazines, had long been in the province of men, but with the increase of women in editorial positions, researchers Lee Joliffe and Terri Catlett asked, "Has the presence of women in positions of control altered the content to women's magazines?"

In the first period of women's activism, 1965 to 1975, Joliffe and Catlett found that the increase in women executives coincided with an increase in positive portrayals of women. Articles increasingly framed women as powerful in their environment, as independent, as knowledgeable, and as self-reliant. But in the second period that was examined, 1975 to 1985, even the increase in women executives could not stop the media reflection of the country's conservative drift. Fewer articles appeared that described women as in charge of their environment, while more were published that represented women as passive dependents and as family servants. Fewer pieces were adult-to-adult informational articles. In both periods, the presence of female executives seemed to make little difference in the increasing number of negative portrayals of women, particularly during the second period, when the women "seem to have adopted stereotypical views of other women." The researchers concluded that the content of the magazines was more likely to represent the cultural climate of the times than the presence of female executives (Joliffe and Catlett 1994).

The relationship of women's issues and women in positions of authority has been only slightly covered, but mass media coverage of women's health has received close attention (Signorielli 1993; Freimuth 1984). However, health care scholars note that while that women's health care has received increasing prominence in the 1990s, it has been in ways that are often premature and unrealistic presentations that are most beneficial to the health-care industry (Ruzek, Oleson, and Clark 1997). A 1999 study found that both women's magazines and general news-magazines covered breast cancer in ways that were most related to prevention but that women's magazines emphasized coping stories, personal experiences, and risk factors, while newsmagazines were more likely to have coverage in an economic frame, including political, insurance, and economic issues of funding and research (Andsager and Powers 1999).

The coverage of breast cancer according to the tried-and-true principles of women's magazines comes at a time when women's magazines are no longer under the jurisdiction of male editors. How the stories are played may have little to do with gender of the executive but rather suggests that the magazines continue to be shaped by the perception that they serve lower-middle-class audiences that are believed to be interested only in stories told in a social or helpful-information frame. Furthermore, the advertising of prescription drugs, once a rarity outside professional journals, is now commonplace in all mass media venues and can only serve to cool (especially in advertising-starved periods of economic recession) institutional attacks, whether in connection with women's health care or in con-nection with health care in general.

What can be interpreted from the overview offered here is that as the women's movement became a national phenomenon, its coverage in the mass media turned to reforms that could be accommodated without much cost to the major culture and, not incidentally, serve as a way to reach new readers or new con-sumers. These changes included more sensitive coverage of rape and rape victims, women's health, the use of women as references in news stories (as women began to move into politics), and the adoption of less prejudicial newspaper headlines and language. For advertisers, women's empowerment served as an advertising theme when coupled with traditional values of youth and beauty. The hope that radical Left ideas would be carried into the daily media mainstream by the new women reporters did not come to fruition. Women reporters as much as male reporters found an appropriate zone of comfort in a reform agenda. Moreover, the chill effect of appearing "strident" was powerful in newsrooms, places in which women still needed to adopt the majority of craft traditions to survive. Like many other Americans, a reform agenda was both appropriate and sufficient for the new women reporters as much as it was for the men.

The War Won

Six years after its Kate Millett cover, *Time* produced another cover article on women in the issue usually reserved for the "Man of the Year." There was no single "Woman of the Year" for 1976. Instead, *Time* devoted its story to "Women of the Year," and a dozen women were pictured as representatives of the changing place of American women in national life. The magazine ticked off women's accomplishments, noted setbacks, and looked toward roads yet to be traveled.

For the casual readers—and most media consumers are—the subheads led the reader through a thicket of not-so-upbeat statistics with a unremittingly upbeat air. Business was still "wholly a men's club," according to the copy, but the section's boldface subhead proclaimed "Inroads to Management." Although the traditional female occupation of teaching still most represented women in the professions, the subhead saw women as "Finally Making It." Most women remained in low-level jobs, a fact interpreted as "Out of Women's Ghettos" by the subhead on the basis that the low-level jobs were once considered male occupations. Women in the military? "Some Amazing Gains," according to the optimistic subhead. Problems in the family? "The Delicate Dilemma." Accompanied by photographs of women in their new achievements, the subheads led the quick reader through a rosy view of women in the national life that did not fit with the majority of statistics in the copy or the limitations of representing a movement in terms of a dozen successes (*Time* 1/5/76: 6–15).

By the late 1990s, at a time when the "new society" had not panned out as envisioned by 1970s marketers, the New York Advertising Women, disturbed by what seemed like a replay of sexist advertising, returned to the old tactic of making embarrassing public presentations bestowing "The Good, the Bad, and the Ugly Awards" on advertisers and their agencies. In 1987, Kathy Bonk was one of two founders of a Washington-based research group, Communications Consortium, that still operates. Friedan founded the media reform group Women, Men, and the Media at the University of Southern California, where she was teaching, and it has served as a dispersal point for hiring trends and for the promotion of local watchdog efforts. The International Women's Media Foundation is governed by a board of directors composed of high-level women journalists from around the world and works to promote international reform of media practices. Freedom and Accuracy in Reporting (FAIR) examines media and gender as part of a overall reform agenda. *Media Report to Women*, founded by Donna Allen in 1972, continues to be published after her death, maintaining her tradition of providing reliable and up-to-date information about women in media. Media critic Jean Kilbourne has produced two updates of her original "Killing Us Softly" video on advertising harmful to women. As Kilbourne illustrates, images of women that would have raised howls of protest in the 1970s are now routinely accepted in mass media advertising (Kilbourne 2000). NOW continues its long-term struggle over the issue. The NOW Foundation established a new media activist group in 1999, and its 2002 report found that programming on the nation's six television networks pandered to adolescent boys while women functioned as decoration (NOW Foundation 2002).

10. Reform Redux

Broadcast

The assumption that once on the inside, women would be able to influence the news agenda was as strongly felt among broadcast reformers as among those in print. Terry Gross, later the host of National Public Radio's *Fresh Air* interview program, began her broadcast career on a woman-staffed feminist radio program. "It didn't matter that I had no radio experience. The producers were almost as committed to training other women as they were to getting the program on the air. They were convinced that the mass media would continue to ignore or misinterpret the women's movement until women were in a position to make editorial decisions and report the stories. And that couldn't happen until there were women who knew their way around the studio and control room" (Gross 1998: 226). Implicit in the goal was the expectation that mass media, properly directed, could change national behavior, a point of view that was held by radical as well as not-so-radical women as part of the resurgence of the "powerful effects" theory of mass communication. The mass media themselves assumed their own power. *Redbook* titled its article on how women across the country perceived the movement " 'Women's Lib? I've Seen It on TV' " (Cadden 1972). The producers who trained Gross clearly believed that negative perceptions could be changed if new hands were on the media levers.

But in the same period there were other indications that if mass media were powerful, this power did not necessarily emanate from their overt messages. *All in the Family* was seen as a breakthrough program that promoted racial tolerance because the bigotry of its lead character was ridiculed. But by the mid-1970s researchers noted that viewers of *All in the Family* tended to take what fit their pre-existing notions and leave out what was not. To some, Archie was a hero, not a buffoon (Brigham and Biesbrech 1976; Vidmar and Rokeach 1974). That latter line of inquiry was more in line with research in Great Britain, where new cultural studies scholars were finding that working-class audiences could be quite resistant to attitudes promoted by media products (Fiske 1986). Anecdotal evidence supported such notions. At a 1970 conference seeking to assess the influence of television on behavior, Nigel Ryan, an editor at Great Britain's Independent Television News, noted that the campaign by the British television industry to diminish racial intolerance had been to no avail. "If you were to attack broadcasting in Britain as not having been objective on any issue, I would say it was here, in constant preaching and in the careful avoidance of the immigration issues for years" ("How" 1970: 26).

Feminist women, however, had little interest in questioning how powerful media really was after what, for some, had been the infuriating television coverage of the Strike for Women, the marginalized roles women played in television dramas and news, and the lack of content in both arenas that reformers believed were important to women. These were longtime NOW interests, and with a cadre of committed and knowledgeable activists, the organization launched a national campaign to change the broadcasting industry in every realm—in news and entertainment content; in employment, both technical and managerial; and across commercial and public broadcasting lines.

The Battle for Women in Broadcast

The world of broadcasting was inhospitable to women. Its first mantra, invoked repeatedly, was that women's voices did not carry authority. Even after Pauline Frederick obtained exclusive stories, she was still turned down for a regular assignment on the basis of voice. "It isn't that you haven't proved yourself," her supervisor admitted, "but when listeners hear a woman's voice, they'll turn off their radios, because a woman's voice just doesn't carry authority." Frederick finally joined NBC-TV in 1953, where she had a distinguished career as the television correspondent for the United Nations although she remained barred from radio (Blau 1990: D18).

Frederick's success stands in contrast to a legion of other women broadcast pioneers who were caught on the shoals of voice prejudice. Growing up in Cleveland, Ohio, Marlene Sanders, later an ABC correspondent, could recall hearing only the "lone, disembodied voice" of radio personality Dorothy Fuldheim, which "got lost in the sea of resonant male sounds" (Sanders and Rock 1988: 5).

Women in broadcasting were generally accepted, if at all, in venues that were expected to appeal to women, exemplified by Mary Margaret McBride's career, which began in the 1930s and lasted until the 1960s. In 1929, Ruth Crane Schaefer translated a clerical position into the advice giver of "Mrs. Page's Household Economy" at WJR in Detroit. Judith Cary Waller was the general manager of WMAQ in Chicago but was downgraded to a public service director when the station was sold to NBC in 1931 (Williamson, M. 1976–77). Women were primarily used as staples of programs about domestic economy. World War II was briefly helpful to women who wanted to do radio reporting. Mary Marvin Breckinridge was for a short time one of "Murrow's Boys," the first woman on the CBS Radio News staff. A few other women found the microphone thanks to the needs of war: Sigrid Schultz, a reporter for the *Chicago Tribune*, broadcast for the Mutual Broadcasting Company, and Margaret Rupil and Helen Hier broadcast for NBC. Their careers were prompted by the exigencies of the time but none of these women was able to parlay her wartime experience into the postwar careers enjoyed by male broadcasters. Not even the exigencies of war could keep Betty Wason on the air. Although Wason was hired by legendary war correspondent William Shirer to report on the invasion of Norway, CBS complained that Wason's voice was "too young and feminine for war news and that the public was objecting to it" (Hosley 1984: 118).

One startling exception was Lisa Sergio, an Italian immigrant who in 1937 became NBC's first female "guest" announcer. Indeed, press attention was attracted precisely for what *Newsweek* called her "golden voice" and what the *New York Times* termed her "fluent phonetics." In 1940, NBC balked at Sergio's proposal to do news commentary, and she moved to New York's WQXR radio, where she remained until 1947, when the station's owner, the New York Times Company, decided to limit commentary to print. Sergio, like other female broadcasters, was sidelined (*Nswk* 12/13/44: 109; *NYT* 7/18/37: 10; *NYT* 6/27/89: B8). In July 1937, a CBS official told the *New York Times* that in radio, men were more successful than women because "men's voices carry authority" (*NYT* 7/18/37: 10). As late as 1971, Reuven Frank, president of NBC News, told a *Newsweek* interviewer, "I have the strong feeling that audiences are less prepared to accept news from a woman's voice than from a man's" (*Nswk* 8/30/71: 63). When Marlene Sanders asked Frank when a woman could be expected to anchor a news program, he responded, "A woman's voice is not authoritative" (Sanders and Rock 1988: 120). In 1974 Lauren Lipton became the first female news anchor for top-forty station WFIL in Philadelphia, and she recalled that the program director told her that the station management was "thrilled they were getting a good reaction. They had been really worried that people would hear a woman and turn their radios right off" (Lipton 1998). The canard was difficult to put away even in face of scholarly research, also conducted in 1974, that found that believability in news was not affected by the gender of the news giver (Whittaker and Whittaker 1976; Stone, V. and Dell 1972).

The traditions of radio were taken into the television. As a student at Duquesne University in Pittsburgh, Eleanor Schano set her sights on a television news career: "Wow, was that a joke in 1950 if you were a female person. There was absolutely no opportunity for women, and I could not see anywhere down the line that there would be." Schano hosted a fifteen-minute, three-day-a-week show, *The Beauty Spot*, on Pittsburgh's WDTV, but she was not permitted to change the format.

"I didn't want it to be The Beauty Spot, I didn't want it to be fluff and frivolous. I tell you this story because it shows you what their mind-set was." Schano spent a decade as a "weather lady." In 1954, the same station hired one of nation's first television news women, Florence Sando, for a morning news program aimed at women. Like Schano, Sando resisted a female ghetto and did not select news items in terms of their perceived appeal to women. "It was the news," she recalled in 1993, "I tore it off the wire, it was film from UP, it was local footage shot by our newsroom cameraman" (Hinds 1995: 126).

Indeed, to be assigned to do "women's news" was to court the broadcast ghetto. Liz Trotta, an ambitious local television reporter, turned down a network assignment when it was connected with Lynda Johnson's wedding gown. "I don't work on women's stories," she told the producer, knowing that while television reporters in general might cover a wide range of subjects and still be taken seriously, "women's stories" were not on the palette (Trotta 1994: 58). The title of her memoir, *Fighting for Air*, suggests the difficulty of being female and seeking a broadcast reporting career in the 1960s.

For most women broadcasters, to be a female in the business was to work the hardest, be paid the least, and to be treated with ridicule. As Ruth Crane Schaefer recalled, "The lowest branch on the organization tree was usually that of the woman who did food, children's programs, women's activities and so on, no matter how well sponsored and notwithstanding this woman in almost all cases was also her own complete staff-writer, program director, producer, public relations, innovator, outside speaker, often saleswoman for her own sponsors, radio or TV and sometimes both. Our efforts were not taken very seriously by our associates even though the announcers and technicians were often the veritable beginners on the staff. And the jokes directed at her were not always innocent" (Beasley and Gibbons 1993: 171). A survey taken in 1960 but not reported until 1966 found low salaries and little chance for advancement. This poll also found that women left the field earlier than men but did not consider that the lack of opportunities played a role, instead concluding that "ambition may not be an outstanding characteristic of women in broadcasting" (D. Smith and Harwood 1966: 347). A 1976 sociological study found that just 10 percent of women in journalism were in radio and broadcasting. Women were "much rarer in broadcast than in print journalism" because women on women's pages—apparently not considered journalism—were included in print employment figures, whereas women who handled informational programming for women were not considered part of news or public information in broadcasting (Johnstone, Slawski, and Bowman 1976: 23).

Finally, broadcast education was not in the forefront of broadcast reform, as indicated by the title of a 1962 journal article, "The Student of Broadcasting: His

Recruitment, Training and Future in Broadcasting" (Lacy et al. 1962). Nor was the issue raised in quasi-public inquiries into the state of television. Of the eighty-eight participants in the duPont-Columbia Seminars on Broadcasting and the Public Interest, just two female names appear (Marya Mannes and Gail Smith). The duPont-Columbia report for 1968–69 called for diversity in programming but did not include anything about women (Barrett, M. 1969). In 1973, Edward Jay Epstein published his highly regarded analysis of the production of television news, *News from Nowhere*, but without one word devoted to women as correspondents or to issues of the second wave as content.

What makes Epstein's lack of notice all the more remarkable was that by 1973 some changes were under way. In 1963, Philadelphia's KYW-TV hired an African-American woman field reporter, Trudy Haynes, because, as Al Primo, the station news director, put it, "That's no secret. We were looking for a black reporter" (Marshall 1999). Liz Trotta was hired in 1965 by New York's NBC flagship when the NBC president Robert Kintner issued a directive: "Find me a girl reporter" (Trotta 1991: 29). On the West Coast, Ruth Ashton, first writing for CBS commentator Robert Trout, was eventually allowed to report for KCBS in Los Angeles by the mid-1960s. In 1961, Barbara Walters, a writer for NBC's *Today Show*, used her talent and the acumen developed as the daughter of a successful theatrical agent to secure a place at the desk and build on what had been a limited anchor position. Sanders, with a background in theater, produced Mike Wallace's 1955 news program and by the early 1960s had broken the voice barrier in radio network news. ABC had a woman, Lisa Howard, on its television network (Sanders and Rock 1988). Most successful for the period was Nancy Dickerson, who began as a producer and by 1963 was the first woman to have her own network news broadcast, a five-minute daytime program aimed at women viewers. When John F. Kennedy was assassinated in 1963, she was prominent among the on-air reporters and during the Johnson administration was recognized by *Variety* as one of the top ten television reporters, "9 Guys and a Doll" (Dickerson 125). By 1972, Catherine Mackin was an NBC convention floor reporter. In the same year, a researcher found that half of the nation's television newsrooms employed at least one newswoman, although news directors still overestimated (by one-third or more) the audience's belief in the credibility given to male reporters (Stone, V. 1973, 1973–74). Nonetheless, Norma Quarles, Linda Ellerbee, Ann Compton, Judy Woodruff, Jane Pauley, Renee Poussaint, Connie Chung, Hillary Brown, Lesley Stahl, and Andrea Mitchell began significant broadcast careers. However, for some news directors, one woman per newsroom was enough. A woman applicant for a position with the *New York Times* Broadcasting Service reported to the EEOC that she was rejected by a news director because he "already had a woman reporter" (Stevens 1985: 13).

As women began to move into television news, negotiation had to occur on several fronts for men to accept them as colleagues. Women first had to distance themselves from what had been defined as traditional women's news to prove themselves on what had been male territory. This view of women's news in the broadcast media, shared by men and many women, meant that women's news was not to be the entrée for serious women's issues stories as it had been in print. When topics that had been introduced by second-wave activists were finally taken into the broadcast fold, generally in local markets, they were included because the topics promised a new avenue for audience building. Less dependent on journalistic craft traditions and closer to the management side of news, the introduction of new topics by male producers was a selective affair that gave precedence to those stories that produced audiences and profits.

News Makes Money

When Nancy Dickerson was reporting, to be in the network news division was to have some prestige but not to be at the industry's profit center. Managers thought of news, national or local, as the main support for broadcasters' claims to be serving the public interest at license renewal time. However, the broadcast reform movement coincided with news as a new profitability center, a discovery that carried significant impact for broadcast reform efforts.

In 1970, broadcasters were no longer permitted to carry cigarette advertising and suffered a major loss of revenue. At ABC that loss was mitigated by the success of the five local stations owned by network, led by its flagship in New York, WABC-TV. WABC-TV contributed most to the corporate revenue thanks to its success with local news, reshaping local television news from a money-losing, behind-the-desk anchor style to the 1968 debut of the snappier—critics said flashier and crasser—"happy talk." It was pioneered by Al Primo, who had tried out the system at KYW in Philadelphia and utilized a "beat" system that put attention on street reporters and brought them into the studio (Powers, *Newscasters*: 151). Primo took the format to New York and by 1972 the popularity of WABC-TV's *Eyewitness News* had helped make WABC the number one New York television station, essential to the profits of its weak network (Allen, C. 1997). The program's innovations included an unapologetic emphasis on stories that would bring in viewers, such as the weather, with a jocular weatherman, and the use of television field reporters involved in the story in flashy ways.

The first woman to be a Monday-through-Friday anchor was Jean Emerson in 1971 at Seattle's KING, whose excellence in news coverage made it the nation's premier local station in the 1970s. Emerson's promotion, however, occurred only after the consulting firm McHugh and Hoffman recommended that the station change to an "Eyewitness News" format with Emerson at the anchor desk. The recommendations by this firm and by consultant Frank Magid were largely responsible for the fact that by the end of the 1970s, most Top 100 stations had male and female anchors. While Emerson would retain her place for the next thirty years, other female anchors left the field because of the public scrutiny (Allen, C. 2003).

Despite critics, the new formats gave new opportunities for minorities and women. Melba Tolliver, Gloria Rojas, and entertainment editor Rona Barrett became part of the original team at WABC-TV. Bantering on the set among the anchors and visiting reporters became the format's hallmark. RoseAnn Scamardella was one of the reporter-anchors, her popularity evidenced by the fact that comedian Gilda Radner used Scamardella as the basis for the character Roseanne Roseannadanna on *Saturday Night Live*. There was no commitment to women or women's issues in the format; on WABC-TV in 1976 the weatherman suggested that women should "enjoy" rape, an off-the-cuff comment that put an end to his on-air career (Powers, *Newscasters*: 35).

Notwithstanding such lapses, the WABC-TV example turned attention to the profitability of local news and encouraged the further rise of consultants. Consultants based their recommendations on audience surveys, assessing attitudes not only toward content but also toward on-air personalities, the visual setting, and the number of news stories. Recommendations were made along these lines and involved making anchors friendly and appealing, designing anchor desks where anchorpeople sat close together, and establishing a lively pace by increasing in the number of stories covered—all these changes aimed at meeting the preferences of the surveyed audience with little concern for the role these changes would make in news coverage. Indeed, consultants had no particular interest in maintaining journalistic traditions or in promoting an agenda of social reform. But one unrecognized benefit of the consultants was that audience surveys leapfrogged over prejudices against female voices. Although the influence of consultants on local television often resulted in fuzzy, happy talk news that was derided by professionals, the formats suggested by the consultants promoted women as reporters and coanchors.

The Emphasis on Local Programming

Women also benefited when local news expanded by the addition of an extra half hour of soft news in what came to be known as a "magazine format" that preceded the local news in many markets. Here, women could be coanchors in the half-hour show of noncritical and nonpolitical news that nonetheless took on the patina of news by the use of an anchor desk and a news format. Such programs were easy and cheap to produce, using a newsroom staff already in place as well as news packages prepared as part of regular reporting duties. Although such programs were not hard-hitting, they were the industry response to the Federal Communication Commission's emphasis on local programming, which had been spearheaded by FCC Commissioner Nicolas Johnson and promoted by President Richard M. Nixon, although for vastly different reasons.

For Johnson, local programming was a way to promote the public interest as outlined in a 1973 FCC survey. Johnson and his team ranked affiliates in terms of their local programming, public service, and employment patterns (Johnson 1975). For Nixon, however, the emphasis on local news was clearly a way to undermine national network news programming. The director of the new Office of Telecommunications Policy, Clay T. Whitehead, took the message to professional gatherings of broadcasters, as reported by *Broadcasting*, a magazine for broadcast executives. "At points in his speech, Mr. Whitehead reportedly indicated that the degree of enthusiasm with which the White House backs license-renewal legislation may depend on how seriously affiliates heed his call to greater independence from networks." Whitehead hardly minced words: "We feel network news is biased" (*BC* 12/18/72: 8). Edward R. Murrow's former producer, Fred W. Friendly, warned that broadcasting was being politicized (Friendly 1972). There was little doubt about that, but the emphasis on the local level had ramifications for women in broadcast, as women were found to be useful as reporters and personalities in the new formats and served to deflect the wave of petitions-to-deny that broadcasters saw threatening their newly discovered pool of profits.

The Broadcast Reform Movement

The broadcast reform movement began in the 1920s in efforts to prevent the commercialization of American radio. The Radio Act of 1927 and its expansion in the Federal Communications Act of 1934 awarded licenses to broadcast corporations whose commitment to the status quo was not in doubt (McChesney 1993). However, in exchange for the privilege of holding broadcast licenses, the broadcast industry was still obligated to operate, in the most famous of industry phrases, "in the public interest." For most of the next forty years, public service was defined narrowly or not at all, and license renewals were fairly automatic. Some unsuccessful efforts were made to challenge licenses. In 1947, the American Jewish

Congress unsuccessfully opposed a license application for an FM station owned by the *New York Daily News*, claiming that the *News* was not a proper custodian of a broadcast license because the paper exhibited antiblack and anti-Semitic views (*NYT* 6/14/47: 3). The next year, the same group, again unsuccessfully, petitioned the FCC for the revocation of the license of KMPV (AM) in Los Angeles, charging the station with slanting the news (*BC* 5/31/48: 1).

The obligations of public service were strengthened after a 1966 court decision gave citizen groups without financial interest in a broadcast outlet legal "standing" and set the stage for challenges of broadcast licenses on the basis of its public service. Soon after the decision, the United Church of Christ joined with two residents of Jackson, Mississippi, to successfully challenge the license of Jackson's WLBT-TV, claiming that the all-white nature of the station's programming did not serve the area's African-American community. This benchmark case led to a subsequent flood of petitions-to-deny from community groups, including those representing women's interests when women were included in the FCC's equal opportunity rule in 1971. *Broadcasting* noted that the Mississippi case "provided practical lessons in how the broadcasting establishment could be challenged" (Powell and Meek 1973: 50).

The United Church of Christ remained active in broadcast reform even as such efforts were taken up by a range of organizations, including the Black Efforts for Soul in Television, the Citizens Communication Center, the National Black Media Coalition, the National Mexican-American Anti-Defamation Committee, the Bilingual Bicultural Coalition for Mass Media, the Gray Panthers, the National Gay Media Task Force, the National Organization for Women, and the American Civil Liberties Union. By 1977, sixty national media reform groups were listed in a directory devoted to the subject (Draves 1977) and together were responsible for several hundred petitions to deny radio and television broadcast licenses for stations considered not to have served in the public interest. From 1972 to 1977, 237 groups filed petitions to deny the licenses of 618 stations (Cole and Oettinger 1978: 205).

The new opportunities to challenge entrenched broadcast practices would not have been possible without low-cost legal representation. The civil rights activism of the 1960s prompted an increase in public-interest law and the establishment of public-interest law firms, some designed solely for achieving change in media reform—the Media Access Project (MAP), the Stern Community Law Firm, the Center for Constitutional Rights, and the Citizens Communications Center in Washington, founded in 1969, which alone was responsible for representing petitions to deny license renewals for more than two hundred stations. The attorneys were likely to be young women and men affected by the social consciousness movements of the time. Like many second-wave activists, female lawyers included women who had begun their activism on behalf of civil rights and shifted to women's issues.

Moreover, filing petitions-to-deny was not so complicated that community groups could not do considerable part of the work. In 1972, at Johnson's prodding, the FCC itself produced for community use a pamphlet on how to file a petition-to-deny (FCC 1972). NOW's Media Project supplied guides for the same purpose, as did the United Church of Christ. This was not good news for broadcasters. It could cost broadcast stations as much as half a million dollars to fight a petition-to-deny (*WSJ* 1/2/75: 1). The broadcast industry was supported in its opposition by the business community as represented by the *Wall Street Journal*, which portrayed broadcasters as victims having to buckle under the pressure of "citizens' demands" (Elliott 1975: 1). As late as 1980, the National Association of Broadcasters (NAB) lobbied the FCC for an inquiry "to determine whether protesters are abusing the petition to deny process" (*BC* 3/3/80: 28), and the FCC seemed inclined to indicate that they were.

By the time the women's movement entered the license fray, the industry was in full battle dress, seeing itself as unfairly besieged by power-mad community groups. "License renewal—no surprise—is everyone's topic at NAB regionals," *Broadcasting* headlined (*BC* 11/7/72: 36). Led by the powerful NAB, the industry had the means to fight on several fronts. Expensive Washington law firms provided seminars on renewal strategies for broadcast executives (*BC* 10/9/72: 32). Broadcasters launched a public opinion campaign, calling community group demands "extortion" at a time when white sympathy for the early civil rights movement had been replaced by suspicion and fear of Black Power (*BC* 10/9/72: 31). Reminiscent of the intensity of the campaign the commercial broadcast lobby waged against educational radio in the 1920s and 1930s, the NAB produced several television public service announcements, in one case equating the U.S. regulatory environment with Nazi Germany. The United Church of Christ complained, but the FCC upheld the NAB's position (Cole and Oettinger 1978).

Broadcasters could only have been pleased when Johnson closed out his six-year term in June 1972—as *Broadcasting* described him, "broadcasters' bête noir in his years as a member of the commission" (*BC* 11/13/72: 26). His retirement buoyed broadcasters' hopes that they would be able to achieve legislation that allowed a longer time between license applications and less FCC scrutiny. Without Johnson, a more conservative FCC issued pronouncements about the "mountains" of petitions and called on community groups to work out difficulties before the license renewal period; formal petitions should be the "last resort" (*BC* 11/13/72: 25). "Nixon makes his move for longer lease term," *Broadcasting* announced a month later (*BC* 12/18/72: 8). Legislators on both side of the aisle expressed concern for the broadcasters' dilemma: "I gather that if the issue [of petitions-to-deny] could be resolved expeditiously, most everything else would fall in line," U.S. Representative Robert H. Macdonald (D-Mass.), chairman of House Communications Subcommittee, soothingly told a group of Texas broadcasters (*BC* 11/20/72: 60).

For their part, broadcasters insisted that they were making meaningful changes. Houston's KPRC-TV offered a promotional photograph of its twenty-eight-member news staff for a December 1972 cover of *Broadcasting*, showing three male African-Americans and three white women as part of its team (*BC* 12/11/72: 1). In 1973, *Advertising Age* reported that the United Church of Christ's monitoring report showed that "Stations Make Progress in Hiring Ethnic Males; Are Remiss on Women" (*AA* 10/29/73: 22).

NOW's Campaign

NOW's broadcast reform efforts coalesced two founding thrusts of the organization, equality in hiring and images of women. On both counts, broadcasting was found wanting: women were discriminated against in employment, and the images of women portrayed on television, like those of the mass magazines that Friedan had attacked, portrayed women in limited ways. For NOW activists as well as for many of the feminists, the two issues were connected. To bring women into the broadcast workforce would be to change content, and to change content was to influence women and the culture in positive ways. Thus, when NOW mounted its legal challenges, it conjoined both employment statistics and images of women.

Many of the feminists' early conclusions about television news were supported by research from the U.S. Commission on Civil Rights. In a 1974 study of network news, the commission found that only 3 out of 230 stories were related to women; that of 141 newsmakers, 9.9 percent were white females and 3.5 percent nonwhite females; most women newsmakers were wives of presidents or experts or who addressed what were considered to be women's topics (U.S. Commission 1977: 49–53). An update of the report two years later found the same patterns (U.S. Commission 1979).

The same kind of statistics were reflected in the employment of women. In its 1973 figures, the FCC found that 22 percent of commercial station employees were women, but just 6 percent of them held jobs in high-paying categories. While women held 10 percent of leadership positions at Boston's WBXZ-TV, KSL-TV in Salt Lake City had none (Johnson 1975: 60–61). Of the women employed at commercial stations, 75 percent were employed in office and clerical jobs. In noncommercial broadcasting, 54 percent of women held in clerical jobs.

In entertainment broadcasting, 72 percent of the lead characters in drama series were men, and 93 percent of voiceovers used men (Mills 1974: 30).

In retrospect, the NOW campaign seems remarkable for an organization that had been in existence for less than five years. NOW representatives testified in front of the Federal Communications Commission and various congressional committees and lent support to a dozen different license challenges, in so doing confronting the experienced and powerful NAB. The enormity of the task may be explained by the optimism of the times and a group of talented young women's belief in the process of change.

One of those young women was Nancy Stanley, who as law student at George Washington University came into contact with broadcast activism of behalf of African-Americans. In a 1971 *Hastings Law Journal* issue devoted to women's legal concerns, she proposed that women were protected by the same set of license requirements as other groups (Stanley 1971).

Stanley's proposal was adopted by another law student, Whitney Adams, who became national coordinator of a NOW FCC Task Force. In that capacity, she testified on broadcast license renewal legislation before the House Communication Subcommittee in 1973 (Mills 1974) and developed a kit for NOW chapters that pointed the way to local license challenges. Adams led a group that challenged the license of Washington's WRC-TV.

Adams influenced a younger woman, Kathleen Bonk, who became national chair of the NOW Task Force on Media and chair of NOW's Media Reform Committee. Unlike women of the Left, however, who usually came to the women's movement by way of the civil rights or antiwar movements, Bonk directly entered the women's movement, less influenced by the leftist politics of the previous decade than by her early successes as president of her high school class, editor of the yearbook, and delegate to Girl's State, a national leadership organization, all alongside a lifelong fascination with mass media television. Bonk's study began modestly. In a University of Pittsburgh mass communication course, she monitored the programming and employment data of the Pittsburgh television stations. The college project resulted in agreements with the three stations scrutinized—a heady beginning. Bonk quickly became the NOW Media Coordinator for Southwestern Pennsylvania and worked on the petition against WABC-TV in New York. By 1973—not long after taking the college mass communication course—she had become an influential figure in the national movement. In 1976, Johnson, devoted his column in the reform publication *access* to the twenty-three-year-old Bonk (Johnson 1976). By 1977, she appeared as a respected and collegial panelist at an NAB convention workshop on working out NOW concerns regarding local television stations (*BC* 4/4/77: 50). She was called "the dean of broadcast reformers" before she had reached the age of thirty (Johnson 1976; Sanders 1991). By 1979, she had testified on behalf of NOW in front of at least three congressional subcommittees (Bonk 1974, 1979; CPB 1975).

There were other important women who were part of the NOW efforts. Notably, NOW's vice president for public affairs, Toni Carabillo, sought changes in the voluntary industry radio and television codes (Carabillo, Meuli, and Csida 1993: year 1973, 1). Cathy Irwin, the organization's public relations director, testified before the congressional committee overseeing the Corporation for Public Broadcasting in 1974 (CPB 1975). National leaders were supported by dozens of activists at local levels (Lewis, C. 1986).

NOW reformers sought to influence the network news by challenging the licenses held by the handful of local stations that the FCC permitted the networks to own. These were flagship stations located in major cities and were major profit centers for their network owners. On 19 August 1970, four chapters of NOW joined with six other women's groups in a Petition to Deny the License Renewal of NBC's WRC-TV in Washington. The petition claimed that the station was discriminatory in hiring, that women's concerns were not reflected in station programming, and, in a new initiative, that the station had violated the Fairness Doctrine by failing to give a balanced picture of the women's rights movement. The suit was prepared by women attorneys from public-interest law firms—Gladys Kessler of Berlin, Rosman, and Kessler in Washington and Elaine Bloomfield of the Citizens Communication Center with the assistance of the Center for Constitutional Rights. Announcing the filings at a press conference, Adams said that while WRC was the worst of the Washington stations in terms of covering the second wave, television programming in general sought "to portray women striving for equal rights as crude, castrating, bra-burning harpies" (BC 9/4/72: 22).

Two years later, the New York chapter of NOW filed a Petition to Deny the License Renewal of ABC's profitable WABC-TV. The NOW petition was eighteen months in preparation by the public-interest law firm the Center for Constitutional Rights, under the direction of NOW officers Judith Hennessee and Joan Nicholson and with the assistance of more than a hundred individuals conducting programming surveys. The 128-page culminating document charged that the station had failed to ascertain the needs and interests of women, had failed to hire and promote women equally with men, and carried programming in which "women are consistently shown as unintelligent, irresponsible, dominated by men, defined by their anatomy and incapable of independent thought or action" (WP 5/2/72: B8). Almost sighing, Broadcasting reported the case as adding to the already existing "mountain of 90 cases," and noted that the "new batch of petitions threatens to jam still further the commission's license-renewal machinery" (BC 5/8/72: 32).

At the same time that the major suits were progressing, NOW—Adams and Bonk at the helm—was encouraging all its chapters to monitor local stations with an eye to license challenges. A Syracuse group affiliated with the United Church of Christ, the Syracuse Coalition for the Free Flow of Information in the Broadcast Media, filed petitions against two of the city's television stations (*BC* 5/8/72: 34). By 1978 NOW chapters had been responsible for twelve of the fifteen license challenges filed by women's groups, a relatively small percentage of the license challenges from all groups in the period (Lewis, C. 1986). Of the sixty-four radio and television licenses that the FCC revoked between 1970 and 1978, none was related to female issues. Eight stations in Alabama were cited for underrepresentation of minorities, but most of problems that local stations experienced with the FCC were related to fraudulent billing practices (Weiss, Ostroff, and Clift 1980). Nonetheless, the threat of license challenges served to promote signed agreements with stations in New York, Detroit, New Orleans, Philadelphia, Syracuse, Fresno, and Pittsburgh (Lewis, C. 1986). And Stanley and her firm also represented NBC's female employees in a discrimination suit under Title VII of the Civil Rights Act and achieved a negotiated settlement in what Stanley recalls as a "historical moment" (Stanley 2003).

The challenges and the discrimination suits that were not far behind also served notice to all stations to examine their hiring. One station had to go no further than its local college. WVOL-TV in Nashville, Tennessee, heavily recruited a nineteen-year-old student at Tennessee State University, a young woman who already had experience in radio news and was a winner of beauty contests to boot. In 1973, thanks in part to a new climate that sought female and African-American representatives on local news, Oprah Winfrey's blazing career—although she was not to stay in news—was on its way.

Jessica Savitch and the Issues of Content

Another station reassessing its local news at the intersection of feminist demands and the corporate push for profitability was KHOU-TV in Houston, Texas. In spring of 1970, the station's news director was ordered by owner Corinthian to hire a woman reporter as a safeguard against a petition-to-deny (as it had ordered the hiring of a black reporter). Jessica Savitch turned out be a fortuitous hire for KHOU, as she would be later for KYW-TV in Philadelphia. She did more than protect the station's license: she proved beyond all shadow of doubt that the real "authority" for women was success in the marketplace. As a reporter, she put herself at the center of the story, as expected in some of the new formats, even if it meant wearing short shorts or "hot pants," in the term of the period, to represent a pinup in a story about World War II airplanes. As a weekend anchor and one of the first woman anchors in the South (Winfrey being another), Savitch honed her legendary anchoring abilities, which made it seem to many viewers that she could look through the camera—a style, according to one biographer, that came only with much practice (Blair 1988). Viewers responded, and KHOU-TV regained the top spot in the market. None of these attributes had to do with journalism or tenets of the feminist movement.

Savitch moved to Philadelphia, the nation's fourth-largest market, under the same circumstances that had drawn her to Houston. Despite the earlier success of the *Eyewitness News* format, by 1972 KYW-TV trailed ABC affiliate WPVI-TV, which was instituting the recommendations offered by the consultant Frank Magid and had its own "action news" format. As she had in Houston, Savitch helped increase her station's ratings by fully utilizing the *Eyewitness News* format emphasizing reportorial involvement.

As a driven careerist in an industry of careerists, Savitch made no claims to organized feminism, but she did not turn away the support of the Philadelphia NOW representative, Linda Ciarrochi. Ciarrochi became a major supporter, urging management to put Savitch in the most prestigious spot, the evening news. It was a major decision for the station, and, when made, it was accompanied by a campaign to promote Savitch as a journalistic presence. Savitch was assigned a number of series, one story to be shown in parts over a week. The advantage of choosing the series format to showcase her was that the promotion of the series was, in actuality, the promotion of Savitch. Moreover, the topics were chosen with an eye to their ease in promotion. Although they seemed to be subjects that had been brought to the news agenda by feminist agitation, they clearly lent themselves to television news packaging and could attract male and female viewers. Savitch was assigned to do a series on childbirth, which included a scene of an actual birth. A second was on rape, "the ultimate violation." In its most-remembered scene, Savitch, her blonde hair highlighted against her white raincoat, walked down a dark street next to a public housing project while she talked about her feelings of vulnerability. However, to walk next to a public housing development in Philadelphia in 1973 was to be in an African-American neighborhood at a time of urban unrest and, in the context of a series on rape, could only call on black stereotypes. The scene had been the idea of Dave Neal, the assignment editor, who had no illusions about its depth: "This wasn't a documentary on public TV. It was commercial TV and you had two or three minutes to create an impression and get people to tune in the next night" (Blair 1989: 145–46).

As in the example of profitability set by WABC-TV, the Savitch mode was to be emulated in other markets. Women in local television came to serve as attractive presences on the anchor desk, African-American women often paired with white males (although the opposite did not occur for some years, which suggested the old prohibitions regarding white women and black men). In the meantime, what had once been dismissed as "women's news" became reframed and popular as "consumer news," a new profitable feature that was taken up by male reporters when it was divorced from the women's ghetto.

The Thrust from Within

The challenges to the networks' flagship stations brought attention to the numbers of women at the network itself and energized women within the networks to argue on their own behalf. Some of these women were well known and could bring public attention by their profile. Yet not all high-profile women participated in the women's groups.

At CBS, the first revolt occurred in 1970, when women refused to obey an order forbidding women to wear pantsuits. A 1973 memo from the CBS president outlined the network's aim to provide equal opportunity and energized women to form a caucus that began to meet with the senior staff. Five on-air women reporters, including one African-American woman, Michelle Clark (who was later killed in an airplane crash), were hired, and other women were hired as producers. But the new women faced old problems. One of the on-air reporters, Sylvia Chase, organized a committee to approach the CBS president about women's issues.

One of the new hires, Lesley Stahl, declined to join the committee and gives evidence regarding the difficulty of building a career and negotiating for social change at the same time. Stahl was working in New York City as a speechwriter for Mayor John Lindsay in 1966, when the women's movement was unfolding. She had worked her way up through researching, producing, and local reporting when, after several attempts, she finally was hired by CBS in 1972. It was difficult for ambitious women who had successfully negotiated the thickets of broadcast prejudice to risk their careers. "I knew that the women's agenda items were taken by men as personal assaults on them," she recalled in her 1999 memoir. "What a coward. Women like Sylvia who confront and make waves are often punished, while the rest of us ride on their backs. I know that I owe them" (Stahl 1999: 46).

Catherine Mackin was hired by NBC's flagship station, WRC-TV, in 1969, perhaps by a farsighted general manager who predicted the next stage of license challenges. Whatever the station's agenda, Mackin did not play and instead became the leader of the twenty-seven women who filed a 1971 discrimination complaint, a fact that did not deter her rise to the network (and her subsequent contributions as a political reporter before her early death) (Beasley and Gibbons 1993: 26). At the network, however, Marilyn Schultz served as the lead plaintiff in the suit charging discrimination in hiring, promotion, and content (WPCF 2002). Buoyed by the EEOC, which had filed its own suit, the women were successful, finally winning a two-million-dollar judgment and a requirement to hire women. In 1982, after eleven years at NBC, Carole Simpson took that experience with her to ABC-TV.

At ABC, women had established a caucus that met regularly with management, and improvements ensued in a generally cooperative arrangement that contrasted with those at NBC and CBS (Sanders and Rock 1988: 138–43). But when Simpson arrived, many of the agreements of the 1970s had been ignored. Simpson was among those establishing the new ABC Women's Group, and it was Simpson, after other efforts had failed, who took advantage of an April 1985 luncheon to honor Barbara Walters, attended by all of the women correspondents and the female executive producers of many of ABC's major programs, to enumerate the continued difficulties. The women had been alerted (although not Walters); they dressed up. At the preluncheon cocktail party, ABC's president, Leonard Goldenson, said they looked like ladies from the garden club. "This was just more ammunition for me." Simpson said, "that we were not seen as serious." To the high-profile women and the male managers, including Roone Arledge, the new head of the news division, Simpson presented a content analysis that had been months in the preparation. After a toast to Walters (who had to leave), Simpson began a presentation that extended late into the afternoon: "I'm telling you, you could hear a pin drop. All eyes were on me. I could see the women smiling. I mean, they were giving me power, because I could tell that they're back here, 'Give it them. Do it, Carole. Do it.'" Arledge, who had already produced the Billie Jean King–Bobby Riggs "Battle of the Sexes" tennis match, seemed surprised that there was a problem. Simpson remembers his response: "I'm not sure what to say" (Simpson 1993: 10–11). As his biographer notes, the women's issue was not on his "radar screen" (Gunther 1994: 197).

Barbara Walters

Arledge was responsible, however, for bringing to ABC several women correspondents—Simpson, Catherine Mackin, Kathleen Sullivan, and broadcast's highest-profile woman, Barbara Walters. Walters occupies a peculiar part in the history of women and broadcasting. She began as a writer at CBS, moved to NBC in 1961, and in 1974 became cohost of the *Today Show*, which developed and showcased her interviewing abilities. Many of the interview coups she achieved during that period occurred because her contract forbade her from interviewing individuals booked through regular channels, forcing her to find her subjects on her own.

Unlike Sanders, Simpson, and Chase, Walters sought to negotiate the tensions of the movement by not associating closely with it, but she did not turn her back on the movement and produced an early special on the subject for WNBC-TV in New York (Walters 1975). Simpson regarded her as a sympathetic colleague, removed from the day-to-day concerns of the ABC women because of her star status but clearly supportive of the women's action in her speech at a later evening function. "I mean, she just echoed and punctuated everything that we had said in the meeting, and sent a strong signal to management that she was on our side" (Simpson 1993: 11).

Walters's major contribution to the broadcast reform movement was in meeting the challenge of being the first woman to anchor a network evening news program. She was generally vilified in the popular press—ridiculed for what was described as a lisp, held up as an example of the popularization of news, and variously characterized as moneygrubbing and aggressive, cold and difficult, or sexy and a tease. Her salary was viewed as exorbitant, and her coanchor, Harry Reasoner, was notably chilly at having to share the anchor desk.

Walters received no kudos in professional circles. After the initial "first wave of nausea" that he reported experiencing on hearing of Walters's hire, Walter Cronkite moved beyond individual criticism to reflect on the problem of consultants and the accompanying lack of news values among the newly hired (Cronkite 1976). Cronkite's view had some validity: ABC indeed had hired Magid to test the market prior to the offer to Walters. However, Cronkite's comment was typical of professional reaction at the time, addressing the changes only in terms of the havoc wreaked by consultants, not the value of reporters who could introduce new sensibilities in the news coverage. In trying to explain the reaction, Judith Hennessee saw the responses less in terms of an attack on news as show business than as an attack on the male ownership of news: "Most of the stories were written by men, expressed male reactions only, and quoted other men exclusively" (Hennessee 1976: 22).

The reaction also drew a response from a television critic: "The curious things about women's ascendancy in TV journalism is the degree of hostility they have encountered among critics as well as their colleagues," Ron Powers wrote in 1977. "Many critics react as though women alone are the interlopers, as though the very presence of a woman on a newscast constitutes a sellout to show business" (Powers, *Newscasters*: 168).

The disinclination of highly placed broadcast women to cover the women's movement left the subject in the hands of craft traditions that had not served it well. Whereas the civil rights movement had been the making of many male journalistic careers, Savitch was among a few on-air reporters to build her career on stories made possible by the women's movement, although she did so in problematical ways. Marlene Sanders was another reporter who sought to put the women's movement on the broadcast agenda movement both through reporting and in documentary work. In 1970 she produced a half-hour documentary, *Women's Liberation,* the first to examine the second wave. In 1972 she examined women's attempt to achieve political power in *The Hand That Rocks the Ballot Box* (Sanders 1970, 1972). However, for the ABC managers, the documentaries were less about public service than about producing inexpensive programming for the nation's lowest-rated network (Sanders and Rock 1988: 117–19). Moreover, the documentaries about women may have been seen to fit a network that was building its strength on the popularity of its programming aimed for women, as in the success of *Marcus Welby, M.D.* As a documentary producer, Sanders was able to take advantage of the window of opportunity offered by the cost benefits. She became a network vice president for documentary production in 1976, but by the late 1980s Linda Ellerbee noted that there were fewer women on air than there had been in 1975, and while the networks "have created a lot of extra vice presidencies," they were "not necessarily a job or a power." Marlene Sanders was succinct: "The boys are running things again" (*USA Today* 4/10/89: 11A).

Women in Management

As the last thrust before his retirement, Nicolas Johnson had his staff survey the FCC reports submitted by 147 local stations for the employment patterns of women in high-paying categories. What emerged was a clear statement of the range of women occupying executive positions, from a high of 25 percent at the CBS affiliate in Philadelphia to none at the CBS affiliate in Salt Lake City. There was, Johnson wrote, "an urgent need for affirmative action programs designed to get more women into high-paying, decision making end of broadcasting" (Johnson 1975: 59).

Three years after the survey, WNBC-TV in New York became the first station in the nation to have a female station manager, Ann Berks, hired in 1976. The NBC network was the first network to have a woman vice president, Lin Bolen, vice president in charge of daytime programming. Two other women vice presidents had joined her by 1974. By that time, CBS had two women vice presidents, out of eighty-five positions, and sixty-one of four hundred managerial positions were filled by women. Sanders was made the first female vice president at ABC, in charge of documentary production. Despite its female vice president, NBC was considered the most contentious shop on the issue of women. This was made clear when Jane Cahill Pfeiffer, a former IBM public affairs vice president and consultant to RCA, NBC's parent corporation, became "chairman" of NBC. It was a bizarre choice, for Pfeiffer did not come from the industry. Her hire was made possible by NBC President Fred Silverman, who sought to protect his power by putting in place an individual who had long championed him. Richard Salant remembered Pfeiffer as "an idealist with a vision of the quality and high standards she thought broadcast could achieve. But she was unsophisticated in the ways of broadcasting and broadcast executives" (Salant 1999: 282). The difficulty she had with the old-time holdovers is represented in the memoir of Reuven Frank, no admirer of women in news: "Pfeiffer was a moralist, cutting a cruel swath through the NBC unit managers, some of whom had indeed been stealing and some of whom had kept quiet rather than lose their jobs. It was a messy situation that had gone on too long, but her handling of it broadened the definition of culprit and showed no sensitivity to a wounded organization. She discovered other transgressions for which people should be fired. Some wag dug into her past as a former religious to coin her widely used nickname: Attila the Nun" (Frank 1991: 365–66).

The choice of Pfeiffer was also atypical for an industry whose executives tended to move from place to place along a skein of personal connections, as described by Sanders. "Often promotions come from within and occur among friends. Women are not usually part of the in-group. Those few women who do advance are often not particularly anxious to help or identify with other women. They have absorbed male values, and tend to play the game the same way as the men. If women are going to change corporate structures, they will only do so when their numbers increase to a critical mass—then, if so inclined, they can act without fear of being overruled or mustered out" (Sanders and Rock 1988: 166). The tendency toward promotion through connections later intensified as a result of what is now endemic in the mass media business—marriages between highly placed men and women in the same business. Such women have the advantages of the friendships that develop through couples' activities outside of the business day, but these influences are apt to reinforce business standards. Connections by marriage are an advantage not available to single women, lesbians, or women married to men in other occupations.

What emerges from the memoirs of television network news executives from the era is the emphasis on high-level politics. Surely no American business, unless it is sports, moves and removes its executives with more frequency than the broadcast industry. This has some relevance for attempts to change the industry. Institutional change from the top is hampered when the time at the top is limited and executives spend much of their time nurturing power and short-term results in the expectation of the next posting.

Although a few high-profile changes occurred, researchers found that management opportunities for women in broadcasting remained limited into the mid-1970s. Research for the 1979 update of *Window Dressing on the Set* upheld such perception. A statistical survey found that there had been an increase in white female correspondents in network news (8.2 percent to 10 percent) but that this growth had occurred at the expense of minority females (who dropped from 3.5 percent to zero) and that no significant gains had occurred in female management (U.S. Commission 1979: 64–65). But there were gains in on-camera presence. In 1979, 37 of the 180 correspondents who appeared on the three commercial television networks were women. Researchers found that women "were assigned more US government stories and less foreign affairs, more social problems and fewer disasters, more 'women issues,' and few stereotypically male-associated topics such as business and sports" (Singleton and Cook 1982: 489). Broadcast reformers may have been pleased that women's issues were on the news agenda, but many ambitious women reporters were not eager to be associated with the new women's beat. Lesley Stahl, a correspondent for CBS in 1974, was one of those reporters cautious about covering the women's movement for fear of being typecast, a reaction shared by "most of the women reporters I knew" (Stahl 1999: 46).

As early as 1971, *Newsweek* suggested that women routinely were part of TV news, and their only major problem was that they were not getting the same kinds of jobs as the male reporters. A female reporter in San Francisco, Christine Lund, remarked, "Everybody's got a woman. . . . It's like having a dog" (*Nswk* 8/30/71: 62). By 1977, as it had for print, the *Time* magazine headline declared the war won. "Prime Time for TV Newswomen" portrayed prominent network anchorwomen and noted only at the end of the article that women composed just 13 percent of on-air newsgatherers (*Time* 3/21/77: 85). Indeed, it was not until the following year that the Public Broadcasting System hired a woman, Charlayne Hunter-Gault, who had integrated the University of Georgia as a student and been a writer for the *New Yorker* and reporter at the *New York Times* before taking the position on the *MacNeil-Lehrer Report*. No matter her credentials, however, her hire came only after the Report of the Task Force for Women in Public Broadcasting pointed to the lack of white and minority women in PBS programming, the slight number of on-air women on National Public Radio, and the low-level positions held by the women who comprised 30 percent of the public broadcasting workforce (Isber and Cantor 1975; *Press Woman* 4/76: 23). It also came after NOW had been active on the federal level. Appearing before House subcommittee hearings on the Public Broadcasting Financing Act in 1975, Irwin and Bonk argued (with large amounts of supporting material) for increased female representation in programming decisions to "ensure a more positive image of women," equal representation with men, and an affirmative action plan for employment—goals that appeared intertwined (CPB 1975).

These new women were often hired as a result of license challenges, Title VII or EEOC concerns, or other pressures, and the task was not easy. Although the women were now inside, they had to perform under scrutiny and criticism and often in an oppressive atmosphere. CBS correspondent Dan Rather noted the sink-or-swim mentality: "Time and time again I have seen a black or a woman put on camera, and if they do not impress, the reaction is, well, we tried and it didn't work" (Rather 1977: 269). Rather comments as a bystander, without mentioning whether he involved himself in those judgments. Sometimes there was intentional harassment. Andrea Mitchell was the target of malicious hazing when she was the first women in the radio newsroom at Westinghouse in 1967 (Marlane 1999: 131). In a bitter episode that she recounted in her memoir, Daniel Schorr accused Stahl of stealing a copy of a secret CIA report he had obtained (Stahl 1999: 51). African-American woman correspondents have had additional burdens related to overcoming African-American stereotypes. Trudy Haynes in Philadelphia recalled photographers who would not work with her (Marshall 1999). Simpson, involved in television since 1970, said in a 1996 interview, "I am still battling. I was sure it would have ended at this point, at my age and with my depth of experience, and it has not. I'm still fighting. As vigorously as I fought race and sex discrimination through the years, I will fight age discrimination" (Marlane 1999: 98).

It is not surprising that the women who survived sought to encourage and support each other rather than become the enemies of popular representation, as with the supposed feud between Barbara Walters and Sally Quinn when Quinn joined the *CBS Morning News* in 1972. Quinn makes it clear that Walters put out the hand of collegial friendship (Quinn 1975). Simpson recalls Walters similarly supportive at ABC (Simpson 2002). Stahl remembers the joyful afternoon she spent with a group of women network correspondents brought together for a *Life* story for yet another pronouncement of the war won. "We all hung around that zany afternoon as long as we could. We loved being with one another because, as one of us said, 'Hey, we're all the same person'" (Stahl 1999: 152).

Did It Matter?

The pressures brought by broadcast reform movement of the early 1970s assisted in opening up opportunities for women. In 1974, Kathy Bonk's Communications Consortium counted that women correspondents reported just under 10 percent of television network stories. Although his research in the 1980s "painted a grim picture of women's visibility on the network evening news," Joe S. Foote found significant changes by the 1990s (1995: 235). In the same period, Sue Lafky noted that gender stereotypes still existed, as in continuing emphasis on youth and beauty for women, particularly on local news (1995: 257). At this writing, the evening news anchors on the over-the-air networks are still male, but the growth of cable news networks has increased women's visibility as anchors and correspondents.

The changes came with difficulty, often as women and minority groups were set against each other. In 1976, as employment of women in broadcasting began to rise at a higher rate than that of black men and women, an FCC official delivered the findings to a Washington-based African-American radio show host, noting that the women's movement and the "minorities movement" had collided over jobs in broadcasting but it was not the role of the FCC to arbitrate disputes between groups. He apparently saw no problem in exacerbating the situation by his appearance on a local program (*BC* 4/1/76: 51–52). By 1978, scholars were calling for a reassessment of the broadcast reform movement, noting that it was at a crossroads as reform groups that could not cooperate for broader goals began to lose volunteers and leaders in a changed regulatory environment (Branscomb and Savage 1978). By the end of the decade, the FCC had become less eager to consider petitions-to-deny and was seeking ways to disallow "frivolous" petitions and petitioners who did not meet a threshold of standing (*BC* 3/8/80: 28).

Finally, it was not clear that the ultimate purpose of broadcast reform had been met. Despite the notable successes of the women's broadcast reform movement, the promise that women in the business would help represent the issues of the women's movement in legitimate ways was problematical. In a discussion of the impact of minorities and women in local television, *Broadcasting* quoted news consultant Pat Polillo as saying that the new groups were "changing the look of news, not anything else" (*BC* 5/76: 86). To succeed or remain in the business, female reporters found it necessary to abide by craft traditions and the directions of their news directors and station managers. Special programs on women (often part of the agreements women had forged in lieu of a license challenge) often had a moderate tone, as in New York's Channel 13 series, *Woman Alive*, which eschewed "militant ideology in favor of pertinent example and quiet celebration" (*NYT* 10/22/75: 91). Still, the 1975 program showed improvement over a 1971 program that "featured brassiere factories, bras being tossed away or burnt" (*Awake and Move* 3/1/71: 1). In her review of the local San Francisco–produced *Women in the Media* program, radical writer Chocolate Waters was not optimistic about the future of television: "We'll still have shows that are violent, racist, and sexist. And we'll still have commercials that are as repugnant as the ones that were inserted in this very special on women. Only now we'll have women who call themselves 'cameramen' doing the shooting, women writing the violent scripts about men killing each other and raping women, and women broadcasting the news that men make about themselves. How very wonderful that women can do the same things that man can do and in the very same ways. How very disappointing" (Waters, "Women in Media": 13).

Waters and other radicals pointed out that industry could hardly change given the role of profit in news. Women began to find doors open in broadcast at a time when broadcasting was under increased pressure to be profitable by any means necessary. On local levels, opportunities began opening up for women, often by way of the formats that called for women on the set. There was hardly a unanimous belief that the new formats were either a service to news or to women, however. In a 1976 article, critic Ron Powers ticked off the stunts to which format reporters resorted, women as much to men: "But there was something missing at the core. Amidst all the self-conscious, the preening, the ingratiation, and the bonhomie, [Edward R.] Murrow might have noticed that in very few cases was there a sense of mission about the TV newscasts, a sense of continuity in the life of the city (or 'market') covered; a palpable willingness to perform the vigorous, adversary check-on-government, intervening role that American journalism has traditionally performed" (Powers 1977: 118). Moreover, the appearance on local news programs of anchorwomen who clearly were not interested in achieving prominence by way of journalistic skills established role models based on attractiveness and careerism rather than on devotion to news, a state of affairs that subsequently impacted the kinds of female students entering college broadcast programs.

Most damning is recent quantitative research that concludes that newsrooms at local stations with females in management are no more likely to produce stories of interest to women than are newsrooms run by men. The same researchers also found no support for their hypothesis that female reporters would contribute to the on-air representation of women by interviewing more female newsmakers and experts. This study suggests that market research, not news managers, dictates news coverage (Smith, Laura and Wright 1998). These conclusions counter feminist beliefs voiced during the period as well as expectations from scholars, including Muriel Cantor, who predicted as late as 1988, "Placing more women in powerful roles in the industry would over time change how women are depicted, which in turn would change their role in society" (Cantor 1988: 81). A substantial number of women in broadcast news may be interested primarily in survival rather than in insuring coverage of a particular agenda. A recent qualitative study of female broadcast managers indicated that finding a way to survive in broadcasting's corporate culture and combining the time demands of a broadcast career with home and family life were the prominent concerns (Phalen 2000).

What clearly did not happen as a result of the broadcast reform movement was a reorientation of news content along reformist lines. Indeed, the consolidation of broadcast properties into fewer and fewer hands has only emphasized what were the dangerous show business trends that so concerned Cronkite in the 1970s but have now become an accepted strategy in a competitive, unregulated environment that seeks the best return on its investment. Special programs on important topics have largely disappeared on network and local levels, not only as cost-saving measures but influenced by a new political environment. Fox News has ushered in a new era of news programming that seeks to make sure that the conservative view is on the news agenda, as liberals thirty years ago sought to put their cause on the agenda.

Finally, the move to reform broadcast came at the heyday of the network news divisions. Few reformers at the time could conceive of the changes that would come to network news because of the impact of cable narrowcasting, convergence of technologies, or the new ways of doing news as a result of ownership patterns. The development of cable along entertainment and profit values, the failure of citizen programming, the blurring of all news into entertainment content, the competition from the Internet, and indeed, the general public disinterest in activist journalism were hardly to be imagined in the optimism of the second wave. Nor did broadcast reformers consider the nature of the broadcast audience. Speaking with unusual frankness considering the United States does not like to deal directly with class issues, Phil McHugh told *Broadcasting* in 1976 that local stations had no choice but to appeal to the largest audience—that is, the 70 percent of the nation composed of the "vast lower middle class and upper lower class" (*BC* 1/6/76: 84). Activists of the second wave—despite their efforts—did not find working-class populations easy to attract. Given the perception that the women's movement was concerned mostly with upper-class women, broadcast managers could conclude only that programming aimed at the largest audience was not likely to succeed if attached to the label of the second wave, whose members comprised only a fraction of viewers. As a result, second-wave issues had to be reframed—domestic violence as a dramatic vehicle for television actress Farrah Fawcett, for example—if they were to become content for a broadcast audience. While this kind of reframing may have been useful for bringing these issues to new audiences, such a treatment also removed from attention the overall, systemic concerns of second-wave feminism and attendant political activism.

Hugh Downs's 1972 comments were prescient: "By its nature, commercial television abandons any real excursion into either end of the spectrum, not so much because it would be some form of journalistic extremism, nor even because of the potential public outcry, but more because of the necessity to avoid controversy at the interface between its offerings and its financial support," he wrote in a magazine piece. "The narrow middle path is itself conservative and somehow patronizing to viewers" (Downs 1972: 67).

11. Rise of the Opposition

Phyllis Schlafly was one of those women writing books in the early 1960s. The self-published *A Choice Not An Echo*, supporting Barry Goldwater for U.S. president, elevated her to the first ranks of conservative leaders and set the way for her to become the nation's most vociferous and public opponent of feminism. When the proposed Equal Rights Amendment to the U.S. Constitution was defeated on 30 June 1982, its extension for ratification having finally run out, it was her moment of glory, which she recalled in 1997 in an article for the magazine *George*. The magazine's editors, even thirty years after the introduction of the amendment, could not resist headlining the Schlafly article "Eyewitness: Beating the Bra Burners." Schlafly recalled, "It was the last day of a ten-year David-and-Goliath struggle waged across America. A little band of women, headquartered in the kitchen of my home on the bluffs of the Mississippi in Alton, Illinois, had defeated the big guns. The odds against us could not have been greater" (Schlafly 1997).

While the image of Schlafly directing the Stop ERA! campaign as an amateur in her kitchen is misleading, to many the passage of the ERA seemed a natural culmination of the women's movement's successes. As early as 1970, census data found that women's attitudes were changing in ways that suggested that passage of the ERA would be the next logical step. That year, in the first Gallup Poll on the subject of the ERA, 56 percent of those interviewed said they favored the amendment (Mansbridge 1986: 14). By 1972 President Nixon had asked the Congress to broaden jurisdiction of the Civil Rights Commission to deal with sex discrimination and called himself an ERA supporter. First Lady Pat Nixon, who in 1973 was ranked by a *Good Housekeeping* poll as the nation's most admired woman, wore a pro-ERA bracelet, as did the Nixons' daughter, Julie, in a pro-ERA campaign sponsored by the League of Women Voters. Twenty-six national organizations came together in a pro-ERA campaign financed by the National Business and Professional Women's Clubs, the longtime supporters of the proposal and an organization that had had much to do with the founding of the second wave. By 1974 the Gallup Poll found that 79 percent of voters backed the ERA (*NYT* 11/4/74: 44). President Gerald R. Ford supported the amendment, as did First Lady Betty Ford, who campaigned for it. Labor, giving up the position on protective legislation that had hindered its early support of the women's movement, also backed the amendment. In a common understanding, activist Pat Keefer said that passage was almost assured by 1975 (*NYT* 1/29/74: 15).

Why the ERA was not adopted has been the subject of discussion since 1982, and the role of media is likely not the reason, even though the ERA presented yet another new conflict story that met craft traditions and provided a platform for the antifeminist messages. Feminists such as Gloria Steinem and Eleanor Smeal put down the loss to the power of the state-regulated insurance business in the state legislatures. In her study of the proposed amendment, Jane J. Mansbridge found no evidence of a conscious insurance-industry campaign against the ERA, although she does not discount that on a subtle level state legislators may have supported the insurance position, seeing it as representing "rugged individualism and nostalgia for a small-business past" as a result of their own connections to small-business occupations such as law, insurance, and real estate (Mansbridge 1986: 150–51). What role those values played in the final votes is not clear. What is clear, despite all the national and sometimes favorable attention the ERA received, as in the League of Women Voters campaign, the defeat of the ERA on a state-by-state level indicated that the women's movement could not replicate on local levels the same kind of accomplishments that had been achieved on the national level. In retrospect, this was not surprising, given the lack of feminist success in securing favorable attention for public actions outside of city settings. Moreover, U.S. state legislatures were and are dominated by men and women from small towns and rural localities, and the connection of feminism to big cities, particularly New York, was likely not an enamoring factor.

Most importantly, however, the campaign to defeat the ERA served as a rallying point for the nation's social conservatives, who utilized a variety of communication networks outside mass media and helped establish a culture that was receptive to political conservatism. Utilizing church, organizational, and technological networks, Catholic, Mormon, and fundamentalist Protestant groups found common ground and built a power base for a new world of revisionist politics that was not envisioned by activists in the early 1970s.

Campaigning for the ERA

Beginning with NOW, many women's organizations outside of those of the New Right supported the ERA and usually did so in activist ways (important exceptions included the General Federation of Women's Clubs and the Republican National

Women's Club). Initially, the activism sought to bring widespread attention to the proposed amendment to reach voters who would pressure elected officials in each state. The various campaigns sought to build on the acceptability of liberal or mainstream feminism by public persuasion.

NOW, of course, was an old hand at such campaigns. Moreover, in the early 1970s NOW was seeking to return to its early style of activism under its new president, Wilma Scott Heide, founder of the activist Pittsburgh NOW chapter. Not only was the chapter active in the broadcast reform movement—Jo-Anne Evansgardener and Kathy Bonk among its members—but Heide herself had led a February 1970 protest in which twenty NOW members interrupted a Senate hearing on the eighteen-year-old vote to call for Senate hearings on the ERA (which, indeed, occurred in May). When Heide became NOW president, her Pittsburgh activism was clearly an influence when she called for a symbolic "tax rebellion" to hurry passage of the ERA (*NYT* 2/13/72: 32). Early the next year, NOW members in Washington, D.C., sold their blood in a fund-raising campaign (*NYT* 1/16/73: 9). At NOW'S 1973 convention in February, Heide called for the women's movement to be more "radical" and for NOW to mount "creative, dramatic actions" (*NYT* 2/19/73: 12). Not surprisingly, the following August, the anniversary of the Nineteenth Amendment was noted in various demonstrations—in the gallery of the American Stock Exchange; a protest outside New York Governor Nelson Rockefeller's office; a mock funeral for women who had died from illegal abortions; and the mock presentations of "Keep Her in Her Place" awards. In the same manner, NOW also chose to emphasize public actions to promote the ERA, sending flowers and valentines to members of the Ohio legislative committee, which was opening hearings on the ERA (*NYT* 2/22/73: 33). Such tactics continued under the NOW presidency of Karen DeCrow, who had come to NOW leadership under Friedan and the public accommodations campaigns, but her NOW presidential campaign "Out of the Mainstream and into the Revolution," distanced Friedan and her supporters, who briefly mounted a counterorganization.

In this whirlwind of political theater, the ERA was not the single or even prime focus of NOW's public actions because of the assumption that the measure would pass easily. NOW's attention was on many other fronts, including print and broadcast reform measures, pornography, what was going to become known as "ageism," sex stereotyping in childhood play activities, in books and in schools, the retention of birth names by married women as well as actions in already delineated subsections of interest (women's health, psychiatric treatment, day care) and issues that emerged from any number of pockets of activity that could be related to feminism, from the naming of tropical storms for men as well as women to arguments over belly dancing. Given the diverse agenda taken on by activist feminists, in and out of NOW, the passage of the ERA sometimes seemed an afterthought.

NOW's emphasis on public actions continued despite what was becoming public and political impatience with those tactics. By 1972 even sympathetic observers were critical of the "theater part" of the movement, as Lady Bird Johnson called it (NYT 1/67/72: 3). An academic warned that the movement needed to make systemic change if it was not to disappear, like the suffragists, "without a trace" (NYT 2/13/72: L33). Criticism also came from inside the movement: the New Jersey coordinator of NOW said that the movement should concentrate on "simple, reasonable goals" rather than "nebulous baloney" (NYT 12/17/72: 90).

Providing the clearest evidence that the tactic of public persuasion did not work was the turnaround of support in the ERA. By the closing months of 1974, rescissions of the ERA had resulted in the need for eight states, rather than three, to approve passage of the amendment. In a sudden realization of the problem, the League of Women Voters opened a national campaign to raise money for the support of the amendment—the sale of ERA bracelets at two dollars each not only raised money but was aimed at providing a way to indicate, woman-by-woman, the breadth of support. Celebrities and public figures as well as ordinary people wore ERA bracelets. But like the red ribbons that later came to represent sympathy with AIDS activism, the ERA bracelets represented broad support—something that was not in doubt, as polls proved—while not necessarily demanding or calling for action from supporters. The purchase of a two-dollar ERA bracelet was a cheap way to share in the cachet of the movement, but it did not demand an investment in the state-by-state local campaign that was needed for the amendment to be approved.

Church and secular organizations also worked together on behalf of the ERA. When it appeared that there was not sufficient time to gain the required number of state approvals, the pro-ERA community—in a final exhaustive effort—achieved an extension. Under Eleanor Smeal, who became the first salaried president of NOW in 1977, the organization mounted a sophisticated and successful campaign for a three-year extension that emphasized not so much large-scale media as the political levers of individual elections on a state-by-state basis. During 1982 NOW was involved in several hundred races at the national and state levels to defeat ERA opponents. Despite many local successes and polls that showed that the majority of women favored the amendment, the organizational effort could not overcome the resources put into the anti-ERA campaign by special-interest groups or counter the gerrymandering of districts to minimize the power of liberal voters (Smeal 1983). Notwithstanding the magnificent culminating efforts of feminists, many of whom put aside personal and other feminist agendas to work for the ERA, the ERA campaign failed to regain its early impetus.

In hindsight, the campaign to pass the ERA put the issue in conflict with the many other feminist issues that were crowding into the media marketplace, including stories deliberately mounted for media as well as feminist stories that emerged from craft traditions. Among the most frequent stories emerging from craft decisions were those of "first women." Every community was beginning to have women in occupations previously closed to them—police officers, firefighters, mail carriers, plumbers, and so on. Then again there were the first women in terms of achievements—in sports, in business, in leadership. First-woman stories offered ways for regional media to localize the national story, to represent changing times, and could even offer opportunity for conflict—altogether a cluster of news values that could hardly be ignored. In her review of first-women stories, Ruth Rosen notes, "I still remember a feature story that made a great impression on me in this period. It profiled a 'lady neurosurgeon' who rose at dawn to train for marathons, made breakfast for her children, operated on six or seven brains, returned home for a few 'quality hours' with her children, cooked a gourmet dinner for her husband, and then, with her children asleep, enjoyed a few hours of intimacy with him" (Rosen 2000: 304).

First-women stories were a mixed blessing, drawing attention to the expectation that every field would be integrated by gender but also suggesting that the new "superwomen" would only enhance rather than replace existing traditions. Moreover, the stories suggested that the war had been won, particularly for those who regarded feminism as calling only for equal pay for equal work. And because there were so many firsts, and they were easy to cover, easy to digest, and positioned the media outlet safely (no argument that media were not covering the movement), the first-women stories came at the expense of other feminist stories without those qualities. While news organizations do not have official quotas for particular subjects, it is certainly part of news managers' judgments to decide how to serve their audiences' interest levels. For most editors, and perhaps for their readers, the first-women stories were more than enough to take care of the second wave. This shift in coverage thus cemented the notion in the public consciousness that the second wave was solely about equal work opportunity.

The media's quick acceptance of the first-women stories helped prompt the ultimate first-woman story, the first modern woman to put herself forward as a candidate for president of the United States. In 1972, as Schlafly was beginning her anti-ERA campaign, supposedly around her kitchen table, the major feminist story of the year was Shirley Chisholm, a member of the House of Representatives from Brooklyn, New York, who sought the Democratic presidential nomination. She had lukewarm support from black leadership groups, but Chisholm saw her candidacy as one not dependent on a black constituency alone, instead drawing support from a variety of groups—women, youth, and older white voters "who had grown impatient with the programs and candidates of the two major parties" (Chisholm, "Good Fight": 38). From the beginning, no one—not even the most ardent feminist or Chisholm worker—or even Chisholm herself—pretended that she could succeed. "Although I could not win," she wrote in her memoir, "I still might help all the people who were offering me support, by increasing their influence on the decision about who would be the Democratic nominee." Even as a token, her campaign was limited—by insufficient funds, by an inexperienced staff, and by discord between white and black supporters. "For me, the conflict between blacks and white women appeared to be a competition over which group was going to own me and my candidacy, and I was determined to keep from becoming the captive of either" (Chisholm, "Good Fight": 44, 166). In the meantime, leading white feminists, including Bella Abzug, Gloria Steinem, and Betty Friedan, preparing to endorse George McGovern, gave Chisholm's candidacy only tentative or late support and then did so in terms of its symbolism rather than actuality. This was not the kind of backing that was likely to persuade African-Americans that the women's movement, which many already distrusted, was as committed to the concerns of African-American women as feminists insistently pronounced.

Nonetheless, Chisholm became a household name and national celebrity because of her candidacy. At the 1972 Democratic National Convention, 151 delegates came out for her on the first ballot as a demonstration of black unity, and her campaign reached its most public point with the jubilant demonstration on her behalf (carried live by the networks) when her name was put into nomination. Yet even at this point, it was clear that the campaign was symbolic, and because it was symbolic rather than representing any real lever of power, feminist support was taken for granted. Feminist delegates were not able to include the abortion plank in the Democratic platform. The feminist choice for vice president, Texas legislator Sissy Farenthold, was ignored in favor of Sargent Shriver. Despite her offers, Chisholm was not invited to be part of the McGovern campaign; similarly uninvited were other minority women and the labor voters that the campaign purported to represent. Nonetheless, several celebrity feminists remained associated with the campaign—Steinem, Shirley MacLaine, Abzug—suggesting to the larger world that the McGovern campaign represented feminism. McGovern's subsequent crushing defeat, taking only one state, connected the second wave only to failed politics. And the defeat could also have reminded feminists that power is often illusionary and perhaps never was as strong as indicated by a *Times*' headline earlier in the year: "Feminists Emerge as a Political Power" (*NYT* 3/4/72: 31).

Chisholm's candidacy drew attention to feminist claims of a male-run political establishment and may have made people consider the possibility of women in high office. It also provided a national platform to an African-American woman, with the corollary that the feminist movement was not simply about white upper-class privilege. But the emphasis on symbolism at a time when supporters were seeking real political commitment to a constitutional amendment may have blurred and confused the political realities and encouraged the example set by the Chisholm candidacy for the ERA also to be considered symbolic.

Internal Divisions

Internal conflict continued to harm the movement as news of divisions leaked into the press and provided a means of "updating" movement stories. At a college lecture, Friedan was reported to have charged Steinem with having "ripped off" the movement for private profit (*NYT* 2/9/72: 28, 6). Friedan said she was misquoted (*NYT* 2/11/72: 19), but the incident marked Friedan's problematical role in the movement and further fueled the conflict metaphor that mass media so frequently used in framing the story. Despite the sobriquet "mother of women's liberation," the approaching tenth anniversary of *The Feminine Mystique*, her ongoing lecture tours, and her role as a public figure, Friedan seemed more famous than loved. At a New York City news conference, Friedan announced her plans to challenge New York's liberal senator, Jacob Javits, but she was upstaged when wild applause was given to Chisholm, introduced by Abzug as the "next President of the United States" (*NYT* 2/17/72: 33). Abzug herself had ambitions for the U.S. Senate and was not above embarrassing Friedan.

However, by 1972, many feminists considered Friedan out of date and even booed her at rallies. Rejected by public feminists Steinem and Abzug, among others, Friedan tried to widen her base and in so doing further alienated many movement feminists. In yet another news conference, Friedan elaborated on the theme of her *McCall's* article that "female chauvinists"—specifically naming Steinem and Abzug as examples—were corrupting the movement and inviting backlash (*NYT* 7/19/72: 4). The remarks brought reactions from Steinem and Abzug and a rush of letters to the *New York Times* (*NYT* 7/20/72: 29).

As Friedan refused to give ground, the *New York Times Magazine* became a very public battlefield. The movement, Friedan said in an article that would further incense former comrades, was in danger of being taken over by "man-haters, lesbians, pseudo-radical infantilists, and infiltrations" (*NYTM* 3/4/73: VI, 8). Her comments resulted in a predictable spate of letters.

This internecine battle in the most public of places did little good in encouraging political change. Abzug failed in her attempt for a Senate seat. By the end of 1972, states had begun to rescind their ERA endorsements. The attention of the country turned to the problem of Vietnam and then to Watergate. Friedan, who had done much to fan the flames of the feminist firestorm, remained out of the center of feminist and political power. Her senatorial ambitions slipped quietly away. In the fall of 1972, she took a job as a guest lecturer in sociology at Temple University in Philadelphia, and she later took other positions at university and think tanks as she made her living for the next thirty years by teaching, speaking, and writing. At Yale in 1974, her course had to be restructured because students— few in the feminist community would have been surprised—complained that she lectured too much (*NYT* 11/11/74: 25). However, the fact that the *New York Times* carried this tiny blip of a story gives evidence to media's ongoing gnawing even at minor issues, if they reflected division. Thus, "Division among Feminists: The Rift Widens" was an unsurprising eight-column *Times* headline in 1975, when the Redstockings accused Steinem of having worked for the CIA (Franks 1975: 32).

The divisions in the movement were not invented by media, but there were widely held suspicions that the CIA was placing operatives in the movement and otherwise promoting rift. Barbara Seaman, a former *Family Circle* health writer and author of a well-received book on women's health, voiced a common perception: "The movement is being ravaged and no one is getting any work done. It is clear to me that there are agents working to bust us up" (Franks 1975: 32). Letty Pogrebin addressed the issue in *Ms.* based on documents obtained under the Freedom of Information Act (Pogrebin 1977). CIA or FBI infiltration of the women's movement long had been contended by Friedan, who viewed the lesbian split as engineered by the CIA or FBI, a point she made to Judy Klemesrud when Steinem held a news conference after Millett was outed by *Time* (*NYT* 12/18/70: 47). In 1975, Friedan's view was taken to a national television news audience when she blamed the CIA for the movement's "paralysis of leadership" (presumably her rejection) (NBC 1975). Many years later, she told Ruth Rosen that CIA infiltration had ultimately defeated the ERA (Rosen 2000: 253).

The suspicions, although often viewed as paranoia and as unpatriotic by the nonfeminist community at the time, clearly were on target: surveillance apparently began as early as 1968 on orders from FBI director J. Edgar Hoover (Rosen 2000: 244–54). What has yet to be explored is how the infiltration affected the drive for the ERA other than by general upset—and that strategy alone may have been sufficient.

In addition to power struggles and the politico-womanist split of the early years, the movement also came to be divided by other diverse points of views.

This was not unexpected in a maturing social movement. In 1976, Jinx Melia, a teacher from Washington, D.C., founded the Martha Movement, which sought to address homemakers' special concerns under the umbrella of the movement: "They want to strengthen their marriages, raise their children, keep their wits, make money when they need to and develop emotional, social, and financial independence" (Sheils et al. 1977: 39). Other feminist organizations marked off territory that rejected parts of the movement, such as abortion, or was aimed at bringing what they considered overlooked issues to the table in the implicit criticism of how the movement had originally been shaped. These were not necessarily divisions as much as discussions of feminism from other points of view.

There was also a natural burnout and turning away from movement activism for personal concerns. By 1976 Jean Curtis represented feminist women who found that sisterhood took second place to her own ambition: "When it comes to my work, I'm mostly rooting for myself" (Curtis, J. 1976: 16). A columnist for *Mademoiselle* magazine wondered how feminists were going to get women to do the work of the movement when most people wanted no more than to "take it easy" (Fader 1972: 36). A 1986 piece in *The Economist* identified what was already occurring ten years earlier: "One trouble with Mrs. Smeal's [new effort on behalf of the ERA] is that it simply redoubles the fury and the determination of right-wing groups without, apparently, arousing much passionate response among young women" (*Economist* 5/23/86: 43). These kinds of views were not part of an antifeminist war but indicated the difficulties of a social change movement maintaining the intensity that many women had felt in consciousness-raising sessions and in actions of the tumultuous 1970s but had lost when they turned back to personal concerns (including new work opportunities that the movement had provided) when faced with the grind of the day-to-day world of feminist activism. Although feminist leaders wrote glowingly of a sense of unity that concluded the 1977 Women's Year Conference in Houston and later at the reinvigoration of the movement after the ERA extension, there was less a sense of this in the general population and certainly nothing like the heady days surrounding the 1970 march. Thus, dissension within the leadership of a movement, an emphasis on symbolic achievement and public events, and overconfidence at a time when feminist women were turning to personal concerns were not surprising characteristics of a movement that had become part of the mass culture in less than a decade. But those characteristics also opened the door to what would turn out to be the major threat to the movement—conservatives, who played a large role in the defeat of the ERA and in less than a decade became powerful enough to elect a U.S. president and to reestablish an agenda that the liberals of the late 1960s and 1970s considered behind them.

New Content for Booksellers

Despite the frequent canard that the women's movement was only of interest to a handful of women, paperback publishers found profit in the subject. Dell reissued a tenth-anniversary edition of *The Feminine Mystique,* Vintage published Robin Morgan's *Sisterhood Is Powerful* in a cheap edition, Quadrangle published Aileen Kraditor's *Up from the Pedestal* in paperback, and Bantam reissued Simone DeBeauvoir's *The Second Sex.* Paperback publishers were also finding interest in the women's movement made a place for paperback originals. Ace published a collection, *Women's Liberation: Blueprint for the Future,* at ninety-five cents, providing a less radical sampling of movement discussion than found in Morgan's book (*NYT* 8/17/70: 32). Another ninety-five-cent book, Margaret Albrecht's *A Complete Guide for the Working Mother,* also gave indication that women's liberation was going to be increasingly interpreted in terms of working (*Saturday Review* 10/31/70: 33).

After the news media had legitimized alternative views as a result of the need to balance the feminist story, publishers were equally eager to publish books reflecting the other side when those views could be profitable. Thus, in 1970, as feminism became hot media property, antifeminism also took hold in the mass media marketplace. These radical Right voices, which had barely existed in the public realm before the second wave, now became as prominent as those of the feminists.

Written in 1963, Helen B. Andelin's manuscript found its way across the desk of Doubleday editor Margaret Cousins in 1965. Cousins, a self-described "warhorse" of the women's magazines, erupted in laughter: "I am very glad you asked me to read this book," she wrote in her evaluation, "as I am now able to understand why I have never married—it is because I laugh loudly and joke, drink by throwing my head back and wear tweeds. Lots of the advice here is quite sound on men-women relationships and actually won't hurt anybody since women are very unlikely to be able to carry it out. If they could it would set women back a couple of thousand years, but maybe that's what they need. I agree with her on a majority of her points, but know I could never accomplish 'bewitching languor' " (Bradley 1995: 84–85).

Andelin chose to self-publish her book from her family's Santa Barbara, California, base. But in 1970, as the women's movement opened a place for feminist and antifeminist works, Andelin's book was republished and received attention, although supercilious in tone, in no less a place than the *New York Times* (*NYT* 9/28/70: 50). *Fascinating Womanhood,* which had been rejected by Doubleday on the basis of silliness, went on to become a best-seller in mass-market paperback and served as the founding document for a magazine and for a national education movement, still extant, that provides women with lessons in how to please their husbands. More importantly, the Fascinating Woman movement, although derided in some quarters, helped politicize antifeminism and thus advance the emerging conservative agenda. Following a similar path, Marabel Morgan published *The Total Woman*, which became a nonfiction best-seller, surpassing even *All the President's Men* (*PW* 2/3/75: 427). The book's popularity not only gave rise to a chapter-by-chapter organization across the nation but also provided yet another new lead for takes on the women's movement.

Antifeminist books flooded the market. In 1972, Midge Decter produced *The New Chastity and Other Arguments against Women's Liberation*, an extension of her *Atlantic* article. In the *Manipulated Man*, Esther Vilar contended that men rather than women were enslaved. In 1973 George F. Gilder wrote in *Sexual Suicide: A Defense of Traditional Love, Marriage, and Sexual Roles* that the woman and home should be "nothing less than the central activity of the human community" (Gilder 1973: 40). This was the first of four books and a television program that helped turn him into a Far Right spokesman. Gilder's celebrity was enhanced during the Reagan administration when his book, *Wealth and Poverty*, arguing that women needed to remain in the home as a mobile labor force to be called on when needed, was embraced by the administration and sold a million copies (Faludi 1991: 289). Interestingly, Gilder's point of view would not have been acceptable had it been presented in terms of an ethnic group, and its acceptance points to the failure of the women's movement to find an equal place with social activism organizations representing race and ethnic groups. For other publishers, antifeminism was an opportunity to get on the national stage. Jarrow Press took out a full-page advertisement in *Publisher's Weekly* ("The Answer to Women's Lib! Or Why the Feminine Mystique Is a Mistake!") promoting David Allen's *The Price of Women* (*PW* 1/25/71: 85).

Publication was now often accompanied by a book tour, considered necessary for promotion since *The Feminine Mystique*. For local television and newspapers interviews, the books represented a new hook on the feminist story. Like the authors of advocacy books, authors of these works often became spokespeople for the positions their books represented, and the book tours segued into paid speaking engagements. Decter was one of the most active on the public circuit, already something of a public figure as a result of her marriage to Norman Podhoretz, editor of *Commentary*. As part of the New York intelligentsia, she received more respectful media attention than did the authors of the Fascinating Woman ideologies. Decter told the Women's National Book Association that the movement helped certain privileged women but led to female "self-hatred." In a prominent feature in the *Washington Post*, she declared, "the movement people are hiding behind the problems of a few unfortunate women" (*WP* 11/5/72: E5). Decter was no Andelin or Morgan, whose ideas were extreme enough for some women to find feminism a viable option. Decter had apparently balanced marriage and family, including four children, and may have indicated to women not ready to embrace feminism that women could have it all without change. The ship of state surely was up to plugging the holes represented by "a few unfortunate women" without changing course.

But even before publishing her book, Decter had been important in putting the antifeminist agenda on the mass media in her role as executive editor at *Harper's*, a magazine that published several articles antithetical to feminism, including the Mailer piece. Decter had a deep and abiding dislike of the women's movement, mostly because of what she saw as its hatred toward men and heterosexual sex. As late as 2001, Decter remained firm in her belief "of the striking influence of lesbianism" in the movement and the responsibility it carried for damage to relationships between the sexes (Decter 2001: 86).

Counterorganizations

The women's movement was able to get on the media agenda by its ability to mount newsworthy events. What were considered extreme positions by the mainstream media called for balance, stories that provided the opposite point of view. The media's choice of what and who would do the balancing was not based on the size of the voice, a tradition that had helped WITCH and other radical groups to attract initial attention. Thus, counter groups merely had to announce themselves with a peg to the women's movement to get mentioned. Antifeminist organizations with acronyms quickly flooded the media. As activities for the 1970 march were getting publicity, a woman described as a part-time legal secretary in New York formed Men Our Masters (MOM), which found newspaper niches even in places such as the *Christian Science Monitor*, which usually eschewed coverage of events considered to have been contrived only for the benefit of media (*CSM* 8/6/70: 16). Later in the month, the new organization presented a MOM award to ERA foe, U.S. Representative Emanuel Celler (D-N.Y.), who accepted it before the acronym was dismantled, which gave an extra fillip to the *Times*'s story (*NYT* 8/29/70: 12:3). One antifeminist organization called Happiness of Womanhood adopted HOW as its acronym for no other purpose than to be a media counterweight for NOW. It announced that it was launching a campaign to battle "those dragging the word 'housewife' though the mud" (*NYT* 4/3/72: 44, 1/15/73: 1). Its first action was to stage a "Happiness Rally" in Los Angeles on the day of the 1970 Women's Strike for Equality. Later in the year, HOW called a press conference at the Miss America Contest, although pageant officials snubbed the group and no one attended the rally (Leone). Nonetheless, the organization's few members received periodic attention from prestige media because it presented an alternative view wrapped in an organizational setting. Lucianne Goldberg, a Washington lobbyist at the time and later involved in the Monica Lewinsky scandal, was among three women who founded a group called the Pussycats that purported to share many of the same goals of feminists, including legalization of abortion, but opposed the "militant'" techniques. "Militant women make war; we make love," said one Pussycat (Goodman 1969: 37).

Phyllis Schlafly

The 1970s women's movement clearly did not produce the Far Right. Its late-twentieth-century version came to national prominence in 1964 with the presidential campaign of Barry Goldwater, who had no greater supporter than Phyllis Schlafly. She wrote and paid to publish and distribute *A Choice Not an Echo*, a campaign book that became a best-seller and a touchstone for conservatives. Goldwater's subsequent defeat, which caused many commentators to predict an end to the Republican Party, energized conservatives to build personal and technologically savvy networks, including a major use of cable and UHF television as those technologies became powerful. Schlafly, who had built her reputation in the conservative movement on the basis of her knowledge of nuclear strategy and public education, turned her energy to the ERA. That energy included a substantial role for major and specialized media in conjunction with the networking opportunities offered by the Republican Party, evangelical churches, and her own organization, the Eagle Forum.

Schlafly was experienced and well connected in conservative and national politics. By the time *A Choice Not An Echo* was published, she had been a three-time delegate to the Republican National Convention. She was also a Phi Beta Kappa graduate of Washington University in St. Louis, earned a master's degree in political science from Harvard University, and obtained a law degree from the Washington University Law School while she was running the anti-ERA campaign. She was married with six children and lived with her husband in Alton, Illinois. In 1972 she began the Eagle Forum as a national volunteer organization. The Stop ERA! organization, which she founded under that umbrella, was significantly financed by the John Birch Society (Boles 1979: 67, 79). The kitchen table analogy did not give credit to the sophistication of her tactics, the depth of her resources, or her unchallenged control of Stop ERA! and the ancillary organizations that supported it—indeed, her total grasp of the levers of propaganda (Tillson 1996). While local chapters operated independently, the loyalty that she engendered staved off challenges to her national leadership. Given the diverse messages that often came from the feminist movement, Schlafly's control of all aspects of the campaign, including its media images, was appropriate to a propaganda campaign as described by Garth Jowett and Victoria O'Donnell: "Successful propaganda campaigns tend to originate from a strong, centralized and decision-making authority that produces a consistent message throughout its structure" (Jowett and O'Donnell 1986: 157). As her biographer describes it, Schlafly's control of the message extended to media opportunities in the smallest detail: "Campaign strategy, set design for TV spots, typeface for brochures, all came under her personal scrutiny" (Felsenthal 1981: 205). A reporter for her local newspaper noted, "Mrs. Schlafly is a creature of the media. . . . She is careful to sit in just the right chair when she is going to be photographed. Like the eager actress she's concerned that the light be adequate for a photograph and that she's always wearing an affable smile." Another reporter commented, "She's always on, she's very serious about the image . . . and that's what makes her so dangerous" (Felsenthal 1981: 299, 300).

Use of Media and the Rise of the New Right

Conservatives had long criticized the mass media, believing that entertainment shows pushed the envelope of the morally acceptable, that news programs served at the beck of the Radical Left, and that insufficient representation of conservative positions occurred in both news and entertainment. The *Washington Post*, the *New York Times*, and CBS television were particular targets for criticism. The most famous attack on the media was made by Spiro Agnew, who in 1969 claimed that national media was not only all-powerful but controlled by a small group of left-leaning elite (Epstein, E. 1973: 200), whom he so famously called "nattering nabobs of negativism." Not surprisingly, as president, Nixon sought ways to disenfranchise national media—by supporting local stations at the expense of networks, changing the composition of the FCC, and compiling an enemies' list of media personalities that his administration chose to shut out.

What was most useful to the New Right was its early adoption of technology—from computers maintaining lists of supporters to the development and use of alternative media, building on the substantive experience U.S. religious movements have had with media since the pre-World War II days when Father Coughlin preached on the CBS radio network. Coughlin also provided an example of how mass media could be circumvented. When he was finally dropped from

CBS for his pro-German messages, he continued to reach a mass radio audience by putting together a group of non–network affiliated stations. In another era, in the 1970s, fundamental religious groups found that they could also build mass audiences by utilizing methods of distribution that were not controlled by the dominant mass media. Religious broadcasters were early adopters of what were at the time the despised ultrahigh frequency television channels. That experience soon led them into cable TV when it was still being dismissed by the mass media. By 1970, the year the Alfred P. Sloan Foundation commissioned an extensive report that came to call cable "the television of abundance," the New Right was among those groups that recognized that the future of cable technology went well beyond its ability to connect communities blocked by mountains.

Network television was at its zenith in the 1970s, seemingly unaware of the competition posed by the multiplying cable systems or the possibility of their consolidation. Similarly dismissed was the Christian Broadcasting Network, which began in 1960 and which owned twenty-three thousand radio stations and thirty-six non–network affiliated television stations by the end of the 1970s. Members of the New Right also sought opportunities to harness craft traditions to spread their word. U.S. Senator Jesse Helms, a Republican from North Carolina, first came to public attention with his daily partisan editorials as the news director of WRAL-TV (also syndicated on radio).

While the New Right came to utilize various venues of broadcast, the Right was also building nonbroadcast channels of media distribution, including publishing houses, religious bookstores, direct mail, and newsletters. These alternatives to mass media were early precursors of the trend of fragmentation that became important in the last years of the twentieth century. Gloria Steinem has been one of the handful of commentators who have noted how the political Right constructed a media of its own, noting in 1993 that "the right wing didn't trust the mainstream media. It didn't sit around waiting for mainstream media to interpret it correctly. It created its own media, its own 'lay your hands on the television set and commune with God' show. It had its own newsletters. It has its own '800' and '900' numbers. And, meanwhile, we goody two-shoes here have been trying to influence the mainstream media" (*Ms.* 9/93: 39).

The mass audience built by the fundamentalist and religious right became a political voice when it adopted the ideology of the political Right. For that powerful partnership to take place, the economic and political ideology of the New Right—that is, the "laissez-faire conservatives," as Rebecca Klatch defined them—only had to shift their rhetoric slightly to appeal to the social conservative views of the religious Right; thus "profamily" had two levels of meaning, the maintenance of the traditional family structures for the social conservatives, who saw women's role as serving in a God-centered universe (not the feminist "me-centered" world), and economic, foreign policy, and libertarian issues that were at the fulcrum of laissez-faire conservative beliefs.

Schlafly was not dramatically changing focus when she turned from the Cold War to the defeat of the ERA. Her laissez-faire ideology could be represented in the framing of the anti-ERA movement. Antifeminism could easily be made to carry the message of opposition to "big government," for example, in ways that resonated with an audience that was most affected by what seemed to be its dismissal by the larger culture. Alan Crawford believes that the New Right built its strength on what he calls the "politics of resentment," a resentment fueled, as the Archie Bunker research noted earlier suggests, by frustration at holding views not reflected in the mass media. Nixon would seek his support from such individuals, whom he would call "the silent majority."

Low Tech

The eventual implementation of the media channels among the political Right was accomplished at the same time as the utilization of low technology, as in the use of the low-tech newsletter. In 1967, Schlafly began publishing the *Phyllis Schlafly Report*, a four-page page monthly newsletter devoted to conservative Cold War issues that continues to be published. In November 1972, following Senate approval of the ERA, Schlafly published the first anti-ERA issue, "What's Wrong with Equal Rights for Women?" which she distributed to the long-established audience that followed her conservative Cold War politics. Schlafly recruited the women who responded to the article to become organizers in their respective states (Davis, F. 1991). Not only did the piece help in recruiting volunteers, but it was subsequently used as a propaganda piece in the Oklahoma state legislature. The single-topic messages of the *Report* iterated messages that feminists would repeatedly have to face (*PSR* 1972–90). Like all propaganda, there was no ambivalence in her message: "There are two very different types of women lobbying for the Equal Rights Amendment. One group is the women's liberationists. Their motive is totally radical. They hate men, marriage and children. They look upon husbands as the exploiters, children as an evil to be avoided (by abortion if necessary), and the family as an institution which keeps women in 'second-class citizenship' or even 'slavery' " (*PSR* 11/72: 7).

The second kind of ERA supporter, Schlafly wrote, was business and professional women who sought equal pay for equal work. That concern could be addressed through the Civil Rights Act and the EEOC. Schlafly's point was not off mark. As Jane Mansbridge writes, it was not clear what the ERA would mean in the workplace, particularly since Title VII of the Civil Rights Act "covers more jobs than the ERA, and it imposes more stringent requirements on employers" (Mansbridge 1986: 40).

The probable effects of an equal rights amendment had been under discussion in NOW since the first Task Force Report on the ERA was issued in 1967. In a memorandum NOW prepared at that time, the likely effects were judged on six points: the amendment would be restricted to governmental action rather than private concerns; the expectation that women would serve on juries and in the military (although not required in certain cases); the lifting of restrictions on property rights for married women; the lifting of restrictive work laws for women; the disallowance of alimony solely on the basis of sex; and the continuance of maternity benefits to mothers (Carabillo, Meuli, and Csida 1993: 182). As the position paper made clear, these were only possible effects, taken from judgments at the time; other effects would depend on court decisions and related interpretations of the Fifth and Fourteenth Amendments. From the beginning of the campaign, then, the passage of the ERA presented no clear message connected to a single issue—hardly a recommendation for a mass media world that operates on simple messages strongly spoken.

Only after the 1972 Senate vote did Schlafly became involved in the anti-ERA movement, concerned, she said, with what she believed to be its implications (Felsenthal 1981: 239–41). Indeed, the ERA's implications and lack of a clear mandate caused furor on both sides of the aisle. The battle over the ERA did not hinge on clearly definable outcomes, as NOW had quickly recognized, since no one really knew what those would be, but rather about ideology. The ERA thus became a battle over dominant hegemony, with the implication there would be a winner and loser.

That was dangerous ground for the second wave, in some regard gambling with its successes for the dubious win of an amendment whose passage, in the end, may have been primarily symbolic given already existing legislation. Moreover, when feminists came to realize the seriousness of the opposition, many of the feminist community's resources and years of effort went into combating the anti-ERA campaign. One upshot of the feminist opposition was that it kept the ERA on the media agenda, but that discussion increasingly did not serve feminists; indeed, in retrospect, the discussion seemed most to promote the ERA as a Trojan horse for the new conservative ideology. Under the rubric of fighting for the ERA, the relatively small number of feminist activists found themselves on the front lines of a larger conservative-liberal battle but without equal resources. It speaks to the long-term strategy of the conservative forces behind the anti-ERA campaign that, by selecting the ERA battle, they were also able to select a relatively weak opponent and take advantage of issues already on the media agenda—stridency, lesbianism, home, and family—to advance a far-ranging agenda in which defeat of feminism was only one part. When Schlafly and her supporters decided to challenge the ERA, they found perhaps the second wave's most vulnerable place: an ill-defined issue that was open to multiple interpretations. Schlafly was to define the subject in ways that were already coming to prominence in the antifeminist movement: as an attack on women and the family. Her November 1972 *Phyllis Schlafly Report* raised the specter that women could lose financial support and that the ERA endangered "The Right to Be a Woman (*PSR* 11/72). Schlafly often used economic arguments in her *Reports* but framed them in an argument of essential difference. The title of her 1977 book, *The Power of the Positive Woman*, for example, echoed the approaches already established in *The Total Woman* and *Fascinating Womanhood*. In *Positive Woman*, Schlafly posited the values of a woman's "fertility as part of her purpose, her potential, and her power" against "independence from men and the avoidance of pregnancy," a trajectory that made it clear that "lesbianism is logically the highest form in the ritual of women's liberation" (Schlafly 1977: 3, 4). Her *Reports* also argued that passage of the ERA would take away women's legal rights and give nothing in return; interfere with states' rights; remove rights from women in education; enshrine abortion and gay rights in the U.S. Constitution; prohibit insurance companies from charging lower rates for women; endanger Social Security; leave divorced women high and dry; and eliminate veterans' preferences—a mix of hot buttons that were most linked to the world of conservative politics (*PSR* 1972–90).

As Schlafly became increasingly connected to the ERA, the *Report* grew from three thousand subscribers to thirty-five thousand and was passed around and copied for many more (Felsenthal 1981: 270). However, the *Report* did not seek masses of readers as much as opinion leaders. Copies were distributed at legislative hearings, and her inclusion of comments by U.S. Senators Sam Ervin (D-N.C.) and Henry Hyde (R-Ill.) in the *Report* added to its authority. Schlafly's use of her newsletter was thus different from the alternative women's press, which aimed to serve and pass on information from the women's Left and to provide an internal forum. In contrast, with a tidy format that never changed (except for her periodic updated and glamorized photographs on the banner), the newsletter was geared not only to regular subscribers but also to outside propagation. The 8½-by-11-inch format made it easy to copy on what were the now ubiquitous photocopiers.

In 1975, after the founding of the Eagle Forum, Schlafly remained with the low-tech style of newsletters by publishing a second newsletter, the *Eagle Forum*

Newsletter, which she used to communicate with her Stop ERA! supporters at the precinct level. This two-sided mimeographed bulletin was aimed at her house-wife supporters and provided step-by-step instructions for raising funds, influencing elected officials, mounting demonstrations, and making good impressions. (She gave annual workshops on how to dress and rewarded volunteers who lost weight; only women who were twenty-five and older were allowed to wear Stop ERA! T-shirts at demonstrations so that the message would be seen to come from responsible adults—or perhaps she did not want her message diluted by men looking at the breasts of the younger women.) The mimeographed format of the newsletter was undoubtedly familiar to an audience that received and read church bulletins. Moreover, it was cheap to produce, and its format conveyed an intimacy that maintained morale. She also found the publication useful for raising anti-ERA funds by direct donations and by the sale of anti-ERA materials and for calling on supporters to demonstrations.

At a time when social change organizations still depended on mass media, Schlafly recognized the power of the simple newsletter. In that sense, she was on the cusp of the developing specialized mass media (as *Ms.* magazine had recognized that specialization in mass magazines). Newsletters are flexible, easy to produce, and give the appearance of providing readers with fresh information not known elsewhere because they are not beholden to mass media values.

Like other parts of the Far Right, however, Schlafly did not ignore sophisticated media techniques. At a time when VCRs were not common and taping still required bulky and expensive three-quarter-inch equipment, Schlafly nonetheless produced training videos in which she critiqued mock ERA debates among her supporters. In 1975, she also produced what public relations professionals would come to call a video news release aimed at wider dissemination. The thirty-minute videotape *A Look at the Eagle Forum* was filled with various images, including those of Ronald Reagan, the American flag, smiling mothers with children, and a woman military leader denouncing the ERA. Other segments, taken from news coverage of Steinem, Abzug, and various marches, framed feminism in a derogatory light. The tape ended with an endorsement by Reagan, who praised the Eagle Forum for helping to elect conservative political candidates (Schlafly 1975).

As Schlafly became the single most recognizable anti-ERA voice, she parlayed her reputation into a regular newspaper column and was a routine subject for interviews, now occupying a fixed place in reporters' telephone files. Schlafly was adept at using radio, serving as a commentator on CBS's *Spectrum* series and on the weekly broadcasts of the National Conference of Christians and Jews. She appeared on television talk shows such as *Donahue,* provided interviews in connection with her lecture tours and with her regularly scheduled debates with Karen DeCrow and

Eleanor Smeal on abortion. Ironically, the feminists she debated in the paid forums contributed to the dispersal of her message because Schlafly might not have been able to draw an audience on her own. In contrast, Steinem had long refused to participate in debates on the rationale that there was no reason why her fame should provide a platform for antifeminism.

Schlafly was not above using political theater to promote her views. Warm apple pies and homemade cookies accompanied leaflets, signs, and buttons distributed to legislators before an ERA vote. At demonstrations, supporters wore bright red to symbolize "stop." She composed new words to popular songs to ridicule the ERA and led the singing of them at pro-ERA demonstrations. She was prominent in actions that were aimed at drawing attention to state votes—rallying support on the steps of state capitols and speaking against the ERA in front of state legislators. But her controlled "demonstrations," without rancor or anger, also reminded legislators and the public of the kind of uncontrolled demonstrations of recent memory. Schlafly would not have expected her demonstrations, by themselves, to prompt support; rather, they served as reminders of all of the demands of the Other—civil rights, student protests, and the women who did not bring apple pies to demonstrations. In 1975, *U.S. News and World Report*, in a special section, "The American Woman on the Move, but Where?" noted that the "counterrevolution" was winning the war of words in "getting across the idea that the proposed amendment imperiled the American family and would usher in a new age of 'unisex toilet' and 'coed' armed forces" (*USNWR* 12/8/75: 55).

Although antifeminism entered the mass media on the hems of balance, Schlafly's tactic not to rely primarily on mass media was wise for her message. While she became the media representative of anti-ERA forces, she herself was not popular with the media. Schlafly's style in most venues relied on a confident recitation of "facts" (although they were not always factual) and emotional images (unfulfilled women, uncared-for children), although not in an emotional or ever humorous style. Her posture tended to be so erect, her hair rigid in a French twist, that she was called "schoolmarmish." Unlike Steinem, Schlafly's public performance alone did not likely charm anyone into agreement with her position. Sally Quinn, writing in the *Washington Post*, noted of Schlafly, "Her outward demeanor and dress is one of a feminine bridge-playing, affluent housewife. She smiles a lot, giggles, worries about her appearance and makes polite conversation. Yet on the podium she comes on like a female George Wallace. She is tough and aggressive, totally unlike the role she espouses for most women" (Quinn 1974: D1).

It speaks to the change in climate that by 1972 much of the national mass news media had accepted liberal feminism and coverage of Schlafly's position was, by some standards, begrudging. Mass women's magazines, attacked by Friedan in the

1960s for being too conservative, were attacked by Schlafly for their support of the ERA (*PSR* 12/79). Indeed, opposition to Schlafly's position occurred not only in *McCall*'s (Grizzuti Harrison 1982) and *Ms.* (Langer 1976), but also *Playgirl* (Dedman 1976) and *Playboy* (1971)—the target of one of Schlafly's derisive lyrics. Nor did the *New York Times Magazine* give to Schlafly the kind of coverage that the early women's movement had received. The *Times*'s review of her 1977 book, buried at the bottom of the page, was dismissive, the reviewer hardly understanding the inspirational role she played for thousands of women who would purchase the book and take her words to heart (Dunning 1977).

As Anita Bryant became the representative of antigay groups, Schlafly was the representative of all antifeminists and was parodied by the feminist theatrical group Ladies against Women (Burbank 1998). The effectiveness of such parody may be questioned, a preaching-to-the-choir technique that took attention away from Schlafly's influence. For feminists, Schlafly's views hardly needed to be parodied, and for her supporters, parody only increased resolve. Some of Schlafly's ongoing canards against militant women seemed verified when, on 17 April 1977 she was smacked in the face with an apple pie during a ceremony to honor her at the Women's National Republican Club, an event caught by a photographer in a widely distributed photo. The attack was mounted by a five-member group calling itself the Emma Goldman Brigade, but the casual news consumer likely attributed the attack to NOW, which was picketing the event (*NYT* 4/17/77: 38).

The International Year of the Woman

By 1976, the managers of the National Conference on Woman no longer took the passage of the ERA for granted. By that time the partnership of the political Right with the religious Right was well under way, and the anti-ERA forces had joined with the strongest arm of the religious Right, the antiabortion crusade. The National Conference of Catholic Bishops (NCCB) had begun to organize immediately after the 1973 *Roe v. Wade* decision, and, like the Protestant Right, used church organizations to build a political action machine. Although instituted by the NCCB, the antiabortion movement soon embraced other members of the opposition, losing its purely Roman Catholic character and bringing into the movement members of the Fundamentalist Right, including groups that may have had an anti-Catholic bias. In retrospect, all of Schlafly's anti-ERA arguments, from women in the military to unisex toilets, seem pale beside the power of the abortion argument, a fact that Schlafly had to admit when the antiabortion forces were invited to join with the Stop ERA! forces in the demonstrations outside the conference. Although antiabortion and the ERA were not legislatively connected, the rhetorical commingling of the two further confused a confused issue. Many years later, in a 1991 *Report* devoted to "The Radical Goals of the Feminists," Schlafly referred to the Houston event as "the occasion when the gender-neutral feminists coalesced with the abortionists and the lesbians to try to force the Equal Rights Amendment down our throats" (*PSR* 12/91: 1).

The partnership of the two groups was not universally accepted in the Right-to-Life circles (MacLean 1979). Nonetheless, for perhaps the majority of antiabortion supporters, it was a natural confluence, particularly given NOW's articulated position that retention of abortion rights would be its top priority once the ERA was ratified. It was a partnership of enormous power, bringing together two well-organized movements in a gathering of Far Right forces that would change the country by the end of the decade.

The Houston Conference

Schlafly's *Report* went into high gear with the announcement of the Houston conference, as she attacked its public funding and confidently announced, "Houston will finish off the women's movement. It will show them off for the radical, anti-family, pro/lesbian people they are" (*PSR* 1/76). Schlafly's words were repeated to the wider world when the *New York Times* provided a lengthy article about the upcoming conference, quoting Schlafly liberally, accompanied by her smiling picture countered by a profile of Friedan, whom the *Times* still regarded as the movement's opinion leader, although she reflected no power bloc in Houston or in the movement. The *Times* also provided yet another restatement of the movement's history, including how it was "brutally split by what became known as 'the lesbian issue'" (Klemesrud 1977: 46).

As the Houston conference approached, the danger posed by Schlafly's opposition was more than clear, and organizers sought to make the National Women's Conference a national platform for the passage of the ERA. It speaks to the increasing mainstream acceptability of the movement that the U.S. Congress, through the efforts of Representative Bella Abzug (D-N.Y.), had allocated five million dollars and convened the conference as an outgrowth of the United Nation's International Women's Year. In Houston, the site of Billie Jean King's victory over Bobby Riggs, delegates met to decide on issues to be included in a national plan of action. From the beginning, when a thousand marchers joined with female athletes carrying a flaming torch and chanting "Hey, hey, what do you say/Ratify the ERA," the ERA was to be placed at the top of the national plan.

The convention was tightly structured (speeches limited, walkie-talkies forbidden, access to microphones controlled) for fear that the meeting would be upset by antifeminist demonstrations. Floor whips emphasized unity, especially on Saturday, when the ERA vote was to be taken. Sponsored by ERAmerica, a new organization formed to promote passage, a demonstration was aimed at encouraging delegates' enthusiasm. First Lady Rosalyn Carter reiterated her support for the ERA and that of the president, as did former First Lady Betty Ford. Liz Carpenter, a Johnson administration figure, raised cheers when she said, "If I die, don't send flowers—just send three more states." Not surprisingly, delegates passed the resolution urging ratification of the amendment. In addition, the convention passed an abortion plank, and a happy snake dance celebrated the inclusion of a lesbian-rights plank, now supported by Friedan. In feminist history, the conference is remembered as "The Glory That Was Houston" (Rosen 2000: 291).

Some of the enthusiasm was reflected in the coverage of the time, although *Newsweek* incorrectly called the abortion vote "a setback for the anti-feminist forces inspired by ERA opponent Phyllis Schlafly" (Sheils et al. 1977: 57). Less glowingly, Barbara Walters's ABC-TV report noted that the conference had been eclipsed by Egyptian President Anwar Sadat's historic visit to Jerusalem, clearly her interest (ABC 1977). NBC's Carole Simpson covered the conference in a lengthy four-and-a-half-minute story that brought attention to the growing opposition to the ERA by the Mormon Church, whose anti-ERA spokeswoman predicted that passage would privilege homosexual rights and lead to the downfall of the family and society along the lines of the destruction of the Grecian and Roman empires (NBC 1977). In the CBS story, Schlafly outlined a similar scenario, but Jane O'Leary, head of the National Gay Task Force, expressed distress that homosexual rights were being used to divide the movement (CBS, "IWY Conference").

The feminist enthusiasm that closed the conference did not stop President Jimmy Carter from canceling his appointment with Abzug to receive the national plan of action (CBS, "IWY Conference"), thus establishing a problematical relationship between feminists and the White House for the rest of the decade. However, in the heady days after Houston, pro-ERA forces were revitalized, establishing a national grassroots effort that achieved a three-year extension in the time for ratification and thereby proving that the movement could organize successfully in support of a definable end. The extension further invigorated the movement. Writing in the leftist *The Progressive*, Judy MacLean noted that one result of the extension was that it produced a "fresh wind of optimism through the feminist movement. Like many other seekers after social justice, feminists need to move from the defensive to the offensive. More experiences like the ERA extension will enable them to say with Eleanor Smeal, 'We are lucky to be part of a time when we are changing the world for the better' " (MacLean 1979: 40).

The extension was achieved despite the formidable opposition posed by the new conjunction of anti-ERA and antiabortion forces. For conservatives, the Houston conference had also been life-changing. Beverly LaHaye, the activist wife of the co-founder of the Moral Majority, was moved to establish a new organization, Concerned Women for America (CWA), aimed at attracting Protestant women to the anti-ERA fight. LaHaye had risen to prominence on the Christian speaking circuits and in 1976 wrote *The Spirit-Controlled Woman*, which she followed up in the same year with a sexual manual for evangelical couples. (In endorsing the clitoral organism, the manual was indebted to Anne Koedt's "Myth of the Vaginal Orgasm.") However, the CWA opposed, as LaHaye was to say, "anything NOW stood for." Most importantly, the conservative group drew new legions of formerly inactive Protestant women to the ERA and abortion opposition. Schlafly's Catholicism was well known and, according to LaHaye, made "Protestant women hesitant to become involved." Schlafly's organization "did not have an open door into many of the Protestant churches." LaHaye said in an interview that she discussed her plans for a new organization with Schlafly, who viewed the decision as one that would assist her ERA activities (LaHaye 2002).

Like Schlafly, LaHaye was an organizer of women who had not been activist and used a kitchen table analogy in her organizing pamphlet, "How to Lobby from Your Kitchen Table." LaHaye chose not to court the mass media in the belief that they distorted ideas. When media coverage was permitted, LaHaye kept tight control on the message. Even state leaders were not permitted to speak to media before completing a media-training program. The CWA soon expanded as it utilized church networks, outlets for religious broadcasting, and newsletters. However, the need for a public relations department was not seen until the 1980s, at which time LaHaye's daily radio program was already nationally syndicated in 120 markets. By the mid-1980s, the CWA was headquartered in Washington, D.C., where it had a twenty-six-member staff, four to five attorneys in a legal division, a six-million-dollar budget (now substantially higher) and a reported membership in excess of half a million "associates" in twenty-five hundred chapters (Cawley 1992; Miller 1985). The CWA worked with Schlafly on various occasions, including the anti-ERA campaign in Illinois, where the CWA supplied workers and paid for 120 television advertisements (by a spontaneous collection taken up at a conference, according to LaHaye).

Despite its thousands of members and the political leverage they represent, the CWA has received overall little attention in the mass media—perhaps a dozen articles in mass magazines and major newspapers in as many years, including one in a warning mode in a 1987 *Ms.* (Paige 1987) but none in the New York–based elite media. Nonetheless, the CWA has assisted in helping achieve the New Right agenda by working in selected legislative races and collaborating with other New Right organizations and has been a contributor to and user of Christian media— radio, bookselling, and now the Internet. In her seventies at the turn of the twenty- first century, LaHaye continued her leadership of the organization, as did Schlafly, who remained at the helm of the Eagle Forum and active in Republican circles. In hindsight, the CWA not only brought to Schlafly's anti-ERA fight new resources, including many more anti-ERA women, but also connected passage of the ERA to the legalization of abortion. Despite the role of U.S. Catholic bishops in anti-ERA funding, the Fundamentalist Protestant groups—by attaching the ERA to an anti- abortion agenda—may have made the difference in the final defeat. By utilizing the ERA to bring opposition to abortion to the national scene, Protestant Fundamen- talists removed abortion as a Catholic-only issue and helped place abortion on the national political agenda, where it remains today.

In retrospect, the Houston convention revitalized feminists but also served notice that the Right, strengthened by antiabortion forces from the Catholic Church, the Mormon Church, and Fundamental Protestantism, endangered not only the passage of the ERA but the *Roe v. Wade* decision. Moreover, antiabortion groups found ways to embed antiabortion rhetoric in public discussion in ways that were not matched by antiabortion rhetorical strategies. As Celeste Michelle Condit argues, the most used of the prochoice images, the coat hanger, appealed only to the already converted, while the images put forth by the antiabortion forces found appeal in all segments (Condit 1990: 92–93).

Even before the Houston conference, CBS singled out abortion as the major thrust of antifeminist activism (CBS, "Abortion"). The Houston conference veri- fied that assessment as proabortion forces not only defined feminism by a pro- choice position but helped to define the Equal Rights Amendment in terms of support for abortion rights. The broad ideological statement represented by the ERA had been helpful in the early ratifications of the amendment, when state leg- islators could vote for it as an expression of their generalized support for women, a position that these legislators could define for themselves. But that advantage was lost when state legislators were asked to support an amendment that was increasingly viewed as a plebiscite on abortion. While ERA supporters continued to argue for the amendment on the basis of its broad ideological appeal, oppo- nents were quick to fill the empty spaces by the delineation of potential outcomes, none more powerful than a connection to support for abortion.

What can be made of political power that came into existence without a place on the mass media agenda? When anti-ERA forces that challenged NOW and other feminist organizations did seek the mass media eye, they were likely to receive little media sympathy. While the early women's movement received a fair share of hostility from the mass media, much of it seemed to result from the culture of the newsroom and the traditions of the trade, neither of which had to with a preference for the ideology of the New Right or its religious underpinnings. Liberal feminism had made major inroads among craft practitioners by the mid-1970s, and media outlets were no open door for New Right ideologues.

However, by the mid- and late 1970s, as the ERA battle moved into high gear, the mass media were becoming less accessible to the rhetoric of the social change movement. Cable and other specialized media came to prominence in a period of deregulation, when no representation of social issues or hiring of underrepresented minority groups was required. Media managers assessed the mood of the country as conservative, as perhaps the managers were, and distanced media products from activism, right or left, as no longer on the cutting edge.

Moreover, even as reform measures were being enacted in mass media circles, these vehicles were losing their preeminent positions in the media marketplace. The large audiences that had watched the evening news would be a thing of the past by the 1980s, as cable programs offered alternatives to network news and to network programming in general. Cable programming, specialty magazines, free entertainment newspapers, the Internet, and video games dispersed the grand audiences that mass media vehicles once had been able to command. The "old media"—newspapers, AM radio, "free TV"—scrambled for audiences in new strategies of survival. The Fox network introduced a style of ownership to over-the-air television that was hardly conciliatory toward social activism and had no interest in constructing a reporting cadre of national prestige, seeking to attract the demographically desirable by whatever means necessary. Ownership patterns changed from corporate to conglomerate, bringing along an emphasis on principles of business management, which meant the amortization of content across many media. The doomsayers of the 1970s were proved correct: entertainment values providing the most profitable return came to dominate in all fields.

For industry professionals of the time, the warnings were clear; what was not so clear to the critics at large was the speedy adoption of the survival strategies that sought to hold off the disintegration. It was the misfortune of the women's movement to come into the mass media marketplace as these strategies were tested.

Conclusion
A Moment of Triumph

The biggest television audience that had ever tuned in for a feminist-related event had nothing to do with organized feminism. It is not noted in histories of the second wave or even in the biography of Roone Arledge, the man who made it possible in seeking to solidify his position as a producer of popular content at ABC. Yet the 1973 Billie Jean King–Bobby Riggs tennis match, the "Battle of the Sexes," transfixed forty million U.S. television viewers (twice the number that tuned in for the Williams sisters' 2001 U.S. Open final), and its audience of more than thirty thousand spectators for a single tennis match has yet to be equaled. The match received front-page coverage in most of the nation's newspapers and was featured prominently on national television news. King appeared on magazine covers and on talk shows. The match was the Town Hall event writ large, the intellectual and elitist gladiators of Germaine Greer and Norman Mailer now replaced by populists Billie Jean King and Bobby Riggs, the new gladiators in the real Houston Astrodome.

The King–Riggs match was not a news event or even a traditional sports event but rather a promotional event that became connected with a news issue to such an extent that it became and was covered as news. The promotion relied so much on the issues of the second wave that there seemed no way to disentangle the two, and coverage of the event was less premised on its place in popular culture than as a plebiscite on the second wave. King's win over Riggs thus seemed to give voter approval to what the match had come to represent, equality in employment. More than a decade after the passage of the Equal Pay Act, King gave evidence that women were equal in the workplace, even if her workplace was the tennis court. King also was proof of what critics of the Equal Pay Act had been saying all along: there could not be equal pay without equal access.

The history of women in sports has some parallels to that of women in the workplace. Like women in the workplace, separate rules existed for women in sports. Not all sports were considered suitable for women, and those that were had special rules for women's play to accommodate women's physical concerns. Women's sports also had rules that distanced women's play from masculine behavior, such as undue competition. Rules of early women's basketball at Smith College, for example, prohibited women from taking the ball from the holder, confined women players to particular areas of the court, and allowed the holder of the ball three bounces. As June Sochen notes, the rise of women in sports coincided with the late-nineteenth-century rise of mass newspapers, which, like Joseph Pulitzer's *World*, covered sports not only as a way to attract readers but also, for Pulitzer at least, as a representation of his philosophy that progress was achieved only by the clash of opposites. Women had no role in the manly occupation of moving the society to its Progressive destiny; thus women's participation in sports at best represented a diversion to maintain the health of a body that would be utilized for the birth of children. As the mass media began to cover female celebrities, women in sports were judged by the same standards of beauty and femininity. However, the extraordinary accomplishments of Babe Didrickson Zaharias—three gold medals in the 1932 Olympics and a subsequent golfing career—came to press attention on the basis of her athleticism and her ambition rather than her beauty or behavior. She clashed with amateur organizations over what clearly appear, from a later perspective, to be class issues, as women's sports were defined in terms of upper-class behaviors. Reporters loved her straightforwardness—as June Sochen describes it, Zaharias was "a female Will Rogers"—as well as for her abilities. She unabashedly endorsed sports products and ventures that would make money, and the Depression generation considered her a woman whose success was clearly related to her efforts (Sochen 1987: 123).

King shared some characteristics with Zaharias, particularly a blue-collar background, a candid and down-to-earth approach with reporters, and an ambition to succeed. Like Zaharias, King enjoyed good press, as her working-class characteristics came to be appreciated by the press corps, themselves representatives of blue-collar upward mobility. She was well known for her slang—"El Barfo," "El Cheapo," and "El Choko." Asking if she had been nervous before the Riggs match, Dan Wakefield made a point of representing her working-class speech: "She grinned widely and said, 'I loved it. Hey—you didn't see me goin' bananas, did ya?'" (Wakefield 1974: 384). When King was on the court, she embodied the working-class individual seeking to prove her worthiness and, in the case of Riggs, did so against the kinds of foolish superiors who have often held power over working-class individuals. Importantly, the tennis court was not just a title, but money—the essential proof of worthiness in the United States. This was not about symbolism: she would be paid for what she did, as in a workplace.

Although the second wave is often cast in the opportunities it opened up for middle-class women, King's success may be considered a voice for working-class women who would seek access to formerly male working-class occupations during the 1970s. Despite the first-women stories, doors to the higher-paying working-class occupations were not so easily opened, and working-class women found themselves, more so than middle-class women, confined to the low-paying pink-collar ghetto, as Louise Kapp Howe (1977) described it, of the expanding service economy. In the inflationary 1970s, the working-class women whose small but nonetheless discretionary income had helped launch *Cosmopolitan* a decade earlier once again flooded the pink-collar marketplace, giving rise to what another writer has called "the second shift" (Hochschild 1989). Given the representation of King as a working-class heroine, her appeal could not have been lost on working-class women who were not participating in the economic benefits that were accruing to other women.

Mass sports draw their largest audiences from working-class populations, and the clear outcomes—a win or a loss—that sports provide is a satisfying emotion for audiences who may not be able to make clear connections between worthiness and success in their individual work lives. Sports—even team sports—with their reliance on extraordinary effort, which can make the difference between a win and a loss, give credence to the notion that individual ability makes a difference. As a result, emphasis on individual effort in sports is useful for mass media in drawing a mass audience and, not incidentally, helps maintain the nation's stability by encouraging a faith in individual effort, whether or not individualism, over the long term, is the most important value to a society or its members.

The immediate context of the match was the passage of the 1972 U.S. Education Act and its Title IX, requiring public schools receiving federal funds to equalize women's opportunities in sports with those for men. For many supporters of male college sports, the law put into high gear concerns that funding for women's sports would impact negatively on funding for the popular men's college sports, basketball and football. While there was no connection between Title IX and the King–Riggs match, the new legislation could only promote the culture of complaint that the match was yet another example of women, as at McSorley's, taking over a man's world. But even before the promotion began, the match was at the eye of a cluster of themes representing the influence of second wave: the attack on male physicality and potency; class issues raised by the perceived elitism of the theoretical feminists versus the bread-and-butter needs of working-class women; equal pay for equal work; the practical aspects of Title IX; the ERA; spectacle as persuasion, as in the 26 August march; and, for one scholar, King as the archetype of Artemis of Greek mythology (Creedon 1994: 11). The complications were swept up, commingled, and essentially simplified by the roil of popular culture.

Until recent years, as media came to be directed into many avenues for specific audiences, popular culture was a tent that unified America's diverse populations in a mode that was distinctively American and celebratory. Even now, sports events, movies, celebrities, certain radio and television programs, popular music, and even brand names offer few barriers to entry and can draw equal participation from Americans representing many different walks of life, ethnicities, and cultures. Like any other popular fad, the King–Riggs event took over the nation's attention. Newspapers, magazines, and each of the three networks provided multiple stories on the upcoming match. At a time when networks often behaved as if the other two did not exist, CBS evening news anchorman Walter Cronkite announced that on the night of the match his network, CBS, had scheduled the television premiere of the popular movie *Bonnie and Clyde*, a rueful admission that the network was bringing out its heavy artillery to combat the expectation that most people would be watching ABC (CBS 1973).

This event, however, had implications beyond those found in other kinds of popular culture events—a sports playoff game, the final episode of a popular television show, the marriage of a celebrity—that can take up the public imagination for a moment or two. Here was an event that seemed implicitly to carry social significance. Not so differently from the Town Hall debate, the match could best be enjoyed by taking sides, each of which saw its outcome as proving some kind of generalized truth.

For the audience as a whole, the success of the King–Riggs promotion may have been because it was refreshing to have an event known for what it was, coming at a time when Americans were tiring of media manipulation, whether by social change groups or the mounted events of political campaigning. A sports event, even a fake one, promised resolution, a comfort at a time when conflicting messages abounded—the lofty goals of the civil rights movement churning into neighborhood busing controversies, Watergate eroding faith in institutions, and a time when even the mainstream media were challenging governmental predictions of the successful end of the Vietnam conflict. Amid urban riots, the assassinations of leaders, and Vietnam protests, the King–Riggs match was a whirlwind of its own, but its either-or outcome promised to put away one of the troublesome issues of the day in an entertaining way.

Riggs was a well-known 1939 Wimbledon winner who had subsequently made a living by promoting private matches between himself and country club stars. When challenging the country club players, Riggs put himself at a heavy disadvantage but did so in entertaining ways—in costume, in a chair on the court, or with one hand tied behind his back. He made his money from bets on the side. In this spirit, he challenged Wimbledon champion Margaret Court to a match for a ten-thousand-dollar purse; had she won, the event would have been as little remembered as the country club matches. Court lost, however, discombobulated by the unexpected publicity prompted by Riggs's bravado. King—the leader in seeking parity with men for women's professional tennis —picked up the fallen glove.

Once the match finally was agreed upon, Riggs and his promoters went into an enlarged version of their old promotional experiences. Riggs was once again on the center court of the media eye. He boasted that no woman athlete, even in her prime, could beat a male athlete, even a has-been such as himself. He took up the rhetoric of the radicals and denatured it by willingly calling himself a "chauvinist pig"; indeed, he readily took up the mantle to represent all men who seemingly had been denigrated as a result of the second wave. But no matter how exaggerated his statements, his style was without rancor, and he took a kind of delight in the angry responses he elicited. For his supporters, his humor and good nature suggested that there could be no greater patronization than failing to take the other side seriously. He clearly enjoyed it all; so did the media. His promotional antics got him on the cover of *Time* in a playful caricature with the sell line "The Happy Hustler" (*Time* 9/10/73).

Riggs's promotional bent was useful to King's goals. Since the beginning of her professional career, King had sought to put women's tennis on the nation's sports agenda. She and her husband, Larry King, worked to promote a new women's tennis league in which the players were expected to take a major role in promotion, from providing interviews to local media to chatting up the fans at intermission. At age twenty-five at the time of the match, King had been the focus of local and national attention for almost ten years, and her ready smile and lively personality, even her emotionality on the court, made her good copy and a contrast to what was often the genteel and constrained behavior of women's tennis players during the 1950s and 1960s. Moreover, the daughter of a fireman and a housewife and a Westerner, her rise to championship levels resulted from instruction that began on public courts. There was little in her background to give her allegiance to the behaviors of traditional women's tennis. Both of her autobiographies suggest that she remained uncomfortable with the class distinctions of Forest Hills Tennis Association and the practice of staying in private homes on tour; her heart was at Wimbledon (despite the still-discriminatory pay between men and women players), perhaps because there she was simply an American and was in a venue where players did not have to depend on the largesse of well-heeled supporters: Wimbledon players stayed in hotels.

Given her working-class background, it may not have been surprising that her commitment to women's tennis was premised on what had become the most popular item on the women's agenda, equal pay for equal work. She had little patience for the "Libbers" or their theoretical positions. "I know for a fact that the Movement has gotten hung up a lot of times on trivia in the interest of radical purity.

Sometimes I think Libbers don't want to move three feet forward if they have to slide an inch to the side at the same time. *Ms.* Magazine, I understand, once turned down a year's worth of advertising and a neat five-figure deal from Virginia Slims because it didn't like the slogan, 'You've Come a Long Way, Baby.' That's ridiculous" (King 1974: 141). Later, she complained that she had been "smothered and used by feminists," politically lumped in with Jane Fonda, Gloria Steinem, Betty Friedan, and Bella Abzug as the "Feminist Athlete Doll" and expected to support the whole feminist agenda. In actuality, her support for feminism was limited to equal pay and abortion rights. She considered feminists long-winded: "Show me a short memo and I'll show you a man" (King 1982: 161).

At the time of the match, these views were still being formed. She was focused on building support for women's tennis, and she was most proud of her tennis accomplishments, including having won one hundred thousand dollars in annual prize money, the first woman to do so. As someone who seemed to have a place in both feminism and the commercial world of professional sports, King seemed to prove that the movement was not out of step with the values of American entrepreneurship. All in all, she was cheerful, ebullient and natural, not an intellectual and, from all indications, no man-hater. She and her husband, Larry, made a classic mom-and-pop team: he ran the business side while she worked the counter. She seemed to have the characteristics of a tomboy, someone's little sister, and her commitment to feminism was not in the lecturing mode of which audiences had grown weary. Even if her workplace was not typical, Billie Jean King's pursuit of equity in women's tennis spoke to women everywhere who worked as hard as men and were paid less.

King was thus a populist heroine, from the tangible demands of equal pay, an issue that resonated with much of her audience, to the role of television as her major leisure activity. When Riggs's representative suggested a new match after his defeat of Court, King saw the proposal as useful to her own goals. She was confident of her ability to work with media, confident enough to refuse to play in the match unless ABC removed an announcer whom she regarded as an enemy of women's tennis. (Howard Cosell, the best-known sports broadcaster of the era, eventually called the match.) She saw the usefulness of promotion and good-naturedly participated in it, although not enough to interfere with her practice time.

In that sense, the King–Riggs match bore some resemblance to Joe Louis's boxing successes in the 1930s. During racially tense times, the Louis matches drew enormous radio audiences, black and white, each of which saw in the matches the nexus of black-white relationships. The black-white symbolism of the 1910 match between African-American Jack Johnson and the reigning white champion led to a white rampage when Johnson won. That did not happen in the 1930s, but not because media ever ignored the question of race (Louis was "dark dynamite," the "tan tornado") or even because race relations were greatly different. What made Louis an acceptable hero to white audiences was that he was characterized in ways that minimized the physical threat that black Americans stereotypically posed to white Americans. Using the nonthreatening images that early civil rights activists found so helpful in getting on the mass media agenda, Louis was portrayed as a humble, prayerful, and well-intentioned man, although perhaps not very clever. During World War II, his reputation for cooperative behavior was increased when he helped raise money for Liberty Bonds (Douglas 1994: 206). Thanks to his rendering in popular culture, white and black communities could agree that Joe Louis was a good citizen, and historians of race relations in the United States generally look at the Joe Louis phenomenon (as they would to Jackie Robinson shortly thereafter) as a step toward improving, in the phrase of the time, "race relations." Standards of acceptability for Joe Louis were decided on by white-owned media. By his association with a white women, Jack Johnson had not met those standards. While events of popular culture appear driven by spontaneous reaction, popular culture events that depend on mass media are necessarily constrained by the media's willingness to permit the popular moment to flourish and the media's decisions about how the event is to be defined. The momentum of a popular culture moment clearly can be lost if the media choose to define an event too differently from how the audience wants to perceive it. Producers of Ed Sullivan's *Toast of the Town* faced such a choice when Elvis Presley was scheduled to appear on the program. Some members of the public considered Presley's hip gyrations obscene, but those motions were also part of the reason why adolescents responded to Presley. The producers sought to negotiate the moment by keeping Presley on the program but televising his performance from the waist up. As a result, Sullivan retained his coup in booking Presley (and the large audience that the performance produced) by a slight modification of the "product" in the transmittal of Presley's performance. Whether Sullivan himself was offended by Presley's pelvic movements was not the issue. What was at stake was maintaining the credibility of the program as a family viewing hour that had made it one of early television's most successful revenue-producing programs. Changing the Sullivan "format" for even as large a popular culture event as Elvis Presley would hardly be worth losing the Sullivan brand name, any more than *Sixty Minutes* is likely to change the kind of stories it utilizes or Barbara Walters is likely to introduce a radically different style of interviewing. Even for what appear to be momentous events of popular culture, the mass media seek to take advantage of the moment without risking what they have at hand.

In terms of mass media, the Joe Louis phenomenon offered great opportunities for radio, but managers were not so willing to risk radio's potential as a commercial medium by alienating white racial attitudes. The presentation of Louis as a humble black man struck a middle road that allowed the Louis phenomenon to continue as a mass media event and helped make radio part of every home, black and white. Similarly, the television miniseries *Roots* might be considered another example of a popular culture explosion that also had to take a middle road. *Roots* presented its African and African-American characters in personal terms that white and black viewers found sympathetic. Like Joe Louis, *Roots* is considered to have contributed to American society by engendering white sympathy for the history of blacks in America while giving black Americans an opportunity to see themselves portrayed in heroic ways.

For this discussion, what is interesting about *Roots* is that its narrative form was the time-tested scenario of family disruption, white cruelty, and black humility. This was hardly the cutting edge of new content given that the same narrative form had been used both by black writers and by white Quaker abolitionists even before the American Revolution. This form of storytelling offers no systemic solutions but works from the premise that sympathy for the downtrodden will result in the adoption of new attitudes by those in charge, which will, in turn, produce change. It is not clear whether *Roots* contributed to productive long-term change in American society, which in any case was to experience increased white flight and deteriorating city schools and black neighborhoods. However, the storytelling technique was surely compelling for the moment, and the weeping audience (like those wearing ERA bracelets) may have come to believe that social change was about responding with the right emotions rather than about the inconvenience, difficulty, or commitment required for institutional change. Social change movements encased in an entertainment frame give a false sense of power to the viewer, whose acceptance of the premise of the story makes it appear as if the goals of the social change movement have been verified when primarily what has been verified is the talent of the popular storytellers. The real coup was for ABC-TV, which could take bows for social responsibility when business acumen had in reality led the network to represent black Americans from the safest perspective possible. It may seem crass to compare Elvis Presley's appearance on *Toast of the Town* to what has become the now-revered production of *Roots*, but the point here is that mass media's commitment to entertainment content is most influenced by the audiences the content can produce. This can best be done by offering content that generally reaffirms rather than opposes national beliefs, simply because that approach is expected to draw the largest audience. From the days when New York's big-circulation newspapers embraced football for that reason, sports reportage has been adept at presenting sports in a narrative that appeals to a broad audience along lines of myth—the ability of individual effort; sports as explications of virtue; the belief that nothing is lost until the last bell; strategy versus strength; and the access of all to the playing field, which, after the King–Riggs match, included women.

The Rise of ABC-TV

As the success of *The Feminine Mystique* has been related to changes in the book business, the success of the Battle of the Sexes had to do with the ABC-TV's efforts to build its revenues by way of mass audiences for "blockbuster" events. Since the network's founding in the 1940s, ABC had trailed the other two networks in original programming, audiences, and prestige. In 1961 the network acquired a new producer who would have a momentous influence on the network. Beginning as producer of ABC's *Wide World of Sports*, Roone Arledge was a vice president by 1963 and president of ABC Sports by 1968. He coupled the new techniques and technology of handheld cameras, split screens, instant replay, and microphones that could pick up sideline conversations with old-fashioned, storytelling narrative and a legendary instinct for editing. Altogether, Arledge's contributions gave ABC a premiere place in sports reporting. His supervision of the coverage of the assassinations of eleven Israeli athletes during the 1972 Olympic Games increased ABC's prestige. By the time of the King–Riggs match, Arledge had not yet been promoted to head of the network's news division, but he was experimenting with entertainment programming, giving to it the same kind of excitement that existed in sports events. During the planning of the King–Riggs match, Arledge was also overseeing Evel Knievel's attempt to jump his motorcycle across Idaho's Snake River Canyon and Frank Sinatra's concert at Madison Square Garden. These events could bring major audiences to ABC's regular programming, as such productions had in sports (Gunther 1994).

Arledge's contribution to sports narrative was bringing to it stories of individual success, and his emphasis in entertainment program utilized the same narrative technique, with *Roots* as the classic example. Such storytelling has long been a staple of mass media content in the United States (and perhaps everywhere) and may be considered one reason why media storytelling helps maintain a nation's stability. The retelling of the same formula—generally individual success over difficult odds—takes on the role of ritual, the American version of the folk dance, endlessly repeated with an occasional change of costume. What is verified is a set of ritualistic beliefs about the nation, including the belief in the individual's ability to overcome all obstacles, even those that come from an institutional setting. By adopting the narrative of individual success, even for blockbuster events, Arledge's genius was to make programs mounted to attract large audiences seem to carry a transcendent value, as if individuals carried the honor of the nation and as most illustrated by the Olympic Games. As an *Esquire* writer observed, "Arledge makes the image of the event more important than the event itself" (Yurick 1974: 54).

The Match

After months of frenzied promotional activity, ABC covered the event live at eight o'clock Eastern time on Saturday night, the time slot of the *Mary Tyler Moore Show*. King was carried into the Astrodome on a litter borne by a half dozen musclemen. Riggs was wheeled out in a rickshaw. At courtside, Riggs presented King with an outsized "Sugar Daddy" candy bar (one of the companies he represented); King gave Riggs a squealing pig named Larimore Hustle to remind him Riggs he was, as he often proclaimed, a "male chauvinist pig." (Larimore was Riggs's middle name.) There was some ribbing; fans shouted encouragement. The *New York Times* called it altogether a "circus atmosphere" (*NYT* 9/23/73: 1) as did the *NBC Evening News* report, which also noted the profit the match was likely to produce (NBC 1973). Yet the match itself has been remembered as a real match—King refusing to take the antics onto the court. She won handily (6-4, 6-3, 6-3) and observers, many of whom who had believed, as had the Las Vegas oddsmakers, that King would surely lose, talked about the age disparity between contestants and Riggs's lack of attention to training. Many observers finally contended, despite all the promotion, that the match did not really prove anything.

From King's perspective, the match proved that a woman athlete was not thrown off by pressure and that women's tennis could bring in a crowd, necessary if women's professional tennis was going to make enough money to equalize prize money between men and women tennis players. Nor was King adverse to the personal finance benefits it brought her by way of her endorsements. She was able to secure substantial commercial endorsements until the early 1980s, when she lost an estimated $1.5 million in upcoming contracts after a female lover, her former secretary, sued her for palimony (King 1982: 213). If the revelation caused a sour note for advertisers and fans alike, it may have resulted from the fact that Billie Jean King was not quite the simple, down-to-earth, "transparent" personality that had made her so acceptable in confusing times.

For others, including feminists, the match proved that the feminist movement had a sense of humor, a peculiarly sensitive spot for feminists, who found themselves defensive as a result of representations of the movement as grim. To other feminists, the match loomed with even larger significance—a matter of upholding women's competency and the women's liberation movement itself—a disturbing amount of value to give to an outcome that could have, for the slightest of reasons, gone the other way. And for many women, the match verified the passage of the 1972 Education Act and encouraged organizations devoted to women in sports. Editors began to consider women as a fresh new sector of readers (*E&P* 10/20/73: 38, 11/10/73: 35).

For the ABC network, the significance of the match was that it drew a blockbuster audience and provided new content for a network seeking to come into its own. And for mass media scholars, the King–Riggs match provides an example of how the mass media, after contributing to a nation's sense of chaos, can also reintroduce a world of order by reduction and simplification. There could be no more simplification than reducing the women's movement to a promotional tennis match. No social change issue of the day was similarly defused at such a minimalist level.

Implications for the Second Wave

Although the activities of women's movement continued for the rest of the 1970s and into the early 1980s, the King–Riggs tennis match marked the decline of the intersection of mass media and the women's movement, an arc that began with the publication of *The Feminine Mystique* as saleable content for the publishing business and continued through the use of the movement as content for a broad television audience as the movement became well known. Once a national audience was established, feminism was vulnerable to the takeover of those parts useful to media. Indeed, a piece of evidence indicating that Billie Jean King was becoming the approved version of feminism for mass media was Dan Wakefield's 1974 article in *Esquire*, "My Love Affair with Billie Jean King." Wakefield provided a paean to King as a sexual being, informally polling other sportswriters to see if they thought she was sexy, which they did, and noting that she wore gold hoop earrings and a thin gold bracelets at her press conferences, providing "a touch of feminine charm" (Wakefield 1974: 384). From a distance, it seems a labored concoction (and Wakefield may have been aware of King's romantic relationship with her secretary, no great secret), and the profile was likely the result of a negotiation to help the launch her new magazine, *WomenSports*, which had a full-page advertisement in the issue of *Esquire* that contained the profile. The art that accompanied the article had King so cosmetically glamorized that the illustration lost all resemblance to its subject and almost became a caricature. Some readers may have had no difficulty in reading it as such.

However, once feminism was in a realm in which its content could be shaped for consumption like any other commodity, there was little incentive for mass media to seek new product. There was surely enough on the agenda for the picking and choosing, as mass media now found it useful to adapt and adopt what had been put on the table. In that sense, the match marked an even more dramatic turn in the media coverage of the movement than the ongoing journalistic search for new leads. Once at rest in the safe harbor of mass media entertainment, certain feminist goals such as equal pay for equal work received the cultural imprimatur of acceptability (furthered on varying levels by the *Mary Tyler Moore Show* and *Maude*). Most importantly, however, the match served as a kind of "happy ending" to the story of the women's movement, and in doing so signaled that the subject was off the news agenda in serious ways. Although feminist reform activities would continue throughout the decade, by 1975 the second wave was drawing to a close. Activists could claim many achievements in a few years' time, but the Nixon administration marked the debut of a conservative era in which activists were generally consolidating their winnings rather than playing a new hand. The King–Riggs match helped set in place a national belief that sufficient strides had been made, thereby making the issue the passage of the ERA no longer the "burning cause" (except in feminist circles) about which Muriel Fox had written in her letter to Friedan ten years earlier. By 1976, with the ERA campaign still alive, "first women" stories abounding, and feminism spreading internationally, *Harper's Bazaar* wondered, "What's Gone Wrong with the Women's Movement?" (*HB* 2/76: 59); by November of that year *Harper's Magazine*, its antifeminist agenda intact, simply declared a "Requiem for the Women's Movement" (Geng 1976: 49).

At the outset of the second wave, when the media broadly dispersed the feminist message, the messages was shaped by media forces, often to the detriment of the original message. But in the King–Riggs match, the media shifted from the shaping of messages to their origination. Under Arledge's direction, the King–Riggs match was imprinted at its inception with a narrative structure that moved feminism from an issue in the public sphere into one of entertainment. King's personality added content by positioning the match as a working-class achievement, a familiar stance for mass media. The difficult parts of feminism were removed. Altogether, the King–Riggs match became a product, made by media for media purposes. It was sold, however, on the basis of a brand name—feminism—that had been constructed in all its myriad voices in the previous decade.

From the publication of *The Feminine Mystique* onward, the women's movement's substantial connection with the mass media infused the presentation of the movement with the secular values that support mass media. These values meant that the movement's goals would be met only in ways that were consistent with the values of commerce—opportunity for work being the most obvious because it was an issue, in the prosperous times before the mid-1970s recession, that offered benefit to the marketplace. The multitude of other issues that concerned feminists subsisted on the margins until those issues were seen as necessary for the support of the majority culture, as when sexual harassment changed from being a joke to the subject of lawsuits.

Equal pay for equal work, which helped to legitimize the second wave on the mass media agenda, in many ways also closed the second wave. Working women became the norm in America, necessary for the economic survival of the family as a result of the ballooning inflation of mid-decade. As well-paying, old-economy jobs disappeared for men, women provided necessary adjunct income from the service industries, and the working class became the working poor, perhaps the nation's most underserved population, a position they retain today (Ehrenreich 2001). For the educated classes, however, the new worlds of work offered career opportunities for women that even the EEOC demonstrators might not have imagined, leading to a standard of living for professional married couples that was equally unimaginable. Early radicals who had decried the women's movement as most beneficial to the middle class were proved, in general, correct.

Still, when Billie Jean King threw her tennis racket in the air at match point, pandemonium raged in the stands, living rooms erupted in cheers, and even those who had not supported her were rueful but not graceless. It was hard not to like King. As she left the court, the crush around her was so great that her husband and secretary were bruised while trying to protect her from her own well-wishers. She was finally able to climb onto a table at courtside, where she could lift her arms high to receive the cheers of the crowd. It was, as everyone agreed at the time, a glorious moment of triumph.

Works Cited

ABC Evening News. "King/Riggs," 9 September 1973, Television News Archives, Vanderbilt University.
———. "Women's Movement/Houston Conference," 21 November 1977, Television News Archives, Vanderbilt University.
ABC-TV. "Philco Presents the World Over: The World's Girls," 25 October 1963, MTR.
Adams, Whitney. *NOW Action to Create a Feminist Broadcast Media: Report on the National Media Task Force.* Washington: NOW, 1974.
Adorno, T. W. "Television and the Patterns of Mass Culture." *Quarterly of Film, Radio, and Television* 8 (1954): 213–35+; reprinted in *Mass Culture: The Popular Arts,* ed. Bernard Rosenberg, 474–88. New York: Free Press, 1957.
Ain't I a Woman [AIAW Collective, Iowa City], 26 June 1970, n.p. [microform].
Albrecht, Margaret. *A Complete Guide for the Working Mother.* Garden City, N.Y.: Doubleday, 1967.
Alexander, Shana. "No Person's Land." *Newsweek,* 18 March 1972, 43.
———. *Happy Days: My Mother, My Father, My Sister, & Me.* New York: Doubleday, 1995.
Allen, Craig. "Tackling the TV Titans in Their Own Backyard: WABC-TV, New York City." In *Television in America: Local Station History from Across the Nation,* eds. Michael D. Murray and Donald G. Godfrey, 3–18. Ames: Iowa State University Press, 1997.
———. "Gender Breakthrough Fit for a Focus Group." *Journalism History* 28:4 (winter 2003): 154–62.
Allen, Martha. "The Development of Communication Networks among Women, 1963–1983." Ph.D. diss., University of Michigan, 1988.
Almquist, June Anderson. "Women's Sections: Are They Opening Windows?" *Editor and Publisher,* 12 May 1973, 28.
Altschuler, Glenn C., and David I. Grossvogel. *Changing Channels: America in TV Guide.* Urbana: University of Illinois Press, 1992.
Andelin, Helen B. *Fascinating Womanhood.* Santa Barbara, Calif.: Pacific Press, 1965; New York: Bantam, 1990.
Andsager, Julie L., and Angela Powers. "Social or Economic Concerns: How News and Women's Magazines Framed Breast Cancer in the 1990s." *Journalism and Mass Communication Quarterly* 76:3 (autumn 1999): 531–50.
The APME Red Book 1976. [Associated Press Managing Editors Association]. "Sex and the Sports Editor," priv. pub., 28–35.
The APME Red Book 1982. "The Equal Rights Amendment," priv. pub., 168.
Armstrong, David. *A Trumpet to Arms: Alternative Media in America.* Boston: Houghton Mifflin, 1981.
Ashley, Laura, and Beth Olson. "Constructing Reality: Print Media's Framing of the Women's Movement, 1966 to 1986." *Journalism and Mass Communication Quarterly* 75:2 (summer 1998): 263–77.
Associated Press. "Michigan Girl Chosen Miss America." *New York Times,* 7 September 1969, 68.
Atkinson, Ti-Grace. *Amazon Odyssey.* New York: Link Books, 1974
Babcox, Peter. "Meet the Women of the Revolution, 1969." *New York Times Magazine,* 9 February 1969: VI, 34–35, 85–88, 90–92.

Barker-Plummer, Bernadette. "News as a Political Resource: Media Strategies and Political Identity in the U.S. Women's Movement, 1966–1975." *Critical Studies in Mass Communication*, 12 September 1995, 306–24.

———. "Producing Public Voice: Resource Mobilization and Media Access in the National Organization for Women." *Journalism and Mass Communication Quarterly* 79:1 (spring 2002), 188–204.

Barrett, Edward W. "Folksy TV News." *Columbia Journalism Review*, November–December 1973, 16–20.

Barrett, Marvin, ed. *Alfred I. duPont–Columbia University Survey of Broadcast Journalism, 1968–1969*. New York: Grosset and Dunlap, 1969.

Baughman, James L. "The Transformation of *Time* Magazine." *Media Studies Journal* 12:3 (fall 1998): 120–27.

Baxandall, Rosalyn Fraad. "Catching the Fire." In *The Feminist Memoir Project: Voices from Women's Liberation*, eds. Rachel Blau DuPlessis and Ann Snitow, 208–24. New York: Three Rivers Press, 1998.

Beasley, Maurine H., and Sheila J. Gibbons. *Taking Their Place: A Documentary History of Women and Journalism*. Washington, D.C.: American University Press in cooperation with the Women's Institute for Freedom of the Press, 1993.

Bender, Marilyn. "And Now, an Organization to Emancipate Men." *New York Times*, 15 April 1969, 38.

———. "Some Call her the 'Karl Marx' of New Feminism." *New York Times*, 20 July 1970, 3D.

Berk, R. H. "Trans-Sexuals: Male or Female?" *Look*, 27 January 1970, 28–31.

Berman, Dr. Edgar P. "The Feminist 'Flim Flam' Won't Bother Housewives." *Atlanta Constitution*, 26 August 1970, 1B–2B.

Berry, Mary Frances. *Why ERA Failed: Politics, Women's Rights and the Amending Process of the Constitution*. Bloomington: Indiana University Press, 1986.

BF-SLRI (1) [box] 49:[folder]1756; (2) 10:388; (3) 10:393;(4) 13:461.

Blair, Gwenda. *Almost Golden: Jessica Savitch and the Selling of Television News*. New York: Simon & Schuster, 1988; New York: Avon, 1989.

Blakemore, Barbara. "When *Redbook* Looks for Stories." *The Writer*, December 1964, 26.

———. "When *McCall's* Looks for Stories." *The Writer*, February 1966, 25.

Blau, Eleanor. "Pauline Frederick, 84, Network News Pioneer, Dies." *New York Times*, 11 May 1990, D18.

Boeth, Richard. "Gloria Steinem: A Liberated Woman Despite Beauty, Chic, and Success." *Newsweek* 16 August 1971, 3.

Boles, Janet K. *The Politics of the Equal Rights Amendment: Conflict and the Decision Process*. New York: Longman, 1979.

Bonfante, Jordan. "Germaine Greer." *Life*, 7 May 1971, 30–33.

Bonk, Kathy. "Statement of the National Organization for Women before the Subcommittee on Communications, Commerce Committee, U.S. Senate at the Hearings of the Operations and Oversight of the Federal Communications Commission," Washington, D.C., 7 November 1975.

———. "Testimony before the House Subcommittee on Communications, Commerce Committee on House Bill 3333," Washington, D.C., 16 May 1979.

———. Interview with author, Sundance, Idaho, July 1999.

Bonk, Kathy, Henry Griggs, and Emily Tynes. *The Jossey-Bass Guide to Strategic Communications for Nonprofits*. San Francisco: Jossey-Bass, 1999.

Botwright, Ken. "Women Toast Freedom in Male Pubs." *Boston Globe*, 26 August 1970, 23.

Boyce, Joseph. "Friendly Skies Thunder with Gals' Protest." *Chicago Tribune*, 15 February 1969, 1:5.

Bradlee, Ben C. *A Good Life: Newspapering and Other Adventures*. New York: Simon & Schuster, 1995.

Bradley, Patricia. "Media Leaders and Personal Ideology: Margaret Cousins and the Women's Service Magazines." *Journalism History* 21:2 (summer 1995): 79–87.

Branscomb, Anne, and Marie Savage. "The Broadcast Reform Movement at the Crossroads." *Journal of Communication* 28:4 (autumn 1978): 27–36.

Brigham, John C., and Linda W. Biesbrech. " 'All in the Family': Racial Attitudes." *Journal of Communication* 26:3 (autumn 1976): 69–74.

Brinkley, David. *David Brinkley.* New York: Knopf, 1995.

Brockway, George. Correspondence with author, September 1998.

Brown, Helen Gurley. *Sex and the Single Girl.* New York: Bernard Geiss, 1962.

———. "New Direction for *Cosmopolitan*". *The Writer* 78:20 (July 1965): 20.

Brown, Rita Mae. "Say It Isn't So." *Rat,* 24 February 1970, 8.

———. "Reflections of a Lavender Menace." *Ms.,* July–August 1995, 40–47.

Brownmiller, Susan. " 'Sisterhood Is Powerful': A Member of the Women's Liberation Movement Explains What It's All About." *New York Times Magazine,* 15 March 1970, 26–27, 127–30, 132, 134, 136, 140.

———. *In Our Time: Memoir of a Revolution.* New York: Dial, 1999.

———. Interview with author, Philadelphia, January 2000.

Buckley, William F., Jr. "Women's Lib Is Opening Door for the Girls." *Los Angeles Times,* 17 August 1970, II:7.

Burbank, Carol Elizabeth. "Ladies against Women: Theatre Activism, Parody, and the Public Construction of Citizenship in U.S. Feminism's Second Wave." Ph.D. diss., Northwestern University, 1998.

Burkhart, Kitsi. "The Frustration of a Woman Fighting Second-Class Status." *Philadelphia Evening Bulletin,* 8 March 1970, 4:1.

———. "Rebellion among Women Parallels the Black Revolt to Erase 'Slave Mentality.' " *Philadelphia Evening Bulletin,* 9 March 1970, 18.

———. "WITCH and NOW Tackle Male 'Oppressors.' " *Philadelphia Evening Bulletin,* 10 March 1970, 42–43.

———. "Men Aren't Enemies . . . They Just Need Education." *Philadelphia Evening Bulletin,* 11 March 1970, 63.

Buzenberg, Susan, and Bill Buzenberg, eds. *Salant, CBS, and the Battle for the Soul of Broadcast Journalism: The Memoirs of Richard S. Salant.* Boulder: Westview, 1999.

CBS Evening News. "Commentary by Eric Sevareid," 26 August 1970, Television News Archives, Vanderbilt University.

———. "King/Riggs," 20 September 1973, Television News Archives, Vanderbilt University.

———. "Abortion," 10 July 1977, Television News Archives, Vanderbilt University.

———. "IWY Conference," 18 November 1977, Television News Archives, Vanderbilt University

Cadden, Vivian. " 'Women's Lib? I've Seen It on TV.' " *Redbook,* February 1972, 88–96.

Calvacca, Lorraine. "Forbidden Four." *Folio,* 15 October 1993, 25.

Cantor, Muriel G. "Women and Public Broadcasting." *Journal of Communication* 27:1 (spring 1977): 14–19.

———. "Feminism and the Media." *Society* 25:5 (July–August 1988): 76–82.

Carabillo, Toni, Judith Meuli, and June Bundy Csida, eds. *Feminist Chronicles, 1953–1993.* Los Angeles: Women's Graphics, 1993; online at http://feminist.org/research/chronicles.

Carroll, Peter N. *It Seemed Like Nothing Happened: America in the 1970s.* New Brunswick: Rutgers University Press, 1990.

Cawley, Janet. " 'Boss Lady': Beverly LaHaye Leads her 600,000 Concerned Women for American Down the Right Path." *Chicago Tribune,* 26 May 1992, 5, 1:2.

Ceballos, Jacqui. "The Turning Point—The Strike That Made Us a Movement." *Veteran Feminists of America* 3:1 (spring 1996): 3–4.

———. Correspondence with author, June 1999.

———. Telephone, e-mail interviews with author, 2000–01.

Charlton, Linda. "Women March Down Fifth in Equality Drive." *New York Times*, 23 August 1970, 1, 30.

Chesler, Ellen. "NOW, Then." *New York Times Magazine*, 1 January 1995, 25.

Chisholm, Shirley. *Unbought and Unbossed*. Boston: Houghton Mifflin, 1970.

———. *The Good Fight*. New York: Harper & Row, 1973.

———. National Women's Political Caucus Convention, Houston, 7 February 1973.

Columbia Journalism Review. "Kissing 'the Girls' Good-Bye: A Discussion of Guidelines for Journalists." May–June 1975, 28–33.

Clark, Alfred E. "Five Women Protest the 'Slavery' of Marriage." *New York Times*, 24 September 1969, 93.

Classen, Steven. "Southern Discomforts: The Racial Struggle over Popular TV." In *The Revolution Wasn't Televised: Sixties Television and Social Conflict*, eds. Lynn Spigel and Michael Curtin, 305–24. New York: Routledge, 1997.

Cole, Barry G., and Mal Oettinger. *Reluctant Regulators: The FCC and the Broadcast Audience*. Reading, Mass.: Addison-Wesley, 1978.

Concerned Women for America. http://www.cwfa.org/about.asp.

Condit, Celeste Michelle. *Decoding Abortion Rhetoric: Communicating Social Change*. Urbana: University of Illinois Press, 1990.

"Congress to Unite Women." *Rat*, 8–21 May 1970, 12.

Corea, Gena. "How Papers Can Conduct Serious Coverage of Women." *Editor and Publisher*, 25 April 1971, 28, 30.

Courtney, Alice E., and Sarah Wernick Lockeretz. "A Woman's Place: An Analysis of the Roles Portrayed by Women in Magazine Advertisements." *Journal of Marketing Research* 8.1 (February 1971): 92–95.

Corporation for Public Broadcasting. *Long-Range Financing for Public Broadcasting: Hearings before the Subcommittee on Communications of the Committee on Interstate and Foreign Commerce, House of Representatives*, 354–55. Serial no. 94-34. Washington: U.S. Government Printing Office, 1975.

Crawford, Alan. *Thunder on the Right: The "New Right" and the Politics of Resentment*. New York: Pantheon, 1980.

Creedon, Pamela. "From the Feminine Mystique to the Female Physique." In *Women, Media, and Sport*, ed. Pamela J. Creedon, 275–99. Thousand Oaks, Calif.: Sage, 1994.

Cronkite, Walter. "On Choosing—and Paying—Anchorpeople." *Columbia Journalism Review*, July–August 1976, 24–25.

Curtis, Charlotte. "Miss America Pageant Is Picketed by 100 Women." *New York Times*, 8 September 1968, 15.

———. "Black Panther Philosophy Is Debated at the Bernsteins." *New York Times*, 15 January 1970, 50.

———. "Women's Liberation Gets into the Long Island Swim." *New York Times*, 10 August 1970, 32.

Curtis, Jean. "When Sisterhood Turns Sour." *New York Times Magazine*, 30 May 1976, 15–16.

Davis, Flora. *Moving the Mountain: The Women's Movement in America since 1960*. New York: Simon & Schuster, 1991.

Davis, Kenneth C. *Two-Bit Culture: The Paperbacking of America*. Boston: Houghton Mifflin, 1984.

Davidson, Sara. "Militants for Women's Rights." *Life*, 12 December 1969, 66–76.

DeCrow, Karen. Letter to "Nan," 24 July 1968. Courtesy Karen DeCrow.

———. Letter to Sylvia Hartman, 5 March 1969. Courtesy Karen DeCrow.

———. "Memo to NOW Board of Directors, Re: Public Accommodations Week," 21 March 1969. Courtesy Karen DeCrow.

———. Interview with author, Syracuse, New York, September 1999.

Decter, Midge. *The New Chastity and Other Arguments against Women's Liberation*. New York: Coward, McCann, & Geoghegan, 1972.

———. "Toward the New Chastity." *Atlantic Monthly*, August 1972, 42–55.

————. *An Old Wife's Tale: My Seven Decades in Love and War*. New York: Regan, 2001.

Dedman, J. "The Conspiracy to Kill the ERA." *Playgirl*, July 1976: 34, 42, 52, 86, 108.

Dell'Olio, Anselma. "Home before Sundown." In *The Feminist Memoir Project: Voices from Women's Liberation*, eds. Rachel Blau DuPlessis and Ann Snitow, 149–70. New York: Three Rivers Press, 1998.

Deutsch, Helene. *The Psychology of Women*. 2 vols. New York: Grune & Stratton, 1944.

DeWolf, Rose. "You're Strong, Weaker Sex Told." *Philadelphia Inquirer*, 9 April 1968, 31.

————. Interview with author, Philadelphia, June 1998.

Diamond, Edwin. " 'Reporter Power' Takes Root." *Columbia Journalism Review*, summer 1970, 12–18.

Dickerson, Nancy. *Among Those Present: A Reporter's View of Twenty-Five Years in Washington*. New York: Random House, 1976.

Dominick, Joseph R., and Gail E. Rauch. "The Image of Women in Network TV Commercials." *Journal of Broadcasting & Electronic Media* 16:3 (summer 1972): 259–65.

Donovan, Hedley. *Right Places, Right Times*. New York: Holt, 1989.

Dougherty, Richard. " 'Shure, and 'Tis no Fit Place for a Colleen, That M'Sorley's." *Los Angeles Times*, 26 August 1970, I:1.

Douglas, Susan. *Where the Girls Are: Growing Up Female with the Mass Media*. New York: Times Books, 1994.

Dowd, Ann Reilly. "Some Moms Who Made It." *Columbia Journalism Review*, July–August 1998, 12–13.

Downs, Hugh. "Television Is Too Conservative." *Columbia Journalism Review*, September–October 1972, 64.

Draves, Pamela, ed. *Citizens Media Directory*. Washington: National Citizens Committee for Broadcasting, 1977.

Dreifus, Claudia. "Playboy after the Dark Ages." *It Ain't Me Babe*, 11 May–20 June 1970, 11.

Drexler, Rosalyn. "What Happened to Mozart's Sister." *Village Voice*, 6 May 1971, 28, 70.

Dudar, Helen. "Women's Lib: The War on 'Sexism.' " *Newsweek*, 23 March 1970, 71–78.

————. "Mailer & the Lib 'Ladies.' " *New York Post*, 1 May 1971, 4, 9.

Dunbar, Roxanne. "Outlaw Women: Chapters from a Feminist Memoir-in-Progress." In *The Feminist Memoir Project: Voices from Women's Liberation*, eds. Rachel Blau DuPlessis and Ann Snitow, 90–114. New York: Three Rivers Press, 1998.

————. Interview with author, San Francisco, January 1999.

Dunning, Jennifer. "Books: Unequal Rights Advocate." *New York Times*, 14 October 1977, III, 25.

Durham, Leona, et al. "APME's 'Guidelines': A Woman's Review." *Columbia Journalism Review* May–June 1971, 55–56.

Dworkin, Susan. *Miss America 1945: Bess Myerson and the Year That Changed Our Lives*. New York: Newmarket, 1998.

Dye, Lee. "L.A. 'Women's Lib' Marchers Greeted by Cheers and Jeers." *Los Angeles Times*, 27 August 1970, 1.

Echols, Alice. *Daring to Be Bad: Radical Feminism in America, 1967–1975*. Minneapolis: University of Minnesota Press, 1989.

Edgar, JoAnne. Interview with author, Sundance, Idaho, July 1999.

Ehrenreich, Barbara. *Nickel and Dimed: On (Not) Getting by in America*. New York: Metropolitan, 2001.

Eldowney, Carol, and Rosemary Poole. "A Working Paper on Media." *Women: A Journal of Liberation* 2:1 (spring 1970): 40.

Elliott, Karen J. "Viewer Power/Broadcasters Give in to Citizens' Demands on Program Content." *Women's Studies Journal*, 2 January 1975, 1, 12.

Ellis, Estelle. Collection, 1944–1999. Smithsonian Archives, Washington, D.C., http://americanhistory.si.edu/archives/d7423.htm, accessed 6 October 2002.

Endres, Kathleen L., and Therese L. Lueck. *Women's Periodicals in the United States: Social and Political Issues*. Westport, Conn.: Greenwood, 1996.

Ephron, Nora. "Women." *Esquire*, July 1972, 42, 44.

———. *Nora Ephron Collected*. New York: Avon, 1991.

Epstein, Barbara. "The Success and Failures of Feminism." *Journal of Women's History* 14:2 (summer 2002): 118–25.

Epstein, Edward Jay. *News from Nowhere: Television and the News*. New York: Random House, 1973.

Epstein, Joseph. "Homo/Hetero: The Struggle for Sexual Identity." *Harper's Magazine*, September 1970, 37–51.

Evans, Sara. *Personal Politics: The Roots of Women's Liberation in the Civil Rights Movement and the New Left*. New York: Knopf, 1979.

Everly, Susan. "Biltmore Men's Bar Bows to Fair Sex." *Rocky Mountain News*, 11 August 1970, 7.

Fader, Shirley Sloan. "An Opinion: Putting Women in Women's Lib." *Mademoiselle*, March 1972, 36, 46.

Fallon, Beth. "A Breakthrough for Women's Rights Ads: Acceptance as Public Service Messages." *New York Daily News*, 10 February 1975, 14.

Faludi, Susan. *Backlash: The Undeclared War against American Women*. New York: Crown, 1991.

Farhi, Paul. "Will There Be a Future for *Ms*. Magazine? Possibly—But Not in the Same Slick, Colorful Form." *Philadelphia Inquirer*, 11 November 1989, D01.

Farrell, Amy Erdman. *Yours in Sisterhood: Ms. Magazine and the Promise of Popular Feminism*. Chapel Hill: University of North Carolina Press, 1998.

FCC. *Report and Order*, docket no. 19269 RMJ-1722. 18 December 1971.

———. *The Public and Broadcasting: A Procedure Manual*. Washington: U.S. Government Printing Office, 1972.

Feldman, Gayle. "Breaking through the Glass Ceiling." *Publisher's Weekly*, 2 July 1997, 82–90.

Felsenthal, Carol. *The Sweetheart of the Silent Majority: The Biography of Phyllis Schlafly*. Garden City, N.Y.: Doubleday, 1981.

Ferraiulo, Perucci. "Women on the Affront Line: Women Broadcasters Like Beverly LaHaye, Ingrid Guzman, Ruth Schofield and Mary Dorr Are Moving Forward as Outspoken and Effective Leaders in the Political Arena." *Religious Broadcasting* 27 (January 1995): 22.

Ferro, Nancy, Coletta Reid Holcomb, and Marilyn Saltzman-Webb. "Statement of Purpose." *off our backs* 1:1 (March 1970): 1; reprinted in *Taking Their Place: A Documentary History of Women and Journalism*, by Maurine H. Beasley and Sheila J. Gibbons, 193–95. Washington: American University Press in cooperation with the Women's Institute for Freedom of the Press, 1993.

Fine, Elsa Honig. *Women and Art*. Montauk: Allanheld and Schram/Prior, 1978.

Fiske, John. "Television: Polysemy and Popularity." *Critical Studies in Mass Communication* 3 (December 1986): 371–408.

Fitzgerald, Edward E. "Woman Leaves *Look* to Become Editorial Director at *McCall's*." *New York Times*, 22 August 1970, 21.

Flaherty, Stacy, and Mimi Minnick. "Marlboro Advertising Oral History and Documentation Project." Smithsonian Institution, http://americanhistory.si.edu/archives/d7198, accessed 6 October 2002.

Flamiano, Dolores. "Covering Contraception: Discourses of Gender, Motherhood, and Sexuality in Women's Magazines, 1938–1969." *American Journalism* 17:3 (summer 2000): 59–87.

Foote, Joe S. "Women Correspondents and the Evening News." In *Women and Media: Content, Careers, and Criticism*, ed. Cynthia M. Lont, 229–37. Belmont, Calif.: Wadsworth, 1995.

Foster, Ann Tolstoi. "Is That Really Me?—Today's Woman Has a Tough Time Recognizing Herself in Those TV Commercials." *TV Guide*, 19 June 1971, 18–20.

———. "Commercials Tend to Ignore Working Women." *Advertising Age*, 10 April 1972, 44.

Fox, Mary Lou. "Made in the Media, Where Talk Is Cheap." *Majority Report*, 6–20 March 1976, 4.

Fox, Muriel. Letter to Betty Friedan, 15 November 1963. Courtesy Muriel Fox.

———. Interviews with author, Tappan, New York, 1998, 1999.

Frank, Reuven. *Out of Thin Air.* New York: Simon & Schuster, 1991.

Frankfort, Ellen. *Vaginal Politics.* New York: Quadrangle, 1972.

Franks, Lucinda. "Dissension among Feminists: The Rift Widens." *New York Times,* 29 August 1975, 32.

Frazier, George. "The Entrenchment of the American Witch." *Esquire,* February 1962, 100–103, 138.

Freeman, Barbara M. *The Satellite Sex: The Media and Women's Issues in English Canada, 1966–1971.* Waterloo, Ontario, Can.: Wilfred Laurier University Press, 2001.

Freeman, Jo. *The Politics of Women's Liberation.* New York: David McKay, 1975.

———. "The Tyranny of Structurelessness." *Ms.,* July 1973, 76–78.

Freimuth, Vicki S. "Covering Cancer: Newspapers and the Public Interest." *Journal of Communication* 34:4 (winter 1984): 62–73.

Friedan, Betty. "We Built a Community for Our Children." *Redbook,* March 1955, 42–45, 62–63.

———. "Why I Went Back to Work." *Charm,* April 1955, 145, 200.

———. "Two Are an Island." *Mademoiselle,* July 1955, 88–89, 100–101.

———. "We Drove the Rackets out of Our Town." *Redbook,* August 1955, 36–39, 86–87.

———. "Now They're Proud of Peoria." *Reader's Digest,* August 1955, 93–97.

———. "The Gal Who Defied Dior." *Town Journal,* October 1955, 33.

———. "The Happy Families of Hickory Hill." *Redbook,* February 1956, 39, 87–90.

———. "Millionaire's Wife." *Cosmopolitan,* September 1956, 78–87.

——— (as told by Julie Harris). "I Was Afraid to Have a Baby." *McCall's,* December 1956, 68, 72, 74.

———. "Day Camp in the Driveway." *Parents' Magazine,* May 1957, 36–37, 131–34.

——— (as told by Marian Stone and Harold Stone). "With Love We Live." *Coronet,* July 1957, 135–44.

———. "Teenage Girl in Trouble." *Coronet,* March 1958, 163–68.

———. "New Hampshire Love Story." *Family Circle,* June 1958, 40–41, 74–76.

———. "The Coming Ice Age: A True Scientific Detective Story." *Harper's Magazine,* September 1958, 39–45.

———. "Business Problems? Call in Plato." *Rotarian,* August 1960, 39–45.

———. "I Say Women Are People Too!" *Good Housekeeping,* September 1960, 59–61.

———. "How to Find and Develop Article Ideas." *The Writer,* March 1962, 13, 15.

———. "Feminine Fulfillment: 'Is This All?' " *Mademoiselle,* May 1962, 146–47, 205–9.

———. "Have American Housewives Traded Brains for Brooms?" *Ladies' Home Journal,* January 1963, 24, 26.

———. "Fraud of Femininity." *McCall's,* March 1963, 81.

———. "GI Bill for Women?" *Saturday Review,* May 18, 1963, 68.

———. *The Feminine Mystique.* New York: Norton, 1963.

———. "Television and the Feminine Mystique." *TV Guide,* 1, 6 February 1964; reprinted in *Television: A Series of Readings from* TV Guide *Magazine,* ed. Barry G. Cole, 267–75. New York: Free Press, 1970.

———. "Woman: The Fourth Dimension." *Ladies' Home Journal,* June 1964, 48–55.

———. Letter to Muriel Fox, 31 August 1966. Courtesy Muriel Fox.

———. "An Opinion: Betty Friedan on the Conventions." *Mademoiselle,* October 1968, 22, 24, 220.

———. "Up from the Kitchen Floor." *New York Times Magazine,* March 4, 1973, 8, 9, 28, 30, 32–35, 37.

———. *"It Changed My Life": Writings on the Women's Movement.* New York: Random House, 1976.

———. *Life So Far: A Memoir.* New York: Simon & Schuster, 2000.

Friendly, Fred W. "The Campaign to Politicize Broadcasting." *Columbia Journalism Review,* March–April 1972, 9–24.

Gans, Herbert. *Deciding What's News.* New York: Vintage, 1980.

Geng, Veronica. "Requiem for the Women's Movement." *Harper's Magazine,* November 1976, 49–56.

Genovese, Margaret. "Her 'Mid-Life Crisis' Is Resolved by Appointment as a Publisher." *presstime,* August 1982, 23.

Gere, Anne Ruggles. *Intimate Practices: Literary and Cultural Work in U.S. Women's Clubs, 1880–1920.* Urbana: University of Illinois Press, 1997.

Gilder, George F. *Sexual Suicide.* New York: Quadrangle, 1973.

———. *Wealth and Poverty.* New York: Basic Books, 1981.

Gillespie, David E. "Women's Liberationists: Impressive." *The Masthead* 22:4 (winter 1970–71): 12–14.

Gingrich, Arnold. "Responsibility of the Press." *Esquire,* July 1959, 6.

———. *Nothing but People; The Early Days at Esquire, a Personal History, 1928–1958.* New York: Crown, 1971.

Gitlin, Todd. *The Whole World Is Watching: Mass Media in the Making and Unmaking of the New Left.* Berkeley: University of California Press, 1980.

Glamour. "A Girl—Signed Herself." February 1964, 101.

Goldman, Ivan. "News Media Action Asked by Feminist." *Washington Post,* 16 May 1971, A28.

Goodman, Ellen. "Pioneer Pussycat." *Boston Globe,* 9 October 1969, 37.

———. "How N.O.W., Betty Friedan." *Boston Globe,* 14 November 1969, 38.

———. "Aileen Hernandez: New at NOW." *Boston Globe,* 3 April 1970, 37.

———. "Keep Her Chained . . . to a Tranquilizer." *Boston Globe,* 16 April 1970, 23.

———. "Feminist to 'Celebrate' and 'Morn' [*sic*] on Aug. 26." *Boston Globe,* 5 August 1970, 20.

———. "Kate Millett's Like Wow!" *Boston Globe,* 23 August 1970, A-1.

———. Interview with author, Boston, September 1999.

Gorney, Cynthia. "Gloria." *Mother Jones,* November–December 1995, 22, 24, 26, 27.

Gornick, Vivian. "The Next Great Moment in History Is Theirs." *Village Voice,* 27 November 1969, 11–12, 48, 50, 52, 54.

———. "Consciousness." *New York Times Magazine,* 10 January 1971, 22–23, 77–83.

———. Telephone interview with author, October 1999.

Graham, Katharine. *Personal History.* New York: Knopf, 1997.

Graham, Virginia. *There Goes What's Her Name: The Continuing Saga of Virginia Graham.* New York: Avon, 1966.

———. *If I Made It So Can You.* New York: Bantam, 1978.

Greenfield, Robert. "A Groupie in Women's Lib." *Rolling Stone,* 7 January 1971, 17.

Greenwald, Marilyn S. *A Woman of the* Times: *Journalism, Feminism, and the Career of Charlotte Curtis.* Athens: Ohio University Press, 1999.

Greer, Germaine. *The Female Eunuch.* New York: McGraw-Hill, 1971.

———. "My Mailer Problem." *Esquire,* September 1971, 90–93, 215.

———. "McGovern, the Big Tease." *Harper's Magazine,* October 1972: 56–71.

Grizzuti Harrison, Barbara. "The Woman Who's Fighting the Law That Most Women Want." *McCall's,* April 1982, 85, 101–4, 106.

Gross, Terry. "Host of NPR's 'Fresh Air.' " In *The Broadcast Century: A Biography of American Broadcasting,* by Robert L. Hilliard and Michael C. Keith, 226–28. Boston: Focal Press, 1997.

Grossman, Edward. "In Pursuit of the American Woman; or, Gulliver at the Gynecologist's." *Harper's Magazine,* February 1970: 47–57, 63–69.

Grossvogel, David I. *Dear Ann Landers: Our Intimate and Changing Dialogue with America's Best-Loved Confidante.* Chicago: Contemporary, 1987.

Grunwald, Henry A. *One Man's America: A Journalist's Search for the Heart of His Country.* New York: Doubleday, 1997.

Gunther, Marc. *The House That Roone Built: The Inside Story of ABC News.* Boston: Little, Brown, 1994.

Haiman, Robert J. "Separating the Winners from the Losers." *presstime,* August 1982: 24–25.

Hammel, Lisa. "They Meet in Victorian Parlor to Demand 'True Equality'—NOW." *New York Times,* 22 November 1966, 44.

Hanisch, Carol. "What Can Be Learned: A Critique of the Miss America Protest." *Women's Liberation,* 11 November 1968, 9–13; reprinted in *Dear Sisters: Dispatches from the Women's Liberation Movement,* eds. Rosalyn Baxandall and Linda Gordon, 185–87. New York: Basic Books, 2001.

———. "The Liberal Takeover of Women's Liberation." In *Feminist Revolution: An Abridged Edition with Additional Writings,* by Redstockings of the Women's Liberation Movement, 163–67. New York: Random House, 1975.

———. "Two Letters from the Women's Liberation Movement." In *The Feminist Memoir Project: Voices from Women's Liberation,* eds. Rachel Blau DuPlessis and Ann Snitow, 197–207. New York: Three Rivers Press, 1998.

Harrison, Cynthia E. "A 'New Frontier' for Women: The Public Policy of the Kennedy Administration." *Journal of American History* 67:3 (fall 1980): 630–46.

Harvey, R. C. "A Baker's Dozen or Two of the Top Cartoonists of the Century." *Comics Journal,* February 1999, 115–22.

Haughton, Rosemary. "Modern Sexuality: Bunk and Debunkery." *Commonweal* 46:20 (8 September 1972): 483–44.

Hayden, Tom. *Reunion: A Memoir.* New York: Random House, 1988.

Healey, Paul. "The Witches of Washington." *New York Daily News,* 28 August 1970, 3.

Heide, Wilma Scott. "Feminism: The Sin Qua Non for a Just Society." Speech presented at the University of Nebraska, Lincoln, 6 March 1972; reprinted in *Vital Speeches of the Day* 30 (1971–72): 404–9.

Heilbrun, Carolyn G. *The Education of a Woman: The Life of Gloria Steinem.* New York: Dial, 1995.

Heins, Ed. "Sports." *Editor and Publisher,* 30 November 1973, 4.

Hennessee, Judith Adler. "The Press's Very Own Barbara Walters Show." *Columbia Journalism Review,* July–August 1976, 22–25.

———. *Betty Friedan: Her Life.* New York: Random House, 1999.

Hennessee, Judith Adler, and Joan Nicholson. "NOW Says: TV Commercials Insult Women." *New York Times Magazine,* 28 May 1972, 11–13, 48–51.

Herman, Edward S., and Noam Chomsky. *Manufacturing Consent: The Political Economy of the Mass Media.* New York: Pantheon, 1988.

Hershey, Lenore. *Between the Covers: The Lady's Own Journal.* New York: Coward-McCann, 1983.

Hills, Rust. "When We Were Young . . . History of 'Esquire' Magazine." *Esquire,* August 1995, 30.

Hinckle, Warren, and Marianne Hinckle. "A History of the Rise of the Unusual Movement for Women Power in the United States, 1961–1968." *Ramparts,* January 1969, 23–31.

Hinds, Lynn Boyd. *Broadcasting the Local News: The Early Years of Pittsburgh's KDKA-TV.* University Park: Pennsylvania State University Press, 1995.

Hochschild, Arlie Russell, with Ann Machung. *The Second Shift: Working Parents and the Revolution at Home.* New York: Viking, 1989; New York: Avon, 1997.

Hoffman, Nicolas. "Women's Page: An Irreverent View." *Columbia Journalism Review,* July–August 1971: 62–64.

Hole, Judith, and Ellen Levine. *Rebirth of Feminism.* New York: Quadrangle, 1971.

hooks, bell. *Feminist Theory: From Margin to Center.* Boston: South End, 1984.

Horowitz, Daniel. "Rethinking Betty Friedan and *The Feminine Mystique*: Labor Union Radicalism and Feminism in Cold War America." *American Quarterly* 48:1 (March 1996): 1–42.

———. *Betty Friedan and the Making of* The Feminine Mystique. Amherst: University of Massachusetts Press, 1998.

Horowitz, David. *Radical Son: A Generational Odyssey.* New York: Simon & Schuster, 1998.

Hosley, David H. *As Good as Any: Foreign Correspondence on American Radio, 1930–1940.* Westport. Conn.: Greenwood, 1984.

Hovey, Susan. "A Radical Vows to Take *Ms.* Back to Its Roots." *Folio*, March 1990, 41–42.

Howe, Irving. "The Middle-Class Mind of Kate Millett." *Harper's Magazine*, December 1970, 110–32.

Howe, Louise Kapp. *Pink Collar Workers: Inside the World of Women's Work*. New York: Putnam, 1977.

"How Influential Is TV News?" *Columbia Journalism Review*, summer 1990, 19–29.

Hunt, Morton. "Up against the Wall, Male Chauvinist Pig!" *Playboy*, May 1970, 94–96, 102–4, 202–9.

Hunter, Marjorie. "Equal Rights Champion Martha Wright Griffiths." *New York Times*, 11 August 1970, 23.

Hyde Park Chapter, Chicago Women's Liberation Union. "Socialist Feminism—A Strategy for the Women's Movement." 1972. Special Collections Library, Duke University http://scriptorium.lib.duke.edu/wlm/socialist, accessed 21 March 2003.

Ireland, Patricia. *What Women Want*. New York: Dutton, 1996.

Isber, Carolyn, and Muriel Cantor. *Report of the Task Force on Women in Public Broadcasting*. Washington: Corporation for Public Broadcasting, 1975.

Janensch, Gail. "We've Come a Long Way, Baby, in Journalism." *The Quill*, November 1970, 30–32.

Jay, Karla. "Ladies' Home Journal." *Rat*, 4–28 April 1970, 4–5, 22.

———. *Tales of the Lavender Menace: A Memoir of Liberation*. New York: Basic Books, 1999.

Jennings, Ralph M. *Television Station Employment Practices: The Status of Minorities and Women*. New York: Office of Communication, United Church of Christ, 1972.

Jezer, Marty. *Abbie Hoffman: American Rebel*. New Brunswick, N.J.: Rutgers University Press, 1992.

Johnson, Nicholas. "Broadcasting in America: The Performance of Network Affiliates in the Top Fifty Markets." *Federal Communication Commission Report*, vol. 42, 2d ser., 10 August 1973–19 October 1973. Washington: U.S. Government Printing Office, 1975.

———. "Kathy Bonk." *access*, 31 May 1976, 5.

Johnstone, John W. C., Edward J. Slawski, and William W. Bowman. *The News People: A Sociological Portrait of American Journalists and Their Work*. Urbana: University of Illinois Press, 1976.

Joliffe, Lee, and Terri Catlett. "Women Editors at the 'Seven Sisters' Magazines, 1965–1985: Did They Make a Difference?" *Journalism Quarterly* 71 (winter 1994): 800–808.

Jones, Beverly, and Judith Brown. *Toward a Female Liberation Movement*. Gainesville, Fla.: Archives Distribution Program, 1968.

Joreen. "Trashing the Dark Side of Sisterhood." *Ms.*, April 1976, 41–51, 92–98.

Jowett, Garth S., and Victoria O'Donnell. *Propaganda and Persuasion*. Newbury Park, Calif.: Sage, 1986.

Kaufman, Sue. "How Women's Lib Looks to the Not-So-Mad Housewife." *Time*, 20 March 1972, 70.

Kearns, Karen. "grove: crimes against women." *off our backs*, 25 April 1970, 6.

Keck, Donna. "The Art of Maiming Women." *It Ain't Me Babe*, 29 April 1970, n.p.

Kennedy, Florynce. *Color Me Flo: My Hard Life and Good Times*. Englewood Cliffs, N.J.: Prentice-Hall, 1976.

———. Interview with author, New York, October 1999.

Kempton, Sally. "Cutting Loose." *Esquire*, July 1970, 53–57.

Kilbourne, Jean, narrator. "Killing Us Softly 3" (video). Media Education Foundation, Northampton, Massachusetts. http://www.mediaed.org/videos/MediaGenderAndDiversity/KillingUsSoftly3, accessed 5 February 2003.

Kilian, Michael. "Liberation: Chicago and across the Country." *Chicago Tribune*, 27 August 1970, 1.

Kinnick, Katherine N., Dean M. Krugman, and Glen T. Cameron. "Compassion Fatigue: Communication and Burnout toward Social Problems." *Journalism and Mass Communication Quarterly* 73:3 (autumn 1996): 687–707.

Kitch, Carolyn. "Reporting on the Birth and Death of Feminism: Three Decades of Mixed Messages in *Time* Magazine." Paper presented at the annual conference of the Association for Education in Journalism and Mass Communication, New Orleans, 1999.

Klatch, Rebecca E. *Women of the New Right*. Philadelphia: Temple University Press, 1987.

Klemesrud, Judy. "It Was a Special Show—and the Audience Was Special, Too." *New York Times*, 17 February 1969, 39.

———. "Coming Wednesday, a Herstory-Making Event." *New York Times Magazine*, 23 August 1970, 6, 14–19, 63–64.

———. "The Lesbian Issue and Women's Lib." *New York Times*, 18 December 1970, 47.

———. "The Disciples of Sappho, Updated." *New York Times Magazine*, 28 March 1971, 38–39, 41, 43, 50

———. "And Now a Word from Our Leader." *New Fashions of the Times*, 4 March 1973, 84, 87, 114.

———. "On Madison Avenue, Women Take Stand in Middle of the Road." *New York Times*, 23 July 1973, 28.

———. "The State of Being Childless, They Say, Is No Cause for Guilt." *New York Times*, 3 February 1975, 28.

———. "Women's Movement at Age 11: Larger, More Diffuse, Still Battling." *New York Times*, 15 November 1977, 46.

———. Papers. Women's Archives, University of Iowa Libraries, Ames.

Koedt, Ann. "Myth of the Vaginal Orgasm." In *Dear Sisters: Dispatches from the Women's Liberation Movement*, eds. Rosalyn Baxandall and Linda Gordon, 158–62. New York: Basic Books, 2001.

Kohler, Pam Sebastian. "Objectivity Ends at the Hemline." *The Quill*, October 1972, 25–27.

Komisar, Lucy. Testimony, "Discrimination against Women," at Special Subcommittee on Education of the Committee on Education and Labor, *U.S. House of Representatives*, 91st Cong., 2d sess., 424. Washington: U.S. Government Printing Office, 1970.

———. "Violence and the Masculine Mystique." *Washington Monthly*, July 1970, 38–48.

———. "Women in Advertising." In *Woman in Sexist Society: Studies in Power and Powerlessness*, eds. Vivian Gornick and Barbara K. Moran, 207–17. New York: Basic Books, 1971.

———. Telephone interview with author, June 1998.

Korda, Michael. *Another Life: A Memoir of Other People*. New York: Random House, 1999.

Kordisch, Karen. "Denver Women's Lib: A Historical Perspective." *Big Mama Rag* 1:4 (1974): 10.

Kovacs, Midge. "Are Your Ads Reaching Those Millions of Women Who Work?" *Advertising Age*, 27 April 1970, 48, 51.

———. "Where Is Woman's Place? Home, Say Ads." *Advertising Age*, 17 July 1970, 48.

———. "Women Simply Don't Recognize Themselves in Many Ads Today." *Advertising Age*, 12 June 1972, 50.

———. "Women's Rights Drive Gets off the Ground." *Advertising Age*, 25 September 1972, 73–74.

———. Interview with author, New York, September 1998.

Kraditor, Aileen S. *The Ideas of the Woman Suffrage Movement, 1890–1920*. New York: Columbia University Press, 1965.

———, ed. *Up from the Pedestal: Selected Writings in the History of American Feminism*. Chicago: Quadrangle, 1968.

Kramer, Marcia. "14 High Heels Stir Sawdust at McSorley's." *New York Daily News*, 11 August 1970, 5.

Kuntz, Mary. "Is Press Stopped for Pioneer *Ms.*?" *Philadelphia Inquirer*, 31 October 1989, E07.

Lacy, Robert, et al. "The Student of Broadcasting: His Recruitment, Training and Future in Broadcasting." *Journal of Broadcasting & Electronic Media* 4:4 (fall 1962): 335–62.

Lafky, Sue. "Women in Broadcast News: More Than Window Dressing on the Set, Less Than Equal with Men." In *Women and Media: Content, Careers, and Criticism*, ed. Cynthia M. Lont, 252–60. Belmont, Calif.: Wadsworth, 1995.

LaHaye, Beverly. *The Spirit-Controlled Woman*. Irvine, Calif.: Harvest House, 1976.

———. Interview with author, December 2002.

Langer, Elinor. "Why Big Business Is Trying to Defeat the ERA: The Economic Implications of Equality." *Ms.*, May 1976, 64–66, 100, 102, 104, 106, 108.

LaRocque, Paula. "Women See Mostly MANagement." *presstime*, August 1983, 4–9.

Lawrence, Mary Wells. *A Big Life (in Advertising)*. New York: Knopf, 2002.

Lawrenson, Helen. "How Women Feel about Other Women." *Esquire*, September 1959, 73–74.

———. "The Feminine Mistake." *Esquire*, January 1971, 83, 146–47, 153–54.

Lawton, Kim. "Powerhouse of the Religious Right?" *Christianity Today* 31 (6 November 1989): 34–37.

Lazarsfeld, Paul F., and Robert K. Merton. "Mass Communication, Popular Taste, and Organized Social Action." In *The Communication of Ideas*, ed. Lyman Bryson, 95–118. New York: Harper and Brothers, 1948; reprinted in *Mass Culture: The Popular Arts in America*, eds. Bernard Rosenberg and David Manning White, 457–74. Glencoe, Ill.: Free Press, 1957.

"Leading Feminist Puts Hairdo before Strike." *New York Times*, 27 August 1970, 30.

Lear, Martha Weinman. "The Second Feminist Wave." *New York Times Magazine*, 10 March 1968, 24–25, 50, 53, 55–56, 58, 60, 62.

Lehmann-Haupt, Christopher. "Books of the Times." *New York Times*, 5 August 1971, 33; 6 August 1970, 33.

Lemann, Nicholas. "A *Long* March." *New Yorker*, 10 February 2003, 86–91.

Leone, Vivien. "Sisterhood Can Be Sorrowful." *New Broadside* 1:2 (November 1970): 1.

Levitt, Laura. *Jews and Feminism: The Ambivalent Search for Home*. London: Routledge, 1997.

Levitt, Leonard. "She: The Awesome Power of Gloria Steinem." *Esquire*, October 1971, 87–89, 200–210, 214–15.

Lewis, Cherie Sue. "Television License Renewal Challenges by Women's Groups." Ph.D. diss., University of Minnesota, 1986.

Lewis, John, with Michael D'Orso. *Walking with the Wind: A Memoir of the Movement*. New York: Simon & Schuster, 1998.

Lichtenstein, Grace. "Feminists Demand 'Liberation' in *Ladies' Home Journal* Sit-In." *New York Times*, 19 March 1970, 51.

———. "For Most Women, 'Strike' Day Was Just a Topic of Conversation." *New York Times*, 27 August 1970, 30.

———. "Women's Lib Wooed by Publishers." *New York Times*, 17 August 1970, 32.

———. Interview with author, Sundance, Idaho, July 1999.

Lichtman, Ronnie. "Getting Together: The Small Group in Women's Liberation." *Up from Under*, May–June 1970, 23.

Life. "Angry Battler for Her Sex." 1 November 1963, 84–87.

———. "The Furious Young Philosopher Who Got It Down on Paper." 31 August 1970, 65.

———. "Gloria in Excelsis: It's the Steinem Look." 11 August 1972, 66–67.

Lipton, Lauren. Interview with author, June 1998.

Lumsden, Linda. " 'You're a Tough Guy, Mary—and a First-Rate Newspaperman': Gender and Women Journalists in the 1920s and 1930s." *Journalism and Mass Communication Quarterly* 72:4 (winter 1995): 913–21.

Lyne, Jack. "Peden and Associates' Katherine Peden: A Woman Who Opened Closed Doors." *Site Selection and Industrial Development*, April 1992, 336–46.

MacDonald, J. Fred. *One Nation under Television: The Rise and Decline of Network TV*. Chicago: Nelson-Hall, 1994; orig. pub. New York: Pantheon, 1990.

MacDougal, Kent. "Clay Felker's New York." *Columbia Journalism Review*, March–April 1974, 36–57.

MacLean, Judy. "Women Fight Back: ERA Extension Has Given the Feminist Movement a Second Wind." *The Progressive*, February 1979, 38, 39, 42.

MacPherson, Myra. "Exploited Women: Female View." *Washington Post*, August 26, 1970, B1, B2.

Maier, Maureen. "Through the Eyes of Newsweek: Themes of the Women's Movement, 1970–72." Unpublished paper, Temple University, in possession of author.

Mailer, Norman. "Prisoner of Sex." *Harper's Magazine*, March 1971, 41–48.

Mainardi, Pat. "Alice Neel at the Whitney." *Art in America*, May–June 1970, 107–8.

Maines, Patrick D., and John C. Olttinger. "Network Documentaries: How Many, How Relevant?" *Columbia Journalism Review*, March–April 1973, 367–42.

Mansbridge, Jane J. *Why We Lost the ERA*. Chicago: University of Chicago Press, 1986.

Mannes, Marya. "Should Women Only Be Seen and Not Heard?" *TV Guide*, 23 November 1968, 6–10.

Marlane, Judith. *Women in Television News Revisited: Into the Twenty-First Century*. Austin: University of Texas Press, 1999.

Marsh, Margaret, and Wanda Ronner. *The Empty Cradle: Infertility in America from Colonial Times to the Present*. Baltimore: John Hopkins University Press, 1996.

Marshall, David. "The Hiring of Trudy Haynes: Factors Which Influenced the Making of a Broadcast Pioneer." Unpublished paper, Temple University, in possession of author.

Marzolf, Marion. *Up from the Footnote: A History of Women Journalists*. New York: Hastings House, 1977.

McCall's. "Gloria Steinem, Woman of the Year." January 1972, 67–69.

McChesney, Robert N. *Telecommunications, Mass Media, and Democracy: The Battle for the Control of U.S. Broadcasting, 1928–1935*. New York: Oxford University Press, 1993.

McCombs, Maxwell E., and Donald L. Shaw. "The Agenda-Setting Functions of Mass Media." *Public Opinion Quarterly* 36:2 (summer 1972): 176–87.

McFadden, Robert. "Carol Sutton, Ranking Editor in Louisville, KY, Dead at 51." *New York Times*, 20 February 1985, B8.

McLuhan, Marshall. *The Gutenberg Galaxy: The Making of Typographic Man*. Toronto: University of Toronto Press, 1962.

McPherson, William. "Exploited Women: Male View." *Washington Post*, 26 August 1970, B1, B2.

Mendocino, Ellen Smith. "A Feminist Takes on the Evergreen." *Rat*, 17 April 1970, 6.

Mercer, Marilyn, "Gloria: The Unhidden Persuader." *McCall's*, January 1972, 67–69.

Merril, Hugh. *Esky: The Early Years at Esquire*. New Brunswick, N.J.: Rutgers University Press, 1995.

Meyer, Elissa. "Community Media Meets Male 'Left' Hassles." *Big Mama Rag*, February 1975, 1.

Meyer, Karl E. "Women Invade *Ladies' Home Journal*, Demand End to 'Demeaning' Articles." *Washington Post*, 19 March 1970, A3.

———. "Women's Lib Asks Boycott of 4 Products." *Washington Post*, 26 August 1970, A1, A10.

Meyerowitz, Joanne. "Beyond the Feminine Mystique: A Reassessment of Postwar Mass Culture, 1946–1958." In *Not June Cleaver: Women and Gender in Postwar America, 1945–1960*, ed. Joanne Meyerowitz, 229–62. Philadelphia: Temple University Press, 1994.

Miller, Holly G. "Concerned Women for America: Soft Voices with Clout." *Saturday Evening Post*, October 1985, 70–71.

Millett, Kate. *Sexual Politics*. Garden City, New York: Doubleday, 1969.

———. "The Pain of Public Scrutiny." *Ms.*, June 1974: 77–78.

Mills, Kay. "Fighting Sexism on the Airwaves." *Journal of Communication* 24:2 (spring 1974): 150–55.

———. *A Place in the News: From the Women's Pages to the Front Page*. New York: Columbia University Press, 1990.

———. "What Difference Do Women Journalists Make?" In *Women, Media, and Politics*, ed. Pippa Norris, 41–55. New York: Oxford University Press, 1997.

Morgan, Edward P. *The 60s Experience: Hard Lessons about Modern America*. Philadelphia: Temple University Press, 1991.

———. "From Virtual Community to Virtual History: Mass Media and the American Antiwar Movement of the 1960s." *Radical History Review* 78 (fall 2000): 85–122.

Morgan, Robin, comp. *Sisterhood Is Powerful: An Anthology of Writings from the Women's Liberation Movement*. New York, Random House, 1970.

———. "The Media and Male Chauvinism." *New York Times*, 27 December 1970, 33.

————. *The Word of a Woman: Feminist Dispatches, 1968–1992.* New York: Norton, 1992.

————. "Goodbye to All That" (1970). In *Dear Sisters: Dispatches from the Women's Liberation Movement,* eds. Rosalyn Baxandall and Linda Gordon, 53–57. New York: Basic Books, 2001.

Morris, Monia B. "Newspapers and the New Feminists: Black-Out as Social Control?" *Journalism and Mass Communication Quarterly* 50:1 (spring 1973): 37–42.

Morton, Frederic. "Sexism—A Better Show Than Sex." *Village Voice,* 6 May 1971: 28, 70.

Moscowitz, Eva. " 'It's Good to Blow Your Top': Women's Magazines and a Discourse of Discontent, 1945–1964." *Journal of Women's History* 8:3 (fall 1996): 66–98.

Ms. "Everything You Wanted to Know about Advertising and Were Not Afraid to Ask." *Ms.,* November 1974, 56–59, 90, 92.

Mungo, Raymond. *Famous Long Ago: My Life and Hard Times with Liberation News Service.* Boston: Beacon, 1970.

Murray, Michael D., ed. *Encyclopedia of Television News.* Phoenix: Onyx Press, 1999.

Myers, Linda. "Friedan's New Agenda: Fairness to Men, Too." *Cornell Chronicle,* 3 December 1998; reprinted in *Interviews with Betty Friedan,* ed. Janann Sherman, 174–76. Jackson: University Press of Mississippi, 2002.

Myerson, Bess, narrator. "Women's Place." NBC, 11 September 1973.

Nader, Ralph. *Unsafe at Any Speed: The Designed-in Dangers of the American Automobile.* New York: Grossman, 1965.

National Advertising Review Board. *Advertising and Women.* New York: NARB, 1975; reprinted as "Advertising Portraying or Directed to Women." *Advertising Age,* 21 April 1975, 72–75.

NBC Evening News. "Riggs/King." 22 September 1973, Television News Archives, Vanderbilt University.

————. "IWY," 11 November 1977, Television News Archives, Vanderbilt University.

NBC-TV. *Meet the Press,* 10 September 1972. Transcript in *Representative American Speeches, 1972–1973,* ed. Waldo W. Brade, 65–66. New York: Wilson, 1973.

Nesbitt, Bonnie J. "No Bra Burning in Rally." *Chicago Daily Defender,* 27 August 1970, 3, 32.

Neuharth, Allen. *Confessions of an S.O.B.* New York: Doubleday, 1989.

Nichols, Wade H. "A Fine Romance, with No Kisses." *The Writer* 77:7 (July 1964): 16–19.

Nichols, William I. "Sex: Our Changing Times." *Vital Speeches of the Day* 33 (October 15, 1966–October 1967): 445–48.

Nobile, Philip. "What is the New Impotence, and Who's Got It?" *Esquire,* October 1972, 95–98, 218.

Noelle-Neumann, Elizabeth. "The Spiral of Silence: A Theory of Public Opinion." *Journal of Communication* 24 (1974): 43–51.

Nordyke, Mrs. Dorothy. "Where the Girls Aren't." *The Masthead* 21:2 (summer 1969): 29–31.

Nourie, Alan, and Barbara Nourie. *American Mass-Market Magazines.* Westport: Greenwood, 1990.

Novick, Peter. *The Holocaust in American Life.* Boston: Houghton Mifflin, 1999.

NOW. Collection. Arthur and Elizabeth Schlesinger Library on the History of Women in America at the Radcliffe Institute for Advanced Study, Cambridge, Massachusetts, 1966 [NOW-SLRI]. "Public Relations Guidelines for NOW Members and Chapters"; "Press Handbook," written by Lucy Komisar, revised by Toni Carabillo, 1971; "Model Agreement with NOW Chapter and KPIG-AM-TV," Washington: NOW, 1974; NOW Media Task Force, "NOW Right to Choose Kit," Washington: NOW, 1974; "NOW Media Project: A Woman's Action Plan against Television and Radio," Washington: NOW, 1974; "Notes on Monitoring Television," Washington: NOW, 1974; " Time Line for Creating a Feminist Media" Washington: NOW, 1974; "Papers of the Public Information Office, 1973–1975."

NOW Foundation. "Watch Out, Listen Up! 2002 Feminist Primetime Report," 2–18, http://www.nowfoundation.org/watchout3/index.html, accessed 28 March 2003.

Newsweek. "Newsgirl," 10 May 1965, 99: "Women's Lib: The War on 'Sexism,' " 23 March 1970, 71–78; "Equal Rights NOW," 2 May 1970, 75; "*Ladies' Home Journal* and the Women's Lib," 3 August 1970, 44; "Women's Lib Growing Pains," 31 August 1970, 47; "Women's Lib's Big Day, 7 September 1970, 15; "The Anti-Lib Pussycats," 21 September 1970, 15; "Women's Lib Invades Churches," 2 November 1970, 81; "Trimming Down," 18 January 1971, 54–55; "Gloria Steinem, the New Woman," 16 August 1971, 51–55; "The New Breed," 30 August 1971, 63–63; "Feminist Forum," 8 November 1971, 104; "The Invisible Woman Is Visible," 15 November 1970, 30; "The *Ms.* Muddle," 6 December 1970, 70; "The Prisoner of Sex," 22 February 1971, 97; "Pronoun Envy," 6 December 1971, 58; "Who's Exploiting Whom?" 20 December 1971, 41; "A New Kind of Candidate: She's Black," 14 February 1972, 24; "The Senate: Woman Power," 23 April 1972, 28. "Girls! Girls! Girls!" 22 May 1972, 105; "Charge Is to *Ms.*," 17 July 1972, 45. "Feminism: A Cry on the Street," 4 September 1972, 58; "The Women vs. ABC," 4 December 1972, 57; "Employment Room at the Top," 4 December 1972, 96; "Executive Lib," 14 December 1972, 127; "The *Ms.* Biz," 15 October 1973: 70; "Is Gloria Steinem Dead?" 2 September 1974, 11.

New York Times-Parkway Village [New York Times-PV]. "20 to 35% Rent Rise Threatens a 585-Family U.N. Community," 29 June 1952, 30; "Parkway Village Faces Rent Rises," 6 July 1952, 31; "U.N. Villagers See Profit on 'Waste,' " 20 July 1952, 13; "U.N. Agency Talks off Saving Village," 24 July 1952, 29; "Banks Firm on Rent Rise," 25 July 1952, 19; "Parkway Villagers Appeal on Rent Rise," 26 July 1952, 21; "U.N. Personnel Get Offer of Rent Cut," 23 September 1952, 8; "U.N. Tells Tenants Pay More or Move," 27 September 1952, 19; "U.N. Tenants Notified in June of Lease End," 28 September 1952: 4; "U.N. Tenants to Vote Today on Rent Rises," 30 September 1952, 4; "U.N. Tenants Reject Rent Offer by Banks," 1 October 1952, 40; "U.N. Tenants Served," 16 December 1952, 32; "12 U.N. Tenants Get Stay," 25 December 1952, 41.

O'Brien, Soledad. "Soledad O'Brien Turns the Spotlight on Lynn Povich." *Women's Wire*, http://www.womenswire.com/plug/splotlight/eo420povich.html, accessed 7 July 1999.

O'Reilly, Jane. *The Girl I Left Behind: The Housewife's Moment of Truth and Other Feminist Ravings*. New York: Macmillan, 1980.

Otte, Mary Lane. "Sexism in Local and Network Television News." Ph.D. diss., Georgia State University, 1978.

Ouellette, Laurie. "Inventing the Cosmo Girl: Class Identity and Girl-Style American Dreams." *Media, Culture, & Society* 21:3 (May 1999): 359–83.

Packard, Vance Oakley. *The Hidden Persuaders*. New York: D. McKay, 1957.

Paige, Connie. "Watch on the Right: Work of B. LaHaye." *Ms.*, February 1987, 24–28.

Parade. "Women on the Warpath." 6 April 1969, 2.

Patterson, Thomas E., and Robert D. McClure. *The Unseeing Eye: The Myth of Television's Power in National Politics*. New York: Putnam, 1976.

Pearson, Patricia. "Gloria Steinem Turns 60." *Chatelaine*, March 1994, 58.

People. "Gloria Steinem Tries to Lower Her Famous Profile." 23 September 1971, 8–9.

Petchesky, Rosalind Pollack. "Anti-Abortion, Anti-Feminism, and the Rise of the New Right." *Feminist Studies* 7:2 (summer 1981): 206–46.

Phalen, Patricia F. " 'Pioneers, Girlfriends, and Wives': An Agenda for Research on Women and the Organizational Culture of Broadcasting." *Journal of Broadcasting & Electronic Media* 44:2 (spring 2000): 230–47.

Playboy. "Playboy after Hours." July 1971, 19, 20.

Pogrebin, Letty Cottin. *How to Make It in a Man's World*. Garden City, N.Y.: Doubleday, 1970.

———. "The FBI Was Watching You." *Ms.*, June 1977, 38–44.

———. "An Open Letter from Your President." *Authors Guild Bulletin*, summer 1999, 4, 37.

———. E-mail correspondence with author, September 1999.

Pollner, Fran. "turn on, tune in, and take over." *off our backs*, October 1972, 4.

Polsgrove, Carol. *It Wasn't Pretty, Folks, but Didn't We Have Fun?* New York: Norton, 1995.

Pottker, Janice, and Bob Speziale. *Dean Ann, Dear Abby: The Unauthorized Biography of Ann Landers and Abigail Van Buren.* New York: Dodd, Mead, 1987.

Powell, Lew, and Edwin E. Meek. "Mississippi's WLBT: After the License Challenge." *Columbia Journalism Review*, May–June 1973, 50–55.

Powers, Ron. "Eyewitness News: Many Local TV News Shows Have Become Cybernetic, Modular Twinkies of the Airwaves." *Columbia Journalism Review*, May–June 1977, 17–23.

———. *The Newscasters.* New York: St. Martin's, 1977.

Prashker, Betty. E-mail interview with author, August 1998.

Press Woman. "Women a Minority in Public Broadcasting Employment/Programs." April 1976, 2–3.

Phyllis Schlafly Report. "The Radical Goals of the Feminists," 25:5 (December 1991); "Facing the Future: Family vs. Feminism," 23:9 (April 1990); "Insights into Feminist Ideology," 23:5 (December 1989); "A Short History of E.R.A.," 20:2 (September 1986); "Women's Magazines Promote ERA—But Deny Equal Rights," 12:12 (December 1979); "E.R.A. and Women's Colleges," 9:7 (February 1976); "Will E.R.A. Make Child-Care the State's Job?" 9:5 (November 1976); "The Ripoff of the Taxpayers Known as the Commission on International Women's Year; or, Bella Abzug's Boondoggle," 9:6 (January 1976); "How ERA Will Affect Social Security," 8:3 (October 1975); "How E.R.A. Will Hurt Men," 8:10 (May 1975); "How E.R.A. Will Affect Athletics," 8:9 (April 1975). "How E.R.A. Will Affect Churches and Private Schools," 8:8 (March 1975); "How E.R.A. Will Affect Our Local Police," 8:7 (February 1975); "ERA Will Doom Fraternities and Sororities," 8:6 (January 1975); "E.R.A. Means Abortion and Population Shrinkage," 8:5 (December 1974); "Why Virginia Rejected ERA," 7:11 (June 1974); "How ERA Will Hurt Divorced Women," 7:10 (May 1974); "Playboy and Rockefeller Foundations Finance ERA," 7:9 (April 1974); "Are You Financing Women's Lib and ERA?" 7:7 (February 1974); "The Precious Rights ERA Will Take Away from Wives," 7:1 (August 1974); "Women in Industry Oppose Equal Rights Amendment," 6:12 (July 1973); "Section 2 of the Equal Rights Amendment," 6:10 (May 1973); "The Right to Be a Woman," 6:4 (November 1972).

Quinn, Sally. "Phyllis Schlafly: Sweetheart of the Silent Majority." *Washington Post*, 11 July 1974, D1, D10.

———. *We're Going to Make You a Star.* New York: Simon & Schuster, 1975.

Radicalesbians. *The Woman Identified Woman.* Pittsburgh: Know, 1970.

Raphael, Chad. "Rethinking Media and Movements." *Radical History Review* 78 (fall 2000): 130–37.

Rather, Dan, with Mickey Herskowitz. *The Camera Never Blinks: Adventures of a TV Journalist.* New York: Morrow, 1977.

Redbook. "When Women Love Other Women: A Frank Discussion of Female Homosexuality." November 1971, 84–85, 186–95.

The Report of the President's Commission on Campus Unrest. Washington: U.S. Government Printing Office, September 1970. http://dept.kent.edu/may4/Campus_Unrest/campus_unrest.htm, accessed 21 March 2003.

Reynolds, Barbara. "Inquiry: Conservative Women Deserve to Be Heard." *USA Today*, 11 November 1989, A11.

Rhode, Deborah L. "Media Images, Feminist Issues." *Signs* 20:3 (spring 1995): 686–710.

Ricchiardi, Sherry, and Virginia Young. *Women on Deadline: A Collection of America's Best.* Ames: Iowa State University Press, 1991.

Rich, Adrienne. *On Lies, Secrets, and Silence: Selected Prose, 1966–1978.* New York: Norton, 1979.

Riesman, David, Nathan Glazer, and Reuel Denney. *The Lonely Crowd: A Study of the Changing American Character.* New York: Doubleday Anchor, 1953; orig. pub. New Haven: Yale University Press, 1950.

Roberts, Willo Davis. "The Heroine Doesn't Have to Be an Idiot." *The Writer*, January 1975, 12–14.

Robertson, Nan. *The Girls in the Balcony: Women, Men, and the* New York Times. New York: Random House, 1992.

Robnett, Belinda. "African American Women in the Civil Rights Movement: Spontaneity and Emotion in Social Movement Theory." In *No Middle Ground: Women and Radical Protest*, ed. Kathleen M. Blee, 65–95. New York: New York University Press, 1998.

Rollin, Betty. "Little Dr. Reuben and His Big Sex Book." *Look*, 14 July 1970, 67–68.

———. "Backlash against Women's Lib! 'They're a Bunch of Frustrated Hags.'" *Look*, 8 March 1971, 15–19.

Rosen, Ruth. *The World Split Open: How the Modern Women's Movement Changed America*. New York: Viking, 2000.

Rowan, Carl T. "News Media under Fire." *Philadelphia Evening Bulletin*, 6 March 1970, 25.

Ruzek, Sheryl B., Virginia L. Oleson, and Adele E. Clark. *Women's Health: Complexities and Difficulties*. Columbus: Ohio State University Press, 1997.

Salant, Richard S. *Salant, CBS, and the Battle for the Soul of Broadcast Journalism: The Memoirs of Richard S. Salant*. Boulder: Westview, 1999.

Sanders, Marlene, narrator. "Women's Liberation." ABC-TV, 25 May 1970.

———, narrator/reporter. "The Hand That Rocks the Cradle." ABC-TV, 26 July 1972.

———. "Ad Liberation." *Television Quarterly* 11:3 (spring 1974): 49–56.

———. "Kathy Bonk: The Great Communicator." *Ms.*, March–April 1991, 90.

———. Interview with author, New York, June 1998.

Sanders, Marlene, and Marcia Rock. *Waiting for Prime Time: The Women of Television News*. Urbana: University of Illinois Press, 1988.

Sandra. "Lesbian Nation Politics: The Ties That Bind." *Big Mama Rag* 2:3A (March 1975): 5.

San Francisco Women's Liberation. Internal newsletter, 16 May 1971.

Schlafly, Phyllis, narrator. *A Look at the Eagle Forum* (videotape). Alton, Ill.: Eagle Forum, 1975.

———. *The Power of the Positive Woman*. New Rochelle, N.Y.: Arlington House, 1977.

———. "Eyewitness: Beating the Bra Burners." *George*, June 1997, http://www.eagleforum/org/george/george.html, accessed 30 October 2000.

Schmidt, Benno. "Access to the Broadcast Media: The Legislative Precedents." *Journal of Communication* 28 (spring 1978): 60–68.

Schudson, Michael. *Discovering the News: A Social History of American Newspapers*. New York: Basic Books, 1978.

Scott, Jim. "Overemphasis on Sex Disturbs Sally Quinn." *Editor and Publisher*, 6 July 1974, 22, 26.

Seaman, Barbara. *Free and Female: The Sex Life of the Contemporary Woman*. New York: Coward, McCann, & Geoghegan, 1972.

Secrest, Merle. "Les Girls." *Washington Post*, 31 August 1969, F1, F8.

"Seize the Press, Sisters." *off our backs*, 25 April 1970, 5.

Sexton, Donald E., and Phyllis Haberman. "Women in Magazine Advertisements." *Journal of Advertising Research* 14:4 (August 1974): 41–46.

Sheehy, Gail. "The City Politic: Teach Me Tonight." *New York*, June 1971, 8–9.

Sheff, Daniel. "*Playboy* Interview: Betty Friedan." *Playboy*, September 1992, 51–54, 56, 58, 60, 62, 149; reprinted in *Interviews with Betty Friedan*, ed. Janann Sherman, 88–116. Jackson: University Press of Mississippi, 2002.

Sheils, Merrill, et al. "State of the Movement." *Newsweek*, 28 November 1977, 59.

Shelton, Elizabeth. "Status of Women." *Christian Science Monitor*, 19 February 1966, 132.

Shenker, Israel. "Norman Mailer vs. Women's Libber." *New York Times*, 1 May 1971, 19.

Sheppard, Eugenia. "Gloria, Hallelujah." *Harper's Bazaar*, February 1970, 142–43.

Sherman, Janann, ed. *Interviews with Betty Friedan*. Jackson: University Press of Mississippi, 2002.

Sherr, Lynn. "She's a Member of the Mod Squad." *The Quill,* November 1972, 36–38.

Shoemaker, Pamela J. "Media Treatment of Deviant Political Groups." *Journalism and Mass Communication Quarterly* 61:1 (spring 1984): 65–66, 82.

Shoemaker, Pamela J., and Stephen D. Reese. *Mediating the Message: Theories of Influence on Mass Media Content.* White Plains, New York: Longman, 1996.

Signorielli, Nancy. *Mass Media Images and Impact on Health: A Sourcebook.* Westport: Greenwood, 1993.

Simpson, Carole. Interview by Donita Moorhus. Women in Journalism Oral History Project of the Washington Press Club Foundation, 8 September 1993, 90–110. http://npc.press.org/ Washington Postforal/sim5.htm, accessed 2 April 2003.

Singleton, Loy A., and Stephanie L. Cook. "Television Network News Reporting by Female Correspondents: An Update." *Journal of Broadcasting & Electronic Media* 26:1 (spring 1982): 487–91.

Smeal, Eleanor. "The Women's Movement; What N.O.W.?" *Social Education* 47:2 (February 1983): 112–21.

Smith, Don C., and Kenneth Harwood. "Women in Broadcasting." *Journal of Broadcasting & Electronic Media* 10:4 (fall 1966): 339–56.

Smith, Howard K. *Events Leading Up to My Death: The Life of a Twentieth-Century Reporter.* New York: St. Martin's, 1996.

Smith, Laura K., and John W. Wright. "Women in Television News Management: Do They Make a Difference?" Paper presented at the annual meeting of the Association for Education in Journalism and Mass Communication, Baltimore, 5–8 August 1998.

Smith, Liz. "Coming of Age in America." *Vogue,* June 1971, 90–92, 150, 158.

———. "Gloria Steinem: Writer and Social Critic, Talks about Sex, Politics, and Marriage." *Redbook,* January 1972, 69–76.

Sochen, June. *Enduring Values: Women in Popular Culture.* New York: Praeger, 1987.

Some Red Witches. "The Sharks Are Coming with Betty Friedan as Pilot Fish." *It Ain't Me Babe,* 6 August 1970, 12.

Spelman, Elizabeth V. *Inessential Woman: Problems of Exclusion in Feminist Thought.* Boston: Beacon, 1988.

The Spokeswoman, 24 August 1970, n.p.

Stahl, Lesley. *Reporting Live.* New York: Simon & Schuster, 1999.

Stambler, Sookie, comp. *Women's Liberation: Blueprint for the Future.* New York: Ace Books, 1970.

Stanley, Nancy E. Interview by Nadia Ramdass, January 2002. Courtesy Nadia Ramdass.

———. "Federal Communications Law and Women's Rights: Women in the Wasteland Fight Back." *Hastings Law Review* 23:1 (November 1971): 15–53.

Steinem, Gloria. "The Moral Disarmament of Betty Coed." *Esquire,* September 1962, 97, 153–57.

———. *The Beach Book.* New York: Viking, 1963.

———. "The Bunny's Tale." *Show,* May, June 1963; reprinted in Gloria Steinem, *Outrageous Acts and Everyday Rebellions,* 29–69. New York: Holt, Rinehart, and Winston, 1983

———. "Visiting Englishmen Are No Roses." *New York Times Magazine,* 29 March 1964, VI 48, 63–64.

———. "The Ins and Outs of Pop Culture." *Life,* August 1965, 72–79.

———. "What's in It for Me." *Harper's Magazine,* 1 November 1965, 169–71.

———. "The City Politic: After Black Power, Women's Liberation." *New York,* 7 April 1969, 8–9.

———. "Why We Need a Woman President in 1976." *Look,* 13 January 1970, 58

———. "After Too Much Moving . . . Cheerful Rooms to Live in, a Private Place to Work." *House and Garden,* July 1970: 52–55.

———. "What It Would Be Like If Women Win." *Time,* 31 August 1970, 22.

———. "What Playboy Doesn't Know about Women Could Fill a Book." *McCall's*, October 1970, 139–40.

———. "A New Egalitarian Lifestyle." *New York Times*, 26 August 1971, 37.

———. "The Machismo Factor." *New York Times*, 6 October 1971, 47.

———. "Sisterhood." *Ms.*, spring 1972, 46–49.

———. "Marilyn Monroe: The Woman Who Died Too Soon." *Ms.*, August 1972, 35–36, 38, 104; reprinted in Gloria Steinem, *Outrageous Acts and Everyday Rebellions*, 233–42. New York: Holt, Rinehart, and Winston, 1983.

———. "The Verbal Karate of Florynce R. Kennedy, Esq." *Ms.*, March 1973, 54, 55, 89.

———. "If We're So Smart, Why Aren't We Rich?" *Ms.*, June 1973, 37–38.

———. "It's Your Year." *Ms.*, January 1975, 45.

———. "Sisterhood." *Ms.*, spring 1972, 46–49; reprinted in Gloria Steinem, *Outrageous Acts and Everyday Rebellions*, 112–18. New York: Holt, Rinehart, and Winston, 1983.

———. "Sex, Lies and Advertising." *Ms.*, July–August 1990, 18–28; reprinted in *Gender, Race, and Class in Media: A Text-Reader*, eds. Gail Dines and Jean M. Humez, 112–20. Thousand Oaks, Calif.: Sage, 1995.

———. *Revolution from Within: A Book of Self-Esteem*. Boston: Little, Brown, 1992.

———. *Moving beyond Words*. New York: Simon & Schuster, 1994.

———. "Finally Real." *Time*, December 2001, G8.

Steiner, Linda. *Construction of Gender in News Reporting Textbooks, 1890–1990*. Journalism Monograph 135. Columbia, S.C.: Association for Education in Journalism and Mass Communication, 1992.

Stern, Sydney Ladensohn. *Gloria Steinem: Her Passions, Politics, and Mystique*. Secaucus, N.J.: Carol, 1997.

Stevens, George M. *Discrimination in the Newsroom: Title VII and the Journalist*. Journalism Monograph 94. Columbia, S.C.: Association for Education in Journalism and Mass Communication, 1985.

Stewart, Debra W. *The Women's Movement in Community Politics in the U.S.: The Role of Local Commissions on the Status of Women*. New York: Pergamon, 1980.

St. George, Donna. "Margaret Congdon, 93, of Villanova." *Philadelphia Inquirer*, 19 August 1988, D10.

Stone, Desmond. "These Women Can Write!" *The Masthead* 23:2 (summer 1971): 35–41.

Stone, Vernon A. "Radio-Television News Directors and Operations: An RTNDA Survey." *RTNDA Communicator*, June 1973, 5–12.

———. "Attitudes toward Television Newswomen." *Journal of Broadcasting & Electronic Media* 18:1 (winter 1973–74): 49–62.

Storm, Jonathan. "How Much Influence Did 'Father' Really Have?" *Philadelphia Inquirer*, 27 July 1998, D5, D7.

Strainchamps, Ethel, ed. *Rooms with No View: A Woman's Guide to the Man's World of the Media*. New York: Harper and Row, 1974.

"Survival/On Our Feet." *off our backs*, 25 April 1970, 16.

Svonkin, Stuart. *Jews against Prejudice: American Jews and the Fight for Civil Liberties*. New York: Columbia University Press, 1997.

Swanberg, W. A. *Luce and His Empire*. New York: Scribner, 1972.

Taeuber, Cynthia. *Statistical Handbook on Women in America*. Phoenix: Oryx, 1991.

Tebbel, John. "Our Shrinking Magazines: Time to Change Your Page Size." *Saturday Review*, 9 October 1971, 70.

Terrace, Vincent, comp. *The Complete Encyclopedia of Television Programs, 1947–1976*. 2 vols. South Brunswick: Barnes, 1976.

Thom, Mary, ed. *Letters to Ms., 1972–1987*. New York: Holt, 1987.

———. *Inside Ms.: 25 Years of the Magazine and the Feminist Movement*. New York: Holt, 1997.

Thomas, Helen. *Front Row at the White House: My Life and Times.* New York: Scribner, 1999.

Tillson, Patricia A. "The Defeat of the Equal Rights Amendment: A Propaganda Analysis of Phyllis Schlafly's STOP ERA Campaign." Master's thesis, University of Houston, 1996.

Time. "People." 21 February 1969, 33; "The New Feminists: Revolt against 'Sexism,' " 21 November 1969, 53–56; "New Victory in an Old Crusade," 24 August 1970, 10–12; "Who's Come a Long Way, Baby?" 31 August 1970, 16–21; "A Second Look at Women's Lib," 14 December 1970, 50; "Women's Lib: Beyond Sexual Politics," 26 July 1971, 36–37; "Ms. Makes It," 25 December 1971, 51; "For the Liberated Female," 28 December 1971, 52; "Ah, Sweet Ms-ery," 20 March 1972, 55; "Womenswar: Womansurge vs. NOW," 1 December 1975, 55; "Women of the Year: Great Changes, New Changes, Tough Choices," 5 January 1976, 6–15; "Prime Time for TV Newswomen," 21 March 1977, 85–86.

Toogood, Alex. "The Gay Life in Television." *Television Quarterly* 11:3 (spring 1974): 22–26.

Trotta, Liz. *Fighting for Air: In the Trenches with Television News.* Columbia: University of Missouri Press, 1994; orig. pub. 1991.

Tuchman, Gaye. "The Impact of Mass Media Stereotypes upon the Full Employment of Women." In U.S. Congress, *American Women Workers in a Full Employment Economy.* Washington: U.S. Government Printing Office, 1978.

———. "The Symbolic Annihilation of Women by the Mass Media." In *Hearth and Home: Images of Women in the Mass Media,* eds. Gaye Tuchman, Arlene Kaplan Daniels, and James Benét, 3–38. New York: Oxford University Press, 1978.

United Electrical Workers. *UE Fights for Women Workers.* Publication 232. June 1952.

U.S. Commission on Civil Rights. *Window Dressing on the Set: Women and Minorities in Television.* Washington: U.S. Government Printing Office, 1977.

———. *Window Dressing on the Set, An Update.* Washington: U.S. Government Printing Office, 1979.

U.S. News & World Report. "Equal Rights for Women? Things May Never Be the Same," 24 August 1970, 69–70; "When the Women Struck for Equality," 7 September 1970, 26–27; "Job Rights for Women: The Drive Speeds Up," 12 November 1972, 90; "Gains for Women Still Snowballing," 11 March 1974, 44; "Women's Rights: Why the Struggle Still Goes On," 27 May 1974, 40–42; "Special Section: The American Woman on the Move—But Where?" 8 December 1975, 54–55.

Van Gelder, Lindsy. "Women's Pages: You Can't Make News out of a Silk Purse." *Ms.,* November 1974, 112–16.

———. "Cracking the Women's Movement Protection Game." *Ms.,* December 1978, 66–68.

———. "The Truth about Bra-Burners." *Ms.,* September–October 1992, 80–81.

———. "Chronicle and Crucible." *The Nation,* 11–18 August 1997, 27–30.

Van Horne, Harriet. "Militants' Mistake." *San Francisco Sunday Examiner and Chronicle,* 23 August 1970, 3.

Venkatesh, Alladi, and Clint B. Tankersley. "Magazine Readership by Female Segments." *Journal of Advertising Research* 19:4 (August 1970): 31–38.

Vidmar, Neil, and Milton Rokeach. "Archie Bunker's Bigotry: A Study in Selective Perception and Exposure." *Journal of Communication* 24:4 (winter 1974): 37–47.

Vilar, Esther. *The Manipulated Man.* New York: Farrar, Straus, and Giroux, 1972.

Wade, Betsy. "Hired as a Token, She Used It for a Ride to Court." *Women's e-News,* http://www.womensenews.org/article.cfm/dyn/aid/119/context/archive, accessed 2 October 2002.

Wainwright, Loudon. *The Great American Magazine: An Inside History of* Life. New York: Knopf, 1986.

Wakefield, Dan. "My Love Affair with Billie Jean King." *Esquire,* October 1974, 136–39, 384–86.

Walker, Nancy A. *Shaping Our Mothers' World: American Women's Magazines.* Jackson: University Press of Mississippi, 2000.

Walters, Barbara, narrator. "New York Illustrated: Equal Rights Anyone?" WNBC-TV, 1 November 1975.

Ware, Susan, ed. *Modern American Women: A Documentary History.* Belmont: Wadsworth, 1989.

Washington Post Service. "Author Decries Ownership of Women." *Milwaukee Journal*, 23 August 1970, 6.

Washington Press Club Foundation. Oral History Project. "Marilyn Schultz." http://npc.press.org/ Washington Postforal/int3.htm, accessed 6 December 2002.

Waters, Chocolate. "Women in the Media: A Disappointing Affair." *Big Mama Rag* 3:5 (1974): 13.

———. "A Non-Interview with Gloria Steinem." *Big Mama Rag* 3:6 (1974): 2.

Watson, Patrick, host. "Signature: Gloria Steinem, Part 1." CBS Cable, 4 November 1981.

Weaver, David. "Women as Journalists." In *Women, Media, and Politics*, ed. Pippa Norris, 21–40. New York: Oxford University Press, 1997.

Weaver, David H., and G. Cleveland Wilhoit. *The American Journalist: A Portrait of U.S. News People and Their Work*. 2d ed. Bloomington: Indiana University Press, 1991.

Weigand, Kathleen. "Vanguard of Women's Liberation: The Old Left and the Continuity of the Women's Movement in the United States, 1945–1970s." Ph.D. diss., Ohio State University, 1994.

Weiss, Fredric A., David Ostroff, and Charles E. Clift III. "Station License Revocations and Denials of Renewal, 1970–1998." *Journal of Broadcasting & Electronic Media* 24:1 (spring 1980): 69–77.

Welles, Chris. "Can Mass Magazines Survive?" *Columbia Journalism Review*, July–August 1971, 7–14.

White, William, Jr., ed. *North American Reference Encyclopedia of Women's Liberation*. Philadelphia: North American Publishing, 1972.

Whittaker, Susan, and Ron Whittaker. "Relative Effectiveness of Male and Female Newscasters." *Journal of Broadcasting & Electronic Media* 20:2 (spring 1976): 177–84.

Whyte, William Hollingsworth. *The Organization Man*. New York: Simon & Schuster, 1956.

Wilkes, Paul. "Mother Superior to Women's Lib." *New York Times Magazine*, 29 November 1970, 27–29, 149–50, 157.

Williamson, Lenora. "Women's Editors Express Concern with Content, Direction of Pages." *Editor and Publisher*, 7 April 1973, 14.

Williamson, Mary E. "Judith Cary Walter: Chicago Broadcasting Pioneer." *Journalism History* 3 (winter 1976–1977): 111–15.

Willis, Ellen. "Letters." *New York Times Magazine*, 2 March 1969, 6, 12.

———. "Conservatism of Ms." In *Feminist Revolution: An Abridged Edition with Additional Writings*, by Redstockings of the Women's Liberation Movement, 170–73. New York: Random House, 1978.

———. "Radical Feminism and Feminist Radicalism." In *No More Nice Girls: Countercultural Essays*. Hanover: University Press of New England for Wesleyan University Press, 1992.

———. E-mail interview with author, October 1998.

Winfrey, Oprah. *The Oprah Winfrey Show*. Transcript. 19 January 1993. Harpo Productions.

Wolf, Naomi. *The Beauty Myth: How Images of Beauty Are Used against Women*. New York: Morrow, 1991.

Wolfe, Thomas A. "Radical Chic: That Party at Lenny's." *New York*, 8 June 1970, 26–56.

Wolfe, Winifred. "Does It Have to Be Dirty to Sell? *The Writer*, February 1970, 20–22.

Women: A Journal of Liberation, summer 1970, 68.

Women, Men, and Media. "The Big Stories: A Woman's Voice is Rarely Heard." Informational packet. Los Angeles: University of Southern California, 1989.

Wyman, David S. *The Abandonment of the Jews: America and the Holocaust, 1941–1945*. New York: Pantheon, 1984.

Yurick, Sol. "That Wonderful Person Who Brought You Howard Cosell." *Esquire*, October 1974, 152–54.

Zelman, Patricia G. *Women, Work, and National Policy: The Kennedy-Johnson Years*. Ann Arbor: UMI Research Press, 1982.

Zoonen, Liesbet van. *Feminist Media Studies*. London: Sage, 1994.

Index

ABC, 87, 119, 159–60, 201, 223, 226, 227, 233, 234, 238, 239–40, 243, 269, 273, 278, 280–83
Abortion rights, 57–58, 75, 105, 121, 152, 183, 184, 188–89, 190, 192, 266, 267–68, 269, 270, 271
Abzug, Bella, 90, 121, 153, 158, 161, 166, 252, 253–54, 265, 268, 269, 278
access, 233
Ace Books, 256
Adams, Whitney, 233, 234–35
Addison-Wesley, 200
Adorno, Theodor W., 17, 195
Advertising Age, 120, 197, 201, 212, 213, 214, 232
Advertising agencies: Batten, Barton, Durstine, and Osborne, 213–14; Benton and Bowles, 72; Black Creative Group, 213; Bozell, 190; Cadwell Davis, 212; Dunkel and Charlies, 213; Faberge, 213; J. Walter Thompson, 213, 216; Leo Burnett, 211; Ogilvie and Mather, 212; Olivetti, 212; Trahey-Wolf, 213; Wells, Rich, Greene, 213; Willie Free, 212; Zebra Associates, 213
Advertising Council, 216–17
African Americans: feminists, 44, 45–46, 71–73, 97, 119, 180–81, 252, 253; media bias, 71–73, 116, 195
Agitprop, 56–66, 68–73, 75; trivialization of, 73–76
Agnew, Spiro, 260
Ain't I a Woman, 50
Albrecht, Margaret, *A Complete Guide for the Working Mother*, 256
Alexander, Dolores, 39, 40, 42, 100
Alexander, Shana, 69, 87, 103, 167, 168, 169, 172
All in the Family, 222
All the President's Men, 257
Allen, David, *The Price of Women*, 257

Allen, Donna, 51, 220
Allen, Pam, 55
Allyn and Bacon, 200
Alpert, Jane, 179
Amarillo (Texas) Globe Times, 202–3
Amatniek, Kathie. *See* Sarachild, Kathie
American Civil Liberties Union (ACLU), 199, 230
American Graffiti (film), 127
American Jewish Congress, 229–30
American Newspaper Publishers Association, 208
American Psychological Association, 73, 129, 135
American Review, 132
American Women in Radio and Television, 33, 34
Andelin, Helen B., 256–57, 258; *Fascinating Womanhood*, 256–57, 264
Andrews, Julie, 127
Andy Awards, 210
Angelo, Bonnie, 202
Angry Arts Week, 58
Anthony, Susan B., 92, 94, 156
Anti-Defamation League, 18, 35
Antifeminism, 256–59, 262–72, 284
Antiwar movement, 51–55, 58, 65, 74
Antupit, Sam, 170
Arledge, Roone, 159–60, 238, 273, 281–82, 284
Armstrong, David, 165
Art in America, 134
Ashton, Ruth, 226
Associated Press, 69, 79, 111, 113–14, 196–97, 199–200, 202, 203, 205; Managing Editors Association, 205; Modern Living Committee, 80
AT&T, 214
Atkinson, Ti-Grace, 52, 66–67, 69, 70, 85, 89, 91–92, 97, 101, 135, 139

Atlanta Constitution, 117
Atlanta Newspapers, 201
Atlantic Monthly, 86, 125
Authors Guild, 174
Avon Books, 132

Babcox, Peter, 93–94, 96
Bagdikian, Ben, 195–96
Bantam, 137, 256
Barefoot and Pregnant Awards for Advertising
    Degrading for Women, 211
Barrett, Rona, 228
Bassin, Amelia Kaufman, 213
Baughman, James, 98
Baxandall, Ros, 69, 70–71, 96, 97, 184
Baxman, Minda, 69
Bayh, Birch, 37
Beauty products, 215
Beauty Spot, The, 224–25
Bell Systems, 46
Bellow, Saul, 150
Bender, Marilyn, 74
Bennis, Ingrid, *Combat in the Erogenous
    Zone*, 127
Benson and Hedges, 213
Benton, Robert, 146–47, 149–50
Berks, Ann, 240
Berle, Milton, 129
Berlin, Rosman, and Kessler law firm, 234
Berman, Edgar F., 86, 117
Bernard, Jessie, 43
Bernstein, Leonard, 154
Betty Crocker Show, 9
Beverly Hills Citizen, 42
Big Mama Rag, 49, 163, 187
Bilingual Bicultural Coalition for Mass Media,
    230
Biltmore Hotel bar, 114, 204
Bird, Florence (Ann Frances), 30–31
Birth control pills, 64, 147
Bishop, Joey, 6
Black, Cathleen, 197, 208, 217–18
Black Efforts for Soul in Television, 230
Black Panthers, 72, 106, 118, 154
Black Power movement, 44
Blackman, Ann, 204
Bloomfield, Elaine, 234
Blystone, Dick, 204
Bohm, David, 15

Bok, Edward, 12, 92
Bolen, Lin, 240
Bonk, Kathleen, 207, 220, 233–34, 235, 242,
    243, 249
Bonwit Teller, 73
Boston Globe, 84, 115, 116–17
Bottini, Ivy, 39
Bowman, Patricia, 9
Bradlee, Ben, 133, 205
Brando, Marlon, 126
Braniff Airlines, 213
Braudy, Susan, 102, 171
Bread and Roses, 115
Breckinridge, Mary Marvin, 224
Bridal Fair at Madison Square Garden, 63–64,
    108
Broadcast reform movement, 229–32
Broadcasting, 229, 230, 231, 232, 234, 244, 246
Brockway, George, 3, 13, 24
Brothers, Joyce, *The Brothers' System for
    Liberated Love and Marriage*, 126–27
Brown, Helen Gurley, 7, 10–11, 68, 209;
    Sex and the Single Girl, 6, 10–11, 22, 144,
    174, 209
Brown, Hillary, 226
Brown, Judith, 55
Brown, Rita Mae, 52, 125, 164
Brownmiller, Susan, 40, 68–69, 70, 74, 135, 197,
    212; *Against Our Will: Men, Women, and
    Rape*, 68
Broyand, Anatole, 140
Brustein, Robert, 139
Bryant, Anita, 267
Buckley, William F., Jr., 87–88, 114
Burstein, Patricia, 157
Business and Professional Women's Club, 12,
    30, 32, 33, 108, 247
Business Week, 217
Byoir, Carl, public relations agency, 34, 35

Cable television, 261, 272
Cadwell, Franchelle, 212, 213
Campbell, E. Simms, 146
Canadian women's movement, 30–31
Cantor, Muriel, 245
Carabillo, Toni, 44–45, 234
Carbine, James T., 173
Carbine, Patricia, 158, 168, 169, 173, 183, 205
Carpenter, Liz, 269

Carter, Jimmy, 269
Carter, John Mack, 68–70, 71, 189
Carter, Rosalyn, 269
"Caspar Milquetoast," 92
Catlett, Terri, 218
Catt, Carrie Chapman, 156
CBS, 78, 87, 119, 120, 196, 201, 224, 226, 237, 238, 240, 242, 243, 260–61, 265, 269, 271, 276
CBS Morning News, 243
Ceballos, Jacqui, 96, 107–8, 109–10, 139, 153
Cell 16, 85, 97–98, 118
Celler, Emanuel, 30, 108, 258
Center for Constitutional Rights, 230, 234
Central Intelligence Agency (CIA), 145, 155, 158, 185–86, 254
Century Association (New York), 200, 202
Cerf, Bennett, 6
Charlie (fragrance), 215
Charlotte (North Carolina) Observer, 203
Charlton, Linda, 116
Charm, 7, 168, 170
Chase, Sylvia, 237, 239
Chassler, Sey, 156
Chavez, Cesar, 45, 53, 153, 154
Chesler, Phyllis, 73; *Women in Madness,* 73
Chevrolet, 180
Chicago Sun-Times, 118
Chicago Tribune, 42, 111, 113, 117–18, 207, 224
Chicago Women's Liberation Union, 75, 130
Child care, 46, 105, 121
Childbearing, 92–93
Chisholm, Shirley, 97, 121, 153, 166, 193, 251–53
Christian Broadcast Network, 261
Christian Science Monitor, 32, 95, 258
Chung, Connie, 226
Ciarrochi, Linda, 236
Citizens Communication Center, 230, 234
Civil Rights Act, 31, 41, 108, 235, 262–63
Civil rights movement, 30, 31, 34, 41–42, 43–47, 52, 72, 120–21, 123, 230–31
Clairol, 189
Clarenbach, Kathryn (Kay), 31, 36, 37, 38
Clark, Michelle, 237
Clubwomen, nineteenth century, 92
Cold War, 12–13, 15
Colgate Palmolive boycott, 63, 108
Collier's, 14

Colorado Springs Sun, 208
Columbia Journalism Review, 204, 205, 217
Columbia University, 17, 53–54, 58
Columbia Women's Liberation, 62
Column writing, 87–88
Commonweal, 127
Communication Consortium, 207, 220, 243
Communist Party, 15
Compton, Ann, 226
Concerned Women for America (CWA), 270–71
Condit, Celeste Michelle, 271
Congress of American Women, 16
Congress of Racial Equality (CORE), 35
Congress to Unite Women, 47, 104
Consumer culture, women in, 11
Corporation for Public Broadcasting, 234
Cosell, Howard, 278
Cosmopolitan, 7, 10, 68, 83, 126, 170, 171, 180, 209, 211, 275
Coughlin, Father, 260–61
Country Life, 146
Court, Margaret, 276–77, 278
Cousins, Margaret, 7, 256
Craft traditions: challenges to, 79; of conflict, 84, 86–87, 90; in news broadcasting, 78–79; in news writing, 77–78; in women's pages, 81
Crawford, Alan, 262
Crawford, Joan, 9
Cronan, Sheila, 67
Cronkite, Walter, 54, 239, 246, 276
Cumming, Adelaide Hawley, 9
Curtis, Charlotte, 60–61, 81–83, 115, 133, 154, 196
Curtis, Cyrus C. K., 92
Curtis, Jean, 255

Daily Defender (Chicago), 118–19
Daily News (New York), 112–13, 119, 121, 153
Daly, Richard, 54
Daniel, Clifton, 38
Darling Lily (film), 127
Daughters Inc., 194
Davidson, Sara, 101, 121
Davis, Angela, 118
DeBeauvoir, Simone, *The Second Sex,* 256
DeCrow, Karen, 41–42, 44, 92, 107, 160, 249, 265–66

Decter, Midge, 90, 103, 125–26, 130, 139, 257–58; *The New Chastity and Other Arguments against Women's Liberation*, 257
Deep Throat, 126
Deliverance (film), 129
Dell Books, 23, 200, 256
Dell'Olio, Anselma, 94, 96, 109
Democratic National Convention: (1968), 54, 58, 59, 62, 160; (1972), 141, 252
Demonstrations, as media events, 53–54, 104–8, 109–10, 115–22
Des Moines Register, 208
Detroit Free Press, 208
Deutsch, Helen, *The Psychology of Women*, 136
DeWolf, Rose, 67
Dialogue on Women's Liberation. *See* Town Hall
Diamond, Edwin, 217
Diary of a Mad Housewife (film), 127
Dick Cavett Show, 74, 102
Dickerson, Nancy, 226, 227
Dickey, James, *Deliverance*, 129
Didrickson, Babe. *See* Zaharias, Babe Didrickson
Divisiveness, in the women's movement, 51, 52, 74, 75, 84, 107, 121, 185–87, 253–55; media coverage of, 84–86, 90, 101, 166, 253
Dog Day Afternoon (film), 129
Dohrn, Bernadine, 94, 96
Dolan, Mary Ann, 207
Donahue, 265
Donovan, Arlene, 23
Donovan, Hedley, 99, 132, 149
Doubleday Company, 6, 7, 23, 131, 200, 218, 256
Douglas, Susan, 104, 116, 119, 120
Downs, Hugh, 246
Dreifus, Claudia, 102
Dudar, Helen, 101
Duffett, Judith, 61
Dunbar, Roxanne, 85–86, 97, 99
DuPont-Columbia Seminars on Broadcasting and the Public Interest, 226

Eagle Forum, 259, 264, 271; newsletter, 264–65
East, Catherine, 32
Eastman, Mary, 32, 40
Economist, The, 255
Edgar, JoAnne, 171, 174–75, 183

Editor and Publisher, 119, 208
Education Act, 275, 283
Education, equal opportunity, 105
Elizabeth Arden cosmetics, 215
Ellerbee, Linda, 226, 240
Ellis, Estelle, 170
Emerson, Jean, 227–28
Emma Goldman Brigade, 267
Employment: equal pay, 30, 32, 46, 251, 277–78, 284, 285; gender discrimination, 35, 47, 66, 105, 175, 195–201, 223–27, 232–33, 234, 235, 237–38, 273; increase of women workers, 11, 30, 251; sexual harassment, 285; women in advertising, 212–13; women in broadcasting, 222, 223–27, 232–33, 234, 235, 237–38, 240–43, 244–46; women in management positions, 207–9, 218, 240–43, 245; women in media occupations, 195–200, 207, 209, 218, 219; women in publishing, 200–1
Ephron, Nora, 142, 161, 162, 204, 207
Epstein, Barbara, 76
Epstein, Edward Jay, 226; *News from Nowhere*, 226
Epstein, Joseph, 129
Equal Employment Opportunity Commission (EEOC), 30, 31, 37, 40, 63, 66, 75, 197, 198, 200, 238, 262
Equal Pay Act, 30, 273
Equal Rights Amendment (ERA), 12, 29–30, 32, 37, 95, 105, 106, 108–10, 111, 115, 118, 183, 247–51, 254, 255, 259, 262–72, 284
ERAmerica, 269
Ervin, Sam, 264
Esquire, 8, 83, 87, 98, 103, 124, 125, 141, 142, 145–49, 151, 154–55, 161, 162, 170, 208, 257, 282, 283
Evansgardener, Jo-Anne, 249
Everly, Susan, 113–14
Everything You Always Wanted to Know About Sex but Were Afraid to Ask (Reuben), 126
Eyewitness News (WABC-TV), 227, 236

Facts on File, 171, 175
Family Circle, 19, 136, 254
Farenthold, Sissy, 252
Fasteau, Barbara Feigen, 157
Fawcett, Farrah, 246
Federal Bureau of Investigation (FBI), 254

Federal Communication Commission (FCC), 78, 229–30, 231, 232–33, 235, 240, 244, 260

Federal Communications Act, 229

Federated Press, 15, 16

Fedus, Diane, 42

Feiffer, Jules, 139

Feigen, Brenda, 171

Felker, Clay, 147, 154, 170, 183, 189

Feminist Majority Foundation, 190

Feminist Press, 194

Feminist Revolution: An Abridged Edition with Additional Writings, 185, 186

Feminists (radical group), 52, 56–57, 62, 67, 101

Fight against Dictating Designers, 73

Fighting Woman News, 50

Fine, Don, 23, 33

Firestone, Shulamith, 55, 69, 70, 97, 184; *The Dialectic of Sex*, 184

First Amendment, 77, 78, 87

First wave feminism, 92–96

"First-women" stories, 251, 284

Flexner, Eleanor, *Century of Struggle*, 92

Folio, 190

Fonda, Jane, 278

Foote, Joe S., 244

Ford, Betty, 247–48, 269

Ford, Gerald, 247

Fortune, 198

Foster, Ann Tolstoi, 213, 214, 216

Fox, Muriel, 27–28, 33–39, 42, 44, 45, 48, 60, 61, 79, 104, 284

Fox Network, 246, 272

Francis, Ann. *See* Bird, Florence

Frank, Reuven, 224, 241

Frankel, Max, 205

Frankfort, Ellen, 73; *Vaginal Politics*, 127

Frankfurt School, 17–18

Frederick, Pauline, 223

Freedom and Accuracy in Reporting, 220

Freedom Trash Can, 59–61

Freeman, Barbara M., 31

Freeman, Jo, 177, 187

Fresh Air, 222

Freud, Sigmund, 13

Friedan, Betty, 3–5, 7, 8, 11–29, 30, 33–35, 51, 88, 90, 99, 116, 118, 139, 157, 162, 168, 169, 207, 215, 232, 252, 268, 269, 278; disputes with other feminists, 84, 85, 101, 104, 106–7, 121, 130, 135, 142, 151, 164, 166, 186, 249, 253–54; *The Feminine Mystique*, 3–5, 11–28, 131, 137, 200, 218, 253, 256, 257, 281, 283; involvement with NOW, 31, 33, 35–40, 42–43, 44–45, 47, 83, 84, 104–7, 130, 195; *It Changed My Life*, 186; radical background, 14–17, 21; *The Second Stage*, 186; as suburbanite, 18–22; television presence, 160, 166

Friedan, Carl, 24

Friendly, Fred W., 229

Fuldheim, Dorothy, 223

Fur, Leather, and Machinist Workers Union, 65

Furness, Betty, 34

Galbraith, John Kenneth, 143, 166

Gannet News Service, 207, 208

Gans, Herbert, 78–79

Gartner, Diane, 213

Geis, Bernard, 174; and Associates, 6, 171

General Federation of Women's Clubs, 30, 248

Gentleman's Agreement, 18

George, 182, 247

Geyer, Georgie Ann, 196

Gilder, George F., 257; *Sexual Suicide: A Defense of Traditional Love, Marriage, and Sexual Roles*, 257; *Wealth and Poverty*, 257

Gillespie, David, 203

Gillespie, Marcia Ann, 190

Gilman, Charlotte Perkins, 156

Gingold, Hermione, 25

Gingrich, Arnold, 145–46

Girl Talk, 25–26, 27, 84

Gitlin, Todd, 13, 51–52

Glamour, 120, 150, 151

Glueck, Grace, 198

Goldberg, Lucianne, 259

Goldenson, Leonard, 238

Goldwater, Barry, 259

Good Housekeeping, 6, 7, 24, 93, 247

Good, the Bad, and the Ugly Awards, The, 220

Goodbye to All That, 65

Goodman, Ellen, 84, 88, 97–98, 115, 206, 207, 210

Gornick, Vivian, 44, 94, 206, 207

Graham, Katharine, 65, 183, 199, 202

Graham, Virginia, 25–26, 27

Grann, Phyllis, 200

Gray Panthers, 230

Greer, Germaine, 94, 137–42, 144, 158, 162, 210, 273; *The Female Eunuch*, 137–38, 168; *The Whole Woman*, 142
Gridiron Club, 202
Griffiths, Martha, 108–9, 113, 115, 158
Grimké, Sarah, 156
Gross, Terry, 222
Grossinger, Tania, 24, 27
Grove Press, 65, 200
Grunwald, Henry, 99, 132–34, 139, 141, 149
Guinzberg, Tom, 150
Guthrie, Janet, 131

Hand That Rocks the Ballot Box, The, 240
Hanisch, Carol, 59, 61, 62, 185
Happiness of Women (HOW), 73, 117, 258–59
Harper's Bazaar, 152, 284
Harper's Magazine, 3, 14, 20, 21, 103, 129–30, 141, 149, 150, 151, 258, 284
Harris, Elizabeth Forsling, 171
Hart, Moss, *Act One*, 6
Hartman, Sylvian, 42
Harvard Law Review, 158
Harvard University, 73
Hastings Law Journal, 233
Hawes, Elizabeth, 16
Hayden, Tom, 54, 55, 145
Hayes, Harold, 146, 147, 148–49, 155, 170
Hayes, Susan, 145, 147
Haynes, Trudy, 226, 243
Health care issues, for women, 219
Hearst Magazines, 208, 209
Hefner, Hugh, 74, 102–3, 149
Heide, Wilma Scott, 130, 157, 216, 249
Heilbrun, Carolyn G., 150, 157, 159, 186
Helms, Jesse, 261
Hemingway, Ernest, 146
Hemphill, Paul, 158
Hencken, Ann, 204
Hennessee, Judith, 234, 239
Hentoff, Nat, 166
Hernandez, Aileen, 104, 105
Hershey, Lenore, 69–70, 71, 209
Hier, Helen, 224
Highlander Folk School, 15
Hills, Rust, 149
Hinckle, Warren, 56, 149
Hochstadt, Joy, 43
Hoffman, Abbie, 58–59

Hoffman, Nicolas, 80, 87
Hole, Judith, *Rebirth of Feminism*, 165
Holiday, 146
Hollywood Citizen-News, 42
Hollywood Toilet Bowl Caravan, 72–73
Holocaust, 18, 19
Holyoke (Massachusetts) Transcript, 206
Homosexuality, 126, 129, 131, 136, 163, 269. *See also* Lesbians
hooks, bell, 180
Hoover, J. Edgar, 254
Horkeimer, Max, 17, 195
Horowitz, Daniel, 15, 21
Houghton Mifflin, 200
House and Garden, 152–53
House Un-American Activities Committee, 16, 63
Houston Chronicle, 207
How to Survive Marriage, 127
Howar, Sally, 152
Howard, Lisa, 226
Howe, Louise Kapp, 275
Humphrey, Hubert, 86
Hunt-Wesson, 214
Hunter-Gault, Charlayne, 202, 242
Hyde, Henry, 264

I Love Lucy, 9
I Married Joan, 9
Images of women: in advertising, 210–11, 213–16; in media, 209–12, 218, 232
Independent Television News, 223
Infiltration, of the women's movement, 254
Inman, Mary, *In Woman's Defense*, 15–16
International Research Service, 145
International Women's Media Foundation, 220
International Women's Year, 182, 186, 195, 207, 255, 268
Institute for Defense Analysis, 54
Irwin, Cathy, 234, 242
Ivins, Molly, 81
Ivory Liquid soap, 211

Jackson State College, 54
Jaffe, Rona, 85
Jarrow Press, 257
Javits, Jacob, 166, 253
Jay, Karla, 61, 64, 66, 68, 69, 70, 164
Jeannette Rankin Brigade, 55–56

Jefferson, Eve, 119

Job listings, sex-segregated, 40, 47, 63

John Birch Society, 259

John Fairfax publishing firm, 190

Johnson, Jack, 278, 279

Johnson, Lady Bird, 240

Johnson, Lynda, 225

Johnson, Lyndon B., 30, 37

Johnson, Nicolas, 229, 231, 233, 240

Johnson, Rafer, 162

Johnston, Jill, 106, 139–41

Joliffe, Lee, 218

Jones, Beverly, 55

Jones, Carolyn, 213

Journal of Liberation: No More Fun and Games, 97, 101

Jowett, Garth, 260

Kaufman, Sue, 100; *Diary of a Mad Housewife*, 100

Katz, Herman, 67

Kazickas, Jurate, 204

Keefer, Pat, 248

Kempton, Sally, 69, 74, 87

Kennedy, Florynce, 40, 50–51, 63, 71–73, 85, 210

Kennedy, Jacqueline, 147, 202

Kennedy, John F., 12, 29, 202, 226

Kennedy, John F., Jr., 182

Kennedy, Robert F., 153

Kent State University, 53, 54

Kerner Commission, 195

Kerrigan, John J., 203

Kessler, Gladys, 234

Kilbourne, Jean, 220–21

Kilian, Michael, 117–18

King, Billie Jean, 268, 273–78, 281–85

King, Larry, 277, 278

King, Martin Luther, Jr., 44, 46, 53, 153

King, Rebecca Ann, 62

Kintner, Robert, 226

Kissinger, Henry, 152

Kitch, Carolyn, 98, 100

Klatch, Rebecca, 261

Klemesrud, Judy, 64, 82–83, 90, 106, 123, 135–36, 142, 157, 206–7, 214, 254

Knef, Hildegard, *The Gift Horse*, 138

Knievel, Evel, 281

Koedt, Anne, 69, 89, 95, 97, 125, 136, 137, 178, 270

Kohler, Pam Sebastian, 203

Komisar, Lucy, 40, 110–14, 119, 131, 139, 210, 211, 212, 214

Korda, Michael, 143

Korda, Reva, 212

Kordisch, Karen, 49

Kovacs, Midge, 40, 120, 123, 212, 216, 217

Kraditor, Aileen, *Up from the Pedestal*, 256

Kurtzman, Harvey, 145

Kushins, Joel, 190

Ladies against Women, 267

Ladies before Gentlemen, 8–9

Ladies' Choice, 9

Ladies' Home Journal, 6, 8, 24, 27, 83, 88, 92, 93, 121, 125, 168, 171, 176, 189, 209; sit-in at, 68–71, 74, 75, 107–8, 151, 184, 197

Lady Golfer, 217

Lafky, Sue, 244

LaHaye, Beverly, 270–71; *The Spirit-Controlled Woman*, 270

Landers, Ann, 88, 202

Lang Communications, 188, 190

Lasswell, Harold, 17

Last Tango in Paris, 126

Lawrence, D. H., 127, 132

Lawrence, David, Jr., 208

Lawrence, Patricia, 109–10

Lawrenson, Helen, 103, 148–49, 155

Lazarsfeld, Paul, 17

League of Women Voters, 247, 248, 250

Lear, Martha Weinman, 91–92

Left press, 49–52; critique of mass media, 49–51

Lemann, Nicholas, 46

Leon, Barbara, 184–85; *Brainwashing and Women: The Psychological Attack*, 185

Leone, Vivian, 69

Lesbian Tide, 178

Lesbians, in the women's movement, 44, 74, 83, 104, 106, 121–22, 123–26, 131, 134–36, 139–42, 156, 162–64, 178–79, 186, 254, 258, 264, 268, 269

Levine, Ellen, *Rebirth of Feminism*, 165

Levine, Susan Braun, 171, 173, 175, 183

Levitt, Leonard, 143, 161

Lewin, Frances, 199, 202

Lewinsky, Monica, 259

Lewis, John, 120–21

Liberation News Service, 51, 58, 102
Liberty Media for Women, 190
Lichtenstein, Grace, 68, 69, 70, 82, 110–11, 116
Life, 7–8, 27, 53, 54, 94, 101–2, 121, 126, 134, 135, 138, 146, 150, 151, 157, 167, 168, 171, 184, 243
Lindsay, John, 237
Linkletter, Art, 6
Lippert, Karen, 174, 183
Lipton, Lauren, 224
Little, Brown, 200
Look, 86–87, 129, 151, 152, 168, 169
Look at the Eagle Forum, A, 265
Los Angeles Herald-Examiner, 83, 207
Los Angeles Times, 36, 73, 80, 83, 113, 114, 117, 207–8, 218
Louis, Joe, 278–80
Louisville Courier-Journal, 80, 207
Louisville Times, 207
Love and Marriage, 7
Love, Barbara, 135
Lucas, George, 127
Luce, Henry, 99, 135
Lund, Christine, 242
Lyon, Phyllis, 178

MacDonald Communications, 190
Macdonald, Dwight, 146
Macdonald, Robert H., 232
Mackin, Catherine, 226, 237, 238
MacLaine, Shirley, 121, 252
MacLean, Judy, 269
Macmillan, 200–1
MacNeil-Lehrer Report, 242
MacPherson, Myra, 115
Mad magazine, 145
Mademoiselle, 24, 39, 171, 255
Magid, Frank, 228, 236, 239
Maier, Maureen, 100
Mailer, Norman, 129–30, 132, 139–41, 154, 258, 273
Mainardi, Pat, 134
Man in the Gray Flannel Suit, The, 12
Management Adviser, 217
Manley, Joan, 132
Mannes, Marya, 139, 226
Mansbridge, Jane J., 248, 263
Marches: (26 August 1970), 104–8, 109, 115–22, 123, 152–53, 204, 216, 258; (26 August 1971), 158
Marjorie Morningstar, 12

Mark, Mary Ellen, 184
Marlboro Man, 124
Marriage, feminist views on, 66–67
Martha Movement, 255
Martin, Del, 178
Mary Tyler Moore Show, 128, 129, 282, 284
Maude, 128–29, 284
Mauldin, Bill, 118
McBride, Mary Margaret, 223
McCade, Bob, 133
McCall's, 6, 7, 13, 21, 24, 69, 88, 151, 153, 156, 158, 166, 167–69, 171, 253, 267
McClendon, Sarah, 202
McGee, Frank, 120
McGovern, George, 141, 152, 153, 252
McGraw-Hill, 137, 205
McHugh and Hoffman consulting firm, 228
McHugh, Phil, 246
McLuhan, Marshall, 159, 165
McSorley's Old Ale House, 111–14, 203
Mead, Margaret, 13, 22, 118
Media Access Project, 230
Media Report to Women, 51, 220
Media Women, 62, 67–68, 120, 197
Media Workshop, 62, 72
Medical Committee for Human Rights, 67
Meet the Press, 103
Melia, Jinx, 255
Men Our Masters (MOM), 258
Merton, Robert K., 17
Metalious, Grace, *Peyton Place*, 23
Meyer, Helen, 23, 200, 218
Meyer, Karl, 68, 69
Midgley, Leslie, 34
Mildred Pierce, 9
Miller, Henry, 132
Miller, Joy, 36, 79, 204
Millett, Kate, 49, 75, 96, 100, 121–22, 123, 131–35, 138, 139, 144, 152, 153–54, 158, 160, 162, 178, 220, 254; *Sexual Politics*, 49, 63, 68, 121, 130, 131–32, 133, 134, 138, 200, 218
Mills, Kay, 218
Milwaukee Journal, 113, 116
Mink, Patsy, 86
Miss America protest, 58–62, 74, 93, 101, 107, 211, 259
Mitchell, Andrea, 226, 243
Monroe (Louisiana) Morning World, 44
Monroe, Marilyn, 164–65
Moral Majority, 270

Morgan, Marabel, 257, 258; *The Total Woman*, 257, 264

Morgan, Robin, 49, 56, 58–62, 63, 64, 65, 139, 177, 180, 187, 190, 192, 200, 218; *Sisterhood Is Powerful*, 256

Morris, Willie, 103, 130, 149

Mott, Lucretia, 156

Ms. Foundation, 182, 186, 190

Ms. magazine, 6, 73, 77, 95, 147, 148, 149, 153, 154, 156, 158, 254, 267, 271; advertising in, 178, 180, 187–90, 197, 210, 217, 278; coverage of abortion, 188–89, 190, 192; coverage of lesbians, 163, 164, 178–79; critics of, 178–81, 183–87, 188–89; editorial direction, 176–81, 187–88, 190–93; financial trouble, 189–90; founding of, 157, 166, 169, 170–72, 175–76; nonprofit status, 190; readership, 171, 172; staff, 171–75; success of, 182–83

Mungo, Raymond, 58

Munsel, Patrice, 9

Murray, Pauli, 32, 36, 203

Murrow, Edward R., 229, 245

Mutual Broadcasting Company, 224

My Little Margie, 9

Myerson, Bess, 18, 35, 61

Myra Breckenridge (film), 129

Nader, Ralph, 45; *Unsafe at Any Speed*, 29

Nassatir, Marcia, 23

Nation, Carrie, 95

National Advertising Review Board, 214

National Advisory Commission on Civil Disorders, 195

National Airlines, 214

National American Newspaper Publishers, 40

National Association of Broadcasters (NAB), 231, 233

National Black Media Coalition, 230

National Conference of Catholic Bishops, 267

National Conference of Christians and Jews, 265

National Conference of Editorial Writers, 202

National Conference on Woman, 267–69

National Federation of Press Women, 202, 217

National Feminist Party, 72–73

National Gay Media Task Force, 230, 269

National Mexican-American Anti-Defamation Committee, 230

National Mobilization Committee, 56

National Organization for Women (NOW), 26, 27–28, 62, 66; Baby Carriage Brigade, 46; black membership, 44, 45–46; campaign against demeaning advertising, 211–12, 214, 216; campaign for broadcast reform, 232–35; disputes within, 47, 66; campaign for ERA, 248–50, 263; founding of, 29, 31–32, 34–36; Legal Education and Defense Fund, 35, 217; male membership, 130, 156; and mass media, 33, 35–37, 38–39, 40–41, 60, 88–89, 195, 221, 230, 231, 233; New York chapter, 37–40, 42–43, 46, 66, 106, 211–12; proactive advertising, 216–17; public demonstrations, 43, 46–47, 75, 249–50; Task Force on the Image of Women, 38–39, 216; women's march, 104–8, 109, 115

National Public Radio, 222, 242

National Review, 87–88

National Women's Press Club, 33

NBC, 119, 120, 223, 224, 226, 234, 235, 237–38, 240–41, 269, 282

Neal, Dave, 236

Neel, Alice, 133–44

Nesbitt, Lynn, 5–6

Nessim, Barbara, 149, 161, 163

Neuharth, Al, 208, 209

New England Feminist Party, 73

New Feminists troupe, 109

New Journalism, 147, 149

New Right, 260–62, 267, 271, 272

New York Advertising Women, 220

New York Daily News, 230

New York Herald Tribune, 80

New York magazine, 147, 151, 152, 153, 154, 157, 170, 183

New York Post, 60, 140

New York Radical Women, 55, 60, 61, 62, 68, 70, 125, 184

New York Times, 19, 36, 37–38, 40, 58, 60–61, 63, 67, 68, 74, 80, 81–83, 85, 106, 108, 110–13, 115, 116, 121, 123, 132, 134, 135, 139, 140, 152, 154, 157, 158, 186, 196, 198–99, 201, 205–7, 208, 224, 226, 242, 252, 253, 254, 256, 258, 260, 268, 282

New York Times Magazine, 27, 41, 43, 61, 62, 66–67, 68, 83, 84, 89, 90, 91, 94, 95, 106, 121, 130, 135, 142, 150, 151, 153, 155, 212, 214, 253, 267

New York Tribune, 198

New Yorker, 49, 146, 172, 242
Newsday, 39
Newspaper Guild, 199, 201
Newsweek, 35, 62, 68, 87, 94, 98, 101–3, 118,
   150, 162, 171, 198, 199, 201, 205, 208, 217,
   224, 242, 269
Nichols, William, 124
Nicholson, Joan, 234
Nixon, Julie, 247
Nixon, Pat, 247
Nixon, Richard, 73, 119, 229, 231, 247, 260,
   262, 284
Nolan, Irene, 207
Nordyke, Dorothy, 202–3
Norton, Eleanor Holmes, 199
Norton, W. W., and Company, 3, 5, 24, 27
Notes from the First Year, 125
Notes from the Second Year: Women's Liberation,
   125

O'Donnell, Victoria, 260
off our backs, 50, 75, 107, 194, 210
Office of Telecommunications Policy, 229
Ogle-ins, 65–66
O'Haire, Catherine, 171
Old Hat Award, 211
O'Leary, Jane, 269
Olivia Records, 194
Olympic Games, 281–82
Oppenheimer, Robert, 15
O'Shea, Anne, 28
Overholser, Geneva, 208

Pacino, Al, 129
Packard, Vance, *The Hidden Persuaders*, 29
Page, Patti, 9
Palmer, Lilli, 9
Parade, 43
Parks, Rosa, 46
Parkway Villager, 18–19
Pasadena Eagle, 73
Paul, Alice, 45, 92, 115
Pauley, Jane, 226
Peacock, Mary, 171
Peden, Katherine, 32
Pee-in at Harvard Yard, 73
Penguin Putnam, 200
Pennsylvania Women's Press Association,
   203

Penthouse, 126
People magazine, 157
Pepper, Claude, 35
Peter Pan brassieres, 215
Peterson, Estelle, 30
Pfeiffer, Jane Cahill, 241
Philadelphia Evening Bulletin, 43, 86, 94, 113,
   117, 204–5
Philadelphia Inquirer, 117
Philco Presents the World's Girls, 27
Phillips, B. J., 132–33, 171–72, 198
Piercy, Marge, 73
Playboy, 20, 102–3, 126, 140, 146, 149, 153,
   267
Playgirl, 126, 209, 267
Plimpton, George, 154
Podhoretz, Norman, 139
Pogrebin, Letty Cottin, 6, 77, 88, 171, 173–74,
   183, 189, 254; *How to Make It in a Man's
   World*, 77, 171, 174
Polillo, Pat, 244
Popular culture, 275–76, 279–80
Poussaint, Alvin, 44, 46
Poussaint, Renee, 226
Povich, Lynn, 198, 199
Powers, Ron, 239, 245
Prashker, Betty, 131–32, 200, 202, 218
President's Commission on Campus Unrest,
   54–55
President's Commission on the Status of
   Women, 12, 29–30, 31–33, 34
Presley, Elvis, 279, 280
Press clubs: in Los Angeles, 73; in Milwaukee,
   64; National Press Club, 64–65, 202. *See also*
   National Women's Press Club
Pressman, Sonia, 30
Primo, Al, 226, 227
Pristine, 211
Procter and Gamble, 180
Progressive, The, 217, 269
Psychology Today, 170
Public accommodations, 41–43, 47, 105,
   110–14, 116
Public Broadcasting System, 242
Publisher's Weekly, 138, 257
Publishers Lunch Club, 200
Pulitzer, Joseph, 274
Purnick, Joyce, 196
Pussycats, 259

Quadrangle Press, 256
Quaker Oats, 214
Quarles, Norma, 226
Queen, 151
Quill, The, 203–4
Quindlen, Anna, 196, 198
Quinn, Sally, 208, 243, 266

Racism, in media, 71–73
Radical Feminism, 125
Radical feminists, 55, 164, 191–92; critiques, 48, 56; disputes among, 56, 74; and mass media, 48–49, 51, 52, 56–57, 59, 61–62, 68–70, 74–75, 89; opposition to New Left, 56, 65, 179
Radio Act of 1927, 229
Radner, Gilda, 228
Ramparts, 56, 149
Randolph, Jennings, 119
Random House, 6, 185, 186, 200
Rankin, Jeannette, 56
Rat, 58, 65, 69, 70–71, 74, 125
Rather, Dan, 243
Rawalt, Margaret, 32, 61, 108
Reader's Digest, 14, 200; Book Division, 171
Reagan, Ronald, 265
Reasoner, Harry, 239
Redbook, 7, 19, 83, 118, 155–57, 178, 222
Redstockings, 56, 57–58, 62, 70, 152, 158, 184–87, 254
Reed, Rex, 154–55
Religious fundamentalism, 261, 267, 270–71
Republican National Convention, 259
Republican Women's Club, 248–49
Revlon, 215
Reynolds, Burt, 126
Reynolds, Debbie, 6
Rice Council of America, 153
Richette, Lisa, 94
Ride, Sally, 183
Riesman, David, *The Lonely Crowd*, 23
Riggs, Bobby, 268, 273–78, 281, 282, 283, 284
Rivers, Joan, 121, 153
Robbins, Harold, *The Carpetbaggers*, 6
Robertson, Nan, 82, 198
Robinson, Jackie, 279
Rocky Mountain News, 113, 118
Roe v. Wade, 267, 271
Rojas, Gloria, 228

Rollin, Betty, 86–87, 126
Rolling Stone, 138, 170
Rooms with No View: A Woman's Guide to the Man's World of the Media, 197
Rooney, Andy, 87
Roosevelt, Eleanor, 156
Roosevelt, Franklin Delano, 15
Roots, 280, 281
Rorum, Ned, 139
Rosen, Ruth, 251, 254
Rosenthal, A. M., 82, 186
Rotarian, 20
Roth, Philip, 139
Royal Commission on the Status of Women, 30–31
Rubin, Jerry, 58
Rudd, Mark, 54
Rupil, Margaret, 224
Rusk, Dean, 58
Ryan, Nigel, 223

Sacramento Bee, 113
Sadat, Anwar, 269
Sagan, Françoise, *A Certain Smile*, 23
Sagaris, 186
Salant, Richard, 241
Salembier, Valerie, 208
San Francisco Examiner and Chronicle, 114, 117, 196, 201
Sanders, Marlene, 34, 39–40, 66, 68, 69, 223, 224, 226, 239, 240, 241
Sando, Florence, 225
Sarachild, Kathie, 55, 57, 177, 184
Saturday Night Live, 228
Saturday Review, 24, 217
Savitch, Jessica, 235–36, 240
Scamardella, RoseAnn, 228
Schaefer, Ruth Crane, 223, 225
Schano, Eleanor, 224–25
Schlafly, Phyllis, 126, 247, 251, 259–60, 262–68, 269, 270–71; *A Choice Not an Echo*, 247, 259; *Eagle Forum Newsletter*, 264–65; *Phyllis Schlafly Report*, 262, 264, 268; *The Power of the Positive Woman*, 264
Schlesinger, Arthur, 39
Schorr, Daniel, 243
Schroeder, Patricia, 196
Schudson, Michael, 85
Schultz, Marilyn, 238

Schultz, Sigrid, 224

Scott, Foresman, 205

Seaman, Barbara, 254; *Free and Female: The Sex Life of the Contemporary Woman*, 136–37

Seattle Magazine, 171, 175

Seattle Times, 206

Seib, Charles, 205

Sensuous Woman, The, 127

September 11 attacks (2001), 160

Sergio, Lisa, 224

Sevareid, Eric, 87, 120

Seventeen, 169–70, 193

Sexist language, 205

Sexuality: in books, 126–27, 129, 136–38; fear of homosexuality, 126, 129, 136; fear of impotence, 125–26; in films, 127, 129; in the media, 124–26, 129–30, 135–36, 138, 141; in the 1960s, 124; in situation comedies, 127–29

Sheehy, Gail, 139, 140, 141

Sheppard, Eugenia, 80

Sherr, Lynn, 203–4

Shirer, William, 224

Show magazine, 145, 149, 151, 171

Shriver, Sargent, 252

Shulman, Alix Kates, 69, 184

Sigma Delta Chi, 202, 203

Signoret, Simone, 27

Silva Thins, 211

Silverman, Fred, 241

Simpson, Carole, 238, 239, 243, 269

Simpson, Ruth, 135

Sinatra, Frank, 281

Sinclair, Upton, 22

Sixty Minutes, 87, 167, 279

Sloane (Alfred P.) Foundation, 261

Smeal, Eleanor, 120, 248, 250, 255, 266, 270

Smith College, 11

Smith, Gail, 226

Smith, Howard K., 87, 119

Smith, Liz, 155–56, 162

Smith, Margaret Chase, 34

Smith, Steve, 139

Sochen, June, 274

Socialist Workers Party, 107

Society for Cutting up Men (SCUM), 63

Society for the Emancipation of the American Male, 73–74

Solanus, Valerie, 63

Sontag, Susan, 139

South Pacific, 18

Sparkman, Muriel, 213

Spectrum, 265

Spelman, Elizabeth, 180

Spillane, Mickey, 13

Sports, 273–78, 280–85

Sports Illustrated, 146, 198

Stahl, Lesley, 196, 226, 237, 242, 243

Stanley, Nancy, 233, 235

Stanton, Elizabeth Cady, 156

Statesman, The, 217

Statue of Liberty, 109–13, 114

Steinem, Gloria, 5, 28, 57, 72, 73, 90, 94, 96, 100, 103, 106, 122, 130, 131, 132, 135, 139, 142, 168, 175, 215, 248, 252, 261, 265, 266, 278; *The Beach Book*, 5, 143, 149–50; in childhood, 144, 175; CIA connection, 145, 155, 158, 185–86, 254; critics of, 165, 179, 181, 184; at *Esquire*, 145–49; feminist awakening, 152–53; freelance career, 151, 152–53; leadership in the women's movement, 155–56, 158, 161, 162, 165–66, 253; as McCall's "Woman of the Year," 169; and *Ms.*, 171, 176–77, 178–79, 182–83, 185–87, 189, 190, 191, 193; at *New York*, 151–53, 154; political interests, 152, 154, 252; reticence to discuss personal life, 161–63; *Revolution from Within*, 162; self-fashioned celebrity, 143–44, 150–52, 153, 154–55, 157–59, 161; sexual ambiguity, 163–64; television appeal, 159, 161, 165; writing style, 147–48, 152

Stereotypes, perpetuated in mass media, 50–51, 62, 79, 84, 85, 90, 92–94, 97, 101, 103, 113, 114, 119, 133–34, 148, 195, 205, 212. *See also* Images of women

"Sterile" characterization, 92–93, 101–2

Stern Community Law Firm, 230

Stern, Sydney, 157

Stone, Desmond, 203

Stonewall riot, 129

Stop ERA! organization, 259–60, 265, 268

Streisand, Barbra, 155

"Strident" characterization, 74–75, 77, 81, 96–97, 190, 216

Strike, by women workers, 104–8, 109, 116, 117–18, 120, 223, 258

Students for a Democratic Society (SDS), 51–52, 54, 55, 94, 184

Stumbo, Bella, 24, 80, 218
Suck, 137
Suffrage movement, 45, 92
Sullivan, Ed, 6, 279
Sullivan, Kathleen, 238
Susann, Jacqueline, 139; *Valley of the Dolls*, 6
Susskind, David, 96–97, 141
Sutton, Carol, 80, 133, 207
Symbolism, in the women's movement, 55, 75
Syracuse Coalition for the Free Flow of
   Information in the Broadcast Media, 235

Talese, Nan, 200
Taylor, Jean Shirley, 80, 207–8
Television: coverage of September 11 attacks,
   160; coverage of women's movement, 69,
   119–20, 159, 160–61, 166; as marketing tool,
   6, 24; news formats, 181, 227–29, 245;
   simplicity of images and messages, 159–60;
   women's themes in programming, 8–10, 24,
   50, 244
Terry, Dian, 47, 84
Thaler, Seymour, 57, 58
Third Woman's Alliance, 116
This Week, 39, 43, 124
Thom, Mary, 171, 175, 183, 185, 188
Thomas, Helen, 196, 202
Thomas, Franklin, 162
Threlkel, Richard, 120
Tiger, Lionel, 139
Time magazine, 35, 43, 95, 98–100, 102, 108–9,
   114, 121–22, 124, 131–35, 149, 153–54,
   162–63, 166, 168, 172, 198, 202, 217, 220,
   242, 254, 277
Time-Life books, 132, 198
Title IX, 275
Toast of the Town, 279, 280
Today Show, 39, 226, 238
Tolliver, Melba, 228
Toogood, Alex, 129
Toward a Female Liberation Movement, 55
Town & Country, 146
Town Hall, 139–41
Town Journal, 19
Trahey, Jane, 213
Transsexuality, 129
Trenton Times, 203
Trilling, Diana, 139
Trotta, Liz, 225, 226; *Fighting for Air*, 225

Trout, Robert, 226
Truman, Harry S., 6
Tuchman, Gaye, 37, 195
Tully, Mary Jean, 216
TV Guide, 10, 24, 208, 214

United Airlines, 41, 42
United Church of Christ, 230, 231, 232, 235
United Electrical, Radio, and Machine
   Workers, 15, 16
United Farm Workers, 45, 154, 211
United Press International, 105, 111, 196,
   205
University Club (New York), 202
Up from Under, 50
Updike, John, *Couples*, 126
U.S. Commission on Civil Rights, 232, 247
U.S. News and World Report, 98, 115–16, 266
USA Today, 207, 208

Van Doren, Abigail, 88
Van Gelder, Lindsy, 60, 79, 81, 180, 195
Van Horne, Harriet, 87, 88, 93, 114
Variety, 226
Veteran Feminists of America, 26
Vidal, Gore, *Myra Breckenridge*, 129
Viking Press, 143, 149–50
Vilar, Esther, *The Manipulated Man*, 257
Village Voice, 38, 49, 68, 73, 106, 127, 140, 185,
   206
Vintage Books, 256
Virginia Slims, 189, 210, 211, 216, 278
Vogue, 139, 151, 162
Voice of the Women's Liberation Movement, 56,
   61
Voting Rights Act, 31
Vreeland, Diana, 139

Wade, Betsy, 198–99
Wakefield, Dan, 274, 283
WaldenBooks, 7
Walker, Alice, 180
Wall Street Journal, 208, 231
Wall Street protest, 63
Wallace, Mike, 26
Waller, Judith Cary, 223
Walters, Barbara, 165–66, 202, 226, 238–39,
   243, 269, 279
Washington Monthly, 131

Washington Post, 36, 65, 68, 69, 80, 94, 113, 115, 118, 132–33, 134, 195, 199, 205, 208, 257, 260, 266

Washington Post Writers Group, 208

Washington Star, 207

Wason, Betty, 224

Waters, Chocolate, 163, 179, 244–45

Watson, Patrick, 163

Weaver, David, 172

Webb, Charles: *The Graduate*, 127; *The Marriage of a Young Stock Broker*, 127

Webb, Marilyn Saltzman, 55–56

Weber, Harold T., 92

Wedemeyer, Dee, 204

Wells, Mary, 213

White House Correspondents Association, 202

Whitehead, Clay T., 229

Whyte, William, *The Organization Man*, 12, 29

Wide World of Sports, 281

Wilhoit, G. C., 172

Wilkes, Paul, 121

Wilkins, Roy, 19

Williams, William B., 72

Willis, Ellen, 4, 49, 61, 172, 177, 184, 185, 187, 188, 192

Wilson, Flip, 129

Wilson, Woodrow, 60

Window Dressing on the Set, 242

Winfrey, Oprah, 143, 144, 235, 236

Wire Service Guild, 199

Wisconsin, University of (Madison), 54

WITCH (Women's International Conspiracy from Hell), 63–66, 258

WLBT-TV, 230

WNEW Radio, 72

WNEW-TV, 72

Wolf, Naomi, 215

Wolfe, Tom, 149, 154

Wolfson, Alice J., 64

Wollstonecraft, Mary, 156

Woman Alive, 244

Woman under the Influence, A (film), 127

Woman's World, 184

Women: A Journal of Liberation, 50

Women against Consumer Exploitation, 73

Women in Love (film), 127

Women in the Media, 244

Women, Men, and the Media, 207, 208, 220

Women of the Free Future, 73

Women's Action Alliance, 166, 171

Women's Action Commission, 74

Women's Health Collective, 75

Women's Home Companion, 93

Women's International Democratic Federation, 16

Women's Liberation (documentary), 240

Women's Liberation: Blueprint for the Future (anthology), 256

Women's Liberation Front, 201

Women's magazines: advertisers in, 167, 189, 197; feminist themes, 156–57, 218; service function, 168, 209; as subjects for antifeminist criticism, 266–67; as subjects for feminist criticism, 67–71, 167–68, 266; themes of the 1950s and 1960s, 7–8, 17; under women executives, 218–19. *See also individual titles*

Women's National Book Association, 257

Women's National Democratic Club, 152

Women's National Republican Club, 267

Women's pages, in newspapers, 79–81, 115

Women's Party, 12

Women's Political Caucus, 97, 175

Women's Strike Coalition, 121

Women's Strike for Equality, 211

WomenSports, 283

Woodruff, Judy, 226

World, 274

World of the Girls, The, 160

World War II, 223–34, 279

Writer, The, 20, 126

Wyden, Peter, 21

Yarborough, Ralph, 64

Yippies, 58–59, 61, 63

Young Socialist Alliance, 107

Zaharias, Babe Didrickson, 274

Zonta, 33